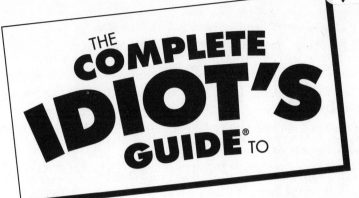

THE COMPLETE IDIOT'S GUIDE TO

Terrific Diabetic Meals

by Lucy Beale, Joan Clark, M.S., R.D., C.D.E.,
and Barbara Forsberg

ALPHA

A member of Penguin Group (USA) Inc.

Lucy: To my husband, Patrick Partridge
Joan: To my children, Tricia, Ryan, and Jenny Clark, my favorite taste testers
Barbara: To my sister-in-law, Chenoa Mittan, who suffered from diabetes and is no longer with us

International Standard Book Number: 1-59257-275-8
Library of Congress Catalog Card Number: 2004108624

06   8   7   6   5   4   3

Interpretation of the printing code: The rightmost number of the first series of numbers is the year of the book's printing; the rightmost number of the second series of numbers is the number of the book's printing. For example, a printing code of 04-1 shows that the first printing occurred in 2004.

Printed in the United States of America

Publisher: *Marie Butler-Knight*
Product Manager: *Phil Kitchel*
Senior Managing Editor: *Jennifer Chisholm*
Senior Acquisitions Editor: *Mike Sanders*
Development Editor: *Nancy D. Lewis*
Senior Production Editor: *Billy Fields*
Copy Editor: *Susan Aufheimer*
Illustrator: *Chris Eliopoulos*
Cover/Book Designer: *Trina Wurst*
Indexer: *Tonya Heard*
Layout/Proofreading: *Ayanna Lacey, Mary Hunt*

Contents at a Glance

Contents

Foreword

Lucy Beale continues to break new ground with her great cookbooks. Her previous book, *The Complete Idiot's Guide to Low-Carb Meals*, which she wrote with Sandy G. Couvillon, was the first low-carb cookbook to incorporate the glycemic index.

Lucy's new cookbook is the first to take it one essential step further by incorporating both the glycemic index (GI) and glycemic load (GL). She provides GI and GL calculations for each of the book's approximately 277 recipes.

Lucy has been a weight-loss expert for almost 20 years. By choosing foods with low glycemic values, many people have been able to achieve substantial weight loss.

About 80 percent of all people with diabetes are overweight. But the GI and GL are not just weight loss aids. In fact, they were developed as tools for people with diabetes, and here they are of the greatest importance.

Whatever type of diabetes you have, your body can't do a good job of using the food you eat. This is because of a disturbance of carbohydrate metabolism that can cause your blood glucose levels to spike, and it is these spikes that led to the complications of diabetes.

In the old days we used to say that "a carb is a carb is a carb." We now know, however, that different carbohydrates have different effects.

Pioneering researchers at the University of Toronto first wrote about the GI in March of 1981. They compared the effects of equivalent amounts of carbohydrate and glucose on groups of volunteers over a two-hour period. Setting glucose to equal 100, the difference between the effects of the 62 foods and glucose was the GI for that food. Over the next quarter of a century researchers applied the concept of the GI to more and more foods.

When a doctor diagnosed me with diabetes in 1994, I found that all the GI research was scattered in myriad professional journals.

Ever since I started my diabetes website, www.mendosa.com, in February 1995, my articles and lists of GI/GL values have received the most attention. Professor Jennie Brand-Miller of the University of Sydney made my site one of the most popular ones dealing with diabetes by authorizing me to reprint her "International Tables" that a professional journal had published in 1995 and enlarged in 2002.

But it wasn't until 1996 that the first book about the GI for the general public appeared. Published in Australia, the book was hard to find in the United States until an American edition appeared in 1999. The 2003 edition, now titled *The New Glucose Revolution*, includes GI and GL values for almost 800 individual foods. The GL takes the GI one step farther by including serving sizes. Sales of books in this series now total more than one million copies.

The GI and GL are the most significant dietary advances of the past quarter century. All that has been lacking are appropriate recipes. Lucy now wonderfully fills that gap with recipes that are both scientifically sound and incredibly appetizing. If you thought that having diabetes meant few food options, it just means that you didn't know her recipes yet.

—Rick Mendosa

Diabetes journalist, editor and publisher of *Diabetes Update*

Introduction

Cooking a great meal that's suitable for persons with diabetes brings double satisfaction. First, you're fixing a meal that provides healthy and restorative nutrition. Second, you're cooking foods that are delicious and satisfying.

Our hope is you'll find this cookbook filled with thoughtfulness and love. Thoughtfulness, because we want you to find recipes that meet all the nutritional requirements of someone with diabetes, whether that someone is yourself or another person. Love, because we want you to enjoy mouth-watering, delicious dishes that you, your family, and your friends will love.

Many are foods you already love to eat. Barbecued ribs and cornbread. Lasagna and Italian vegetables. Cheesecake and pudding. Other recipes will delight you with new tastes and food combinations. You can prepare these recipes for yourself, for family meals, or for special occasions.

Oh, you can also expect lots of compliments on your cooking!

How This Book Is Organized

This book is divided into eight parts:

Part 1, "Eating for Pleasure and Health," gives you the most up-to-date information on meals and eating for persons with diabetes. You'll learn all about the glycemic index and glycemic load and which kinds of fats are good for you. We also introduce you to the New Diabetes and Weight Management Food Guide Pyramid.

Part 2, "Breakfasts and Lunches," features recipes to perk up your mornings, jumpstart your metabolism, and give you sustained energy throughout your day. Recipes for fabulous brunches are included, too.

Part 3, "Appetizers, Snacks, and Side Dishes," is filled with recipes for delicious, healthy appetizers and midday snacks. You'll also find dozens of appealing vegetable, salad, and fruit side dishes.

Part 4, "Lean Meat Entrées," contains recipes for lean beef, pork, ground meat, poultry, veal, and lamb dishes. You'll find recipes for everything from simple family meals to gala parties.

Part 5, "Shellfish and Fish Entrées," gives you recipes for the bounty of our oceans, streams, and lakes. You'll discover both fish and shellfish recipes for varied meals with a healthy focus.

Part 6, "Combination Main Dishes," features recipes that offer meats or fish, plus vegetables and wonderful seasonings. Choose from one-pot meals, soups and stews, or main-dish salads.

Part 7, "Favorite Cuisines," gives you plenty of healthy low-glycemic recipes for some of your favorite ethnic cuisines, such as Italian, Mexican, and Asian.

Part 8, "Extras: Starches, Desserts, and Beverages" offers finishing touches for your meals, with low-glycemic recipes for bread, grains, and legumes. Plus, you'll find recipes for scrumptious low-glycemic desserts, such as cheesecakes, brownies, and cookies.

Healthy Bites

The sidebars in this book offer diabetic health notes and tips, recipe variations, warnings, and definitions. Here's what to look for:

Words for Well-Being
Definitions of words that increase your knowledge of cooking for persons with diabetes.

In the Danger Zone
Warnings on how to avoid cooking and meal-planning pitfalls. Watch out!

Healthy Notes
Good information on healthful cooking and nutrition for persons with diabetes.

Palate Preview
Recipe overviews that tell you about the recipe and how it will taste.

Delightfully Different
Suggestions for interesting recipe variations.

Acknowledgments

A special ingredient went into every recipe in this book. It's the love and devotion of everyone who contributed to the book's publication.

As a great team creating this cookbook, the authors want to thank each other: Joan Clark for cheerfully working on recipes, recipe analyses, and joyously sharing her nutritional and cooking expertise. Barbara Forsberg for compiling a superb collection of recipes and for guiding the recipe selection. Lucy Beale for organizing and writing recipes and the book. And for her leadership and living what she teaches.

Lucy thanks her husband, Patrick Partridge, for editing suggestions and encouragement. "Pat, you are my inspiration and foundation. I appreciate your patience with my long hours writing and with all the 'date nights' we had to postpone."

Lucy also extends thanks to Rick Mendosa for generously sharing his knowledge of the glycemic index and glycemic load; to Judy Webb for her uplifting friendship and for sharing recipes; to Jane Pennington for happily keying recipes; to Dr. Brian Martin for coaching, and to her clients who continually inspire and challenge her.

Joan dedicates this book to her children—Tricia, Ryan, and Jenny Clark—her favorite taste testers. She's very grateful for their long-term support, patience, and encouragement.

Joan is also grateful to Dr. Dana Clarke, medical director of the Utah Diabetes Center, for his support, kindness, and professional input. A sincere thank-you also goes to all her co-workers at the Utah Diabetes Center.

Barbara Forsberg gives special thanks to her husband, Ian, for his patience and encouragement in getting the recipes researched and perfected in a timely manner; to her children, Conner and Isaac, for their constant computer support; and to her friend, personal assistant, and fabulous cook, Sandra Lekas, for keying recipes on a moment's notice.

Barbara also thanks her late friend Mayetta St. John for teaching her how to cook at an early age. And she thanks her good friend Annie Brown for her willingness to try new foods with her all around the world.

We all thank Marilyn Allen of the Allen O'Shea Literary Agency for her constant support and unwavering faith in this project. And we thank Mike Sanders, our editor at Alpha. We love working with you, Mike. And we thank our editors, Nancy Lewis and Karen Berman, for diligently assuring the accuracy and readability of the text and recipes.

Special Thanks to the Technical Reviewer

The technical reviewer for *The Complete Idiot's Guide to Terrific Diabetic Meals* was Karen Berman, a Connecticut-based writer and editor who specializes in food and culture. She is a contributing editor to *Wine Enthusiast* magazine whose work has appeared in numerous magazines, newspapers and newsletters. She is the author of *American Indian Traditions and Ceremonies* and has worked in various editorial capacities on numerous cookbooks.

Trademarks

All terms mentioned in this book that are known to be or are suspected of being trademarks or service marks have been appropriately capitalized. Alpha Books and Penguin Group (USA) Inc. cannot attest to the accuracy of this information. Use of a term in this book should not be regarded as affecting the validity of any trademark or service mark.

Part 1

Eating for Pleasure and Health

The new principles for diabetic cooking recommend eating lean meats, healthy fats, and low-glycemic carbohydrates to give you mouth-watering and healthy meals. The principles are explained in the *New Diabetes and Weight Management Food Guide Pyramid* developed at the Utah Diabetes Center at the University of Utah.

The ingredient section details the lean meats, good fats, and low-glycemic carbohydrates called for in the recipes. You'll learn about the condiments and seasonings that help modulate your blood sugar levels, plus the best sweeteners for desserts.

And finally, learn how to use the glycemic index combined with the glycemic load values of recipes so that you can stop counting calories and carbohydrates while losing weight and easily regulating your blood glucose levels.

Cooking for Health and Pleasure

In This Chapter

- ◆ Eating for your health pays off
- ◆ Learning which foods make you healthier
- ◆ Avoiding eating pitfalls
- ◆ Using this cookbook for great family meals

If you have diabetes, food and eating probably mean more to you than to the average person. It just isn't simple for you any more. Even though you have diabetic concerns, like all people everywhere, you enjoy eating and want to savor great-tasting food. But you now face more eating constraints and requirements than you ever thought possible. It can all seem, well, odd. And maybe unfair.

By now you most likely have personally experienced how food can be either your friend or your enemy. The friendly foods make you feel great, boost your energy, and keep your blood sugar levels in a safe zone. The enemy foods undermine your daily life and get in your way of having fun. In this book, we focus on the friendly ones. We give you recipes that you can use for everyday eating, not only for yourself but also to serve your family and guests.

Here's our promise. You will no longer need to apologize for serving "diabetic" foods. Your family members will eventually ask you to cook up many of these recipes simply because they taste great, and some of these recipes will become family favorites.

The Health Condition of Diabetes

If you're reading this book, either you or someone you know and love has diabetes. Here's a short overview about diabetes to clue you in on what it's all about.

Having diabetes means that a person's blood glucose levels are too high, which isn't good for a person's health. It can lead to serious health problems including heart disease, obesity, high blood pressure, and loss of vision or limbs.

Ideally, the blood carries glucose to all the body's cells. The hormone, insulin, excreted by the pancreas glands, helps the glucose in the blood move into the cells for nourishment. If the body doesn't make enough insulin or if the insulin doesn't work the way it should, glucose can't get into the cells. Instead, the glucose stays in the blood and blood glucose levels then get too high.

A person can get diabetes at any age. There are three main types:

◆ Type 1 diabetes, formerly called juvenile diabetes or insulin-dependent diabetes. In this type of diabetes, the beta cells of the pancreas no longer make insulin because the body's immune system has attacked and destroyed them.

◆ Type 2 diabetes, formerly called adult-onset diabetes or non-insulin-dependent diabetes, is the most common form of diabetes. In type 2 diabetes, the pancreas does not make enough insulin, and the fat, muscle, or liver cells do not use it properly. Being overweight can increase the chances of developing type 2 diabetes.

◆ Some women develop gestational diabetes during pregnancy. Although this form of diabetes usually goes away after the baby is born, a woman who has had it is more likely to develop type 2 diabetes later in life.

Fortunately, a person's diet can help keep blood glucose levels in a healthy range. All the recipes in this book are specifically created to help keep your blood glucose levels in a healthy range.

Eating for Health

Many individuals, not only persons with diabetes, are concerned about eating and foods. Fortunately, many of the principles for healthy eating apply to everyone. Healthy eating assists with such conditions as obesity and overweight, high blood pressure, heart disease, mood disorders, attention deficit disorder, autoimmune diseases, diabetes, and even some cancers. The list of healthy eating habits reads something like this:

- Reduce salt intake.
- Eat less fat.
- Eat fewer saturated fats.
- Eat more "good for you" fats.
- Avoid refined wheat and refined wheat products. In fact, avoid all refined grains and refined grain products.
- Eat 5 to 10 servings of fruits and vegetables a day.
- Avoid eating fatty meats.
- Eat whole grains such as whole wheat, barley, slow-cooking oatmeal, cornmeal, and brown rice.
- Eat nuts and seeds because they are good for you.
- Eat plenty of fruits and vegetables because they contain important antioxidants.
- You can't go wrong eating green vegetables.
- Stay away from junk foods and highly processed foods.
- Minimize your intake of artificial preservatives, colorings, and flavorings.
- Eat nutrient-filled snacks during the day.
- Eat high-quality protein at every meal, meaning at least three times a day.
- Eat plenty of fiber because it's "better than great" for you.
- Limit your intake of coffee and other beverages containing caffeine.
- Enjoy dark chocolate in moderation because it's filled with health-giving antioxidants.
- Exercise, exercise, exercise. It makes everything better.

 Healthy Notes

Trans-fatty acids are perilous to the health of your heart. They adhere readily to artery walls and may cause heart disease. Avoid all foods with ingredients labeled "partially hydrogenated fats." Also, when you heat most vegetable oils, the chemical composition changes and trans-fatty acids are formed.

- Take a daily vitamin and mineral supplement—just in case.
- Eat low- to moderate-glycemic carbohydrates.
- Reduce sugar intake.
- Avoid trans-fatty acids because they directly clog arteries and cause heart disease.

What's interesting is that these recommendations fit just about everyone, *and* they are the guidelines that persons with diabetes should use. What's healthy for you is what's healthy for the general public.

Changing Eating Preferences

But wait a minute. Changing eating patterns isn't so easy to do. Most of us have eating habits we absolutely don't want to change no matter what the scientific research suggests. Even just trying to eat 5 to 10 servings of fruits and vegetables a day can cause a whole family to rebel and propel some members to drastic actions (such as spending their allowance at a burger joint rather than on new CD releases and video games). Perhaps even you have wanted to stash jellybeans and donuts under the bed and eat "privately"!

Changing eating habits takes time and perseverance and a bit of trial and error. That's why this book emphasizes foods that are familiar yet downright good for you! You'll find healthy recipes in this book that have lots of zing that use ingredients you've grown accustomed to eating.

The recipes in this book will help you …

- Keep your blood sugar levels in the healthy range and out of the danger zone.
- Keep your blood sugar levels even all day.
- Manage medication timing and amounts.
- Reduce or eliminate your need for medications.
- Get the nutrients—vitamins, minerals, antioxidants, and other substances—that you need for great health.
- Enjoy eating.

Living in the Safe Zone

Managing diabetes gets easier every day. New information is available about how certain foods or activities can let you lead an easier and healthier life ... not to mention a more normal life. Here's what we know helps.

Eating Monounsaturated Fats

Yes, you can eat fat, and some kinds are better than others. Some of the best are the *monounsaturated* fats. Monounsaturated fats are also called the omega-9 fatty acids. It appears that these types of fats may help reduce insulin resistance. The following food sources are some of the highest in the monounsaturated fats:

- Avocados
- Olive oil
- Cold-pressed canola, sesame, and peanut oils
- Olives, both black and green
- Nuts and seeds, such as almonds, cashews, peanuts, pecans, hazelnuts, sesame seeds.
- Nut and seed butters made from the nuts and seeds. (The best kinds are fresh ground.)
- Tahini or sesame paste

> **Words for Well-Being**
>
> **Monounsaturated** fats are liquid at room temperature and can help lower high blood cholesterol levels when they are part of a lower-fat diet. Monounsaturated fats and polyunsaturated fats are both forms of unsaturated fat—fat that has room in its chemical structure for additional hydrogen atoms, which tends to make it more biologically active and healthy.

A good goal is to have at least one third of your daily fat intake come from monounsaturated fats. You can do this by eating avocados regularly and by using olive oil for your salad dressings. Of course, you still need to moderate your total fat intake, but a significant proportion of the fats you consume should be of the monounsaturated variety.

Eating Vegetables and Fruits

The more research done on antioxidants and how they work in the body, the more we learn we need them. Foods rich in antioxidants in their natural forms—that is, in fruits and vegetables—are especially good for you. The exception is that too much fruit can be too much of a good thing as far as your blood glucose levels go.

Biologically speaking, antioxidants neutralize the free radicals in the body. Free radicals damage cells and are created by stress, sun, illness, bacteria, viruses, and just by normal daily living. Antioxidants are thought to help prevent or reduce the severity of high blood pressure, heart disease, diabetes, autoimmune diseases, arthritis, depression, anxiety, ADHD, and cancer.

Specific beneficial antioxidants include flavonoids, quercetin, resveratrol, vitamin C, alpha lipoic acid, and carotinoids such as betacarotine, anthocyanidins, and bioflavinoids. Vitamin E is also antioxidants.

Eating 5 to 10 servings of fruits and vegetables every day seems like a lot. It is. But it makes a huge difference. A serving is generally defined as ½ cup cooked vegetables, and 1 cup raw. This cookbook includes plenty of yummy vegetable recipes that offer many health-giving benefits.

> **Healthy Notes**
> Carotinoids (betacarotine is one of them) are present in orange and yellow vegetables and fruits, and have been shown to increase glucose uptake in body cells. You'll find recipes in this book that contain carrots, sweet potatoes, red peppers, mangoes, and others. They aren't simply good; they're good for your blood glucose regulation.

Pour on the Acid

Acidic foods, such as vinegar and lemon juice, are excellent for you. The acid lowers the glycemic index of your meal and, thus, the glycemic load of a meal. Only 4 teaspoons of vinegar in your salad dressing can reduce the glycemic effect by 30 percent.

This means that simply by using acidic foods you can more easily maintain optimal blood glucose levels. This book offers plenty of recipes made with acidic ingredients.

Acid foods that can help reduce the glycemic load of your food intake include …

♦ Citrus fruits such as lemons, limes, oranges, and grapefruit.

♦ Vinegars.

♦ Sauerkraut.

♦ Capers and pickled foods, such as olives or pickled garlic (just be careful you don't get too much sodium).

♦ Pomegranates.

> **Healthy Notes**
> You can learn more about how to get to your ideal size without dieting from *The Complete Idiot's Guide to Weight Loss.* You'll learn simple and elegant ways to eat, think, and act plus get healthier at the same time.

You can eat these foods often and even with every meal.

Botanical Benefits

Many foods are beneficial for reducing blood glucose levels. Here's a list:

- **Cinnamon**. This is a wonderful addition to your foods. Why? Because it reduces blood glucose levels. Sprinkle it on your food and enjoy this luscious spice. Add it to vegetables, sweet potatoes, and acorn squash. Pair it with baked apples or pears. Use it to flavor yogurt and milks.

- **Garlic**. By now you've heard so much about garlic that you think it must be a miracle food. Indeed, it is. Garlic mildly lowers blood glucose levels, so you can consume garlic regularly. Eat it any way you can. Try it raw. Eat it pickled. Add garlic to your main dish recipes or top a salad with chopped garlic and toss well. Serve roasted garlic cloves as a delightful condiment.

> **In the Danger Zone**
> Keep the use of acidic foods in perspective. Don't even think of eating 4 or 5 donuts or bagels and then drinking a stiff vinegar cocktail to offset the glycemic load. Besides the fact that you would be overeating, you would be doing way more harm than good.

- **Hot peppers**. Those wonderful chili peppers that spice up our food and make it so delicious also help in lowering blood glucose levels. So enjoy salsas and Southwestern recipes, as well as Southeast Asian dishes and countless others that contain hot peppers.

- **Bitter melon**. This is an Asian fruit that lowers blood glucose levels. We've included one recipe using bitter melon in Chapter 21. Most likely you won't find it at a regular grocery store but can find it at a health food store or Asian market.

- **Fenugreek**. This is a spice that can also help normalize blood sugar levels. Try the vegetable recipe for Split Yellow Peas with Vegetables in Chapter 22 and the Poached Cod in Spicy Tomato Sauce in Chapter 8.

Dietary Fiber

Dietary fiber occurs naturally in all vegetables and fruits. Whole grains contain plenty, too. As you know, people with diabetes benefit greatly from diets high in fiber. Fiber slows down digestion and can prevent starches and sugars from quickly raising blood sugar levels.

When possible, always choose the food form that contains the most fiber. For instance, eating an orange gives you more fiber than drinking orange juice. When you eat an orange, you eat the pulp and fibrous membranes, but those fiber-containing parts of the orange are filtered out of orange juice.

The Least You Need to Know

- A diabetic diet is a super-healthy way to eat. The whole family will enjoy these recipes.
- Exercise and eating the right foods can help you limit your use of medications and reach your ideal size.
- Check your blood glucose levels regularly and keep your doctor informed about your health. The recipes in this book can also help you regulate blood glucose levels.
- Monounsaturated fats, fruits, vegetables, acidic foods, selected spices such as cinnamon and fenugreek, and dietary fiber help control diabetes.
- The glycemic index and load counts are provided for each recipe to assist you in eating low to moderate glycemic.
- Keep yourself informed about how certain foods or activities can let you lead an easier and healthier life.

The Glycemic Index for Food Choices

In This Chapter

- Eating low- and moderate-glycemic foods
- Utilizing glycemic load
- Losing and maintaining weight with low-glycemic eating
- Eating fats, proteins, and carbohydrates
- Reading the nutritional analysis summaries

The "newest" news in eating to monitor and control blood glucose is the glycemic index. Health results indicate that the glycemic index is here to stay. While it has an unusual name and could seem to be a complicated system, it's fast becoming a worldwide standard. In this chapter, we explain how the glycemic index works and show you how to use it.

We don't stop there. For every recipe in this cookbook, we tell you not only the glycemic index but also the glycemic load. From now on, you'll find it easier to predict how a recipe or a meal will affect your blood glucose levels.

Healthy eating encompasses other important factors as well. Because you want to be in charge of your eating and your health, we give you the tools and information you need. Our nutritional analysis summary of every recipe puts you in the know about the exact quantities of carbohydrates, fiber, fats, sodium, and other things you are eating.

Glycemic Index: All Carbohydrates Are Not Created Equal

Up until about 10 years ago, it was thought that all carbohydrates boosted blood glucose levels more or less identically. For example, it was believed that carbohydrates from an apple affect your body just like a slice of white bread does. Then some researchers in Australia took another look. They discovered that different carbohydrate-containing foods react differently in the body.

Some carbs, such as white bread and rice crackers, send blood glucose levels really high very fast, while others, such as vegetables and legumes, have only a slight effect. This was revolutionary news at the time, as well as great news for persons with diabetes and for individuals who wanted to lose weight.

In the Danger Zone

You can tell if a food has too high a glycemic value, or if the food you ate is too high in carbohydrate, by checking your blood sugar level two hours after the meal. If your blood sugar is over 140, then you either ate a food or foods high in glycemic index, or, you ate too much carbohydrate at one time.

What does this discovery mean to you? It means that you and everyone else you know with diabetes can eat carbohydrates with low glycemic indexes and still keep blood glucose levels in the safe range.

Following their initial discovery, the researchers got down to quantifying their results. They gathered groups of individuals to test carbohydrate-containing foods. In controlled studies, the groups ate certain amounts of a food and their blood glucose levels were tested. This data was compiled into what we now know as the glycemic index, or GI.

The glycemic index values of different foods were measured using glucose as a standard. It was assigned a value of 100. All other carbohydrates fall either above or below glucose, from 0 to about 115.

Generally speaking, and we'll cover the specifics later, refined starches, such as white bread, rice crackers, and maltodextrins (modified food starch) have high GIs. Table sugar, sucrose, and some fruits come next. Most fruits are in the group after that. And most nonstarchy vegetables are at the bottom of the glycemic index.

Pure fats, such as oils and butter, and animal-based proteins, such as meats and poultry, have a GI of 0. However, some dairy products such as yogurt or milk are tricky because they contain some carbs and some have higher GIs. Non-sweetened dairy products have a low glycemic value.

Foods are categorized this way:

♦ **High GI:** Over 70
♦ **Moderate GI:** Between 55 to 70
♦ **Low GI:** Lower than 55

The healthiest ideal is simple. Eat most of your carbohydrate-containing foods from the low-glycemic index range. Only occasionally eat foods that are moderate glycemic index. Avoid eating high-glycemic index foods.

Most likely you already have a glycemic listing brochure given to you by your nutritionist or certified diabetic educator (C.D.E.) and have used it to look up individual foods. We sure hope so. You'll definitely benefit from it!

Glycemic Load: Too Much of a Good Thing

Not everyone has great results using only the glycemic index. A person could eat only low-glycemic carbohydrates and still have a dramatic rise in blood glucose levels.

How could this happen? Because they ate too much of a good thing! For example, even though green peas have a GI rating of 48, definitely in the low glycemic range, a person could eat a whole pound—about 3 cups—and experience a marked increase in blood glucose levels. Likewise, a person could eat three or four jellybeans, which have a high GI rating of 78, and not experience any adverse reaction. Why? Because the quantity consumed matters. A lot. Enter the concept of glycemic load.

Glycemic load factors in the amount of food eaten plus the glycemic index rating of the food consumed. The lower the glycemic load of a given amount of a carbohydrate-containing food, the less it will increase your blood glucose levels.

Healthy Notes

Years ago dieters thought that grapefruit helped burn fat. That theory has been disproved. Yet grapefruit, which is quite acidic, does give an edge in losing weight. Acidic foods decrease the glycemic index and glycemic load of a meal. If you eat 4 teaspoons of vinegar with a meal, the effective glycemic index decreases by 30 percent. Include acidic foods often in your meals.

The following are accepted glycemic load (GL) standards:

- **Low GL:** 10 or less
- **Medium GL:** 11 to 19
- **High GL:** 20 or more

If you're striving to eat low glycemic, your glycemic load for a day should be about 70 or lower. If you eat a mixture of low and moderate glycemic foods, your glycemic load should be about 100. Remember though, not to "save up" carbohydrates by skipping meals and eating big at a later meal. Spread out carbohydrates fairly evenly throughout the day for best blood glucose control.

Here's a chart to show you what it looks like to eat meals that add up to a glycemic load of 70 or lower versus eating meals that add up to a glycemic load greater than 100.

Breakfast

Low Glycemic Load Food	GI	Carb	GL	Higher Glycemic Load Food	GI	Carb	GL
1 cup cooked thick-cut oats	42	30	13	1 cup cooked instant oatmeal	75	30	22
8 halves dried apricots	32	15	5	2 TB raisins	64	15	10
1 cup no-sugar added yogurt	14	15	2	½ cup yogurt w/sugar	40	15	6
Breakfast Total			20				38

Lunch

Low Glycemic Load Food	GI	Carb	GL	Higher Glycemic Load Food	GI	Carb	GL
Chicken	0	0	0	Chicken	0	0	0
2 cups broccoli	<1	10	<1	⅔ cup beets	64	10	6
⅔ cup long-grain brown rice	50	30	15	⅔ cup sticky white Asian rice	98	30	29
Lunch Total			15				35

Dinner

Low Glycemic Load Food	GI	Carb	GL	Higher Glycemic Load Food	GI	Carb	GL
Salmon	0	0	0	Salmon	0	0	0
6 oz. yam	37	30	11	6 oz. russet potato	85	30	25
½ cup peas	48	15	7	½ cup corn	60	15	9
2 cup vinegar/oil spinach salad	<1	5	0	2 cup vinegar/oil spinach salad	<1	5	0
Dinner Total			18				34

Snack

Low Glycemic Load Food	GI	Carb	GL	Higher Glycemic Load Food	GI	Carb	GL
Large pear	38	30	11	Microwave popcorn ½ bag	72	30	22
Snack Total			11				22
Day Total			64				129

You can determine the daily load that is best for you by keeping a food diary with glycemic load and a chart of blood glucose levels over a week or two. Then figure out the glycemic load that keeps you the healthiest and aids you in maintaining or losing weight.

The Role of Fiber

Foods high in fiber generally speaking have a lower glycemic index value. Bread made from white flour is about 70; bread made from whole-wheat flour is 71. But 100 percent stone-ground whole wheat bread is low glycemic at 53. The difference is that the first two breads are light and fluffy with an even texture. The stone ground bread is chewier and has an uneven texture with noticeable bits of partially ground wheat. The larger the particles of fiber, the lower the glycemic index.

> **Healthy Notes** _____
>
> Pasta is notable for its high-carbohydrate content. In general, though, it has a lower glycemic index than bread. And, if you cook regular pasta for only 6 minutes, to a very al dente state, it will have an even lower glycemic index.
>
> The pasta recipes in this book suggest you cook pasta for only 6 to 10 minutes so it's low-glycemic. As a substitute, you can cook the vegetable, spaghetti squash and use it exactly as you would spaghetti. Spaghetti squash, a nonstarchy vegetable, has fewer carbs—only 5 per ½ cup. Al dente pasta has 22 carbohydrates per ½ cup. So, the spaghetti squash has a lower glycemic load than pasta.

Fiber helps slow the intestinal absorption rate of glucose, and low-glycemic foods are the ones high in fiber. Thus it makes sense that higher fiber foods would be low glycemic.

Getting More Information

These websites offer information about the glycemic index.

- **diabetes.about.com/library/mendosagi/ngilists.htm.** Print out a com-prehensive list of the glycemic index with glycemic load values. Plus, sign up to receive Rick Mendosa's newsletter, "Diabetes Update."
- **www.glycemicindex.com.** From the University of Sydney in Australia, this site offers great information about eating low glycemic.
- **www.phelpsteam.com/glycoload/glycoload.htm.** Offers computer software that automatically calculates the glycemic load of foods, based on the food's glycemic index and quantity. The price is right at $15.95.

Daily Recommended Food and Nutrient Plan

Here are recommendations for your daily food and nutrient intake. By following these guidelines, you can regulate your blood glucose levels and enhance your overall health:

- **Glycemic index.** Eat low-glycemic, under 55. All the recipes in this book are low glycemic. Only occasionally eat foods that are moderate glycemic, from 56 to 69. Avoid eating foods that are high glycemic, over 70.

◆ **Glycemic load.** Keep your total for the day between 70 and 100. Be sure to eat three to five meals or snacks every day and spread out the glycemic load among all meals and snacks. Don't save up your glycemic load count to eat at one big meal because this causes glycemic loading, which results in high blood glucose levels.

◆ **Calories.** Eat 1,600 to 2,500 calories per day, depending on your height and activity level. Check with your certified diabetic educator to determine the right amount of calories for you.

◆ **Protein.** Eat 60 to 100 grams. Eat at least two thirds of your protein from animal sources so that you get plenty of complete protein or essential amino acids. Eat only one third or less of your daily protein from vegetable and plant sources.

◆ **Carbohydrates.** Eat 90 to 250 grams, depending on your height and activity level. Ask your Certified Diabetes Counselor for the amount you need on a daily basis.

◆ **Dietary fiber.** Eat at least 30 grams of dietary fiber. For the diabetic population the range is 30-45 grams per day. Primary sources are vegetables, fruits, nuts, seeds, legumes, and grains. The grains highest in fiber are whole grains, rather than refined grains.

◆ **Net Carbohydrate.** The amount of carbohydrate available for the body to convert into blood glucose. The fiber part of the total carbohydrate is subtracted out to give you net carbohydrates. Fiber is seldom digested and absorbed as glucose.

Healthy Notes _____

If you take a rapid-acting insulin medication before meals, subtract the grams of fiber from the total grams of carbohydrate in the meal. This is necessary if the fiber content of your meal is 4 grams or more. For example:

Food	Fiber grams	Total carbohydrate grams
½ cup 100% bran cereal	14	24
¾ cup blueberries	3	15
¾ cup milk	0	9
Total	17	48

48 − 17 = 31 grams of carbohydrate

This calculation is done for you in all the recipes in this book.

- **Fat.** Eat 30 percent or less of your calories from fat. Ideally, eat about 10 percent as monounsaturated fats and about 10 percent as polyunsaturated fats.

- **Saturated fat.** Eat 10 percent or less of your daily calorie intake from saturated fat.

- **Cholesterol.** 250 grams or less. Persons with diabetes have a much higher risk of heart disease, so it's best to restrict cholesterol intake.

- **Sodium.** 2,500 milligrams (2.5 grams) or less. Diabetes increases the risk of heart disease, as does an elevated blood pressure. Restricting sodium intake helps control blood pressure.

The Glycemic Index and Losing Weight

The glycemic index and glycemic load are used to lose weight by many individuals, including persons without diabetes. Why? Because losing weight becomes far easier when you use the glycemic index. By eating low glycemic you keep your insulin levels from rising too high. When the body contains too much insulin, it stores more and more fat. This is true for persons who don't have diabetes, too.

This link between weight gain and insulin creates a double whammy for persons with diabetes. You know that losing weight will help reduce blood glucose levels. That's good. Unfortunately, taking insulin or insulin secreting medications often stimulates weight gain. That's bad. You're caught between the need to watch your weight and your need to take medications to control blood glucose levels. That stinks!

The answer: Take charge by eating low glycemic! Doing so will help you avoid over-stimulating your body to produce insulin which can create more insulin resistance. You will start to gain control and reduce your weight down to your ideal size. If you are on insulin or insulin-secreting medication, you need to carefully manage your food intake and your medicine schedule for best blood glucose control. Check with your diabetes physician and diabetes educator to learn more about how your medication and/or insulin works in your body.

The Food Guide Pyramid for Weight Management and Type 2 Diabetes

An excellent food pyramid for Type 2 diabetes and weight management was developed by two medical professionals at the Utah Diabetes Center at the University of

Utah hospitals and clinics. The authors are Dana Clarke, M.D., C.D.E., who is the medical director of the Utah Diabetes Center and Joan Clark, M.S., R.D., C.D.E., one of the authors of this book and a dietitian counselor at the Center.

The Food Guide Pyramid for Weight Management and Type 2 Diabetes has five levels. At the top of the pyramid are the foods to eat only once in a while, and the foods at the bottom of the pyramid are the foods to eat more frequently. Serving sizes are indicated for each. Foods near the top of the pyramid increase blood glucose levels more than foods at the bottom.

Food Guide Pyramid
for Type 2 Diabetes and Weight Management

Foods near the top increase blood sugar to a greater degree than the foods near the bottom of the food pyramid

High glycemic index carbohydrates
With very low nutrient value sugar, syrup, sweets, flavored beverages w/sugar, most candy.
Occasionally

Higher Carbohydrate Foods
15 gm carbohydrate or more per serving

Refined Cereal

High glycemic index carbohydrates
With nutrient value
Cheerios, Grapenuts, sticky white rice, instant rice, dates, raisins
2 or fewer servings per day

Moderate glycemic index carbohydrates
Yams, sweet potatoes, apricots, bananas, oranges, peaches
2-4 servings per day

Eat less total fat, especially saturated fat.
Saturated fats are foods like butter, lard, bacon, some red meat, etc.

Oats

Yogurt

Low glycemic index carbohydrates
Milk, nonsweet Yogurt, dried peas and beans, wheat bran, rice bran, aldente past, cherries, grapefruit, apples, strawberries
2-4 servings per day

Very low Carbohydrate Foods
5 gm carbohydrate or fewer per serving

Nonstarchy vegetable
Broccoli, green beans, salad green, cucumber, peppers, cauliflower
4-9 servings per day

Healthy fats
Olive and canola oil, flax seed, nuts and seeds, avocado
2-6 servings per day

Healthy protein
Fish, chicken, turkey, very lean beef and pork, low fat cottage cheese
2-4 servings per day

Food Guide Pyramid for Weight Management and Type 2 Diabetes

Here is a detailed explanation of the Food Guide Pyramid:

- **High-glycemic index carbohydrates (with very little nutritional value— these foods are usually not nutrient dense).** Sugar, syrup, sweets, flavored beverages with sugar, and most candy. Eat only occasionally, which means infrequently.

- **High-glycemic index carbohydrates (with some nutritional value).** Un- sugared and sugared breakfast cereals, sticky white rice, dates, and raisins. If you eat these at all, have only two or fewer servings per day.

- **Moderate-glycemic index carbohydrates that are nutrient dense.** Sweet potatoes, apricots, bananas, oranges, peaches. Eat only two to four servings per day.

- **Low-glycemic index carbohydrates are nutrient dense.** Milk, unsweetened yogurt, dried peas and beans, wheat bran, rice bran, al dente pasta, cherries, grapefruit, apples, strawberries. Eat two to four servings per day.

The bottom of the pyramid has three categories of foods. These foods have the fewest carbohydrates. Eat mostly these kinds of foods for best blood glucose control:

- **Nonstarchy vegetables are nutrient dense.** Broccoli, green beans, salad greens, cucumbers, peppers, cauliflower, and other "free" foods. Eat four to nine servings per day.

- **Healthy fats are nutrient dense.** Olive and canola oils, flaxseed, nuts and seeds, avocado. Eat two to six servings per day.

- **Healthy protein is nutrient dense.** Fish, chicken, turkey, very lean beef and pork, low-fat cottage cheese, and other lean animal protein foods. Eat two to four servings per day.

Use these guidelines to determine serving sizes:

- **Protein.** 3 to 4 oz. meat, poultry, or fish; ¾ cup to 1 cup of cottage cheese; ¾ cup to 1 cup liquid egg substitute or egg whites. Each of these servings are 21 to 28 grams of protein.

- **Fats.** 1 teaspoon oils; 1 to 2 tablespoons or equivalent nuts/seeds; ¼ small avo- cado; 1½ tablespoon peanut butter. Each of these servings are 5 grams of fat.

- **Nonstarchy vegetables.** 1 cup raw or lightly cooked; ½ cup cooked well; ½ cup vegetable juice. Each of these servings are approximately 5 grams of carbohydrate.

Use these guidelines for serving sizes of foods higher in carbohydrates:

♦ For starches like potatoes, pinto beans, bran cereals, oatmeal, corn, and peas, ½ cup cooked is a serving and equals 15 grams of carbohydrate. For pasta and rice, ⅓ cup cooked is a serving and also equals 15 grams of carbohydrate.

♦ For fruits and fruit juices like oranges, pineapple, applesauce and pears, ½ cup is a serving. For melons (watermelon, cantaloupe, honeydew) and berries (strawberries, raspberries, blueberries), 1 cup is a serving. For dried fruit like raisins and prunes, about 2 tablespoons is a serving. All fruit servings are equal to about 15 grams of carbohydrate.

♦ For milk and sugar-free yogurt, 1 cup is a serving and this equals approximately 12 to 15 grams of carbohydrate.

In the Danger Zone
Don't go by the serving size on the package. They may not be correct for persons with diabetes. Instead, use the recommendations in this section as you plan your meals.

The recipes in this cookbook were written to be compatible with these guidelines. You can be certain that your dietary health needs are the highest priority in every recipe. Taste and flavor for your eating enjoyment are a strong second in priority for the recipes.

Keeping Up with Proteins

Eating high-quality protein is an important part of a balanced diet. Ideally, you should eat about .8 to 1 gram of protein per pound of lean body weight. Two thirds of this protein should be from animal sources to obtain all nine *essential amino acids*. So, for a 120-pound woman, with 20 percent of her body counted as fat and a lean mass of about 96 pounds, she would need between 77 to 96 grams of total protein, and 51 to 64 grams of animal protein per day. Three ounces of poultry, fish, meat, or the equivalent to this three times a day, would provide approximately 63 grams of animal protein per day.

For individuals with kidney disease, the recommended amount of protein is lower. Generally recommended is 4 to 6 ounces of a meat, poultry, or an equivalent for the day.

Words for Well-Being
Essential Amino Acids are comprised of nine amino acids that need to be ingested everyday for optimal health. Other non-essential amino acids can be manufactured in the body, but the body can't manufacture essential amino acids.

One exception is if your kidneys are compromised. If you have kidney problems it's recommended that you decrease your protein intake to about 1- to 2-ounce portions, two or three times a day, or about .6 grams of protein per pound of lean body weight.

At times, you can substitute vegetable proteins, such as legumes and soy, for animal protein, but it's best to eat them only occasionally. Vegetable protein doesn't contain all nine amino acids. Many forms of vegetable protein are difficult to digest so the protein may not be fully digested and assimilated in your body.

The Many Varieties of Fats

Yes, you need fats. Although you need less fat than you may have eaten before, you still need fat. Fats can be health giving, if you eat the good-for-you fats and reduce other fats. Fat increases absorption of fat-soluble vitamins and helps with metabolism of many bodily functions, including brain neurotransmitters, skin integrity, and a healthy heart. Current thinking suggests you can have between 20 to 30 percent of the calories you consume as fat. Ideally, your daily fat intake should follow these guidelines:

- ⅓ from monounsaturated fats
- ⅓ from polyunsaturated fats
- ⅓ from saturated fats

Here's what you need to know about these fats and what foods to find them in.

Healthy Notes

Peanut butter contains plenty of healthy monounsaturated fats. The old-fashioned kind of peanut butter that separates is best. You can usually still find it in the grocery stores and also at health food stores.

Monounsaturated Fats

Recent research tells us that monounsaturated fats assist the body in lowering blood glucose levels. They are found in olive oil, canola oil, and peanut oil. Avocados are high in them, as are olives, almonds, cashews, peanuts, and pecans. Sesame seeds and sesame butter are also great sources. You'll find plenty of monounsaturated fats in the recipes in this book.

Polyunsaturated Fats

Polyunsaturated fats are available in foods such walnuts and pumpkin and sunflower seeds, corn, safflower, and soybean oils. They are also found in mayonnaise and mayonnaise-like salad dressings, such as Miracle Whip. They're good for you if they comprise only 10 percent of your diet. When eaten in larger quantities, they can cause inflammation. Both polyunsaturated and monounsaturated fats contain essential fatty acids.

Saturated Fats

Saturated fats are solid fats and come from fat in meat, poultry, some dairy products, and in many processed foods such as crackers, chips, and so on. Most processed foods contain hydrogenated vegetable oil, a saturated fat that is added in fairly large quantities to many products. Saturated fats are thought to increase the risk of heart disease, especially in those persons who overeat them. A small amount is fine and actually unavoidable in a balanced diet.

Here's how to limit your saturated fat to 10 percent of your food consumption, or about one third of your daily fat intake:

◆ Grill, broil, or bake meats, because this lets the fat drip off during cooking.

◆ Slow cook meats and pour off the fat before serving.

◆ Avoid eating high-fat meats such as sausages and bacon.

◆ Cut off all visible fat from the meat before you cook it.

◆ Remove skin from poultry before you cook it. If this isn't possible, remove the skin and discard before serving.

◆ Avoid eating fried seafood, fish, and meats. In fact, avoid all fried foods.

◆ Avoid eating a lot of convenience foods that contain hydrogenated vegetable oil.

Butter is a saturated fat but doesn't need to be avoided entirely. You can use a small amount to sauté vegetables or meats.

Essential Fatty Acids

Essential fatty acids (EFAs) are good for everyone. In fact, we have to ingest EFAs regularly for health. EFAs ease aches and pains, act as mood enhancers because they modulate brain chemicals, and promote heart health.

They have the designation "essential" because they can't be manufactured in the body. The only way to get them is to ingest them. EFAs are contained in both the monounsaturated and the polyunsaturated fats. EFAs are important for mood regulation, healthy skin and nails, to reduce inflammation, assure a healthy heart, and aid in weight loss.

The primary essential fatty acids are linoleic acid and alpha-linolenic acid. The best sources of these are polyunsaturated fats, which include omega-3 and omega-6 fatty acids. Most people eat plenty of omega-6s in their diet by eating corn, safflower, and soybean oils and by eating seeds and nuts such as pumpkin seeds, sunflower seeds, walnuts, and Brazil nuts.

> **Healthy Notes**
> Certainly you've heard the tales about Grandmother and cod-liver oil. Perhaps you had to swallow it down as a child. Well, Grandma knew what she was doing. For what is in cod-liver oil, but essential fatty acids? In fact, you could take cod-liver oil daily, but only if you like the taste.

It's the omega-3's, the alpha-linolenic acids that are less readily available because they're unstable at room temperatures. The best sources of the omega-3 fatty acids are salmon and other coldwater fish, such as albacore tuna and cod. Other good sources of omega-3s are fish oil, flax seed oil, and flaxseed.

Another way to ingest enough essential fatty acids is to take a supplement, either in liquid or capsule form. Take about two tablespoons of liquid EFAs per day. In addition, you can also sprinkle ground flaxseed on your salads to increase the amount of EFAs in your diet.

The Nutritional Analysis

A nutritional analysis summary per serving appears at the end of every recipe in this book. Here's a sample nutritional analysis summary with each item explained. Because the nutritional values of foods vary from season to season, and grower to grower, the numbers are close but not exact.

We calculated the nutritional values based on information in *The Complete Book of Food Counts* by Corinne T. Netzer (Dell, 1997), and by the USDA National Nutrient Database. For the information on glycemic index and glycemic load we used a nifty computer program called GlycoLoad. You can order this program from this website: www.phelpsteam.com/glycoload. The program costs $15.95 and gives both the glycemic index of common foods and glycemic load based on either grams or ounces.

Nutritional Analysis per Serving: Glycemic Index 4 • Glycemic Load 3 • Calories 253 • Protein in grams 25 • Animal Protein 25 • Vegetable Protein 0 • Carbohydrates 5 grams • Dietary Fiber 1 • Net Carbohydrates 2 grams • Fat 7 grams • Saturated Fat 2 grams • Cholesterol 129 mg. • Sodium 5 mg. • Exchanges 6 lean meat, 1 fat, ½ fruit

♦ **Glycemic Index.** To get this number, we compiled the GI of all the ingredients in their corresponding ratios.

♦ **Glycemic Load.** This number represents the GI of the recipe, created by factoring in the amount of each ingredient. Generally it should be between 60 and 100.

♦ **Calories.** Total number of calories in a serving.

♦ **Protein.** Total amount of protein in a serving.

♦ **Animal Protein.** Total amount of animal protein in the serving. Contains all nine essential amino acids. Use this to calculate your daily protein intake.

♦ **Vegetable Protein.** Total amount of vegetable protein in the serving.

♦ **Carbohydrates.** Total grams of carbohydrates in the serving.

♦ **Fiber.** Total amount of fiber in the meal. If the number is greater than 4, you can subtract the number from the amount of carbohydrates to get the total effective carbohydrates in the meal.

♦ **Net Carbohydrates**. Carbohydrates less fiber and sugar alcohol equals the amount of carbohydrates available. In this book sugar alcohol is not used, and not recommended. Common sugar alcohols end in "ol" and include mannitol, sorbitol, xylitol, and lactitol. Sugar alcohols that don't end in "ol" include iso-malt and hydrogenated starch hydrolysates. Sugar alcohols can cause stomach bloating and diarrhea in some individuals. If you choose to use foods with sugar alcohol, you need to count them. They do increase blood sugar. The rule is to subtract ½ of the grams of sugar alcohols from the total carbohydrate.

♦ **Fat.** Total amount of all fats in the serving. Daily total of all fats should be under 30 percent of your daily calorie intake.

♦ **Saturated Fat.** Total saturated fat in the serving. Keep this daily total below 10 percent of your daily calorie intake.

♦ **Cholesterol.** The American Heart Association recommends no more than 300 mg. of cholesterol per day.

♦ **Sodium.** Keep your daily sodium intake to 2,400 mg (2.4 grams) or less.

♦ **Exchanges.** Gives the diabetic food exchange equivalents for the recipe. These are the four major carbohydrate exchanges:

Carbohydrate exchanges are starches, fruits, milk products, and sweets and desserts. One fruit or one starch exchange equals 15 grams of carbohydrate.

One milk exchange equals 12 grams of carbohydrate.

One sweets and dessert exchange equals 15 grams of carbohydrate.

Proteins like poultry, fish, cheese, eggs, and some vegetable protein make up the meat exchanges. The meat exchanges include four different categories: very lean, lean, medium fat, and high fat. A very lean meat exchange is equal to about 35 calories and 1 gram of fat, a lean meat exchange equals about 55 calories and 3 grams of fat, a medium-fat meat exchange is about 75 calories and 5 grams of fat, and a high-fat meat exchange equals about 100 calories and 8 grams of fat.

Fats such as butter, oils, nuts, and seeds make up the fat exchange. Each fat exchange equals about 45 calories and 5 grams of fat.

By using the nutritional analysis summaries you can create healthful meals that are also delicious and satisfying.

The Least You Need to Know

- ◆ Knowing the glycemic index of carbohydrate foods helps you keep your blood glucose levels in the safe zone.
- ◆ Glycemic load lets you know how much of each food you may eat on a day-to-day basis.
- ◆ Eating high-quality protein will help you maintain your energy and health.
- ◆ Some fats, such as monounsaturated fats, are good for you, so eat them daily; some kinds of fats, such as saturated fats, need to be eaten sparingly.
- ◆ The nutritional analysis summary for each recipe in this book gives you all the information you need to eat healthfully.

Chapter 3

Ingredients for Your Health

In This Chapter

- ◆ Using everyday ingredients
- ◆ Adding exotic and unusual flavors
- ◆ Shopping with an eye for healthier ingredients
- ◆ Desserts you can trust
- ◆ Incorporating healthy cooking techniques

Cooking can be lots of fun when you're cooking the foods you love. All that slicing and dicing, measuring and mixing, and boiling and broiling seem much more worthwhile when you know you're going to be munching down on some wonderful tasty dish.

Sure, cooking for persons with diabetes has restrictions and limitations, but you don't want to limit yourselves to a bland diet either. You aren't going to be frying up batches of high-cholesterol, high-sodium, high-calorie foods. You've already given up those gooey, yeasty, puffy breads. But at the same time, you still want to eat foods with familiar tastes that are good for you.

In this chapter, you learn how to do just that. You'll discover which ingredients to keep on hand and which ones you don't need anymore.

You'll learn cooking techniques for preparing the delicious flavors you love in ways that meet your dietary needs.

Everyday Ingredients

Perhaps you've noticed that the foods available in your grocery store have changed dramatically over the last 10 years. Sure, there's more junk food and more foods with unnatural colors and a plethora or artificial ingredients. Regrettably, you'll also find plenty of highly processed packaged foods that you already know to avoid.

> **In the Danger Zone**
> Be careful when purchasing foods labeled as health foods. Even the ones marked organic and natural could be filled with modified food starches and other high-glycemic ingredients. Reading the nutritional label and the ingredient list lets you know if the food will serve you well.

But somewhere in most grocery stores is a health food section. Or, as is true in many stores, the health foods have been integrated onto the regular store merchandise shelves. You can find unsweetened natural fruit juices, whole grains, brown rice, bulk nuts and seeds, and whole-grain flours.

These healthier selections are now a part of the everyday diets of many people. Food companies now recognize that many of us want better and healthier food. The choices are expanding. For instance, you can purchase absolutely delicious, even exotic, low-fat cheeses. In addition, low-fat and even non-fat mayonnaise and very lean ground meats are universally available.

If you don't have an adequate selection of these kinds of foods at a store near you, do two things. First, ask your grocer to start stocking healthier foods. Second, go online and order them. Fortunately, healthy foods are now only a click away.

Ingredients

The ingredients for the recipes in this book have been selected to give you the best nutrition. The cooking methods for these foods have been chosen to preserve as much of their natural nutrients as possible. Your job is to purchase the best-looking, most wholesome ingredients you can find.

Meats and Poultry

Choose lean cuts of meat for grilling and broiling. You can use fattier cuts for slow cooking and some roasting. Purchase fresh meats. You can freeze them when you get home if you aren't going to eat them in a couple of days. For those of you who care about the purity of your food, often you can find drug-free meats at the grocer. Look for terms like "no antibiotics," "no hormones" and "no animal byproducts in feed" on the labels.

Before cooking meats, cut away all visible fat. If the recipe calls for browning the meat, cook it in a very small amount of olive oil or butter, or both. A little olive oil keeps the butter from burning.

Remove the skin from poultry before cooking unless you are roasting a whole bird. The recipes in the poultry chapter mostly use skinless chicken breasts. When roasting poultry, you can keep the skin on, but be sure to remove and discard it before eating.

The white dense meat of pork is actually low in fat. It's the other pork cuts—like bacon and ribs—that are quite fatty. If you like the taste of ribs, be sure to remove all visible fat before parboiling, grilling, or slow cooking. After cooking, be sure to pour off the fat and discard it. It's best to simply avoid bacon because it's high in sodium, high in fat, and usually full of preservatives, such as nitrates. Nitrates are best avoided if possible.

Ham is an acceptable meat. But it's usually high in sodium, fat, and preservatives. One excellent method for reducing the amount of sodium and fat in a ham is to place the ham, either precooked, or uncooked, in a large pot, cover it with water, and boil it for two to four hours. Then pour off the water. Lots of the salt and much of the fat dissolves into the cooking water. It's completely cooked, and you can then roast the ham to bring out more flavor, or simply slice and eat it. Ham is great for quick breakfasts and lunches.

> **In the Danger Zone**
> Food preservatives are designed to reduce spoilage and extend shelf-life of many foods. They are deemed safe by the Food and Drug Administration (FDA). However, many are believed to carry their own health hazards— some, such as nitrates, have been linked to increased risk of cancer. It's best to read labels carefully and limit your consumption of food preservatives.

Fish and Seafood

Protein from the seas adds variety to your weekly meal plan. Fish and seafood are generally high in protein and filled with good-for-you fats. Studies show that having even one serving of cold-water fish a week can lower the risk of heart attack.

Healthy Notes _____
Cold-water fish, such as salmon, tuna, and cod contain the important omega-3 essential fatty acids. Try to consume some regularly.

If possible, purchase your fish and seafood fresh and cook it within a day or two. Ask for fish that's caught wild, and don't purchase farmed-raised fish. As of this writing, farmed fish contains toxins, such as dioxins and PCBs. Canned salmon and sardines are always wild, and not farmed fish.

Chapter 16 gives you seafood recipes; Chapter 17 contains fish recipes. They are so good you may want to have protein from the sea two or more times a week.

Vegetables

It's virtually impossible to say anything bad about vegetables. Most of them are low glycemic and well-suited to a diabetic eating plan. Only a couple are moderate glycemic, but even those have relatively low glycemic loads.

The only vegetables to avoid are white potatoes and corn. They are full of starch and high on the glycemic index. However, you can eat yams, because they are low glycemic. You can make them either mashed or baked.

So with vegetables … have a feast! Nutritionists recommend that we all eat at least 5, preferably 10, servings of vegetables and fruits every day, because studies have shown that ingesting these quantities reduces the risk of heart disease, diabetes, and cancer. Eat them all the time!

In the Danger Zone _____
While white potatoes are classified as a vegetable, the glycemic index counts are really high. Mashed potatoes are 92; baked potatoes are 85. If you love baked potatoes, give baked yams a try. They bake up just like a regular potato and taste delicious but their glycemic index is a low 37.

Try to eat a "rainbow" of foods. The more colors of food you eat, the merrier. And the healthier. Red foods? Eat purple cabbage, red bell peppers, tomatoes, radishes, and beets. A little orange or yellow food? Think carrots and squash. Green veggies? There are so many! Broccoli, peas, green beans, bean sprouts, lettuce, and many more. How about white food? There's onions, jicama, garlic, cauliflower, celery root, and turnips. There's nothing healthier than a salad tossed with a colorful palate of vegetables from your garden, the farmer's market, or a nearby grocery store.

Purchase either fresh or frozen vegetables. When the nutritionists suggest we eat vegetables, they don't mean canned ones. Avoid the canned vegetables if possible because they're already overcooked, mushy, and most likely full of sodium. Plus, they no longer contain some of the vitamins, minerals, and *phytonutrients* found in their fresh cousins. Sad but true, canned vegetables are "nutrient deprived."

You can eat vegetables raw all by themselves. Or add zest to raw vegetables with any of the many condiments listed in the later section, "Condiments Make a Feast."

Steaming is the preferred cooking method for vegetables. Boiling in a very small amount of water comes in second. Studies show that microwaving vegetables destroys some nutrients, so avoid using the microwave for vegetables whenever possible. After all, why purchase good ingredients to ultimately rob yourself of some of their health value?

> **Words for Well-Being**
> **Phytonutrients** are found in fruits and vegetables. These molecules play an important role in disease prevention. They neutralize free radicals that can cause diseases such as cancer, diabetes, skin cancer, heart disease, and minor colds and flu.

However, microwaving is here to stay. It's convenient and a natural part of everyone's everyday cooking. Some recipes in this cookbook call for microwaving vegetables. If you prefer to retain virtually all of the nutrients, go ahead and steam cook for higher nutritional value.

We have packed our vegetable side dish chapter with a veritable rainbow of delicious recipes for both you and your family to enjoy—there's even a chapter on side salads.

Fruits

Can you eat fruit? Absolutely yes! Most fruits are moderate glycemic, and some are low glycemic. Fruits generally also have a low-glycemic load factor. You may think they are high in sugar, and certainly they contain sugar, but overall, fruits are good for you. Fruits are high in fiber and are filled with important phytonutrients. Phytonutrients help to strengthen your body and prevent disease.

Add fruit to your daily food rainbow. Eat any kind of berry—blueberries, raspberries, strawberries, blackberries, or others. Enjoy cherries, oranges, pomegranates, plums, peaches, and melons. The list of delectable fruits is vast.

Chapter 11 on fruit side dishes offers many creative recipes that will increase your appreciation and taste for these wonderful natural foods.

Whole Grains

Far and away, your best choices for starchy foods are the least refined ones. Here's why. The more refined a grain, the higher its glycemic index. Refined grains, such as wheat and quick-cooking oatmeal, have been so highly processed that they are essentially white. The fiber has been removed, and the wheat or oatmeal is light and fluffy. Because of this, more of the starch is available when they're cooked and eaten. When you eat a refined starch, with its glycemic rating of 70 or more, your blood glucose levels soar.

Most processed foods use highly refined starches. Such products include white bread, bagels, muffins, cookies, cakes, rice crackers, donuts, quick-cooking oatmeal, boxed breakfast cereals, crackers, and cookies. You get the picture. Most of them are high glycemic.

Unfortunately, this doesn't necessarily mean that whole-wheat bread is any better for you. Regular whole wheat bread has a high glycemic rating of 71, which is actually higher than white bread. While the fiber hasn't been removed, the wheat is ground exceptionally fine, and usually sugar and caramel coloring are added to the bread. The result is still high glycemic.

In the Danger Zone

Shop for bread carefully. Read the label and watch out for several ingredients that may indicate the bread is high glycemic. Avoid breads with caramel coloring. It is often used to make bread appear to have a higher content of whole wheat. If the list of ingredients includes several kinds of flour and at least one is called wheat flour or enriched flour, don't buy it.

So just how can you get a decent slice of low or even moderate glycemic bread? Find bread that has pieces of grain still in it. Look for stone-ground wheat bread with "stone ground wheat" as the only type of flour in the ingredient list.

Here's the ingredient list for a package of bread labeled, Stone Ground Wheat Bread: Wheat Flour Bleached, Water, Soy Fiber, Vital Wheat Gluten (Wheat Protein), High Fructose Corn Syrup, Wheat Bran, Yeast, Molasses, Whole Wheat Flour, Salt, Dough Conditioners. You may be asking, so what ingredient makes this bread stone-ground? The answer is: none of them. This bread has a deceptive label. The first ingredient is plain old white flour, which doesn't belong in your diet.

Don't be fooled when you go shopping. Ideally, stone-ground bread's first ingredient is stone-ground whole wheat flour. Add to that some yeast, water, salt, and a bit of sweetener, and you would have stone-ground bread. Coarse breads without added coloring or refined flours are your best choices. Coarse rye bread with intact kernels such as whole-grain pumpernickel bread is great. Barley-kernel bread with 50 percent intact kernels is also great. You can also make your own bread, such as whole-grain bread with added psyllium or whole-grain bread with at least 50 percent whole oats or wheat bran. Choose hearty breads that are naturally heavy to the feel and thick in texture.

The same rules apply for choosing crackers. Anything with a coarse texture and 100 percent whole grain is probably good for you. But be sure to read the label carefully to verify the manufacturer hasn't added refined flour, modified food starch, or another high-glycemic ingredient.

The least refined oatmeal and consequently the best oatmeal for you is called Irish steel-cut oats. If your grocer doesn't stock this item, purchase it at a health food store. Steel-cut oats take a long time to cook, perhaps an hour or two, so cook up a batch and reheat portions during the week.

Psyllium and Bran

These ingredients add fiber to the recipes. Psyllium is a very mild tasting grain that's very low-glycemic and very high in fiber. Wheat and oat bran are very high in fiber, but contribute more to the glycemic load of a recipe than psyllium.

You can purchase psyllium in bulk at the health food store. Also, you may be able to find bran at the grocery store—but don't look in the cereal aisle. Instead, look in the health food section.

Rice

Rice is interesting because its glycemic index varies all over the place but mostly it's in the 50-60 range. The range is either in the high range of low, or the low range of moderate glycemic. Use brown rice, white rice, basmati rice, and even converted white rice. Just be sure to use only the amount specified per serving to keep your blood glucose levels stable. Avoid Asian glutinous rice, sticky rice, and jasmine rice as those are usually high glycemic.

Rice crackers and rice cakes are high glycemic. We once thought they made a great snack because they had so few calories. What rice cakes lack in calories, they make up for with their high-glycemic rating at 78.

Pasta

Cook pasta for a very short time, less than 6 minutes, or for a very short time, less than 6 minutes, or about half the recommended cooking time and it remains low glycemic. Cook it for 12 minutes or more, and it becomes high glycemic. Cook *fresh* pasta and other varieties, such as angel hair pasta only half as long as recommended in the cooking instructions.

If you want to avoid the situation all together, use a vegetable called "spaghetti squash" as a substitute. It is absolutely delicious with spaghetti sauce, because it readily picks up the delightful Mediterranean flavors. And spaghetti squash counts as one more vegetable serving for the day. Spaghetti squash is low glycemic.

Nuts and Seeds

Eaten in moderation, unsalted nuts and seeds make a delicious addition to your eating plan. They all contain fats that are good for you—the monounsaturated fats and the polyunsaturated fats.

Purchase nuts and seeds that are fresh. You can purchase them in bulk in many grocery and health food stores. You can also purchase nuts and seeds prepackaged, but be sure to check the expiration label, because both can get rancid if old.

At home, store nuts and seeds in the refrigerator or freezer. That way, they'll stay fresh until you finish eating the bag.

Sugars

No food has been more controversial for persons with diabetes than sugar. First it was bad. Then it was okay once in a while. Artificial sweeteners seemed like a great alternative. But animal test results indicate that artificial sweeteners may not be healthy and could be risky to use.

Because no one can say with total confidence that artificial sugars are actually good for you, we decided to simply avoid the issue. We chose not to cook with them.

Instead, the recipes in this book use the following two sweetener choices:

◆ **Fructose.** Fructose is relatively inexpensive and is available at most grocery stores in powder form. If you can't find it locally, order over the Internet.

The glycemic index of fructose is very low, at 19. Regular table sugar (sucrose) is 61, although fructose tastes slightly sweeter than sucrose. Fructose can be used in cooking, for baked goods, and for desserts.

♦ **Stevia with FOS (fruit ogliosaccharides).** Stevia is made from stevia leaf, a South American herb originally used as a healing herb by the native peoples. Stevia is 300 times sweeter than table sugar, so a little goes a long way.

Stevia has a slightly odd aftertaste that some people don't like. Manufacturers are now combining it with *FOS*, which mitigates the aftertaste and is actually good for you. If you can't find stevia with FOS, it's perfectly okay to use stevia without FOS. Stevia comes in a powdered and a liquid form; however, recipes in this book use powdered stevia.

Stevia with FOS is about 10 times sweeter than table sugar. Its glycemic index is zero. It holds up fine to both heat and freezing temperatures. You'll find stevia with FOS in many of our dessert recipes.

You may need to visit your local health food store to purchase stevia, or you can shop via the Internet.

 Healthy Notes Fruit ogliosaccharides (FOS) selectively nourish the friendly bacteria in the intestines and thus increase the number of good bacteria that support gastrointestinal health. FOS may improve regularity, cleanse the colon, assist and strengthen the immune system, prevent yeast overgrowth syndrome and help control the formation of free radicals. Wow! Amazing to think that a sweetener can help do all that.

 **Healthy Notes** The many varieties of honey average 55 on the glycemic index. Its position is at the cut off point between low and moderate glycemic. So you can use it sparingly as a sweetener. Sparingly means about 1 teaspoon a couple times a week, always eaten as part of a balanced meal or snack.

Oils and Fats

The recipes in this book use olive oil, peanut oil, and canola oil. Olive oil is easy to purchase because it's always cold-expeller pressed (or cold pressed, as it's sometimes called) from olives, then bottled. The lighter tasting olive oils are pale and come from second and third pressing of the olives; the richer tasting ones are darker and even slightly cloudy and they come from the first pressing of the olives. This is labeled virgin olive oil and contains more antioxidants than the lighter oils. You may want to use the richer ones for Italian and Mediterranean recipes and the paler olive oils for cooking where a lighter taste is desired. For general purpose cooking, you can use either.

We recommend cooking spray for pans, cookie sheets, and your grill to avoid sticking when sautéing, baking, or grilling. Use a general-purpose cooking spray and

In the Danger Zone

A little butter, preferably unsalted butter, now and then—say, a teaspoon—is probably fine to eat. But cooking with lots of butter can overload your body with saturated fat. Unfortunately, most butter substitutes, such as margarines, contain trans-fatty acids, which definitely aren't good for you. Use olive oil, or cold-expeller pressed canola oil, and peanut oil for general cooking.

spray lightly, using just enough to very lightly coat the surface of the pan or grill. You can purchase flavored cooking sprays, but you don't need to. The recipes all call for the unflavored types.

Purchase canola and peanut oils that are also cold-expeller pressed. This means that the oil wasn't heated when processed. Cold-expeller pressing preserves all the goodness of the oil. The alternative to cold-expeller pressed is heat-extracting. Heat extracting causes oils to form trans-fatty acids, which are known to cause heart disease, so it's important for everyone to avoid them. Keep your eyes open because the Food and Drug Administration is requiring that all packaged goods list the amount of trans-fatty acids on the nutritional label.

Condiments and Seasonings Make a Feast

Condiments and seasonings are the herbs, spices, sauces, and other flavorings that can dress up even the plainest of foods. Yes, persons with diabetes can enjoy a full range of tasty condiments and seasonings. In fact, the list of these flavorings that you can enjoy is quite long. Most likely our list includes some you've never tried before and perhaps haven't even known about.

Some of these condiments and seasonings can be used liberally, while others require a lighter touch because they contain either lots of sodium or lots of starches and sugars.

Surprise! Some condiments and seasonings actually help modulate blood glucose levels. Those that are beneficial for modulating blood sugar levels include: These condiments can be used freely:

Healthy Notes

Vinegar adds acidity to your meals. Choose from apple cider, balsamic, rice, red wine, white wine, champagne vinegar, and vinegars flavored with herbs and fruits.

- Cinnamon
- Garlic
- Vinegar
- Lemon juice and lime juice
- Chili peppers and chili powder
- Ground peppercorns (black, red, white, pink, green)

- Plain horseradish (but not the kind prepared with cream and other ingredients)
- Herbs and spices (such as rosemary, basil, sage, tarragon, coriander, cardamom, parsley, chives, thyme, fennel, cloves, mustard seed, celery seed, anise seed, and virtually any other spice in your spice cabinet)
- Prepared mustards and all the wonderful flavored mustards (if your mustard is sweet, then use in small amounts)

Use just a tiny bit of the following condiments. They contain enough sodium that you need to use them with a light touch. Fortunately, a little goes a long way toward dressing up your meal.

- Low-salt soy sauce. Avoid using regular soy sauce as it is filled with sodium.
- Bragg's Liquid Aminos. Used as a soy sauce substitute and as a salad dressing. Available at the health food store. But go easy, it still contains sodium.
- Dill pickles. Rinse in water before serving to wash off some of the sodium.
- Capers. Again, rinse before eating.
- Onions, scallions, and chives.

The following condiments count as a fat or vegetable exchange if you have more than just a teaspoon. Be sure to figure them into you overall daily tally.

- Parmesan cheese. As little as a teaspoon can add zest to many foods.
- Peanut butter or other nut butters, such as almond, filbert, or cashew. If you feel adventurous, mix with some chili powder or cinnamon!
- Toasted sesame seeds, pumpkin seeds, or sunflower seeds.
- Chopped nuts and seeds.
- Ground flaxseed.
- Homemade salsa. Today salsa is a bigger seller at the grocery stores than ketchup. Store-bought salsa typically contains way too much sodium and some-times sugar, so check the label for sodium and sugar content, or best yet, pre-pare salsa fresh at home.
- Sun-dried tomatoes.
- Pesto, which is traditionally a combination of pine nuts, fresh basil, garlic, and olive oil. You can vary the type of nuts if you wish, add sun-dried tomatoes, or make it with parsley or cilantro instead of basil. Your choices are quite varied. Plus, pesto is really easy to make. If you add cheese to your pesto, be sure to count the added sodium and fat in your daily meal plans.

The very words "condiment" and "seasoning" connote small amounts—like a teaspoon or at most a tablespoon. Much more than that and you are having a serving. Having a serving isn't what condiments and seasonings are all about.

Be sure to include these seasonings and condiments with your meals. A touch of this and a dab of that can change the most common food into something delightfully different. And many of them are quite good for your health!

For Your Sweet Tooth

Desserts are important. They taste good. They satisfy one's sweet tooth. Fortunately, desserts aren't forbidden food. And just to prove it, Chapter 26 is filled with many yummy recipes to satisfy your yearning for that "something sweet."

The dessert recipes are all low glycemic and have low enough glycemic loads that one dessert a day can easily fit into your daily food plan.

The recipes are made with a wide variety of dessert favorites: fruits, chocolate, and nuts. There are cheesecakes, parfaits, puddings, cookies, cakes, and cobblers. And plenty of choices so that your dessert palate won't get bored.

The topping to use for your desserts is frozen nondairy whipped topping. Popular commercial brands include Cool Whip and Dream Whip. These are a free food for persons with diabetes. An average size dollop for topping a desert is 2 tablespoons.

The Least You Need to Know

- Healthier foods can also be more delicious.
- Some sugars and sweeteners are actually good for you.
- The cooking methods you use can make all the difference in your health.
- Using ingredients that are low glycemic makes for a successful recipe and a satisfying food plan.
- Healthy ingredients can be found at the local grocery store or the local health food store.

Part 2

Breakfasts and Lunches

The quality of your most important meal of the day, breakfast, can make or break your energy level and health. These breakfast and brunch recipes will perk up your mornings, jumpstart your metabolism, and give you wonderful long-lasting energy and health.

The lunch recipes offer you a variety of delicious sandwiches and salads with a balanced combination of proteins, vegetables, and fats.

Chapter 4

Quick Breakfasts

In This Chapter

- ◆ Eating your most important meal of the day
- ◆ Preparing quick and healthy breakfasts
- ◆ Making mini-feasts on a mini-timeline
- ◆ Feeling energized all day long

You've heard for years that breakfast is the most important meal of the day. Eating a good breakfast prepares you for high energy and stable blood glucose levels throughout the day. Sounds simple enough, right?

But let's be honest about the realities of eating breakfast. It takes time. It takes thought. It takes preparation. And most likely, it's the last thing you want to deal with as you try to get yourself and your family out the door on time.

When you use the recipes in this chapter, eating a good breakfast will become considerably easier. These breakfasts are quick to make; many you can take with you in the car. And the tastes will satisfy the whole family.

Instead of fretting about poor breakfasts, from now on you should plan to have nutritious, enjoyable breakfasts. This chapter shows you how.

Breakfast Basics

By now you know that skipping breakfast is a bad idea. It makes your blood glucose levels unstable, and it robs you of energy later in the day. But we don't want to sound preachy about breakfast. We know how hard it can be to squeeze breakfast into a busy morning.

In the Danger Zone

Don't get so discouraged about having to deal with breakfast that you shortchange your health. A Danish and coffee for breakfast isn't good for anyone. Ditto presweetened cereal. It's best to give yourself a morning health boost, and keep your energy high.

So what should you eat for breakfast? Sometimes it gets confusing. What you ate for breakfast years ago gets failing marks today. Add to that your time crunch. Preparing breakfasts when you have time to cook—for example, on the weekend—is quite different from trying to prepare them as you are rushing to get out the door. You need something both healthy and quick. Of course, you also want food that is delicious and pleasurable. In other words, you want a mini-feast on a mini-timeline.

The Least You Need to Know

- Quick breakfasts can be healthy breakfasts.
- Many breakfast recipes can be ready-made to take with you on your way to work.
- Good quick breakfast recipes meet the needs of the whole family.
- Jump-start your day with the best nutrition possible.

Cottage Cheese Cup

Prep time: 5 minutes   •   Cook time: none   •   Serves: 1   •   Serving size: 1 cup

Nutritional Analysis per Serving: Glycemic Index 37   •   Glycemic Load 3   •   Calories 120 • Protein in grams 16   •   Animal Protein 15   •   Vegetable Protein 1   •   Carbohydrates 9 grams   •   Dietary Fiber 1½ grams   •   Net Carbohydrate 8 grams   •   Fat 2 grams • Saturated Fat 1 gram   •   Cholesterol 9 mg   •   Sodium 458 mg   •   Exchanges 2 lean meat, ½ fruit

½ cup 2% low-fat cottage cheese

½ cup berries (such as blueberries, strawberries, raspberries)

⅛ tsp. stevia with FOS

Combine cottage cheese, berries, and stevia in a serving bowl. Serve.

Palate Preview _____

This simple recipe is great tasting, for a sweet and nutritious start to your day. If you are in a big rush, you can put it in a plastic or glass container and take it with you to work. Besides, berries always seem luxurious.

Delightfully Different _____

If you don't have fresh or frozen berries on hand, you can substitute other fruit. Try fresh, sliced apples or pears. You can even use canned fruit, if it's canned in its own juice without added sweeteners (drained, of course).

Egg Salad

Prep time: 15 minutes • Cook time: none • Serves: 2 • Serving size: ½ cup

Nutritional Analysis per Serving: Glycemic Index (not significant) • Glycemic Load (not significant) • Calories 156 • Protein in grams 7½ • Animal Protein 7 • Vegetable Protein ½ • Carbohydrates 3 grams • Dietary Fiber <1 gram • Net Carbohydrate 3 grams • Fat 12½ grams • Saturated Fat 3 grams • Cholesterol 211 mg • Sodium 30 mg • Exchanges 1 medium-fat meat, 1 fat

2 hard cooked eggs, diced	2 TB. chopped pecans or sunflower seeds
2 TB. low-fat mayonnaise	2 TB. diced carrots
3 TB. diced celery	¼ tsp. freshly ground black pepper

Combine eggs, mayonnaise, celery, pecans, or sunflower seeds, carrots and black pepper in a bowl. Mix to moisten.

Palate Preview

Cook the eggs the night before. In fact, you can make the salad the night before so it's waiting when you arrive in the kitchen. You can easily double or triple the recipe to serve everyone in your family. Also great for a mid-afternoon snack.

Cold Cut Roll-ups

Prep time: 10 minutes • Cook time: none • Serves: 2 • Serving size: 4 rollups

Nutritional Analysis per Serving: Glycemic Index (not significant) • Glycemic Load (not significant) • Calories 73 • Protein in grams 12 • Animal Protein 12 • Vegetable Protein 0 • Carbohydrates 0 • Dietary Fiber 0 • Net Carbohydrate 0 • Fat 1½ grams • Saturated Fat ½ gram • Cholesterol 8 mg • Sodium 360 mg • Exchanges 2 lean meats

16 lettuce leaves

8 slices low-salt deli cold cuts (such as ham, turkey, or roast beef)

8 thin tomato slices

2 TB. plus 2 tsp. low-fat mayonnaise

Freshly ground black pepper

On a cutting board or working area, stack two lettuce leaves, one slice meat or poultry, one slice tomato, and one teaspoon mayonnaise. Sprinkle with black pepper. Roll up and secure with a toothpick. Repeat for all ingredients.

Palate Preview _____ Gives you a delicious, meaty flavor as you head out to work—or play. And it takes only one hand to eat!

Delightfully Different _____ If you like chilies and a Southwestern taste even for breakfast, add a teaspoon of diced green chilies to the stack before rolling.

Breakfast Burrito

Prep time: 5 minutes • Cook time: 30 seconds • Serves: 1 • Serving size: 1 burrito

Nutritional Analysis per Serving: Glycemic Index 30 • Glycemic Load 9 • Calories 260 • Protein in grams 21 • Animal Protein 17 • Vegetable Protein 4 • Carbohydrates 32 grams • Dietary Fiber 2 grams • Net Carbohydrate 30 grams • Fat 3 grams • Saturated Fat 1 gram • Cholesterol 28 mg • Sodium 420 mg • Exchanges 2½ lean meat, 2 starch

¼ cup cooked, diced chicken, beef, or pork (from leftovers)	2–3 TB. diced vegetables (such as celery, carrots, broccoli, tomatoes)
1 whole-grain, medium-size flour tortilla	1 TB. nonfat sour cream
2 TB. shredded low-fat or non-fat cheese	1 TB. Picante sauce

Place chicken, beef, or pork in center of tortilla, top with cheese, and microwave on high power for 30 seconds. Top with vegetables, sour cream and sauce. Fold over or roll.

Palate Preview

Whole-wheat tortillas come in handy for holding yummy ingredients. Plus, the glycemic index of a whole-wheat tortilla is low at 30. Vary the meats and vegetables to get new tastes and eliminate food boredom.

Breakfast Pizza

Prep time: 20 minutes   •   Cook time: 20–30 minutes   •   Serves: 6   •   Serving size: ⅙ pizza

Nutritional Analysis per Serving: Glycemic Index 47   •   Glycemic Load 14   •   Calories 287   •   Protein in grams 27   •   Animal Protein 21   •   Vegetable Protein 6   •   Carbohydrates 34 grams   •   Dietary Fiber 5 grams   •   Net Carbohydrate 29 grams   •   Fat 8 grams   •   Saturated Fat 3 grams   •   Cholesterol 56 mg   •   Sodium 278 mg   •   Exchanges 2 lean meat, 1 medium-fat meat, 2 starch

1 cup warm water	1 cup tomato sauce
1 cup slow-cooking rolled oats	2 cups chopped raw or lightly cooked vegetables (such as broccoli, spinach, or mushrooms)
½ cup unprocessed wheat bran	
1 pkg. (1 TB.) active dry yeast	¼ cup diced onion
⅛ tsp. salt	2 cups cooked, diced lean meat or poultry
1 TB. fructose	1 TB. chopped fresh oregano
1 cup whole-wheat flour, preferably stone ground	1 TB. chopped fresh basil
	2 cups shredded low-fat or nonfat cheese

Add oats and bran to warm water. Stir in yeast, salt, and fructose. Let stand for 15 minutes. Add flour. Knead into a ball of dough. Let stand for ½ hour. Preheat oven to 350 °F. Press dough flatly and evenly onto a round pizza pan. Spread tomato sauce evenly over surface. Add vegetables, onion, and lean meat or poultry. Sprinkle with oregano, basil, and cheese. Bake for 30 minutes. Serve immediately or eat throughout the week cold or heat in microwave for 30 seconds to warm.

Palate Preview

This pizza is filled with way more meat and vegetable topping than you'll get at the store. Prepare this breakfast pizza when you have the time, and you have just made breakfast for six days of the week. If you like your pizza cold, as many of us do, don't bother with heating it up in the microwave.

Breakfast Tempeh

Prep time: 10 minutes • Cook time: 5 minutes • Serves: 6 • Serving size: ⅙ square tempeh

Nutritional Analysis per Serving: Glycemic Index 15 • Glycemic Load 1 • Calories 80 • Protein in grams 7 • Animal Protein 0 • Vegetable Protein 7 • Carbohydrates 5 grams • Dietary Fiber 4 grams • Net Carbohydrate 1 gram • Fat 5 grams • Saturated Fat 1 gram • Cholesterol 0 • Sodium 102 mg • Exchanges 1 medium-fat meat

1 square pkg. (8 oz.) plain *tempeh*

2 TB. water

1 TB. low-salt soy sauce

1 TB. minced garlic

3 TB. finely chopped onion

3 TB. finely chopped fresh cilantro

Words for Well-Being

Tempeh is a fermented soybean product that gives you all the health benefits of soy in an easy-to-digest form. This recipe has a savory taste enhanced by the soy sauce.

Slice tempeh lengthwise, then crosswise into 12 equal pieces. Heat 2 tablespoons water and 1 tablespoon soy sauce in a frying pan set over medium-high heat. Place tempeh pieces into pan. Top with onion and cilantro. Simmer for about 2 minutes. Turn and simmer until water/soy liquid evaporates.

High Protein Chocolate Shake

Prep time: 5 minutes   •   Cook time: none   •   Serves: 2   •   Serving size: 1 cup

Nutrition Analysis per Serving: Glycemic Index 32   •   Glycemic Load 4   •   Calories 170   •   Protein in grams 20   •   Animal Protein 20   •   Vegetable Protein 0   •   Carbohydrates 12 grams   •   Dietary Fiber <1 gram   •   Net Carbohydrate 12 grams   •   Fat 2½ grams   •   Saturated Fat 1 gram   •   Cholesterol 6 mg   •   Sodium 308 mg   •   Exchanges 2 lean meat, 1 skim milk

1½ cup frozen skim milk or soy milk

½ cup frozen 2% low-fat cottage cheese

2 TB. whey protein powder

¼ tsp. stevia with FOS or to taste

1 TB. unsweetened cocoa powder

Soften milk and cottage cheese in microwave for about 30 to 45 seconds. Pour milk, cottage cheese, whey protein powder, stevia, and cocoa powder in a blender and blend well for about 2 minutes.

High-Protein Fruit Smoothie

Prep time: 5 minutes   •   Cook time: none   •   Serves: 1   •   Serving size: 2 cups

Nutritional Analysis per Serving: Glycemic Index 32   •   Glycemic Load 6   •   Calories 170   •   Protein in grams 15   •   Animal Protein 14   •   Vegetable Protein 1   •   Carbohydrates 21 grams   •   Dietary Fiber 1 gram   •   Net Carbohydrate 20 grams Fat 1 gram   •   Saturated Fat <1 gram   •   Cholesterol 10 mg   •   Sodium 178 mg   •   Exchanges ½ skim milk, 2 lean meat, 1 fruit

¾ cup nonfat plain yogurt or skim milk

1 cup fresh or frozen unsweetened fruit, chopped

2 TB. whey protein powder

¼ cup 2% low-fat cottage cheese

¼ tsp. stevia with FOS or to taste

Place yogurt or milk, chopped fruit, whey protein powder, cottage cheese, and stevia in a blender and blend until smooth. Serve cold.

Oatmeal with Nuts and Raisins

Prep time: 5 minutes • Cook time: 1 minute • Serves: 1 • Serving size: 1 cup

Nutritional Analysis per Serving: Glycemic Index 53 • Glycemic Load 17 • Calories 281 • Protein in grams 18 • Animal Protein 14 • Vegetable Protein 4 • Carbohydrates 36 grams • Dietary Fiber 3 grams • Net Carbohydrate 33 grams • Fat 10 grams • Saturated Fat 2 grams • Cholesterol 4 mg • Sodium 350 mg • Exchanges 2 starch, 2 lean meat, 1 fat

1 cup water

⅓ cup dry old-fashion or thick-cut oatmeal

1 TB. raisins

Pinch of salt

½ tsp. ground cinnamon

¼ tsp. ground ginger

1 TB. nutritional yeast or whey protein powder

1 TB. ground flaxseed (ground in a small coffee grinder)

¼ cup 2% low-fat cottage cheese

6 whole raw almonds

Palate Preview

Bet you'd make this recipe even if it weren't so healthy for you. Imagine a thick bowl of oatmeal filled with seeds and raisins, then topped with cottage cheese and nuts. You'll love it.

Bring water to a boil. Add oatmeal, raisins, and salt. Stir. Bring to a boil again. Reduce heat, cover, and cook about one minute. Turn off heat. Add cinnamon, ginger, nutritional yeast or protein powder, and ground flaxseed. Stir. Pour into bowl and top with cottage cheese and almonds.

Chapter 5

Brunches

In This Chapter

- ◆ Taking time for a leisurely breakfast
- ◆ Delicious recipes for weekends
- ◆ Cooking with health-filled ingredients
- ◆ Mastering the art of pleasurable eating

What a delightful meal breakfast can be—especially when you have plenty of time to relax and savor the flavors. Turn on some favorite music, set the table, gather the family, and serve up some of these delicious recipes.

Leisurely breakfasts can be veritable feasts. That's because breakfast foods are truly wonderful. Rich flavors. Sensuous textures. Great aromas. Plus, a leisurely breakfast is special in itself because you probably prepare such a treat only once or twice a week and more likely, once, on the weekend.

Glance through the recipes in this chapter and go ahead and plan your weekend breakfasts right now. That way, you'll have plenty of time to purchase the ingredients you'll need.

Breakfast Ingredients

The recipes in this chapter offer you standard breakfast and brunch fare. You'll find quiches and pancakes, sausages, and egg casseroles.

You can also make breakfasts more "diabetes friendly" by choosing your ingredients carefully. Here are some examples:

♦ **Sausage.** As you know, regular prepackaged breakfast sausage is out of bounds because of saturated fat and sodium. The Spicy Breakfast Sausage recipe included here offers you a delicious, savory version of sausage. It calls for ground pork, beef, and veal. You add in seasonings from your spice cabinet along with fresh garlic, scallions, and green bell pepper.

♦ **Flour.** Some recipes call for flour. White flour and finely ground whole-wheat flour are both high on the glycemic index at 70 for white flour and 71 for whole-wheat flour. Less finely ground flour, such as stone ground or seven-grain flour are lower on the glycemic index—at about 58. The coarser flours are also much higher in fiber. It's worth a trip to the health food store to get the coarser flours.

♦ **Cheese.** Regular, full-fat cheeses are used sparingly. A dusting of Parmesan can greatly enhance the flavor of virtually any egg dish, so go ahead and use a teaspoon now and then. Remember, though, that it's high in sodium. For most recipes, we recommend low-fat or nonfat cheeses. The "Nutritional Analysis per Serving" is based on using low-fat cheese.

♦ **Eggs**. Most of the egg recipes in this chapter call for egg whites or liquid egg substitute (made from egg –whites and available at the grocery store). Whole eggs are high in cholesterol and fat, so use them only once in a while, as we have here.

By changing out some of your regular ingredients for "upgrades," so to speak, you can create breakfasts that more healthfully fuel your body.

The Least You Need to Know

♦ Make leisurely breakfasts a part of your weekly routine.

♦ These breakfast recipes use regular everyday ingredients, although some feature specific low-glycemic ingredients.

♦ These recipes include egg-cheese combinations, pancakes, sausage, and other dishes that are both sweet and savory.

♦ An appealing environment and the right frame of mind make your meals healthier and happier.

Vegetable Quiche

Prep time: 20 minutes • Cook time: 40 minutes • Serves: 1 serving • Serving size: 1 quiche

Nutritional Analysis per Serving: Glycemic Index (not significant) • Glycemic Load (not significant) • Calories 159 • Protein in grams 14 • Animal Protein 11 • Vegetable Protein 3 • Carbohydrates 12 grams • Dietary Fiber 2 grams • Net Carbohydrate 10 grams • Fat 3 grams • Saturated Fat 1 gram • Cholesterol 6 mg • Sodium 173 mg • Exchanges 1 lean meat, ½ high-fat meat, 2 vegetable

Olive oil cooking spray	⅛ red bell pepper, cored, seeded, chopped
⅛ onion, chopped	½ cup broccoli florets
½ clove garlic, minced	1 TB. shredded low-fat cheddar cheese
⅛ green bell pepper, cored, seeded, and chopped	2 egg whites
	1 TB. seven-grain flour

Preheat oven to 350°F. Spray a 1-quart casserole and a large a skillet with olive oil spray. Set skillet over medium-high heat, the add onions, the garlic, and peppers, and sauté, stirring frequently, until tender. In a steamer, steam the broccoli for about 6 minutes or until tender. Mix the sautéed vegetables, broccoli, and ½ TB. cheese, and spoon into prepared casserole. In a small bowl, mix together egg whites and flour until thoroughly combined. Pour mixture over vegetables and sprinkle with remaining cheese. Bake for about 40 minutes or until set.

Palate Preview

This vegetable mix of red and green peppers combined with broccoli and garlic makes a unique one-person crustless quiche. Your meal comes out of the oven in 40 minutes. Just enough time to get in some exercise while it cooks.

Crab and Pork Omelet

Prep time: 15 minutes • Cook time: 30 minutes • Serves: 2 • Serving size: ½ omelet

Nutritional Analysis per Serving: Glycemic Index (not significant) • Glycemic Load (not significant) • Calories 238 • Protein in grams 22 • Animal Protein 21 • Vegetable Protein 1 • Carbohydrates 1 gram • Dietary Fiber <1 gram • Fat 13 grams • Saturated Fat 5 grams • Cholesterol 115 mg • Sodium 80 mg • Exchanges 3 medium-fat meat

¼ lb. ground pork, browned and drained

¼ lb. cooked crabmeat, rinsed and drained

1 egg

1 small onion, chopped

1 clove garlic, chopped

2 white mushrooms, chopped

Salt and freshly ground black pepper to taste

Preheat oven to 350°F. Mix together pork, crabmeat, egg, onion, garlic, mushrooms, and salt and pepper, and pour into an 8-inch square baking dish. Bake for about 30 minutes, or until eggs are firm and all other ingredients are heated through. Cut into halves.

Palate Preview _____

The combined flavors of ground pork and crabmeat make an unusual dish with a taste slightly reminiscent of Southeast Asia. Add a tossed green salad (or side salad from Chapter 10) to complete your meal.

Broccoli Strata

Prep time: 20 minutes plus 4 hours refrigeration time • Cook time: 45 to 55 minutes •
Serves: 6 • Serving size: 1 square (2½ × 4 inches)

Nutritional Analysis per Serving: Glycemic Index 44 • Glycemic Load 10 • Calories 231
• Protein in grams 18 • Animal Protein 15 • Vegetable Protein 3 • Carbohydrates
22 grams • Dietary Fiber 4 grams • Net Carbohydrate 18 grams • Fat 6 grams •
Saturated Fat 3 grams • Cholesterol 22 mg • Sodium 106 mg • Exchanges
2 medium-fat meats, 1 starch

Vegetable oil cooking spray	1 cup shredded Italian cheese blend
1 medium onion, chopped	1½ cups nonfat milk
1 cup julienne-cut (2 × ⅛ × ⅛-inch) carrots	1 cup refrigerated or frozen fat-free egg substitute, thawed
2 cups frozen broccoli florets, thawed	
6 slices day-old whole-wheat bread, preferably stone-ground	1 tsp. salt-free garlic-pepper blend

Spray an 8-inch square (2-quart) glass baking dish and
a large nonstick skillet with cooking spray. Heat the
skillet over medium-high heat. Add onion and carrots,
and cook, stirring, for 3 to 4 minutes. Add broccoli,
and cook, stirring, for 2 to 3 minutes more or until vegetables are crisp-tender.

Palate Preview ___
Cook this layered egg-
and-vegetable dish for your family
and also for guests at brunch.
You'll love the cheesy egg base
with delicious vegetables.

Cut bread into large cubes and pour into prepared baking dish in a single layer. Spoon broccoli mixture over
bread. Sprinkle cheese evenly over top.

In a medium bowl, combine half-and-half, egg substitute, and garlic-pepper blend, and beat
until smooth. Pour over broccoli mixture. Cover and refrigerate for at least 4 hours or
overnight.

Preheat the oven to 350°F. Cover strata and bake for 45 to 55 minutes or until a knife inserted
in the center comes out clean. Let stand 5 minutes before cutting into squares.

Spicy Breakfast Sausage

Prep time: 15 minutes plus 3 hours refrigeration   •   Cook time: 5 minutes   •   Serves: 12
•   Serving size: 1 (3-ounce) sausage patty

Nutritional Analysis per Serving: Glycemic Index (not significant)   •   Glycemic Load (not significant)   •   Calories 226   •   Protein in grams 21   •   Animal Protein 21   •
Vegetable Protein 0   •   Carbohydrates 0   •   Dietary Fiber 0   •   Net Carbohydrate 0   •
Fat 13 grams   •   Saturated Fat 7 grams   •   Cholesterol 78 mg   •   Sodium 82 mg   •
Exchanges 3 medium-fat meat

1 lb. lean ground pork	2 tsp. ground cumin
1 lb. lean ground beef	1 tsp. dried thyme
1 lb. ground veal	1 tsp. fennel seeds
4 cloves garlic, minced	Pinch ground nutmeg
1 bunch scallions (green onions, white part and 2 inches green), minced	Crushed red pepper flakes, to taste
	Olive oil cooking spray
1 large green bell pepper, cored, seeded, and minced	

Mix pork, beef, and veal thoroughly in a large mixing bowl. Add garlic, scallions, green pepper, cumin, thyme, fennel seeds, nutmeg, and red pepper flakes. Mix thoroughly with your hands.

To make sure seasoning is to your taste, fry 1 teaspoon in a skillet until it is no longer pink. Taste and adjust if necessary.

Palate Preview With this recipe you can make your own spicy, aromatic sausage without all the added fat and sodium found in store-bought brands. Cook ahead for the week, and you can have sausage every morning simply by warming in the microwave.

Divide remaining meat mixture in half. Roll each half into a log 7 inches long and about 2 inches wide. Wrap logs separately in plastic wrap and refrigerate at least 3 hours or up to 2 days.

When you are ready to cook, unwrap the sausage logs and cut them into ½-inch slices. Spray a skillet with cooking spray and sauté the patties over medium-high heat until well browned on each side.

Delightfully Different One of the greatest kitchen conveniences to come along in a long time is fresh (not dried) minced garlic in a jar. It saves you the time of peeling and mincing garlic. And it saves you the smelly hands. To substitute, figure ½ teaspoon minced garlic for each medium-size clove.

Cinnamon Apple Whole-Wheat Pancakes

Prep time: 25 minutes • Cook time: 15–20 minutes • Serves: 6 • Serving size: 2 (4-inch) pancakes

Nutritional Analysis per Serving: Glycemic Index 59 • Glycemic Load 9 • Calories 98 • Protein in grams 4 • Animal Protein 2 • Vegetable Protein 2 • Carbohydrates 16 grams • Dietary Fiber 2 grams • Net Carbohydrate 14 grams • Fat 2 grams • Saturated Fat ½ gram • Cholesterol 40 mg • Sodium 169 mg • Exchanges 1 starch

¾ cup whole-wheat flour, preferably stone-ground

¼ cup unprocessed wheat bran

2 tsp. baking powder

2 tsp. ground cinnamon, or more to taste

⅛ tsp. salt

¾ cup skim or 1% low-fat milk, or more if needed

1 egg or 2 egg whites

1 tsp. canola oil

½ cup unsweetened applesauce

Vegetable oil or vegetable oil cooking spray

1½ cup sliced apple wedges

6 TB. water

1 tsp. stevia with FOS

Mix together whole-wheat flour, wheat bran, baking powder, cinnamon, and salt. Add milk, eggs, oil, and applesauce. Mix. Add a little more milk if a thinner consistency is desired. Grease a griddle or frying pan with a little vegetable oil or vegetable oil spray and set over medium-high heat. Scoop 2 tablespoons batter for each pancake into pan, being careful not to crowd pan, and cook until bubbles form on top and the edges begin to look dry. Turn the pancake with a spatula and cook until golden brown and cooked through. Repeat with the remaining batter. Place apple wedges in microwavable bowl. Add water to apples. Cover and microwave on high power for 2 minutes or until of desired consistency. Sweeten with stevia with FOS. Serve with pancakes. Sprinkle more cinnamon on top if desired.

Palate Preview

Yes! Everyone loves pancakes and these are sure to be a hit. These are topped with apple slices and cinnamon.

High-Fiber Wheat Bran and Oats Pancakes

Prep time: 20 minutes • Cook time: 3 minutes per pancake • Serves: 6 • Serving size: 1 pancake

Nutritional Analysis per Serving: Glycemic Index 52 • Glycemic Load 7 • Calories 82 • Protein in grams 4 • Animal Protein 2½ • Vegetable Protein 1½ • Carbohydrates 14 grams • Dietary Fiber 2 grams • Net Carbohydrate 12 grams • Fat 1 gram • Saturated Fat <1 gram • Cholesterol 33 mg • Sodium 202 mg • Exchanges 1 starch

1 cup buttermilk (or skim milk with 1 TB. lemon juice)

⅔ cup slow-cooking rolled oats

½ cup unprocessed wheat bran

2 egg whites or 1 egg

¼ cup whole-wheat flour, preferably stone-ground

1 tsp. fructose

⅛ tsp. salt

¾ tsp. baking soda

Palate Preview

These pancakes offer you a down-home country taste with an interesting and satisfying texture. Serve with the Spicy Breakfast Sausage Recipe also found in this chapter. Add some fruit or a vegetable for a complete meal.

Vegetable oil or vegetable oil cooking spray Combine milk, oats, and bran in a large bowl. Let stand until rolled oats soften. Add egg and blend. Mix in flour, fructose, salt, and baking soda. Grease a griddle or frying pan with a little vegetable oil or vegetable oil spray and set over medium-high heat. Pour about ¼ cup batter into the pan and cook for about 3 minutes or until bubbles form on top and the edges begin to look dry. Turn the pancake with a spatula and cook for 1 to 2 minutes, or until golden brown and cooked through. Repeat with the remaining batter. Serve hot with unsweetened jam or syrup.

Vegetable and Meat Frittata

Prep time: 10 minutes • Cook time: 5 minutes • Serves: 1 • Serving size: 1½ cups

Nutritional Analysis per Serving: Glycemic Index (not significant) • Glycemic Load (not significant) • Calories 130–140 • Protein in grams 29 • Animal Protein 27 • Vegetable Protein 2 • Carbohydrates 5 grams • Dietary Fiber 1 gram • Net Carbohydrate 4 grams • Fat 2–5 grams • Saturated Fat 2 grams • Cholesterol 9 mg • Sodium 172 mg • Exchanges 3 lean meat, 1 vegetable

¼ cup fat-free liquid egg substitute

¼ cup cooked lean meat or chicken

1 TB. grated Parmesan cheese

Vegetable oil cooking spray

⅔ cup chopped fresh or cooked vegetables

¼ cup shredded nonfat or low-fat cheese

Preheat the broiler. Combine egg substitute, meat or chicken, and Parmesan cheese in a bowl. Spray a non-stick skillet with cooking spray and set over medium-high heat. Add vegetables and cook for 1 minute. Reduce heat and add egg mixture. Cover and cook without stirring for 3 to 5 minutes or until egg is set. Sprinkle shredded cheese over egg mixture, transfer the skillet to the broiler and broil for about 1 minute, or until cheese is melted and golden.

Palate Preview

You get plenty of high-quality protein in this frittata, plus a serving of vegetables. Just a sprinkle of Parmesan cheese spices up the meal. And you can use up your leftover meat or chicken and vegetables deliciously.

Chapter 6

Lunches

In This Chapter

- ◆ Eating light and nutritious lunches
- ◆ Using low-glycemic breads
- ◆ From burgers to spicier fare
- ◆ Dishes for everyday meals

You know how easy it is to forget to eat lunch. Your agenda is filled, your computer continually beeps with meeting alarms, and the phone seems attached permanently to your ear. Where could you ever find the time?

Yet people do. Even really busy people find time to stop and eat lunch. They make themselves slow down enough to actually enjoy it, too. People who easily manage their weight don't skip meals.

Eating a nutritionally balanced lunch keeps your metabolism engine stoked until your afternoon snack. Your blood glucose levels stay regulated. And if you take time to slow down and savor, eating lunch is terrific for lowering your stress levels.

With the recipes in this chapter, you'll come to appreciate lunch in a brand-new way. For a small amount of prep time, you get added value in terms of nutrition and delightful tastes. Plus, you get to take a big, long breath, and relax midday.

Not on the Run

Catching something to eat on the run for lunch works against your goals of eating well. It works against anyone's health goals.

Rushing when eating makes for a confused stomach. The food goes in fast. Often, it's fast food. Often the food isn't as much chewed as simply swallowed. Your stomach, in fact your whole body, is looking for nutrients to keep on going for somewhere between three to five hours.

If you eat a meal devoid of good nutrients, your stomach will be still searching for satisfaction. In its search, you get hungry again soon, and if you give in to the urge to eat, you could easily overload on calories. That means weight gain. And if you eat nutrient-poor foods again, the cycle has no end.

The lunch recipes in this chapter offer you excellent nutrients to satisfy both your stomach and your body. As you eat these foods, think pleasure, enjoyment, and health.

The Least You Need to Know

- Make lunch a time for a relaxing and nutritious meal.
- A good lunch helps keep blood glucose levels regulated all afternoon.
- A nutritious lunch can keep your energy high until dinner time.
- The recipes in this chapter are quick and easy to prepare.

Slow Cooked Barbecued Turkey Sandwiches

Prep time: 15 minutes • Cook time: 10 hours • Serves: 12 • Serving size: 1 whole-wheat sandwich bun with ½ cup turkey mixture and 1½ tablespoons coleslaw

Nutritional Analysis per Serving: Glycemic Index 55 • Glycemic Load 18 • Calories 290 • Protein in grams 22 • Animal Protein 20 • Vegetable Protein 2 • Carbohydrates 34 grams • Dietary Fiber 2½ grams • Net Carbohydrate 32 grams • Fat 5 grams • Saturated Fat 2 grams • Cholesterol 78 mg • Sodium 146 mg • Exchanges 3 lean meat, 2 starch

Vegetable oil cooking spray	2 TB. hot pepper sauce (Louisiana style)
4 turkey thighs (2½ to 3 lb.), skin removed	1 tsp. coarsely ground black pepper
2½ TB. fructose	½ tsp. crushed red pepper flakes
3 TB. prepared mustard	12 stone-ground whole-wheat buns or bread
3 TB. ketchup	½ pint (1 cup) low-fat coleslaw
2 TB. cider vinegar	

Spray a 4- to 6-quart slow cooker with cooking spray and place turkey into it. In a small bowl, combine fructose, mustard, ketchup, vinegar, hot pepper sauce, black pepper, and red pepper flakes. Mix well and pour over turkey, turning turkey as necessary to coat.

Cover and cook on low heat setting for 8 to 10 hours.

Remove turkey from the slow cooker and place on a large plate, leaving broth in the slow cooker. Remove meat from bones and discard bones. Shred turkey with two forks. Return turkey to broth in slow cooker and mix well to add moisture and broth taste to the meat.

To serve, with slotted spoon, place about ½ cup turkey mixture onto bottom half of each bun. Top each with a rounded tablespoon of coleslaw. Cover with bun tops and serve.

Palate Preview

Barbecue is always a mouth-watering treat, and it's easy when prepared in a slow cooker. Try these tender and spicy turkey thigh sandwiches. With coleslaw (try the recipes in Chapter 10), they make a complete meal. This recipe serves twelve, so you can prepare for a party or freeze half as a reserve for the next week's lunches.

Middle Eastern Beef Pita Pockets

Prep time: 15 minutes • Cook time: 10 minutes • Serves: 4 • Serving size: ½ whole-wheat pita pocket with 2 cups salad mix

Nutritional Analysis per Serving: Glycemic Index 48 • Glycemic Load 14 • Calories 460 • Protein in grams 39 • Animal Protein 33 • Vegetable Protein 6 • Carbohydrates 31 grams • Dietary Fiber 4 grams • Net Carbohydrate 27 grams • Fat 18 grams • Saturated Fat 4 grams • Cholesterol 96 mg • Sodium 397 mg • Exchanges 4 lean meat, 3 fat, 2 starch

Vegetable oil cooking spray

1 lb. London broil or other tender cut of steak

1 large onion, quartered

4 cups torn romaine lettuce

½ English cucumber, quartered and sliced

1 cup drained canned chickpeas, rinsed

Lemon-Mint Dressing:

¼ cup fresh mint leaves

¼ cup chopped fresh parsley

2 garlic cloves, chopped

3 TB. fresh lemon juice

3 TB. canned, fat-free, low-sodium chicken broth

2 TB. extra-virgin olive oil or herb flavored oil

2 whole-wheat pita pockets, cut in half

Palate Preview

Whole-wheat pita bread is moderate glycemic at 57. Fill the pockets with steak, vegetables, and chickpeas. Then top with lemon-mint sauce. Easy enough for an at-home or brown-bag lunch.

Delightfully Different

Use leftover sliced beef in this recipe and you can save the cooking time.

Spray a grill rack or broiler pan with cooking spray. Prepare a medium-hot fire in a charcoal or gas grill, with the rack set 3 to 4 inches above the heat, or preheat the broiler. Place the London broil and onion quarters on the grill or broiler pan and cook for 4 to 5 minutes, turn and cook 3 to 4 minutes more for medium. For well-done meat, cook an additional 4 minutes on each side. Remove from heat and set aside.

In a large bowl, mix lettuce, cucumber, and chickpeas.

To make dressing: Process mint leaves, parsley, garlic, lemon juice, broth, and oil in a blender until smooth. Slice meat into thin strips, chop onion, and add both to salad. Pour dressing over salad, toss, and stuff 2 cups of salad into each half pita pocket, and serve.

East Indian Chicken Kebabs

Prep time: 15 minutes plus 2 hours to marinate • Cook time: 4 to 6 minutes • Serves: 6 • Serving size: 1 (4-oz.) chicken skewer

Nutritional Analysis per Serving: Glycemic Index (not significant) • Glycemic Load (not significant) • Calories 187 • Protein in grams 28 • Animal Protein 28 • Vegetable Protein 0 • Carbohydrates 1 gram • Dietary Fiber 0 • Net Carbohydrate 1 gram • Fat 7 grams • Saturated Fat 1½ grams • Cholesterol 68 mg • Sodium 80 mg • Exchanges 4 lean meat, 1 fat

6 (4-oz.) boneless, skinless chicken breasts	1 tsp. ground turmeric
3 garlic cloves	½ tsp. ground allspice
¼ tsp. salt	¼ tsp. freshly ground black pepper
Juice of 3 large limes	½ tsp. ground cumin
2 TB. olive oil	Tomatoes, onions, red or green bell peppers, cut into bite-size pieces, optional
6 TB. low-fat plain yogurt	
Vegetable oil cooking spray	6 wooden skewers, soaked in warm water for 1 hour

Cut chicken into 1½- by 2-inch pieces and place in large bowl. Pound garlic with salt with mortar and pestle. Pour lime juice into small bowl and whisk in garlic mixture, olive oil, and yogurt. Add turmeric, allspice, freshly ground black pepper, and cumin. Whisk to blend. Pour over chicken and toss well. Cover and refrigerate for 2 to 4 hours, tossing occasionally.

When you are ready to cook, spray a grill rack or broiler pan with cooking spray. Prepare a medium-hot fire in a charcoal or gas grill, with the rack 3 to 4 inches above the heat, or preheat the broiler. Remove the chicken from the marinade and pour the marinade into a small pot. Bring the marinade to a boil. Skewer chicken, alternating with your choice of vegetables if you wish, and grill or broil for 4 to 6 minutes, turning and basting often with boiled marinade, until the chicken is cooked through, no longer pink and any juices run clear. Serve with rice or other grains.

Palate Preview _____

Don't let the exotic sound of this recipe scare you off. The chicken is marinated in garlic, and lime juice—both are excellent and tasty ingredients for your meal plan.

Roasted Chicken Caesar Salad

Prep time: 15 minutes • Cook time: none • Serves: 4 • Serving size: 2 cups salad

Nutritional Analysis per Serving: Glycemic Index (not significant) • Glycemic Load (not significant) • Calories 205 • Protein in grams 22 • Animal Protein 21 • Vegetable Protein 1 • Carbohydrates 3 grams • Dietary Fiber 1 gram • Net Carbohydrate 2 grams • Fat 11 grams • Saturated Fat 2 grams • Cholesterol 98 mg • Sodium 188 mg • Exchanges 3 lean meat, 2 fats

1 (10-oz.) pkg. chopped hearts of romaine	4 TB. low-sodium Caesar salad dressing
2 cups cubed cooked chicken	Freshly ground black pepper to taste
2 TB. shaved Parmesan cheese	

Toss romaine lettuce with chicken, Parmesan cheese, and salad dressing. Season with black pepper.

Palate Preview

This simple and elegant luncheon recipe can be put together for a crowd or just for yourself.

Garlic Turkey Burgers

Prep time: 15 minutes   •   Cook time: 8 to 10 minutes   •   Serves: 4   •   Serving size: 1 (4-ounce) patty

Nutritional Analysis per Serving: Glycemic Index 78 (hash browns)   •   Glycemic Load 3   •   Calories 134   •   Protein in grams 21   •   Animal Protein 20   •   Vegetable Protein 1   •   Carbohydrates 4 grams   •   Dietary Fiber 0   •   Net Carbohydrate 4 grams   •   Fat 4 grams   •   Saturated Fat 1 gram   •   Cholesterol 133 mg   •   Sodium 137 mg   •   Exchanges 3 lean meat

1 lb. lean ground turkey	¼ cup sliced
½ cup frozen shredded hash brown potatoes, thawed	2 TB. grated Parmesan cheese
	⅛ tsp. freshly ground black pepper

Preheat the broiler. In a medium bowl, combine turkey, potatoes, green onions, cheese, and black pepper. Mix well. Shape into four patties (½-inch thick). Place patties on broiler pan.

Broil 4 to 6 inches from heat for 8 to 10 minutes or until no longer pink in center and thoroughly cooked, turning once.

Palate Preview _____
We all like burgers and these burgers are sure to please you. They are low in fat and high in flavor.

Salmon Salad Wraps

Prep time: 20 minutes • Cook time: none • Serves: 5 • Serving size: 1 (9-inch) whole-wheat tortilla with 1 cup salmon salad

Nutritional Analysis per Serving: Glycemic Index 30 • Glycemic Load 10 • Calories 388 • Protein in grams 28 • Animal Protein 24 • Vegetable Protein 4 • Carbohydrates 34 grams • Dietary Fiber 3 grams • Net Carbohydrate 31 grams • Fat 12½ grams • Saturated Fat 7 grams • Cholesterol 58 mg • Sodium 289 mg • Exchanges 3 medium-fat meat, 2 starch

2 cups flaked, poached, or grilled salmon	1 cup diced fresh tomatoes
1 cup diced cucumber	½ cup low-fat ranch salad dressing
¼ cup chopped green onions	5 large lettuce leaves
2 TB. chopped fresh dill or ½ tsp. dried dill	5 (10- to 12-inch) whole-wheat tortillas
1 medium red bell pepper, cored, seeded, and diced	

Palate Preview

Tortillas are a wonderful way to wrap up food. Wrap up flaked salmon with vegetables and you have a complete meal in a wrap.

In a medium bowl, combine salmon, cucumber, green onions, dill, bell pepper, tomatoes, and dressing. Mix well.

Heat tortillas as directed on package to soften. Place 1 lettuce leaf in center of each tortilla. Spread about 1 cup salmon mixture evenly over each. Fold up bottom quarter of each tortilla and fold sides toward center.

Cajun Chicken Salad

Prep time: 10 minutes • Cook time: 10 minutes • Serves: 4 • Serving size: 1½ cups

Nutritional Analysis per Serving: Glycemic Index 49 • Glycemic Load 7 • Calories 175 • Protein in grams 12½ • Animal Protein 11 • Vegetable Protein 1½ • Carbohydrates 15 grams • Dietary Fiber 2 grams • Net Carbohydrate 13 grams • Fat 8½ grams • Saturated Fat 1½ grams • Cholesterol 30 mg • Sodium 27 mg • Exchanges 1½ lean meat, 2 fat, ½ vegetable

1 cup uncooked instant white rice	1 medium green bell pepper, cored, seeded, and diced
1 cup water	Dressing:
4 cups diced cooked chicken breast	2 TB. cider vinegar
1 cup diced celery	2 to 3 tsp. salt-free Cajun seasoning
⅓ cup chopped green onions	2 TB. olive oil
1 large tomato, diced	

Cook rice in water as directed on package. Place in freezer for 5 minutes to cool.

In large bowl, combine chicken, celery, green onions, tomato, bell pepper, and cooked rice. Stir gently to combine.

In small bowl, combine vinegar and Cajun seasoning, and mix well with wire whisk. Whisk in oil until well blended. Pour dressing over salad and toss to coat. Serve immediately, or cover and refrigerate until serving.

Palate Preview
A delightfully mild Cajun flavor—you can add more hot pepper seasoning if you like more bite in your salad.

Stuffed Tomatoes with Tofu Salad

Prep time: 25 minutes • Cook time: none • Serves: 4 • Serving size: 1 tomato filled with ¾ cup tofu salad

Nutritional Analysis per Serving: Glycemic Index 20 • Glycemic Load 2 • Calories 140 • Protein in grams 8 • Animal Protein 0 • Vegetable Protein 8 • Carbohydrates 10 grams • Dietary Fiber 2 grams • Net Carbohydrate 8 grams • Fat 9 grams • Saturated Fat 1 gram • Cholesterol 5 mg • Sodium 163 mg • Exchanges l lean meat, 2 fat, 1 vegetable

4 medium tomatoes

1 (12.3-oz.) pkg. firm or extra-firm tofu

¼ cup low-fat mayonnaise

2 tsp. prepared mustard

¼ tsp. salt

⅛ tsp. freshly ground black pepper

½ cup chopped celery

3 TB. chopped green onions, or more to taste

4 lettuce leaves

Palate Preview
Tofu can be a nice departure from meat for lunch. It's high in vegetable protein and blends well with the onions and mustard in this salad.

Delightfully Different
You can substitute chicken or tuna for tofu in this recipe and still enjoy the fresh taste.

Cut a thin slice off the bottom of each tomato. Cut off the stem end from each tomato. Scoop out and discard pulp. Drain tomato shells well.

Drain tofu if necessary. Gently press between layers of paper towels to remove excess moisture.

In a medium bowl, combine mayonnaise, mustard, salt, and black pepper, and blend well. Add tofu, celery, and green onions. Stir gently with a fork until well mixed and tofu is crumbly.

To serve, line individual plates with lettuce leaves. Place a tomato shell on each leaf. Spoon equal amounts of tofu mixture into tomato shells. If desired, garnish with additional chopped green onions.

Tropical Spinach Pasta Salad

Prep time: 15 minutes   •   Cook time: 6 minutes   •   Serves: 4   •   Serving size: 1½ cups

Nutritional Analysis per Serving: Glycemic Index 37   •   Glycemic Load 21   •   Calories 266   •   Protein in grams 6   •   Animal Protein 0   •   Vegetable Protein 6   •   Carbohydrates 56 grams   •   Dietary Fiber 3 grams   •   Net Carbohydrate 53 grams   •   Fat 8 grams   •   Saturated Fat 1 gram   •   Cholesterol 0 mg   •   Sodium 147 mg   •   Exchanges 3 starch, 1 vegetable

5 oz. (2 cups) uncooked bow tie whole-grain pasta (farfalle)

1 cup julienne-cut (2 × ⅛ × ⅛-inch) jicama

1 medium mango, peeled, pitted, and cubed

½ medium red bell pepper, cored, seeded, and cut into thin strips

4 cups fresh baby spinach

2 TB. finely chopped fresh cilantro

Dressing:

½ tsp. grated lime zest

2 TB. fresh lime juice

2 TB. olive oil

2 TB. fructose

½ tsp. ground ginger

¼ tsp. salt

Cook pasta for 6 to 8 minutes. Drain and rinse with cold water to cool. Drain well.

In a large bowl, combine cooked pasta with jicama, mango, bell pepper, spinach, and cilantro. Toss gently.

In a small glass or ceramic bowl, combine lime zest, lime juice, olive oil, fructose, ginger, and salt, blending well. Pour dressing over salad and toss gently to coat.

Delightfully Different

If you can't readily find mangoes, you can substitute peaches, papaya, or apricots. The flavors will stay sunny and bright.

Palate Preview

By using more exotic fruits, vegetables and herbs like mangoes, jicama, and cilantro, you get a sunny tropical taste. To balance out your meal, have some protein such as sliced chicken breast or flaked salmon on the side. If you haven't tried jicama, now is the time. It's a white root vegetable that's quite crunchy and has a sweet light taste. And it's so low glycemic that it's a free food.

Cashew Chicken Melts

Prep time: 15 minutes • Cook time: 20 minutes • Serves: 6 • Serving size: ½ whole-wheat English muffin with ½ cup chicken salad

Nutritional Analysis per Serving: Glycemic Index 60 • Glycemic Load 9 • Calories 280 • Protein in grams 22 • Animal Protein 18 • Vegetable Protein 4 • Carbohydrates 16 grams • Dietary Fiber 1 gram • Net Carbohydrate 15 grams • Fat 12 grams • Saturated Fat 2½ grams • Cholesterol 39 mg • Sodium 443 mg • Exchanges 2 lean meat, 1 high-fat meat, 1 starch

2 cups cubed cooked chicken breast	2 TB. sliced green onions
⅓ cup coarsely chopped unsalted cashews	3 whole-wheat English muffins, split and toasted
⅓ cup low-fat mayonnaise	6 (¾-oz.) slices low-fat cheddar or American cheese
¼ cup sliced celery	

Preheat oven to 350°F. In medium bowl, combine chicken, cashews, mayonnaise, celery, and scallions. Mix well.

Cut a 36 × 12–inch piece of heavy-duty aluminum foil and place it on a baking sheet. Place muffin halves on foil and spoon equal portions of chicken mixture onto each. Top each with 1 slice cheese. Make a "tent" over muffin halves with a second sheet of foil, using double-fold seals and allowing space between cheese and top of packet to prevent cheese from sticking (by inserting toothpicks into two of the muffin halves to hold the foil up)

Palate Preview

Expect a creamy, bready, cheesy texture with all the fixings for a great lunch—chicken and cashews. Everyone is sure to love these.

Bake for 20 minutes or until sandwiches are hot. Carefully remove from foil and serve hot.

Seasoned Turkey Cheeseburgers

Prep time: 5 minutes • Cook time: 10 minutes • Serves: 4 • Serving size: 1 (5-ounce) turkey burger on ½ stone-ground whole-wheat hamburger bun

Nutritional Analysis per Serving: Glycemic Index 68 • Glycemic Load 13 • Calories 319 • Protein in grams 34 • Animal Protein 28 • Vegetable Protein 6 • Carbohydrates 20 grams • Dietary Fiber 2 grams • Net Carbohydrate 18 grams • Fat 8 grams • Saturated Fat 2 grams • Cholesterol 113 mg • Sodium 320 mg • Exchanges 4 lean meat, 1 fat, 1½ starch

Vegetable oil cooking spray	2 tsp. finely chopped onion
1 lb. lean ground turkey	4 (¾-oz.) slices low-fat American cheese
¼ cup low-sodium Italian-style bread crumbs	2 stone-ground whole-wheat buns, split
2 TB. ketchup	Lettuce, tomato slices, onion slices, optional
1 tsp. salt-free garlic-pepper blend	

Spray grill rack with cooking spray. Prepare a medium-hot fire in a charcoal or gas grill, with the rack placed 4 to 6 inches above heat. In a large bowl, combine turkey, bread crumbs, ketchup, garlic pepper, onion, and cheese. Mix well and shape mixture into four patties, 4 inches in diameter.

Place patties on grill rack and cook for 10 to 14 minutes or until patties are thoroughly cooked and no long pink in the center, turning once.

Or if you prefer to use the oven, preheat the broiler. Place the patties on broiler pan and cook for 4 to 5 minutes, turn and cook 3 to 4 minutes more for medium.

Palate Preview ___ Heat up the grill and get ready for burgers, seasoned to perfection. For condiments, select from the following: salsa, mushrooms, garlic, mustard, chopped onions, or dill pickles rinsed in water.

During last 1 to 2 minutes of cooking time, top each patty with 1 cheese slice and cook until melted. If desired, also place buns on grill, cut side down. Cook 1 to 2 minutes or until lightly toasted.

Serve patties on bun halves. If desired, top patties with lettuce, tomato, and onion slices.

Greek Chicken Whole-Grain Pita Pockets

Prep time: 30 minutes • Cook time: none • Serves: 4 • Serving size: one pita bread pocket

Nutritional Analysis per Serving: Glycemic Index 52 • Glycemic Load 19 • Calories 436 • Protein in grams 34 • Animal Protein 28 • Vegetable Protein 6 • Carbohydrates 38 grams • Dietary Fiber 5 grams • Net Carbohydrate 33 grams • Fat 15 grams • Saturated Fat 3 grams • Cholesterol 95 mg • Sodium 388 mg • Exchanges 4 lean meat, 3 fat, 2 starch

4 (7-inch) whole-wheat pita pockets	4 (4-oz.) boneless, skinless chicken breast halves
½ cup low-fat mayonnaise	½ cup chopped cucumber
2 tsp. minced garlic	½ cup chopped tomato
2 tsp. no-salt Greek seasoning blend	

Palate Preview ___ A superb Mediterranean taste in a tidy pita pocket.

Spray grill rack with cooking spray. Prepare a medium-hot fire in a charcoal or gas grill, with the rack placed 4 to 6 inches above heat, or preheat the broiler and place broiler rack 4 to 6 inches from heat. Wrap pita pockets together in foil and set aside. In a small bowl, combine mayonnaise and garlic, blending well. Refrig-erate until serving time. Sprinkle Greek seasoning over chicken breast halves.

When ready to cook, place chicken on grill or broiler pan. Cook for 12 to 15 minutes or until chicken is tender, no longer pink and juices run clear, turning once.

During last the 5 minutes of cooking time, place foil packet of pita pockets on grill or broiler pan and heat until warm, turning foil packet once.

To serve, spread warm pita bread with garlic mayonnaise. Thinly slice chicken. Fill each pita pocket with equal portions of chicken, cucumber, and tomato. If desired, secure with toothpicks.

Chicken and Artichoke Pizza

Prep time: 20 minutes • Cook time: 5 minutes • Serves: 6 • Serving size: 1 (6-inch) whole-wheat tortilla with ⅔ cup filling

Nutritional Analysis per Serving: Glycemic Index 33 • Glycemic Load 6 • Calories 256 • Protein in grams 16 • Animal Protein 13 • Vegetable Protein 3 • Carbohydrates 21 grams • Dietary Fiber 4 grams • Net Carbohydrate 17 grams • Fat 12 grams • Saturated Fat 2 grams • Cholesterol 34 mg • Sodium 328 mg • Exchanges 1 starch, 2 lean meat, 2 fat

1 (14-oz.) can artichoke hearts, packed in water, well drained and rinsed, coarsely chopped	6 (6-inch) whole-wheat tortillas
⅓ cup low-fat mayonnaise	1½ cups diced cooked chicken breast
¼ tsp. hot pepper sauce	⅓ cup chopped (cored and seeded) red bell pepper
⅓ cup finely shaved Parmesan cheese	2 TB. pine nuts

Spray grill rack with cooking spray. Prepare a medium-hot fire in a charcoal or gas grill, with the rack placed 4 to 6 inches above heat, or preheat the broiler and place broiler rack 4 to 6 inches from heat. In medium bowl, combine artichokes, mayonnaise, hot pepper sauce, and ½ of Parmesan cheese. Mix well.

Spread artichoke mixture over tortillas. Top with equal portions chicken, bell pepper, remaining cheese, and pine nuts.

When ready to cook place tortilla pizzas on grill or broiler and cook for 3 to 5 minutes or until thoroughly heated.

Palate Preview

Artichokes make all meals special. They are wonderful on this chicken pizza. They add a unique flavor along with the pine nuts and always make a meal more festive.

Nutty Chicken Salad Lettuce Wraps

Prep time: 15 minutes • Cook time: none • Serves: 4 • Serving size: 2 lettuce leaves with ⅓ cup filling per leaf

Nutritional Analysis per Serving: Glycemic Index 31 • Glycemic Load 2 • Calories 193 • Protein in grams 16 • Animal Protein 15 • Vegetable Protein 1 • Carbohydrates 7 grams • Dietary Fiber <1 gram • Net Carbohydrate 7 grams • Fat 10 grams • Saturated Fat 2 grams • Cholesterol 42 mg • Sodium 206 mg • Exchanges 2 lean meat, 2 fat, ½ fruit

½ cup halved seedless red grapes

1½ cups cooked cubed chicken breast

¼ cup chopped, toasted, unsalted cashews

¼ cup diced celery

¼ cup low-fat mayonnaise

8 large leaves Bibb lettuce

Combine grapes, chicken, cashews, celery, and mayonnaise in a bowl and stir gently. Place 2 lettuce leaves on each plate and top each leaf with about ⅓ cup chicken salad mixture.

Fold lettuce over to cover chicken salad and serve.

Palate Preview

Using lettuce as a sandwich wrap keeps the glycemic index and the glycemic load very low. Plus, you get one more serving of vegetables for the day. The grapes and cashews give this salad a fresh, sweet taste.

Easy BBQ Beef Sandwiches

Prep time: 20 minutes • Cook time: 10 hours • Serves: 20 • Serving size: 1 whole-wheat bun with ⅓ cup barbecue beef

Nutritional Analysis per Serving: Glycemic Index 56 • Glycemic Load 22 • Calories 359 • Protein in grams 26 • Animal Protein 21 • Vegetable Protein 4 • Carbohydrates 40 grams • Dietary Fiber 3 grams • Net Carbohydrate 37 grams • Fat 9 grams • Saturated Fat 3 grams • Cholesterol 67 mg • Sodium 181 mg • Exchanges 2 starch, 3 meat, ½ fruit

3½ to 4 lbs. beef round steak, trimmed of fat, and cut into 1-inch pieces	½ cup ketchup
1 cup finely chopped onions	⅓ cup cider vinegar
¼ cup fructose	1 (12-oz.) can light beer
1 TB. salt-free chili powder	1 (6-oz.) can tomato paste
	20 whole-wheat sandwich buns, split

In 3½- to 4-quart slow cooker, combine beef, onions, fructose, chili powder, ketchup, vinegar, beer, and tomato paste. Mix well.

Cover and cook on low setting for 10 hours.

With slotted spoon, remove beef from sauce and place in large bowl. Using 2 forks, pull beef apart to shred. Add 2 cups of sauce from the slow cooker and mix well. Place 1 bun on each plate and spoon equal portions of beef on each. If desired, serve with extra sauce.

Palate Preview

After cooking the round steak for 10 hours in your slow cooker all the alcohol content of the beer is gone, but the flavor remains. Add a side salad to this barbecued beef (perhaps from Chapter 10) and you'll have a balanced meal. Eat as an open face sandwich with knife and fork, or eat as a sandwich with your hands.

Fish Tacos

Prep time: 20 minutes • Cook time: 10 minutes • Serves: 6 • Serving size: 2 corn taco shells with ½ cup filling per shell

Nutritional Analysis per Serving: Glycemic Index 42 • Glycemic Load 15 • Calories 606 • Protein in grams 34 • Animal Protein 28 • Vegetable Protein 6 • Carbohydrates 38 grams • Dietary Fiber 7 grams • Net Carbohydrate 31 grams • Fat 20 grams • Saturated Fat 4 grams • Cholesterol 46 mg • Sodium 386 mg • Exchanges 2½ starch, 4 lean meat, 4 fat, 1 vegetable

2 avocados	½ tsp. chili powder
2 TB. chopped fresh cilantro	½ tsp. salt
⅓ cup low-fat Thousand Island salad dressing	1½ lb. halibut, skin removed, cut into 1-inch pieces
12 corn taco shells	1 cup shredded lettuce or mixed salad greens
1 TB. vegetable oil	
1½ tsp. no-salt lemon-pepper seasoning	1 small tomato, diced

Palate Preview
Fish tacos are a terrific way to eat fish. Combined with south-of-the-border flavors and avocados, you get a highly healthy lunch. And it also tastes great.

Delightfully Different
Substitute any other kind of fish or seafood for the halibut. Use salmon, shrimp, crab, tuna, or red snapper.

Cut 1 avocado in half. Carefully insert widest part of a sharp knife blade into pit and twist knife slightly. Remove and discard pit. Slice the flesh of the avocado half into small dice while still in the shell by cutting several times in one direction and then several times in the other. Scoop out the flesh into a medium bowl. Repeat with remaining half and other avocado.

In a medium bowl, combine avocado, cilantro, and salad dressing. Toss to coat avocado. Set aside. Heat taco shells as directed on package.

Spray grill rack or broiling pan with cooking spray. Prepare a medium-hot fire in a charcoal or gas grill, with the rack placed 4 to 6 inches above heat, or preheat the broiler. In large bowl, combine oil, lemon-pepper seasoning, chili powder and salt. Mix well. Add halibut and toss gently to coat.

When ready to cook, place halibut in a grill basket or on broiling pan. Place the basket on grill or the broiling pan in oven and cook for 5 to 10 minutes or until fish is opaque and flakes easily with a fork, rearranging twice.

To serve, place equal portions fish, lettuce, avocado mixture, and tomato in heated taco shells.

Part  3

Appetizers, Snacks, and Side Dishes

We know you need your daily between-meal snacks. This chapter offers you both yummy hot appetizers and satisfying cold snacks. Both you and your family will find them delicious and satisfying.

Eating plenty of vegetables, salads, and fruits is in everyone's eating plan. They provide you with powerful antioxidant health benefits, dietary fiber, and delightful and varied tastes. Plus, these recipes complement the tastes of main dishes. You'll find dozens of appealing choices here.

Chapter 7

Appetizers

In This Chapter

- ◆ Appetizers to fit your nutritional needs
- ◆ Delicious bites of flavor
- ◆ Serving at parties or meals
- ◆ Easy and quick to cook

There's a great reason appetizers qualify for a food classification all their own. They're awesome! Bite-size delights! Fabulous finger food!

Generally, appetizers are not served in large enough quantities to qualify as a main dish. They aren't supposed to fill you up, or even come close. The purpose of an appetizer is to whet your appetite and prepare your palate for the meal that's to come.

But sometimes appetizers do constitute a meal. Perfect for entertaining, appetizers have come into their own as party fare. A buffet table abounding with appetizers lets a person eat enough nibbles to qualify as a meal, albeit a stand-up meal.

The appetizer recipes in this chapter show you how to prepare irresistible bites of food, such as shrimp, smoked trout or salmon, and beef or chicken skewers seasoned to perfection. You'll also find recipes for a salsa dip for vegetables and the highly popular warm artichoke-cheese dip.

Think in Bites

You can tell as you page through this chapter, the serving sizes are small for persons with diabetes, only one or two tidbits per serving. While the servings aren't particularly generous, appetizers by definition are supposed to be small amounts of really delectable food served as the first course of a meal, before the salad and entrée. So keep that in mind so you don't ruin your appetite.

Certainly, you could make an entire entrée or meal from any of these appetizers, but be sure to calculate your daily intake of carbohydrates, fats, and proteins based on how many servings you eat.

Appetizers as Snacks

Most of the time you'll serve these appealing appetizers as a first course before your main meal of the day. But you can also serve them as a snack, perhaps in the late afternoon right after work or school. These appetizers typically have enough nutrition, especially protein, to stave off hunger pangs until it's time for dinner in two or three hours. Of course, if you're closely tracking your daily intake of carbohydrates, fats, and proteins, you'll need to add the snack totals, too.

The Least You Need to Know

♦ For the person with diabetes, appetizers should usually be eaten in small servings.

♦ Shrimp, smoked trout, salmon, beef, or chicken make delicious bites of food.

♦ Serve appetizers for a cocktail buffet, for a first course, or even as a late afternoon snack.

♦ If you make a meal of appetizers, refigure your nutritional counts based on the number of servings you eat.

Cucumber Slices with Smoked-Trout Mousse

Prep time: 30 minutes • Cook time: none • Serves: 10 • Serving size: 2 pieces

Nutritional Analysis per Serving: Glycemic Index (not significant) • Glycemic Load (not significant) • Calories 25 • Protein in grams 6 • Animal Protein 6 • Vegetable Protein <1 • Carbohydrates <1 gram • Dietary Fiber <1 gram • Net Carbohydrate 0 • Fat 1 gram • Saturated Fat <½ gram • Cholesterol 3 mg • Sodium 140 mg • Exchanges 1 very lean meat

5 oz. smoked trout, no salt added	Cayenne to taste
3 oz. fat-free cream cheese	20 (½-inch thick) cucumber rounds
½ tsp. grated lemon zest	1 tsp. paprika
1 TB. fresh lemon juice	20 fresh dill sprigs

Combine smoked trout, cream cheese, lemon zest, and lemon juice in blender. Pulse to a smooth paste. Add cayenne and process just until mixed in. Fill pastry bag fitted with a large tip with mousse and pipe onto cucumber slices (or drop mousse by spoonfuls). Dust each with paprika and garnish with dill sprigs.

Delightfully Different
You can substitute salt-free smoked salmon for the trout in this recipe.

Palate Preview
An excellent appetizer for a group or potluck. The cucumber forms the base for a smoked-trout and cream-cheese mousse. Don't worry if you don't have a pastry bag; you can also drop spoonfuls of mousse on the cucumber slices.

Beef or Chicken Sate

Prep time: 20 minutes plus 3 hours to marinate • Cook time: 6 minutes • Serves: 12 • Serving size: 2 skewers

Nutritional Analysis per Serving: Glycemic Index <5 • Glycemic Load <1 • Calories 270 • Protein in grams 16 • Animal Protein 8 • Vegetable Protein 8 • Carbohydrates 6 grams • Dietary Fiber 1½ grams • Net Carbohydrate 5 grams • Fat 20 grams • Saturated Fat 4 grams • Cholesterol 28 mg • Sodium 156 mg • Exchanges 1 very lean meat, 1 high-fat meat, 2 fats

1 lb. tender beefsteak or 1 lb. skinless, boneless chicken breast

Marinade:

1 TB. low-salt soy sauce

4 TB. white wine vinegar

1 TB. canola or sunflower oil

1 tsp. ground coriander

1 tsp. ground cumin

1 tsp. no-salt chili powder

1 tsp. ground ginger

1 tsp. granulated sugar

Peanut Sauce:

1½ TB. canola or sunflower oil

2 garlic cloves, finely chopped

½ tsp. crushed red pepper flakes

1 tsp. ground ginger

1 tsp. brown sugar

½ tsp. salt

1 TB. fresh lemon juice

1½ cups unsalted all-natural, no-sugar-added peanut butter

1½ cups fat-free, low-sodium chicken broth

24 (5-inch) wooden skewers, soaked in warm water for 1 hour

Cut steak or chicken into strips. In a medium bowl, combine soy sauce, vinegar, oil, coriander, cumin, chili powder, ginger, and sugar. Add steak or chicken to the bowl, and toss to coat. Cover and refrigerate for at least 3 hours.

For the Peanut Sauce, heat oil in a heavy-bottom pan over medium-high heat, and stir-fry garlic, red pepper flakes, ginger, brown sugar, and salt until browned, being careful that the ingredients don't burn. Add lemon juice and peanut butter, and stir until smooth. Stir in chicken broth and cook until the liquid reduces in volume slightly. Allow to cool.

Palate Preview

Sate, a Malaysian treat of skewered meats with spicy peanut sauce, is so delicious.

When you are ready to cook, preheat the broiler. Remove steak or chicken from marinade and discard marinade. Thread steak or chicken strips onto the skewers, portioning strips as evenly as possible between skewers. Broil for 2 to 3 minutes on each side, until brown. Serve hot, with peanut sauce.

Snow Pea-Shrimp Skewers

Prep time: 40 minutes • Cook time: 1 minute • Serves: 10 • Serving size: 2 skewers

Nutritional Analysis per Serving: Glycemic Index (not significant) • Glycemic Load (not significant) • Calories 20 • Protein in grams 3 • Animal Protein 3 • Vegetable Protein <1 • Carbohydrates 2 grams • Dietary Fiber 0 • Net Carbohydrate 2 grams • Fat <1 gram • Saturated Fat <1 gram • Cholesterol 21 mg • Sodium 108 mg • Exchanges ½ very lean meat

½ cup nonfat mayonnaise

2 TB. fresh lemon juice

20 large snow peas

20 large shrimp, cooked and peeled

20 (6-inch) wooden skewers

Blend mayonnaise and lemon juice together in small bowl. Refrigerate until ready to serve.

Bring a pan of water to a boil over high heat. Prepare a bowl of cold water. Add snow peas and boil for 1 minute. Drain and plunge them immediately into cold water for 30 seconds to stop cooking process and set color. Drain again and pat dry with paper towels.

Thread 1 shrimp and 1 snow pea on each skewer. Cover and refrigerate for 30 minutes. Serve chilled with lemon mayonnaise.

Palate Preview
Try this easy appetizer as a late afternoon snack or for a cocktail party. It has no carbohydrates and the mayonnaise-lemon sauce gives the shrimp and snow peas plenty of zing.

Note: You can skewer shrimp and snow peas up to 8 hours in advance along with the mayonnaise lemon juice mixture. Store both containers in an airtight container in the refrigerator.

Lamb Brochettes with Mint-Yogurt Sauce

Prep time: 20 minutes plus 30 minutes to marinate • Cook time: 6 minutes • Serves: 10
• Serving size: 2 skewers

Nutritional Analysis per Serving: Glycemic Index (not significant) • Glycemic Load (not significant) • Calories 57 • Protein in grams 8 • Animal Protein 8 • Vegetable Protein <1 • Carbohydrates 1 gram • Dietary Fiber 0 • Net Carbohydrate 1 • Fat 2 grams • Saturated Fat 1 gram • Cholesterol 22 mg • Sodium 139 mg • Exchanges 1 lean meat

Mint-Yogurt Sauce:

¾ cup low-fat yogurt

½ cup finely chopped fresh mint

½ cup finely chopped fresh parsley

Juice of ½ lemon

Lamb Brochettes:

¾ lb. lean ground lamb

½ medium onion, finely chopped

2 tsp. chopped garlic

2 tsp. ground cumin

½ tsp. ground coriander

Grated zest of 1 lemon

2 TB. finely chopped fresh cilantro

½ tsp. salt

¼ tsp. cayenne

20 (6-inch) wooden skewers, soaked in warm water for 1 hour

Vegetable oil cooking spray

Palate Preview
Dip these lamb brochettes into the mint-yogurt sauce and it will satisfy your mid-meal or pre-meal appetite.

Combine yogurt, mint, parsley and lemon juice in a small ceramic or glass bowl. Mix well, cover and refrigerate until ready to serve.

Place lamb, onion, garlic, cumin, coriander, lemon zest, cilantro, salt, and cayenne in a food processor. Pulse until combined and slightly pasty. Divide into 20 equal-size pieces. With your wet hands, roll pieces into oval shapes.

Thread 1 oval onto each skewer. Cover and refrigerate for 30 minutes to allow flavors to blend. Preheat a gas grill to medium-high or prepare a medium-hot fire in a charcoal grill, with the rack placed 4 to 6 inches above the heat, or preheat the broiler. Place brochettes on broiler rack or grill and cook until browned, about 3 minutes on each side. Serve hot with chilled Mint-Yogurt Sauce.

Thai Shrimp Skewers

Prep time: 10 minutes plus 1 hour to marinate   •   Cook time: none   •   Serves: 10   •
Serving size: 2 skewers

Nutritional Analysis per Serving: Glycemic Index (not significant)   •   Glycemic Load (not
significant)   •   Calories 15   •   Protein in grams 1   •   Animal Protein 1   •   Vegetable
Protein 0   •   Carbohydrates 1 gram   •   Dietary Fiber 0   •   Net Carbohydrate 1   •
Fat <1 gram   •   Saturated Fat <1 gram   •   Cholesterol 18 mg   •   Sodium 5 mg   •
Exchanges ½ very lean meat

20 medium shrimp, cooked and peeled	1 tsp. granulated sugar
2 garlic cloves, finely chopped	1 TB. fish sauce
1 TB. grated fresh gingerroot	Juice of 1 lime
½ tsp. crushed red pepper flakes	20 (3-inch) wooden skewers or long tooth-picks, soaked in warm water for 1 hour

Pat shrimp dry with paper towels. Combine shrimp,
garlic, ginger, red pepper, sugar, fish sauce, and lime
juice in a glass or ceramic bowl. Cover and refrigerate
for 1 hour. Skewer 2 shrimp onto each skewer. Serve
chilled.

Note: You can marinate shrimp up to 6 hours in
advance; skewer shrimp up to 3 hours in advance.
Store in an airtight container in the refrigerator.

Palate Preview
No cooking required if
you buy precooked shrimp. Just
thread the marinated shrimp on
skewers, chill, and eat. You can
also serve the marinated shrimp on
lettuce leaves as a first course.

Salsa Catalan

Prep time: 20 minutes plus 30 minutes refrigeration   •   Cook time: 10 minutes   •
Serves: 16   •   Serving size: 2 tablespoons

Nutritional Analysis per Serving: Glycemic Index 42   •   Glycemic Load 1   •   Calories 48
•   Protein in grams 1½   •   Animal Protein 0   •   Vegetable Protein 1½   •   Carbohydrates
3½ grams   •   Dietary Fiber 1 gram   •   Net Carbohydrate 2   •   Fat 3 grams   •
Saturated Fat <½ gram   •   Cholesterol 0   •   Sodium 20 mg   •   Exchanges ¼ starch, ½ fat

1 TB. olive oil

½ cup blanched almonds or pine nuts

2 slices day-old stone-ground whole-wheat
bread, cubed

1 roasted red pepper, no sugar added

2 garlic cloves, chopped

¼ tsp. cayenne

½ tsp. paprika

1 cup chopped fresh parsley

2 tomatoes, chopped

2 TB. sherry vinegar

Palate Preview
Just one taste of this
savory dip is all you need to know
you've found an all-time favorite.
The flavorful salsa is spicy with garlic and cayenne, and rich with
roasted red pepper, almonds or
pine nuts, stone-ground bread, and
fresh parsley.

Heat oil in a pan set over medium heat. Stir-fry
almonds or pine nuts with bread cubes for about 5 minutes, or until golden. Drain on paper towels.

Place nut-and-bread mixture, red pepper, garlic,
cayenne, paprika, parsley, tomatoes, and vinegar in a
food processor or blender. Pulse until well blended but
still slightly coarse. If the mixture is too dry, gradually
add water, 1 tablespoon at a time.

Cover and refrigerate for 30 minutes to allow flavors to
blend. Serve chilled with raw vegetables.

Salmon-Stuffed Cherry Tomatoes

Prep time: 20 minutes • Cook time: none • Serves: 6 • Serving size: 3 tomatoes

Nutritional Analysis per Serving: Glycemic Index 28 • Glycemic Load 1 • Calories 81 • Protein in grams 9½ • Animal Protein 9 • Vegetable Protein ½ • Carbohydrates 3 grams • Dietary Fiber ½ gram • Net Carbohydrate 3 • Fat 3 grams • Saturated Fat ½ gram • Cholesterol 24 mg • Sodium 102 mg • Exchanges 1⅓ lean meat, ½ vegetable

18 cherry tomatoes	1 TB. finely chopped onion
1 cup cooked boned salmon or canned	½ tsp. dried dill weed
2 TB. nonfat mayonnaise	4 sprigs fresh parsley
1 TB. capers, drained, optional	

Line a baking sheet with two layers of paper toweling. Cut a thin slice from the bottom of each tomato. Scoop out seeds and pulp, leaving the flesh around the edges intact. Invert onto the paper towels to drain.

In a small bowl, combine salmon, mayonnaise, capers (if desired), onion, and dill, and mix well. Spoon about 2 teaspoons of filling into each tomato. Garnish with small parsley leaves.

Palate Preview
Great finger food. The cherry tomatoes hold a salmon mixture made with capers, dill, and onion. Great for parties or late-afternoon snacks.

Delightfully Different
You can make a delicious luncheon entrée with this recipe. Instead of cherry tomatoes, use three large tomatoes, and fill with the salmon-mayonnaise mixture.

Artichoke-Cheese Dip

Prep time: 15 minutes • Cook time: 25 minutes • Serves: 12 • Serving size: 2 tablespoons

Nutritional Analysis per Serving: Glycemic Index 17 • Glycemic Load 1 • Calories 56 • Protein in grams 3½ • Animal Protein 2½ • Vegetable Protein 1 • Carbohydrates 7 grams • Dietary Fiber 1 gram • Net Carbohydrate 6 • Fat 1 gram • Saturated Fat ½ gram • Cholesterol 4 mg • Sodium 174 mg • Exchanges 1 vegetable, ⅓ milk

1 (14 oz.) can artichoke hearts in water, drained, rinsed, and coarsely chopped	½ cup grated Parmesan cheese
1 cup nonfat sour cream	2 TB. sliced green onions
½ cup nonfat mayonnaise	½ tsp. garlic powder
	½ tsp. hot pepper sauce

Preheat the oven to 350°F. In a medium bowl, combine artichoke hearts, sour cream, mayonnaise, cheese, green onions, garlic powder, and hot pepper sauce, and mix well. Spread in an ungreased 9-inch quiche dish, a glass pie plate, or a shallow 1-quart casserole. Bake for 15 to 25 minutes or until thoroughly heated. Serve warm with fresh vegetables as dippers.

Palate Preview

There's something about artichokes in a creamy cheese sauce that's appealing and satisfying to almost everyone. Serve with vegetables, such as broccoli, jicama, carrots, or celery, for dipping.

Beef Tenderloin Canapés

Prep time: 20 minutes   •   Cook time: 40 minutes   •   Serves: 12   •   Serving size: 2 canapés

Nutritional Analysis per Serving: Glycemic Index 42   •   Glycemic Load 13   •   Calories 330   •   Protein in grams 25   •   Animal Protein 19   •   Vegetable Protein 6   •   Carbohydrates 31   •   Dietary Fiber 2 grams   •   Net Carbohydrate 29   •   Fat 10 grams   •   Saturated Fat 3 grams   •   Cholesterol 70 mg   •   Sodium 464 mg   •   Exchanges 2 starch, 2 ½ medium-lean meat, ½ fat

Beef:

1 (2½ lb.) beef tenderloin

1 TB. olive oil

2 tsp. Mrs. Dash Original Flavor Seasoning Blend

24 coarse-kernel cocktail-size rye bread

Radicchio and watercress leaves

Sauce:

½ cup nonfat mayonnaise

5 TB. finely chopped green onions

1 TB. capers, drained

2 TB. Dijon mustard

1 TB. horseradish

Preheat the oven to 450°F. Place beef tenderloin in an ungreased, ovenproof skillet. Rub beef with oil and sprinkle with Mrs. Dash seasoning. Set pan over medium-high heat and sear beef for 30 seconds to 1 minute on each side, until browned on all sides.

Palate Preview _____
Tender, succulent beef served as canapés on rye bread with a tangy horseradish sauce. They're sure to satisfy.

Transfer the skillet to the oven and immediately reduce the oven temperature to 375°F. Bake for 30 to 35 minutes or until a meat thermometer inserted in the center of tenderloin registers 140°F.

Remove beef from the oven. Cool for 30 minutes or until completely cooled. If desired, wrap and refrigerate until you are ready to serve.

Meanwhile, in a small bowl, combine mayonnaise, onions, capers, mustard, and horseradish. Mix well, cover, and refrigerate until you are ready to serve.

To serve, slice beef thinly. Spread rye-bread slices with sauce. Top each with a small piece of radicchio, beef slice, and watercress.

Stuffed Mushrooms

Prep time: 10 minutes • Cook time: 20 minutes • Serves: 6 • Serving size: 3 mushrooms

Nutritional Analysis per Serving: Glycemic Index 46 • Glycemic Load 2 • Calories 72 • Protein in grams 3 • Animal Protein 1 • Vegetable Protein 2 • Carbohydrates 6 grams • Dietary Fiber 1½ grams • Net Carbohydrate 5 • Fat 4 grams • Saturated Fat 2 grams • Cholesterol 10 mg • Sodium 142 mg • Exchanges ½ vegetable, ⅓ starch, 1 fat

18 cremini or white button mushrooms, with stems

Vegetable oil cooking spray

1 TB. unsalted butter

1 cup frozen chopped broccoli, thawed

¼ cup dry bread crumbs, white or whole wheat

2 oz. (¼ cup) crumbled chèvre (goat cheese)

2 TB. chopped fresh chives, optional

 **Palate Preview**

Mushrooms stuffed with a mixture of broccoli, goat cheese, and chives. These are fantastic.

Preheat the oven to 350°F. Remove stems from mushrooms. Chop stems to make about ¾ cup and set aside.

Place mushroom caps, hollow side down, in an ungreased 15×10×1 baking pan, in a single layer. Spray mushrooms lightly with cooking spray. Bake for 10 minutes.

Meanwhile, melt butter in medium saucepan over medium heat. Add chopped mushroom stems and broccoli. Cook, stirring, for 3 to 4 minutes or until tender. Stir in bread crumbs and cheese.

Remove mushrooms from the oven. Turn mushrooms hollow side up. Spoon some broccoli mixture into each. Sprinkle with chives if desired.

Return to the oven and bake an additional 10 minutes or until thoroughly heated. Serve warm.

Chapter 8

Snacks

In This Chapter

- ◆ Preparing food for between-meal snacks
- ◆ Quick and convenient recipes
- ◆ Snacks as nutrition boosters
- ◆ Keeping healthy snacks on hand

Snacking is a habit that's here to stay. Once upon a time, experts thought snacking was a bad habit to be avoided at all costs. Not that people stopped snacking. They simply sneaked food between meals.

What a turnaround snacking has made! Today, experts consider snacking to be a good habit and an important one for persons with diabetes. Snacking between meals helps regulate blood glucose levels and provides ongoing energy throughout the day. Snacking even two or three times a day is fine if you watch the quantity you consume.

Great snacks come in small serving sizes. Snacking isn't meant to replace a meal, but rather to replenish you between meals. The best snacks are low in carbohydrates, sodium, and fat, yet provide you with complete protein, some good fats, and even vegetables. The snacks in this chapter give you all that and more. They satisfy your palate and your body.

A Healthy Bite of Nutrition

The recipes for snacks in this chapter give you great nutrition in small bites. Think of snacks as supplements to your already healthy food plan. Snacks are a wonderful way to increase your daily intake of valuable nutrients.

These snacks can give you one more serving of vegetables, or one more exchange of complete protein, and often more "good for you" monounsaturated fats. Many of the recipes offer you all three in delicious and savory bite-sized amounts.

Serving Dips and Snacks

Many of the recipes call for you to scoop up the dips and snacks on vegetables and to avoid using high-carbohydrate crackers and chips. So plan to keep fresh vegetables on hand in your refrigerator. You can cut them up yourself or purchase precut vegetables at the grocery store.

Good vegetable choices are those that are "free" foods such as celery, carrot strips, jicama slices, green or red bell pepper spears, broccoli or cauliflower florets, cucumber slices, and mushrooms. If you like, try radishes, snow peas, Belgian endive, or Chinese cabbage.

The Least You Need to Know

- Snacking is a good and healthy habit, so feel free to snack two or three times a day.
- Think of snacks as small amounts of food that keep your blood glucose levels regulated and your energy high.
- The recipes in this chapter give you excellent nutritional choices.
- Use vegetables for scooping up dips and salsas.

Tomato Guacamole

Prep time: 10 minutes • Cook time: none • Serves: 8 • Serving size: ½ cup

Nutritional Analysis per Serving: Glycemic Index 4 • Glycemic Load <1 • Calories 167 • Protein in grams 2 • Animal Protein 0 • Vegetable Protein 2 • Carbohydrates 9 grams • Dietary Fiber 7 grams • Net Carbohydrate 2 • Fat 14 grams • Saturated Fat 2 grams • Cholesterol 0 • Sodium 77 mg • Exchanges 1 vegetable, 3 fat

4 ripe avocados	¼ teaspoon salt
1 cup minced red onion	4 tsp. fresh lemon juice
1 cup diced tomato	1 bunch fresh cilantro, stemmed and chopped

Cut 1 avocado in half. Carefully insert the widest part of a sharp knife blade into pit and twist the knife slightly. Remove and discard the pit. Slice the flesh of 1 avocado half into small dice while it is still in the shell by cutting several times in one direction and then several times in the other. Scoop out the flesh into a medium bowl. Repeat with the remaining half and the other three avocados.

Healthy Notes _____

Be sure to add the tomato and lemon juice to the avocado as soon as it is diced. Avocados will turn brown quickly otherwise.

Immediately add onion and tomatoes to avocados. Season with salt and lemon juice and add cilantro. Mix guacamole until everything is just blended. Serve at once, or cover with plastic wrap so the wrap touches the entire surface of guacamole and set aside. Can be refrigerated for up to eight hours before serving

Palate Preview _____

You'll appreciate the wholesome goodness of this tomato guacamole. It tastes great and it's very good for your health. Eat with a spoon, or serve with cut-up vegetables, such as jicama or celery.

Italian Spinach Dip

Prep time: 10 minutes plus 2 hours refrigeration • Cook time: none • Serves: 8 • Serving size: 2 tablespoons

Nutritional Analysis per Serving: Glycemic Index 27 • Glycemic Load 1 • Calories 33 • Protein in grams 3 • Animal Protein 2 • Vegetable Protein 1 • Carbohydrates 4 grams • Dietary Fiber 1 gram • Net Carbohydrate 3 • Fat 0 • Saturated Fat 0 • Cholesterol 1 mg • Sodium 201 mg • Exchanges ½ vegetable, ½ very lean meat

1 cup frozen cut leaf spinach

1 (3-oz.) pkg. nonfat cream cheese, cut into pieces

½ cup nonfat sour cream

1 TB. zesty no salt added Italian dressing mix

Assorted vegetable such as sliced carrots, jicama, broccoli, zucchini, broccoli, cauliflower, green pepper, radishes

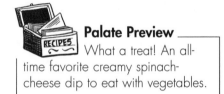

Palate Preview ___ What a treat! An all-time favorite creamy spinach-cheese dip to eat with vegetables.

Place spinach in a microwave-safe medium bowl. Cover with plastic wrap and vent. Microwave on high power for 3 to 4 minutes or until hot. Drain well and chop.

Add cream cheese to spinach and stir until cream cheese is softened. Add sour cream and dressing mix, blending well. Cover and refrigerate for at least 2 hours or until chilled. Serve with assorted vegetables.

Healthy Notes _____ If you substitute low-fat cheese and cream in this recipe, the fat content would increase. As best you can use nonfat products when specified in each recipe.

Spiced Party Nuts

Prep time: 10 minutes • Cook time: 30 minutes • Serves: 16 • Serving size: 2 tablespoons

Nutritional Analysis per Serving: Glycemic Index 18 • Glycemic Load 1 • Calories 108 • Protein in grams 4 • Animal Protein <½ • Vegetable Protein 4 • Carbohydrates 5 grams • Dietary Fiber 2 grams • Net Carbohydrate 3 • Fat 9 grams • Saturated Fat 1 gram • Cholesterol 0 • Sodium 146 mg • Exchanges ⅓ fruit, 2 fats

2 cups blanched almonds

1 TB. egg white (about ½ egg white)

2 tsp. dark brown sugar

1 tsp. salt

½ tsp. cayenne

1 TB. finely chopped fresh rosemary leaves

Preheat the oven to 300°F. Spread blanched almonds on a baking sheet in a single layer. Roast almonds, shaking the pan occasionally, for about 15 minutes or until lightly golden. Remove from the oven and cool slightly. Beat egg white until frothy and add almonds, brown sugar, salt, cayenne, and rosemary. Toss ingredients together to coat each almond well. Return almonds to the oven. Roast for about 20 minutes or until fragrant and golden. Cool. Serve at room temperature.

Delightfully Different
You can use other nuts, such as pecans, peanuts, or cashews in this recipes and still benefit from monounsaturated fats.

Palate Preview
Almonds contain plenty of monounsaturated fats that are good for you. But the best part of Spiced Party Nuts is the eating. They taste great.

Celery Boats with Blue-Cheese Filling

Prep time: 20 minutes • Cook time: none • Serves: 10 • Serving size: 2 pieces

Nutritional Analysis per Serving: Glycemic Index (not significant) • Glycemic Load (not significant) • Calories 61 • Protein in grams 4 • Animal Protein 3 • Vegetable Protein 1 • Carbohydrates 3 grams • Dietary Fiber 1 gram • Net Carbohydrate 2 • Fat 3½ grams • Saturated Fat 1 gram • Cholesterol 5 mg • Sodium 110 mg • Exchanges ½ lean meat, ½ vegetable, ½ fat

8 large celery stalks	1 tsp. paprika
4 oz. blue cheese, crumbled	24 walnut pieces for garnish
1 (4 oz.) pkg. nonfat cream cheese	Cut celery stalks on the diagonal to make 24 pieces, each 2 × 2 inches.
Freshly ground black pepper	

Beat blue cheese and cream cheese in mixer, food processor, or by hand until well combined. Add pepper to taste. Spoon about 2 teaspoons of the cheese filling into each piece of celery. Dust with paprika and garnish with one walnut.

Palate Preview

Celery seems naturally made to hold treats. This blue-cheese filling will please you with its tangy cheese taste. The walnut garnish enhances the flavor of the blue cheese.

Eggplant Caviar

Prep time: 20 minutes • Cook time: 40 minutes • Serves: 16 • Serving size: 2 tablespoons

Nutritional Analysis per Serving: Glycemic Index (not significant) • Glycemic Load (not significant) • Calories 31 • Protein in grams 1 • Animal Protein 0 • Vegetable Protein 1 • Carbohydrates 4 grams • Dietary Fiber 2 grams • Net Carbohydrate 2 • Fat 2 grams • Saturated Fat < ½ gram • Cholesterol < ½ gram • Sodium 70 mg • Exchanges ½ vegetable, ⅓ fat

2 medium eggplants, pierced with a fork	¼ tsp. cayenne
1 garlic clove, minced	20 mint springs for garnish
Juice of ½ lemon	1 tsp. paprika for garnish
2 TB. olive oil	Vegetables such as green and red bell peppers, cauliflower, pea pods, broccoli, celery, carrots, jicama
1 TB. whole-milk plain yogurt	
½ tsp. salt	

Preheat the oven to 350°F. Place the eggplants on a baking sheet and bake for approximately 1 hour, or until skin is black and blistered and flesh feels soft. Remove from the oven and when the eggplant is cool enough to handle, peel off charred skin. Use your hands to squeeze out as much moisture as possible from flesh.

Place eggplant, garlic, lemon juice, olive oil, and yogurt in a food processor or blender and pulse to a smooth puree. Add salt and cayenne and pulse to blend. Cool completely and transfer to a serving bowl. Garnish with mint sprigs and sprinkle paprika. Serve at room temperature with raw vegetables.

Palate Preview _____
The baked eggplant readily picks up the flavors of the garlic, lemon juice, olive oil, and cayenne in this recipe. Keep some in the refrigerator to use for quick snacks.

Roast-Beef Roll Ups

Prep time: 10 minutes plus 1 hour refrigeration • Cook time: none • Serves: 8 •
Serving size: 4 pieces

Nutritional Analysis per Serving: Glycemic Index 34 • Glycemic Load 1 • Calories 78
• Protein in grams 10 ½ • Animal Protein 10 • Vegetable Protein ½ •
Carbohydrates 3 grams • Dietary Fiber ½ gram • Net Carbohydrate 3 • Fat 1 gram
• Saturated Fat <½ gram • Cholesterol 13 mg • Sodium 377 mg • Exchanges
1½ lean meat, ½ vegetable

½ lb. thinly sliced cooked lean roast beef
(from the deli, about 8 slices)

¾ cup nonfat cream cheese, softened

½ cup sun-dried tomato pesto

Spread each slice of roast beef with equal portions of cream cheese. Carefully spread each with sun-dried tomato pesto. Roll up each slice tightly and place on a large platter or baking sheet. Cover and refrigerate for at least 1 hour or until firm.

To serve, cut each roll into 4 pieces. Secure each with cocktail toothpicks.

Palate Preview

Sun-dried tomato pesto adds a unique, sweet, concentrated flavor to this roast beef and cream cheese snack. The taste is exciting and satisfying.

Tuna Pate

Prep time: 10 minutes plus 3 hours refrigeration   •   Cook time: none   •   Serves: 8   •
Serving size: 2 tablespoons

Nutritional Analysis per Serving: Glycemic Index 31   •   Glycemic Load 1   •   Calories 103
•   Protein in grams 13   •   Animal Protein 13   •   Vegetable Protein 0   •   Carbohydrates
2 grams   •   Dietary Fiber 0   •   Net Carbohydrate 2 grams   •   Fat 5 grams   •
Saturated Fat 3 grams   •   Cholesterol 56 mg   •   Sodium 194 mg   •   Exchanges 1 lean
meat, 1 medium fat meat

1 (8-oz.) pkg. low-fat cream cheese

2 TB. chili sauce

2 tsp. chopped fresh parsley

½ tsp. hot pepper sauce, such as Tabasco

2 (6½-oz.) canned water-packed tuna, drained

1 tsp. dried minced onion

Vegetables such as cauliflower, cherry tomatoes, red bell pepper, jicama, broccoli, carrots, celery

Blend cream cheese, chili sauce, parsley, hot pepper sauce, tuna, and minced onion together; put in bowl, cover and refrigerate for about 3 hours. Serve with cut-up "free" vegetables.

Palate Preview

After you taste this, you'll want to keep canned tuna on hand to prepare this quick and easy snack.

Shrimp Dip

Prep time: 10 minutes   •   Cook time: none   •   Serves: 16   •   Serving size: 2 tablespoons

Nutritional Analysis per Serving: Glycemic Index 31   •   Glycemic Load 1   •   Calories 60   •   Protein in grams 4   •   Animal Protein 0   •   Vegetable Protein 4   •   Carbohydrates 2 grams   •   Dietary Fiber 0   •   Net Carbohydrate 2 grams   •   Fat   •   4 grams Saturated Fat 3 grams   •   Cholesterol 27 mg   •   Sodium 61 mg   •   Exchanges ½ medium fat meat, ½ fat

1 (8 oz.) pkg. low-fat cream cheese

1 (8 oz.) pkg. low-fat sour cream

½ (6-oz.) pkg. zesty, salt-free Italian dressing mix

1 TB. lemon juice

1 (4½ oz.) can can small shrimp, rinsed and drained

Vegetables such as radishes, celery, carrots, broccoli, cauliflower, red and green bell peppers, jicama

Delightfully Different

Substitute canned crab-meat for the shrimp in this recipe.

Blend cream cheese and sour cream with an electric mixer set at medium speed. Add dressing mix and lemon juice. Mix thoroughly and add shrimp. The mixer will dice up shrimp. Serve with vegetables.

Palate Preview

Baby shrimp blended with cream cheese and sour cream then seasoned with lemon juice and Italian dressing mix. Makes a perfect midday snack.

Chapter 9

Vegetable Side Dishes

In This Chapter

◆ From A to Z: artichokes to zucchinis

◆ Delicious health-giving side dishes

◆ Getting 5 to 10 servings every day

◆ Traditional favorite recipes

Vegetables are a veritable goldmine filled with nutritional wealth. And that wealth is waiting for you at the nearest grocery store or farmers market. Simply by preparing and eating a wide variety of vegetables, you can boost your health quotient within weeks and keep it up for a lifetime.

The truth is you simply can't go wrong eating green vegetables. You can't go wrong eating "free food" vegetables. And provided you eat root vegetables, such as carrots and sweet potatoes or yams in modest quantities, you can't go wrong eating those either.

In this chapter, you'll find all-time favorite vegetable recipes that satisfy your taste buds, such as Green Beans with Almonds, Summer Squash with Mushrooms and Herbs, Glazed Carrots, Steamed Asparagus, Boiled Artichokes, and Baked Tomatoes Provencal. Included are some more unusual recipes such as Spaghetti Squash Italian Style and Brussels Sprouts with Orange.

Spicing Things Up

Plainly cooked vegetables that are steamed and seasoned with only salt and pepper are delicious all by themselves. They make good everyday side dishes for serving with main dishes such as meat and seafood.

Ah, but you can also spice up those same vegetables simply by adding garlic and onions. The recipes in this chapter contain a wide variety of spices and seasonings. Some seasonings used are sun-dried tomatoes and fresh herbs such as dill and basil. Add to those lemon juice, curry powder, and mustard seed. You'll even find cinnamon, ginger, and brown sugar.

Vegetables can be spiced up so many ways that the possibilities are limitless. We hope these recipes inspire you to make your vegetables anything put plain, and increase your appetite for eating more vegetables. Yes, you can eat 5 to 10 servings a day.

Capturing Nutrients

Of all the ways to cook vegetables, steaming stands head and shoulders above the rest for retaining valuable nutrients, such as antioxidants and flavinoids. In one study, steaming caused a loss of only 10 percent of the flavinoids, whereas microwaving vegetables resulted in a loss of up to 97 percent.

It just isn't worth your while to microwave vegetables. Sure, microwaving can save a few minutes, but it also ruins the whole point of your meal—to get the most and best nutrition possible. If you haven't already, invest in a stainless-steel vegetable steamer. One costs less than $10, and when you purchase it, you're making a terrific investment in your health. While you're at it, consider owning two. That way you can steam two vegetable dishes at mealtime.

The Least You Need to Know

- ◆ Vegetables provide a treasure trove of healthful nutrition.
- ◆ You can eat root vegetables—such as carrots, sweet potatoes, and yams—just in modest quantities.
- ◆ Seasonings and spices perk up vegetable recipes and keep you from being bored with eating vegetables.
- ◆ Steaming vegetables best preserves their nutrient value.

Broccoli with Pine Nuts and Sun-Dried Tomatoes

Prep time: 10 minutes • Cook time: 20 minutes • Serves: 6 • Serving size: ¾ cup

Nutritional Analysis per Serving: Glycemic Index 12 • Glycemic Load 1 • Calories 107 • Protein in grams 3 • Animal Protein 0 • Vegetable Protein 3 • Carbohydrates 7 grams • Dietary Fiber 1½ grams • Net Carbohydrate 6 grams • Fat 8 grams • Saturated Fat 1 gram • Cholesterol 0 • Sodium 72 mg • Exchanges 1½ vegetable, 1½ fat

4 cups broccoli florets	2 TB. minced garlic
½ cup oil-packed sun-dried tomatoes, drained, slivered	1 TB. olive oil
	4 TB. pine nuts, toasted

Combine broccoli with enough water to cover in a saucepan. Boil until crisp tender. Drain and cool.

Sauté sun-dried tomatoes and garlic in olive oil in a skillet until garlic is light brown. Add broccoli. Sauté until heated through. Stir in pine nuts. Serve immediately.

Palate Preview

Be sure to try this broccoli recipe that's dressed up with sun-dried tomatoes and pine nuts. Broccoli never tasted so good.

Broccoli and Cauliflower with Almonds

Prep time: 20 minutes • Cook time: 7 minutes • Serves: 8 • Serving size: 1 cup

Nutritional Analysis per Serving: Glycemic Index (not significant) • Glycemic Load (not significant) • Calories 57 • Protein in grams 2½ • Animal Protein 0 • Vegetable Protein 2½ • Carbohydrates 5 grams • Dietary Fiber 2 grams • Net Carbohydrate 3 grams • Fat 3 grams • Saturated Fat <1 gram • Cholesterol 0 • Sodium 100 mg • Exchanges 1 vegetable, ½ fat

4 cups broccoli florets

4 cups cauliflower florets

2 TB. white wine vinegar

1 TB. olive oil

¼ tsp. salt

¼ tsp. freshly ground black pepper

¼ cup sliced almonds, toasted

Palate Preview
A wonderfully healthy vegetable dish with an added bonus: It's sprinkled with toasted almonds.

Preheat the oven to 350°F. Place almonds in a single layer on a cookie sheet. Bake for ten minutes or until lightly browned.

Pour 1 inch of water into a large saucepan and bring to a boil. Add broccoli and cauliflower. Reduce heat to low. Cover and simmer 5 to 7 minutes or until vegetables are crisp-tender. Drain.

Add olive oil, white wine vinegar, salt, pepper, and almonds. Stir and serve.

Summer Squash with Mushrooms and Herbs

Prep time: 10 minutes • Cook time: 10 minutes • Serves: 6 • Serving size: ⅔ cup

Nutritional Analysis per Serving: Glycemic Index (not significant) • Glycemic Load (not significant) • Calories 36 • Protein in grams 1½ gram • Animal Protein 0 • Vegetable Protein 1½ • Carbohydrates 3 grams • Dietary Fiber 1 gram • Net Carbohydrate 2 grams • Fat 1½ grams • Saturated Fat <1 gram • Cholesterol 0 • Sodium 55 mg • Exchanges 1 vegetable, ½ fat

1 TB. olive or vegetable oil	1½ cups (4 oz.) fresh mushrooms, sliced
2 small zucchinis, sliced	1 TB. chopped fresh basil
2 small yellow summer squash, sliced	⅛ tsp. salt
2 tsp. chopped garlic	⅛ tsp. freshly ground black pepper
1 small onion, thinly sliced	

Heat oil in a large skillet over medium-high heat. Add zucchini, summer squash, garlic, and onion. Cook, stirring frequently, for 2 to 3 minutes until onions begin to soften.

Stir in mushrooms, basil, salt, and pepper. Cook, stirring occasionally, for 3 to 5 minutes, or until vegetables are crisp-tender and any excess cooking liquid has evaporated. Serve.

Palate Preview

A popular skillet-cooked medley of zucchini and yellow squash with onions, mushrooms, and basil. A great accompaniment for any main dish.

Glazed Carrots

Prep time: 10 minutes • Cook time: 20 minutes • Serves: 4 • Serving size: 1 cup

Nutritional Analysis per Serving: Glycemic Index 55 • Glycemic Load 11 • Calories 75 • Protein in grams 1 • Animal Protein 0 • Vegetable Protein 1 • Carbohydrates 20 grams • Dietary Fiber 3½ grams • Net Carbohydrate 17 grams • Fat 2 grams • Saturated Fat 1 gram • Cholesterol 5 mg • Sodium 147 mg • Exchanges 2 vegetable, ½ fruit

1 lb. carrots, peeled and cut into ¼ inch rounds

2 tsp. unsalted butter

1 TB. honey

⅛ tsp. salt

½ tsp. dried ground ginger

1 TB. chopped fresh parsley

Palate Preview _____ This recipe is wonderful. The carrots are glazed in a sauce of honey, butter, and ginger. Yummy.

Place carrots in a saucepan and barely cover with water. Bring to a boil. Reduce the heat and simmer, for 10 to 15 minutes, uncovered until carrots are tender. Drain. Add butter, honey, salt, and ginger, and heat thoroughly. Sprinkle with chopped parsley. Serve at once.

Steamed Asparagus

Prep time: 5 minutes • Cook time: 5 to 8 minutes • Serves: 4 • Serving size: 4 ounces Asparagus or ¼ recipe

Nutritional Analysis per Serving: Glycemic Index (not significant) • Glycemic Load (not significant) • Calories 23 • Protein in grams 2½ • Animal Protein 0 • Vegetable Protein 2½ • Carbohydrates 5 grams • Dietary Fiber 2 grams • Net Carbohydrate 3 grams • Fat 0 • Saturated Fat 0 • Cholesterol 0 • Sodium 2 mg • Exchanges 1 vegetable

1 lb. asparagus

Try to select medium-size asparagus. Break off tough ends and discard. Wash stalks in cold water.

Place a skillet of water over high heat and bring to a boil. Add asparagus. Boil for 5 to 8 minutes, or until tender, depending on the thickness of spears.

Remove asparagus with tongs and drain. Serve immediately, at room temperature, or very slightly cooled.

Palate Preview
Asparagus stands on its own in this simple, though elegant, recipe. It doesn't need any dressing or even salt and pepper to be totally delicious.

Delightfully Different
You can add many different and interesting seasonings to the asparagus. Try one tablespoon butter with salt and pepper, vinaigrette dressing, lime juice, or lemon juice.

Easy Grilled Vegetables

Prep time: 10 minutes • Cook time: 15 minutes • Serves: 6 • Serving size: 1 cup vegetables

Nutritional Analysis per Serving: Glycemic Index 4 • Glycemic Load <1 • Calories 58 • Protein in grams 3 • Animal Protein 0 • Vegetable Protein 3 • Carbohydrates 8 grams • Dietary Fiber 3 grams • Net Carbohydrate 5 grams • Fat 2 grams • Saturated Fat <1 gram • Cholesterol 0 • Sodium 128 mg • Exchanges 1½ vegetable, ⅓ fat

Vegetable oil cooking spray

6 pattypan squash (about 4 inches each)

2 medium red bell peppers, cored, seeded, and cut into 1-inch strips

⅓ cup low-calorie Italian dressing

1 large red onion, cut into ½ inch round slices

12 large white mushrooms

Delightfully Different

You can also cook the vegetables in a low-heat skillet. First add one tablespoon of olive oil and then stir until cooked. Then add dressing.

Spray a grill rack with cooking spray. Prepare a medium-hot fire in a charcoal or gas grill, with the rack placed 4 to 6 inches above heat. Grill squash and peppers for 5 minutes, turning and brushing them with dressing once or twice.

Place onion and mushrooms on the grill. Grill for 5 to 10 minutes, turning and brushing vegetables with dressing 2 to 3 times, until tender.

Palate Preview

A grilled array of vegetables: pattypan squash, red bell peppers, and mushrooms. You'll love the taste of the grill, which is made succulent by basting with Italian dressing.

Grilled Stuffed Mushrooms

Prep time: 15 minutes • Cook time: 10 minutes • Serves: 8 • Serving size:
4 mushrooms

Nutritional Analysis per Serving: Glycemic Index 40 • Glycemic Load 2 • Calories 61
• Protein in grams 3 • Animal Protein 2 • Vegetable Protein 1 • Carbohydrates
6 grams • Dietary Fiber 1 gram • Net Carbohydrate 5 grams • Fat 2½ grams •
Saturated Fat ½ gram • Cholesterol 2 mg • Sodium 210 mg • Exchanges
1 vegetable, ½ lean meat, ½ fat

1 (3-oz.) pkg. nonfat cream cheese, softened	12 oz. large white mushrooms, stems removed (about 32)
¼ cup nonfat mayonnaise	
3 TB. shaved Parmesan cheese	Olive oil cooking spray
3 TB. finely chopped green onion	¼ cup dry bread crumbs
1 (6½-oz.) jar marinated artichoke hearts, drained and finely chopped	1 TB. olive oil
	½ tsp salt-free Mrs. Dash Seasoning Blend or salt-free seasoning of choice

Preheat a gas grill to medium-high or prepare a medium-hot fire in a charcoal grill, with the rack placed 4 to 6 inches above the heat. In a medium bowl, combine cream cheese, mayonnaise, cheese, green onions, and artichoke hearts. Mix well.

Spray the rounded side of mushroom caps with cooking spray. Spoon approximately 1 scant tablespoon cheese-artichoke mixture into each mushroom cap. In a small bowl combine bread crumbs, oil, and Mrs. Dash seasoning, mixing well. Sprinkle equal amounts on top of each stuffed mushroom.

When you are ready to grill, place mushrooms in a 10-inch grill basket or on a piece of foil, in a single layer, stuffed side up. Place the basket or foil on the grill and cook for 8 to 10 minutes or until mushrooms are tender and filling is thoroughly heated.

Palate Preview
These mushrooms are stuffed with cheeses and artichoke hearts. A proven taste pleaser.

You can also bake in the oven at 350°F for 15 minutes or until done.

Boiled Artichokes

Prep time: 10 minutes • Cook time: 45 minutes • Serves: 2 • Serving size: 1 artichoke

Nutritional Analysis per Serving: Glycemic Index <5 • Glycemic Load 1 • Calories 76 • Protein in grams 5 • Animal Protein 0 • Vegetable Protein 5 • Carbohydrates 17 grams • Dietary Fiber 8 grams • Net Carbohydrate 9 grams • Fat 0 • Saturated Fat 0 • Cholesterol 0 • Sodium 430 mg • Exchanges 2 vegetable

2 firm, large artichokes

¼ tsp. salt

1 lemon, cut into quarters

1 tsp. dried oregano

Delightfully Different
Serve boiled artichokes with low-fat mayonnaise mixed with lemon juice and/or a small amount of Dijon mustard.

Palate Preview
Boiled artichokes are fun food, mostly because they have a unique and appetizing flavor, but also because you get to eat them with your fingers.

Wash artichokes under cold water, making sure the water runs between the leaves.

With a sharp knife, cut off stems at the base and remove small bottom leaves and any discolored or particularly tough-looking outer leaves.

With scissors, snip off the pointed ends of outside leaves. With a sharp knife, cut off the top ½ to 1 inch of each artichoke.

Stand artichokes in a saucepan just large enough to hold them snugly if possible. Add enough water to come 2 to 3 inches up the side of the pan. Add salt, lemon quarters, and oregano. Cover and bring to a boil. Boil for 30 to 45 minutes or until bottom of artichokes can be pierced with a fork and base of leaves are tender. Remove from the saucepan with tongs or a slotted spoon, drain and serve hot.

Marinated Artichoke Coleslaw

Prep time: 10 minutes • Cook time: none • Serves: 6 • Serving size: ⅔ cup

Nutritional Analysis per Serving: Glycemic Index 8 • Glycemic Load <1 • Calories 28 • Protein in grams 2 • Animal Protein 0 • Vegetable Protein 2 • Carbohydrates 5 grams • Dietary Fiber 2 grams • Net Carbohydrate 3 grams • Fat 0 • Saturated Fat 0 • Cholesterol 0 • Sodium 169 mg • Exchanges 1 vegetable

3 cups shredded green cabbage

½ cup chopped (cored and seeded) red bell pepper

2 green onions, thinly sliced

2 TB. nonfat mayonnaise

1 (6-oz.) jar marinated artichoke hearts, drained and chopped

2 TB. nonfat Italian dressing

In large bowl, combine cabbage, bell pepper, green onions, mayonnaise, artichoke hearts, and dressing and toss gently to coat. Serve immediately, or cover and refrigerate up to 6 hours before serving.

Palate Preview _____
The marinated artichoke hearts and chopped red bell pepper add interest to this coleslaw.

Green Beans with Lemon and Garlic

Prep time: 15 minutes • Cook time: 10 minutes • Serves: 6 • Serving size: ⅔ cup

Nutritional Analysis per Serving: Glycemic Index (not significant) • Glycemic Load (not significant) • Calories 49 • Protein in grams 1 • Animal Protein 0 • Vegetable Protein 1 • Carbohydrates 3 grams • Dietary Fiber 1½ grams • Net Carbohydrate 2 grams • Fat 5 grams • Saturated Fat 2 grams • Cholesterol 10 mg • Sodium 161 mg • Exchanges 1 vegetable, 1 fat

1 lb. fresh green beans or 16 oz. frozen, thawed	2 tsp. fresh lemon juice
1 tsp. minced garlic	⅛ tsp. salt
2 TB. unsalted butter, melted	⅛ tsp. coarsely ground black pepper
	¼ tsp. hot sauce such as Tabasco

Palate Preview

Green beans tossed with garlic, lemon juice, and seasonings are an easy-to-make side dish that's simply wonderful to eat.

Place beans in a steamer basket. Place the basket in a large saucepan and add about 1 to 2 inches of water. Cover. Bring water to a boil and steam for 7 to 10 minutes or until beans are crisp-tender. Remove beans from the steamer and place beans in a serving bowl.

Combine garlic, butter, lemon juice, blending well. Add garlic mixture, salt, pepper, and hot sauce to green beans, tossing to mix.

Baked Tomatoes Provencal

Prep time: 10 minutes • Cook time: 20 minutes • Serves: 4 • Serving size: ½ tomato with 1 tablespoon Topping

Nutritional Analysis per Serving: Glycemic Index 52 • Glycemic Load 5 • Calories 53 • Protein in grams 3 • Animal Protein 1 • Vegetable Protein 2 • Carbohydrates 9 grams • Dietary Fiber 1 gram • Net Carbohydrate 8 grams • Fat 1 gram • Saturated Fat ½ gram • Cholesterol 2 mg • Sodium 141 mg • Exchanges 1 vegetable, ⅓ starch

Vegetable oil cooking spray

2 large tomatoes cut in half crosswise

Topping:

2 TB. bread crumbs

2 TB. grated Parmesan cheese

1 tsp. dried basil

½ to 1 tsp. salt-free lemon-pepper seasoning

Preheat the oven to 375°F. Spray an 8-inch square baking dish with cooking spray. Place tomatoes into it in a single layer, cut side up. In a small bowl mix bread crumbs, cheese, basil, and seasoning. Top each tomato half with about 1 TB. bread-crumb mixture.

Bake for 15 to 20 minutes or until soft and thoroughly heated.

Palate Preview

Baked tomatoes offer a familiar cheesy au gratin taste that you'll enjoy.

Peachy Sweet Potatoes

Prep time: 15 minutes • Cook time: 3½ hours • Serves: 10 • Serving size: ½ cup

Nutritional Analysis per Serving: Glycemic Index 47 • Glycemic Load 11 • Calories 164 • Protein in grams 2 • Animal Protein 0 • Vegetable Protein 2 • Carbohydrates 24 grams • Dietary Fiber 3½ grams • Net Carbohydrate 21 grams • Fat 7 grams • Saturated Fat 2 grams • Cholesterol 9 mg • Sodium 37 mg • Exchanges 1½ starch, 1 fat

Vegetable oil cooking spray

2¼ lb. sweet potatoes, peeled

1 cup frozen peach slices, thawed and chopped

2 TB. unsalted butter, melted

1 tsp. grated fresh gingerroot

⅛ tsp. salt

Topping:

1 TB. brown sugar

1 TB. unsalted butter

¼ tsp. ground cinnamon

½ cup coarsely chopped pecans, toasted

Palate Preview
An excellent way to serve sweet potatoes for the holidays. The slow cooker makes the sweet potatoes tender, with a soft and comforting texture. As an added plus, the recipe contains peaches, pecans, cinnamon, and butter.

Spray a 4- to 6-quart slow cooker with cooking spray. Halve larger sweet potatoes lengthwise and cut each potato into ½-inch slices. Place in slow cooker. Add peaches, butter, gingerroot, and salt, mixing well to coat potatoes.

Cover and cook on high setting for 2½ to 3½ hours or until tender.

When you are almost ready to serve, prepare the topping: In a small skillet, combine brown sugar, butter, cinnamon, and pecans and cook over medium heat for 2 to 3 minutes or until bubbly and glazed, stirring frequently.

To serve, gently stir potatoes and sprinkle with topping.

Curried Cabbage and Carrots

Prep time: 5 minutes • Cook time: 15 minutes • Serves: 6 • Serving size: ½ cup

Nutritional Analysis per Serving: Glycemic Index 19 • Glycemic Load 1 • Calories 37 • Protein in grams 2 • Animal Protein 0 • Vegetable Protein 2 • Carbohydrates 5 grams • Dietary Fiber 1½ grams • Net Carbohydrate 4 grams • Fat 2 grams • Saturated Fat 1 gram • Cholesterol 5 mg • Sodium 93 mg • Exchanges 1 vegetable, ⅓ fat

4 cups (1 lb.) coarsely chopped green cabbage	¼ tsp. mustard seed
1 cup shredded carrots	½ cup water
¼ tsp. salt	1 TB. unsalted butter
½ tsp. curry powder	

In a large skillet, combine cabbage, carrots, salt, curry powder, mustard seed, water, and butter. Cover and cook over medium heat until crisp-tender, about 15 minutes, stirring occasionally.

Palate Preview

Serve Curried Cabbage and Carrots with any main dish meat or seafood. It lends a slightly exotic taste to your meal.

Summer Vegetable Sauté

Prep time: 10 minutes   •   Cook time: 10 minutes   •   Serves: 6   •   Serving size: ¾ cup

Nutritional Analysis per Serving: Glycemic Index (not significant)   •   Glycemic Load (not significant)   •   Calories 54   •   Protein in grams 2   •   Animal Protein 1   •   Vegetable Protein 1   •   Carbohydrates 4 grams   •   Dietary Fiber 2 grams   •   Net Carbohydrate 2 grams   •   Fat 4 grams   •   Saturated Fat 2 grams   •   Cholesterol 7 mg   •   Sodium 42 mg   •   Exchanges 1 vegetable, 1 fat

1 TB. unsalted butter

2 cups thinly sliced zucchini

2 cups thinly sliced yellow squash

½ cup coarsely chopped red onion

½ tsp. dried basil

½ tsp. dried oregano

1 TB. finely minced garlic

2 medium tomatoes, cubed

3 TB. grated Parmesan cheese

Palate Preview _____ Serve this vegetable sauté any time of year. It's a colorful array of vegetables seasoned with Italian spices.

Melt butter in a large skillet over medium heat. Add zucchini, squash, and onion. Cook, stirring, for 3 minutes. Sprinkle with basil, oregano, and garlic. Cook, stirring, for an additional 3 to 5 minutes or until vegetables are crisp-tender. Stir in tomatoes and cook 1 minute or until tomatoes are thoroughly heated. Sprinkle with cheese.

Zucchini and Carrots with Fresh Herbs

Prep time: 10 minutes • Cook time: 15 minutes • Serves: 6 • Serving size: ¼ cup

Nutritional Analysis per Serving: Glycemic Index 22 • Glycemic Load 1 • Calories 55 • Protein in grams 2 • Animal Protein 0 • Vegetable Protein 2 • Carbohydrates 4 grams • Dietary Fiber 1½ grams • Net Carbohydrate 3 grams • Fat 4 grams • Saturated Fat 2 grams • Cholesterol 10 mg • Sodium 61 mg • Exchanges 1 vegetable, 1 fat

2 medium carrots, sliced	1 tsp. chopped fresh or ¼ tsp. dried dill weed
4 medium zucchinis, cut into julienne strips	2 tsp. fresh lemon juice
2 TB. unsalted butter	⅛ tsp. salt
1 TB. chopped fresh or 1 tsp. dried thyme	¼ tsp. freshly ground black pepper

Place a steamer basket in ½ inch of water in a saucepan (water should not touch the bottom of the basket). Place carrots in the basket. Cover tightly and heat to boiling. Reduce heat and steam carrots 5 minutes. Add zucchini and steam 4 to 6 minutes or until carrots and zucchini are crisp-tender.

Melt butter in a 12-inch skillet over medium heat. Stir in carrots, zucchini, thyme, dill, lemon juice, salt, and pepper. Cook uncovered, stirring gently for 2 to 3 minutes, or until hot.

Palate Preview
This zucchini and carrot dish holds a seasoning surprise with its fresh thyme and dill weed.

Green Beans with Almonds

Prep time: 10 minutes • Cook time: 15 minutes • Serves: 4 • Serving size: ½ cup

Nutritional Analysis per Serving: Glycemic Index (not significant) • Glycemic Load (not significant) • Calories 67 • Protein in grams 2 • Animal Protein 0 • Vegetable Protein 2 • Carbohydrates 6 grams • Dietary Fiber 3 grams • Net Carbohydrate 3 grams • Fat 4 grams • Saturated Fat 2 grams • Cholesterol 7 mg • Sodium 82 mg • Exchanges 1 vegetable, 1 fat

2 cups (16 oz.) frozen cut green beans, thawed	¼ cup sliced celery
1 TB. unsalted butter	2 TB. slivered almonds

Palate Preview

A classic dish prepared simply. You add almonds and butter to the green beans and cook until the celery is just barely tender.

Place a steamer basket in ½ inch of water in a saucepan (water should not touch the bottom of the basket). Place beans in the basket. Cover tightly and heat to boiling. Reduce heat and steam beans 10 to 12 minutes. Drain.

Meanwhile, in a medium skillet over medium-high heat, melt the butter. Add celery and almonds and cook 5 minutes or until celery is crisp-tender. Add beans and toss gently.

Peas with Mushrooms and Pine Nuts

Prep time: 10 minutes • Cook time: 10 minutes • Serves: 6 • Serving size: ¾ cup

Nutritional Analysis per Serving: Glycemic Index 40 • Glycemic Load 5 • Calories 120 • Protein in grams 5 • Animal Protein 0 • Vegetable Protein 5 • Carbohydrates 12 grams • Dietary Fiber 4 grams • Net Carbohydrate 8 grams • Fat 6 grams • Saturated Fat ½ gram • Cholesterol 0 • Sodium 178 mg • Exchanges ½ starch, ½ vegetable, 1 fat

1 TB. olive oil	2 TB. water
¼ cup pine nuts	½ tsp. salt-free Mrs. Dash Seasoning Blend
1 (16-oz.) pkg. frozen peas, thawed	¼ tsp. freshly ground black pepper
2 cloves garlic, minced	2 cups sliced white mushrooms
¼ tsp. salt	

In a large skillet heat oil over medium heat. Add pine nuts and cook, stirring for 1 to 2 minutes or until nuts are lightly browned. Remove nuts from the skillet with a slotted spoon, reserving oil in skillet.

Add peas, garlic, water, salt, Mrs. Dash Seasoning Blend, and pepper to skillet, stirring gently to coat. Cook, covered, over medium-low heat for 5 minutes.

Add mushrooms. Cook, uncovered, stirring, for 3 to 5 minutes more or until tender and heated through. Stir in toasted pine nuts.

Palate Preview

Peas are combined with garlic, mushrooms, and pine nuts—an interesting combination of tastes and textures.

Brussels Sprouts with Orange Peel

Prep time: 10 minutes • Cook time: 15 minutes • Serves: 8 • Serving size: ½ cup

Nutritional Analysis per Serving: Glycemic Index <5 • Glycemic Load 1 • Calories 53 • Protein in grams 3 grams • Animal Protein 0 • Vegetable Protein 3 • Carbohydrates 7 grams • Dietary Fiber 3 grams • Net Carbohydrate 4 grams • Fat 3 grams • Saturated Fat 1½ gram • Cholesterol 7 mg • Sodium 12 mg • Exchanges 1 vegetable, ½ fat

1½ lb. fresh Brussels sprouts	2 tsp. grated orange peel
2 TB. water	4 to 5 drops hot sauce such as Tabasco
2 TB. unsalted butter	

Palate Preview
Orange peel and hot sauce lend delicious flavor to tenderly cooked Brussels sprouts.

Trim ends of Brussels sprouts. Cut a small X in each stem end. Arrange Brussels sprouts in a 2-quart microwave-safe casserole. Add 2 tablespoons water. Cover and microwave on high power for 8 to 10 minutes or until vegetables are crisp-tender, stirring once. Drain.

Place butter in a small microwave-safe bowl. Microwave on high for 15 to 20 seconds or until melted. Stir in orange peel and Tabasco sauce. Pour over cooked Brussels sprouts.

Spaghetti Squash Italian Style

Prep time: 15 minutes   •   Cook time: 35 minutes   •   Serves: 8   •   Serving size: ½ cup

Nutritional Analysis per Serving: Glycemic Index 10   •   Glycemic Load 1   •   Calories 68   •   Protein in grams 3   •   Animal Protein 1   •   Vegetable Protein 2   •   Carbohydrates 9 grams   •   Dietary Fiber 2 grams   •   Net Carbohydrate 7 grams   •   Fat 3 grams   •   Saturated Fat 1 gram   •   Cholesterol 3 mg   •   Sodium 97 mg   •   Exchanges 2 vegetable, ½ fat

1 spaghetti squash (1½ lb.)	⅛ tsp. salt
1 TB. olive oil	¾ tsp. chopped fresh or ¼ tsp. dried oregano
1 medium onion, chopped	¾ tsp. chopped fresh or ¼ tsp. dried basil
1 small green bell pepper, cored, seeded, and chopped	¼ tsp. fennel seed
	⅛ tsp. freshly ground black pepper
1 TB. finely chopped garlic	¼ cup grated Parmesan cheese
2 large tomatoes, chopped	

Pierce whole squash in several places. Wrap in a paper towel. Microwave on high power, uncovered, for 8 to 15 minutes, turning squash over after 5-6 minutes, until tender. Let stand uncovered 10 minutes.

Heat oil in a 3-quart saucepan over medium heat. Add onion, bell pepper, and garlic. Cook, stirring occasionally, for about 5 minutes, or until onion is tender. Stir in tomatoes, salt oregano, basil, fennel seed, and pepper. Simmer uncovered, stirring occasionally, for 5 minutes.

Palate Preview

Prepare this spaghetti squash recipe as a side dish with any meat main dish. It gives your meal a decidedly Italian aroma and taste.

Cut squash in half and remove seeds and fibrous center. Using two forks, remove squash strands and transfer them to a large serving bowl. Toss with cheese. Spoon tomato mixture over squash and toss gently.

Green Beans with Pecans and Blue Cheese

Prep time: 10 minutes • Cook time: 8 to 10 minutes • Serves: 6 • Serving size: ¾ cup

Nutritional Analysis per Serving: Glycemic Index <5 • Glycemic Load 1 • Calories 201 • Protein in grams 4½ • Animal Protein 1½ • Vegetable Protein 3 • Carbohydrates 10 grams • Dietary Fiber 5 grams • Net Carbohydrate 5 grams • Fat 7 grams • Saturated Fat 3 grams • Cholesterol 5 mg • Sodium 125 mg • Exchanges 2 vegetable, 3 fat1 TB. olive oil

2 tsp. white wine vinegar	3 TB. blue cheese, crumbled
½ tsp. Dijon mustard	1 cup pecans, toasted and coarsely chopped
1½ lb. fresh green beans	⅛ tsp. freshly ground black pepper

In a small bowl whisk together olive oil, vinegar, and Dijon mustard.

Preheat the oven to 350°F. Place pecans on a cookie sheet in a single layer. Place in oven and bake for ten minutes or until lightly toasted.

Palate Preview _____ These green beans are anything but boring. You'll love the tastes and textures of pecans and blue cheese added to the beans.

Bring a saucepan of water to a boil, add the beans and boil for about 8 minutes, or until just tender. Drain and cool. Combine beans with mustard dressing in a salad bowl and toss to coat. Add cheese and half of pecans and toss gently. Season with pepper.

Sprinkle remaining pecans over the top of the salad. Serve at room temperature.

Side Salads

In This Chapter

- ◆ Fresh salads to accompany your meals
- ◆ Many varieties of greens
- ◆ Dressings that add zest
- ◆ Delicious servings of vegetables

Side salads are standard fare in most restaurants and many homes. We've come to expect a small tossed salad of lettuce, a couple of vegetables, and dressing with our meal. There are plenty of good reasons for keeping with this time-tested tradition, and plenty of options to make side salads special.

Side salads offer a serving or two of fruits and vegetables, fiber, and healthful oils. Salads are usually low in carbohydrates, sodium, and glycemic load, so they are superb for the eating plans of persons with diabetes. Many experts recommend eating side salads because the lettuces are thought to aid digestion because they contain enzymes that aid digestion.

In this chapter, you'll find recipes for everyday popular salads, such as Tossed Garden Salad; Orange, Almond, and Avocado Salad; and Layered Vegetable Salad. Plus you'll find salad recipes that feature Thai, Mediterranean, and French influences.

Varying Lettuces

You could prepare all of your salads with the old standby, iceberg lettuce. Which is actually a member of the cabbage family! But the recipes in this chapter call for a wide variety of lettuces, all of which are packed with important vitamins and minerals.

We've included recipes calling for varieties such as arugula, romaine, Bibb lettuce, and Belgian endive. In addition, you'll find recipes with spinach and cabbage.

Yes, you can interchange lettuces in these recipes, based on what you already have on hand. Then when you get to the grocery store again, stock up on some of the many lettuce varieties.

The Dressing Makes the Salad

While lettuces and other vegetables comprise the bulk of these salads, the dressing gives a salad its final flourish. The dressings for each recipe have been chosen to add just the right zing to the vegetables.

Healthy Notes
Be sure to dress and toss salads right before serving. If you do this too far in advance, the salad greens will wilt.

Making a dressing from scratch takes very little—just the amount of time it takes to put the ingredients into a container and shake, typically less than 5 minutes. The time is worth it, because the dressings include the spices and seasonings that make each salad totally scrumptious to eat.

Several recipes call for nonfat French dressing. It offers good and balanced flavoring for salads and you may want to keep a bottle on hand.

The Least You Need to Know

- Side salads give you plenty of nutrition and taste in a small to medium package.
- Many recipes call for lettuces such as arugula, romaine, Bibb, Belgian endive, as well as spinach and cabbage.
- Experiment by interchanging the wide variety of lettuces as called for in the recipes in this chapter.
- Make your own salad dressings to enjoy the special spices and seasonings in each salad.

Thai Cucumber Salad

Prep time: 10 minutes plus 30 minutes refrigeration • Cook time: none • Serves: 4 •
Serving size: ½ cup

Nutritional Analysis per Serving: Glycemic Index 14 • Glycemic Load 1 • Calories 27
• Protein in grams 1 • Animal Protein 0 • Vegetable Protein 1 • Carbohydrates
9 grams • Dietary Fiber 1 gram • Net Carbohydrate 8 grams • Fat 0 • Saturated
Fat 0 • Cholesterol 0 • Sodium 88 mg • Exchanges 1 vegetable, ¼ fruit

Salad:

2 medium cucumbers, peeled

1 medium tomato, cut into 8 wedges

2 green onions, cut into ½ inch pieces

2–4 TB. chopped fresh cilantro

Dressing:

2 tsp. fructose

2 TB. fresh lime juice

2 tsp. low-salt soy sauce

Dash of cayenne, optional

Cut each cucumber lengthwise into 8 spears. Cut each spear crosswise into ½-inch slices. Cut
tomato wedges in half crosswise. In a large bowl, combine fructose, lime juice, soy sauce, and
cayenne (if desired), and blend well. Add cucumbers, tomato pieces, green onions, and cilantro,
and toss lightly to coat. Cover and refrigerate about 30 minutes to allow flavors to blend.

Palate Preview

A quick and easy salad with tomatoes and cucumbers. The dressing makes this
salad interesting and fresh tasting. The recipe calls for peeled cucumbers, but you can
leave the peel if you prefer the taste.

Dried-Cherry, Walnut, and Goat-Cheese Salad

Prep time: 15 minutes • Cook time: none • Serves: 6 • Serving size: 1 cup salad

Nutritional Analysis per Serving: Glycemic Index 46 • Glycemic Load 6 • Calories 204 • Protein in grams 5 • Animal Protein 3 • Vegetable Protein 2 • Carbohydrates 14 grams • Dietary Fiber 2 grams • Net Carbohydrate 12 grams • Fat 15 grams • Saturated Fat 4 grams • Cholesterol 10 mg • Sodium 97 mg • Exchanges 1 vegetable, ½ fruit, ½ high fat meat, 2 fat

Salad:

4½ cups salad greens

½ cup dried cherries

2 oz. (about ¼ cup) crumbled goat cheese

½ cup coarsely chopped walnuts, toasted

Dressing:

1 TB. white wine vinegar

2 tsp. nonfat mayonnaise

½ tsp. Dijon mustard

⅛ tsp. salt

⅛ tsp. freshly ground black pepper

2 TB. canola oil, cold-expeller pressed

Palate Preview

A green salad tossed with dried cherries, goat cheese, and toasted walnuts. Add a dressing made of vinegar, Dijon mustard, and mayonnaise, and you have a tangy, sweet, and cheesy combination.

Preheat the oven to 350°F. Place walnuts in a single layer on a cookie sheet. Bake for ten minutes or until lightly browned. Remove from oven and cool before using.

In a small bowl, combine vinegar, mayonnaise, mustard, salt, and pepper. Beat well with wire whisk. Slowly beat in canola oil until well blended. Cover and refrigerate until serving time.

Just before serving, in a large bowl, toss lettuce with dressing. Divide evenly onto 6 salad plates. Sprinkle each with equal portions of cherries, cheese, and walnuts.

Zesty Vegetable Coleslaw

Prep time: 15 minutes plus 1 hour refrigeration • Cook time: none • Serves: 8 •
Serving size: 1 cup

Nutritional Analysis per Serving: Glycemic Index 29 • Glycemic Load 3 • Calories 45
• Protein in grams 1½ • Animal Protein 0 • Vegetable Protein 1½ •
Carbohydrates 10 grams • Dietary Fiber 2 grams • Net Carbohydrate 8 grams •
Fat 0 • Saturated Fat 0 • Cholesterol 0 • Sodium 252 mg • Exchanges
1 vegetable, ⅓ fruit

1 (16-oz.) pkg. coleslaw blend	¾ cup bottled nonfat Italian salad dressing
2 cups small fresh broccoli florets	½ tsp. celery seed
¼ cup sliced green onions	1 (11-oz.) can mandarin orange segments, drained

In a large bowl, combine coleslaw blend, broccoli, and
green onions. Stir gently to mix.

In a small bowl, combine salad dressing and celery
seed, blending well. Pour over coleslaw mixture and
toss to coat. Add mandarin orange segments, tossing
gently. Cover and refrigerate for 1 hour or until ready
to serve.

Delightfully Different
Add an Asian flare to
this salad by topping with 2-3 TB.
slivered almonds.

Palate Preview
This coleslaw recipe is truly easy to make and totally delicious. The orange segments add a sweet fruit flavor.

Jicama Coleslaw

Prep time: 20 minutes plus 20 minutes none 0 minutes   •   Serves: 6   •   Serving size: ¾ cup

Nutritional Analysis per Serving: Glycemic Index 30   •   Glycemic Load 2   •   Calories 50   •   Protein in grams 2   •   Animal Protein 0   •   Vegetable Protein 2   •   Carbohydrates 7 grams   •   Dietary Fiber 2 grams   •   Net Carbohydrate 5 grams   •   Fat 2½ grams   •   Saturated Fat ½ gram   •   Cholesterol 0   •   Sodium 93 mg   •   Exchanges 1½ vegetable, ½ fat

½ cup unsweetened pineapple juice

1 TB. fresh lime juice

1 TB. olive oil

¼ tsp. ground coriander

¼ tsp. ground cumin

¼ tsp. salt

⅛ tsp. coarsely ground black pepper

1 small jicama, peeled cut in julienne strips (3×1-inch) (about 2 cups)

3 large carrots, cut in julienne strips (3×1-inch)

¼ cup chopped fresh cilantro

¼ cup chopped green onions

In a bowl large enough to hold all of the salad ingredients, whisk together pineapple juice, lime juice, olive oil, coriander, cumin, salt, and pepper. Add the jicama, carrots, cilantro, and green onions and toss gently. Cover and refrigerate for 20 minutes and serve.

Palate Preview
Jicama gives this coleslaw a fresh and succulent taste, while the pineapple juice adds sweetness. Add in the spices of coriander and cumin and you'll love the eating.

Tomato and White-Bean Salad

Prep time: 10 minutes • Cook time: none • Serves: 4 • Serving size: 1½ cups greens with ¾ cup salad

Nutritional Analysis per Serving: Glycemic Index (not significant) • Glycemic Load (not significant) • Calories 170 • Protein in grams 8 • Animal Protein 0 • Vegetable Protein 8 • Carbohydrates 25 grams • Dietary Fiber 10 grams • Net Carbohydrate 15 grams • Fat 4 grams • Saturated Fat ½ gram • Cholesterol 0 • Sodium 144 mg • Exchanges 1 very lean meat, 1 starch, 2 vegetable, ½ fat

1 TB. extra-virgin olive oil	2 medium tomatoes, chopped
1 tsp. red wine vinegar	¼ cup sliced green onions
⅛ tsp. salt	1 (15.5-oz.) can Great Northern beans, drained and rinsed
¼ tsp. coarsely ground black pepper	6 cups salad greens

In a medium bowl, combine oil, vinegar, salt, and pepper, blending well. Add tomatoes, greens, onions, and beans. Stir gently until well mixed. Serve at once.

Palate Preview

This hearty salad will help satisfy a big appetite. The white beans add starch and protein to this green salad with tomatoes.

Spinach, Pear, and Blue-Cheese Salad

Prep time: 15 minutes • Cook time: none • Serves: 6 • Serving size: 1½ cups salad

Nutritional Analysis per Serving: Glycemic Index 29 • Glycemic Load 5 • Calories 149 • Protein in grams 5 • Animal Protein 2 • Vegetable Protein 3 • Carbohydrates 18 grams • Dietary Fiber 3 grams • Net Carbohydrate 15 grams • Fat 3 grams • Saturated Fat 1½ grams • Cholesterol 7 mg • Sodium 190 mg • Exchanges ½ fruit, 1 vegetable, 1 fat, ½ high fat meat

1 (10-oz.) pkg. spinach, stems removed, washed well and torn

2 pears, cored and cut into bite-size cubes

½ cup coarsely chopped walnuts, toasted

2 oz. crumbled blue cheese

¼ cup bottled non-fat raspberry vinaigrette

Palate Preview ____ The sensuous combination of ingredients—spinach, walnuts, blue cheese, and pear—makes this salad taste terrific.

Preheat the oven to 350°F. Place walnuts on a cookie sheet in a single layer. Bake for ten minutes or until lightly browned. Remove from oven and cool completely before using.

In a large bowl, combine spinach, pears, walnuts, and cheese and toss gently.

Pour dressing over salad, tossing to coat. Serve immediately.

Tossed Garden Salad

Prep time: 15 minutes • Cook time: none • Serves: 4 • Serving size: 2 cups salad

Nutritional Analysis per Serving: Glycemic Index 41 • Glycemic Load 8 • Calories 132 • Protein in grams 5 • Animal Protein 2 • Vegetable Protein 3 • Carbohydrates 20 grams • Dietary Fiber 2½ grams • Net Carbohydrate 18 grams • Fat 3 grams • Saturated Fat 1 gram • Cholesterol 5 mg • Sodium 229 mg • Exchanges 2 vegetable, ½ fruit, ¼ high-fat meat, ½ fat

6 cups bite-size pieces romaine or red leaf lettuce

⅔ cup cucumber, peeled and chopped

¾ cup tomato, chopped

¼ cup chopped red onion

¼ cup raisins

2 TB. sunflower seeds, toasted

1 oz. or 2 TB. blue cheese, crumbled

¼ cup bottled nonfat French dressing

Toss lettuce, cucumber, tomato, and onion in a large bowl. Sprinkle with raisins, sunflower seeds, and cheese. Pour dressing over salad, tossing to coat. Serve immediately.

Palate Preview

This is an everyday tossed garden salad enhanced with sunflower seeds, blue cheese, and raisins. The crunchy texture adds interest and makes a tossed garden salad anything but plain.

Delightfully Different

You can create many variations of this tossed garden salad. Substitute different kinds of nuts and seeds such as pine nuts, flaxseeds, pecans, and pistachios for the sunflower seeds. In place of the raisins, you can use dried cherries or cranberries. You can even substitute feta cheese or Parmesan for the blue cheese.

Elegant Green Salad

Prep time: 15 minutes plus 1 hour refrigeration • Cook time: none • Serves: 8 • Serving size: 1½ cups salad

Nutritional Analysis per Serving: Glycemic Index (not significant) • Glycemic Load (not significant) • Calories 55 • Protein in grams 2 • Animal Protein < ½ • Vegetable Protein 1½ • Carbohydrates 4 grams • Dietary Fiber 2 grams • Net Carbohydrate 2 grams • Fat 3 grams • Saturated Fat 1 gram • Cholesterol < 1 mg • Sodium 88 mg • Exchanges 1 vegetable, ½ fat

Salad:	Cheese-Mustard Dressing:
4 cups arugula	2 TB. olive oil
1½ cups sliced fresh white mushrooms	1 TB. red wine vinegar
4 cups Bibb lettuce, torn into bite-size pieces	2 tsp. grated Parmesan cheese
4 cups romaine lettuce, torn into bite-size pieces	2 tsp. Dijon mustard
	¼ tsp. salt

In a small bowl, whisk together olive oil, vinegar, cheese, mustard, and salt. Cover tightly and refrigerate at least 1 hour.

Place arugula, mushrooms, and lettuces in a large bowl and toss with dressing. Serve immediately.

Palate Preview _____

This recipe makes a great start to a main dish meat or seafood meal. The arugula lends a peppery taste and the dressing makes the salad lively.

Orange, Almond, and Avocado Salad

Prep time: 15 minutes • Cook time: none • Serves: 4 • Serving size: 1½ cups salad

Nutritional Analysis per Serving: Glycemic Index (not significant) • Glycemic Load (not significant) • Calories 136 • Protein in grams 2 • Animal Protein 0 • Vegetable Protein 2 • Carbohydrates 16 grams • Dietary Fiber 2 grams • Net Carbohydrate 14 grams • Fat 16 grams • Saturated Fat 1 gram • Cholesterol 0 • Sodium 141 mg • Exchanges 1½ vegetable, ½ fruit, 2 fat

2 TB. snipped fresh parsley or 1 TB. parsley flakes	1 avocado, cubed
1 TB. granulated sugar	¼ cup sliced almonds, toasted
2 TB. canola oil	4 cups bite-size pieces Bibb lettuce (about 2 heads)
1 TB. vinegar	1 cup chopped celery
¼ tsp. salt	2 green onions with tops, thinly sliced
Freshly ground black pepper to taste	½ cup mandarin orange segments, drained

Preheat the oven to 350°F. Place almonds on a cookie sheet in a single layer. Bake for ten minutes or until lightly browned. Remove from oven and cool before using.

In a large bowl, whisk together parsley, sugar, oil, vinegar, salt, and pepper.

Cut the avocado in half. Carefully insert the widest part of a sharp knife blade into the pit and twist the knife slightly. Remove and discard the pit. Slice the flesh of 1 avocado half into small dice while still in the shell by cutting several times in one direction and then several times in the other. Scoop out the flesh into the bowl with the dressing and repeat with remaining half. Toss gently.

Add almonds, lettuce, celery, green onions, and oranges and toss. Serve immediately.

Palate Preview

Adding avocado to this all-time favorite orange and almond salad gives you healthy monounsaturated fats and a richer taste.

Mediterranean Vegetable Salad

Prep time: 15 minutes plus 1 hour refrigeration • Cook time: none • Serves: 6 •
Serving size: 1½ cups salad

Nutritional Analysis per Serving: Glycemic Index 6 • Glycemic Load 1 • Calories 145
• Protein in grams 4 • Animal Protein 3 • Vegetable Protein 1 • Carbohydrates
15 grams • Dietary Fiber 2 grams • Net Carbohydrate 13 grams • Fat 11 grams •
Saturated Fat 3 grams • Cholesterol 10 mg • Sodium 48 mg • Exchanges
3 vegetable, ½ high fat meat, 1 fat

3 TB. tarragon vinegar

3 TB. olive oil

2 TB. chopped fresh oregano leaves (or 2 tsp.
dried)

½ tsp. fructose

½ tsp. dry mustard

⅛ tsp. salt

½ tsp. freshly ground black pepper

2 cloves garlic, finely minced

2 large yellow bell peppers, cored, seeded and
sliced into thin rings

3 large tomatoes, cut into 1-inch chunks

6 cups fresh spinach leaves, washed well and
trimmed

2 oz. or ¼ cup crumbled goat cheese

12 pitted Kalamata olives, rinsed and chopped

Delightfully Different
You can substitute red
or green bell peppers for the yellow bell peppers in this recipe.

In a large glass or ceramic container, whisk together
vinegar, oil, oregano, fructose, mustard, salt, pepper,
and garlic. Add bell peppers and tomatoes, and toss.
Cover tightly and refrigerate at least 1 hour to blend
flavors.

Line a serving platter with spinach. Drain tomato-
pepper mixture and place on spinach. Sprinkle with
cheese. Garnish with olives.

Palate Preview
Superbly satisfying. The spinach, goat cheese, Greek olives, and Mediterranean
spices make this salad sunny and robust.

Layered Vegetable Salad

Prep time: 25 minutes • Cook time: 5 minutes • Serves: 8 • Serving size: 1 cup

Nutritional Analysis per Serving: Glycemic Index (not significant) • Glycemic Load (not significant) • Calories 60 • Protein in grams 2 • Animal Protein 0 • Vegetable Protein 2 • Carbohydrates 14 grams • Dietary Fiber 2 grams • Net Carbohydrate 12 grams • Fat <1 gram • Saturated Fat 0 • Cholesterol 0 • Sodium 184 mg • Exchanges 1½ vegetable, ½ fruit

Salad:

1 cup chopped fresh cauliflower florets

1 cup chopped fresh broccoli florets

2 cups thinly sliced fresh spinach leaves

½ cup chopped red onion

1 cup frozen green peas, thawed

1 cup chopped, seeded cucumber

1 cup chopped tomato

Dressing:

½ cup nonfat mayonnaise

¼ cup bottled reduced-calorie French salad dressing

2 TB. chopped fresh parsley

Bring a saucepan of water to a boil and prepare a bowl of ice water. Add the cauliflower and broccoli to the boiling water and boil for about 5 minutes, or until just tender. Drain and immediately plunge cauliflower and broccoli into ice water for 30 seconds to set color and stop the cooking process. Drain.

In a 1½- to 2-quart glass baking dish with straight sides, layer salad starting with a layer of cauliflower, followed by a layer of broccoli, a layer of spinach, a layer of onion, a layer of peas, a layer of cucumber, and finally a layer of tomato.

In a small bowl, combine mayonnaise, French dressing, and parsley, and mix well. Spread over top of salad. Serve immediately, or cover and refrigerate until ready to serve. If desired, toss before serving.

Palate Preview
Take this layered salad to potlucks and church dinners. It's an all-time favorite that everyone appreciates. Plus, you can eat it comfortably, knowing it's plenty good for you.

Endive and Walnut Salad

Prep time: 20 minutes • Cook time: none • Serves: 6 • Serving size: 1½ cups

Nutritional Analysis per Serving: Glycemic Index 2 • Glycemic Load <1 • Calories 95 • Protein in grams 3 • Animal Protein 1 • Vegetable Protein 2½ • Carbohydrates 8 grams • Dietary Fiber 1½ grams • Net Carbohydrate 7 grams • Fat 8 grams • Saturated Fat 1 gram • Cholesterol 0 • Sodium 42 mg • Exchanges 1½ vegetable, 1½ fat

Salad:

1½ lbs. Belgian endive

1 bottled roasted red pepper, diced

¼ cup broken walnut pieces, toasted

Dressing:

2 TB. red wine vinegar

1 TB. fresh lemon juice

1 tsp. Dijon mustard

⅛ tsp. salt

½ tsp. freshly ground black pepper

¼ tsp. crumbled dried tarragon (or ½–1 tsp. minced fresh)

2 TB. olive oil

½ cup nonfat plain yogurt

Palate Preview Try this simple, yet elegant salad as a side dish with a meat or seafood entrée. The Belgian endive has a slightly bitter taste that goes well with the walnuts and roasted red pepper.

Preheat the oven to 350°F. Place nuts on a cookie sheet in a single layer. Bake for 10 minutes or until lightly browned. Remove from oven and cool before using.

Wash endives and pat them dry. Cut them into thick slices. In a medium bowl, toss endive with red pepper and walnuts.

In a small bowl, whisk together vinegar, lemon juice, mustard, salt, pepper, and tarragon. Whisk in oil and yogurt and combine thoroughly. Toss with endive mixture just before serving.

Note: All ingredients and dressing can be prepared several hours in advance. Dry endives and seal in a plastic bag. Place the dressing in a lightly covered container in the refrigerator.

Chapter 11

Fruit Side Dishes

In This Chapter

- ◆ The health benefits of fruit
- ◆ Fruit recipes you can enjoy
- ◆ A healthy, natural carbohydrate
- ◆ Eating fruits in moderation

You can't find a more natural food than fruit. Humans have been eating various fruits, well, since we've been humans! Fruits are sweet, filling, and healthy. They provide many health benefits, such as vitamins, minerals, antioxidants, and fiber, including soluble fiber.

So what's not to like? Unfortunately, fruits are a "be careful" food source for persons with diabetes. Fruits contain fructose, a form of sugar that when eaten in large amounts can give persons with diabetes high blood glucose levels.

However, when fruits are eaten in their natural form and in moderation, they can be a welcome and nutritious treat as part of your daily food intake. In this chapter, we offer you fruit-based recipes that meet your dietary needs and also your culinary desires.

Fruits Are a Natural

Fruits are a luscious gift of nature that contain more carbohydrates than most vegetables. Still, most fruits are low to moderate glycemic—with a few at the moderate level—and can play an important role in your overall eating plan. Prepare a fruit for a dessert or as a side dish, and you'll enjoy a delightful taste treat that contains many important nutrients for your well-being.

But watch out for dried fruits and fruit juices. These less natural forms of fruits are higher on the glycemic index. That's because the sugar content in dried fruits and juices is higher. To fill a 4-ounce glass requires the juice of three to four oranges. That's way more sugar and far less fiber than a person receives from simply eating an orange. Small amounts are acceptable, but avoid consuming lots of juice or dried fruit on a day-to-day basis.

In this chapter, we give you recipes for fruit side dishes seasoned with "sweet" spices, such as cinnamon, coriander, mint, cloves, nutmeg, and vanilla. The spices add interesting flavors of the fruit, and in themselves, the spices are beneficial to one's health.

The Least You Need to Know

- ◆ Fruit side dishes can fit in well with your eating plan and nutritional needs.
- ◆ Fruits offer vitamins, minerals, antioxidants, and fiber, plus luscious good taste.
- ◆ Most fruits are low to moderate glycemic.
- ◆ Dried fruits and fruit juices are higher on the glycemic index.

Strawberry-Pineapple Compote

Prep time: 10 minutes plus 30 minutes to marinate • Cook time: none • Serves: 6 •
Serving size: ¾ cup

Nutritional Analysis per Serving: Glycemic Index 35 • Glycemic Load 7 • Calories 83
• Protein in grams 4 • Animal Protein 3 • Vegetable Protein 1 • Carbohydrates
20 grams • Dietary Fiber 2 grams • Net Carbohydrate 18 grams • Fat 0 •
Saturated Fat 0 • Cholesterol 0 • Sodium 45 mg • Exchanges 1 fruit, ½ skim milk

1 pt. strawberries, quartered

½ medium pineapple, cored, peeled, and cut
into ½-inch pieces (about 2 cups)

3 TB. fresh orange juice

2 tsp. fructose

1 TB. rum (optional)

1 TB. fresh lemon juice

1½ cups nonfat, plain yogurt

6 fresh mint sprigs, for garnish

In a bowl combine strawberries, pineapple, orange
juice, fructose, rum (if desired), and lemon juice.
Cover and let stand at room temperature, stirring
once or twice, for 30 minutes.

Spoon equal portions of fruit into four stemmed gob-
lets. Spoon any juices from the bowl over fruit, dividing
them equally. Top fruit with equal portions of yogurt.
Garnish with mint sprigs and serve immediately.

Palate Preview

The strawberries and
pineapple are topped with nonfat
yogurt for a creamy sweet side
dish. Serve for any meal or snack,
including breakfast.

Baked Fruit Compote

Prep time: 20 minutes • Cook time: 45–60 minutes • Serves: 8 • Serving size: ¾ cup

Nutritional Analysis per Serving: Glycemic Index 44 • Glycemic Load 15 • Calories 133 • Protein in grams 1 • Animal Protein 0 • Vegetable Protein 1 • Carbohydrates 34 grams • Dietary Fiber 4 grams • Net Carbohydrate 30 grams • Fat 0 • Saturated Fat 0 • Cholesterol 0 • Sodium 6 mg • Exchanges 2 fruit

Vegetable oil cooking spray

5 apples, cored and sliced

4 ripe but firm medium-size pears, peeled, cored, and sliced

2 TB. raisins

3 TB. pure maple syrup or honey

¾ tsp. ground cinnamon

½ tsp. freshly grated nutmeg

¼ tsp. ground cloves

2 TB. fresh lemon juice

1 cup apple juice

Palate Preview
Baked winter fruits—pears, apples, and raisins—make a comforting and delicious treat. Plus, the aromatic baking spices of cinnamon, nutmeg, and cloves make your house smell wonderful.

Preheat oven to 375°F. Spray a baking dish large enough to accommodate all of fruit with cooking spray.

Place apples and pears into prepared dish along with raisins. Drizzle with syrup or honey. Sprinkle with cinnamon, nutmeg, and cloves. Mix together lemon juice and apple juice. Toss with fruit. Cover with foil. Place in the oven and bake for 45 minutes to 1 hour, until fruit is very soft. Stir every 10 to 15 minutes. Remove from the oven. Serve hot or at room temperature.

Lemon-Spice Applesauce

Prep time: 30 minutes • Cook time: 40 minutes • Serves: 8 • Serving size: ½ cup

Nutritional Analysis per Serving: Glycemic Index 31 • Glycemic Load 12 • Calories 144 • Protein in grams 1 • Animal Protein 0 • Vegetable Protein 1 • Carbohydrates 38 grams • Dietary Fiber 3 grams • Net Carbohydrate 35 grams • Fat 0 • Saturated Fat 0 • Cholesterol 0 • Sodium 5 mg • Exchanges 2½ fruit

3 lb. cooking apples, such as Granny Smith or Golden Delicious, cored and sliced (8 cups)

1¼ cups water

¼ cup fructose

1 TB. finely shredded lemon zest, fresh or dried

¼ cup fresh lemon juice, or to taste

1 tsp. ground cinnamon

1 tsp. vanilla extract

In a 6-quart heavy kettle or Dutch oven combine apples, fructose, lemon zest, lemon juice, and cinnamon. Bring to a boil. Reduce heat and simmer, covered, for 40 minutes or until apples are very soft, stirring occasionally.

Remove from the heat. Stir in vanilla. Mash mixture lightly with the back of a large wooden spoon. Serve warm or cover and refrigerate before serving.

Palate Preview

Yes, you can eat applesauce. In this homemade version, leave on the apple skins and simmer the apples with lemon peel and lemon juice. A healthful treat any time of year.

Fresh Fruit Platter with Fruit Dip

Prep time: 45 minutes • Cook time: none • Serves: 20 • Serving size: ¾ cup with 1½ TB. dip

Nutritional Analysis per Serving: Glycemic Index 46 • Glycemic Load 11 • Calories 104 • Protein in grams 3 • Animal Protein 1 • Vegetable Protein 2 • Carbohydrates 24 grams • Dietary Fiber 2½ grams • Net Carbohydrate 22 grams • Fat 0 • Saturated Fat 0 • Cholesterol 0 • Sodium 22 mg • Exchanges 1½ fruit

Fruit:

1 honeydew melon

1 ripe cantaloupe

1 lb. watermelon chunks (about 4 cups)

1 ripe pineapple, cored, peeled, and cut into ½-inch pieces (about 2 cups)

1 pt. ripe strawberries, with hulls

10 apricots

4 medium-ripe but firm peaches

4 ripe but firm nectarines

1 lb. cherries, with stems

Fruit Dip:

2 cups nonfat plain yogurt

1 tsp. vanilla extract

1 TB. fructose

Palate Preview

A succulent medley of fresh fruits, including melons, strawberries, pineapple, apricots, peaches, nectarines, and cherries. This recipe makes 20 servings, so prepare this dish for a family outing or invite over guests to share it.

Using a melon baller, scoop out balls from flesh of honeydew, cantaloupe, and if using a whole one, watermelon.

Hull strawberries and halve them lengthwise. Halve and pit apricots. Halve, pit, and slice peaches and nectarines.

Mix together yogurt, vanilla, and fructose.

Arrange melon, pineapple, strawberries, apricots, peaches, nectarines, and cherries on a decorative platter and serve fruit dip in a small bowl placed in the center of the platter.

Baked Apples

Prep time: 20 minutes   •   Cook time: about 12 minutes   •   Serves: 4   •   Serving size:
1 apple with Spice Mix

Nutritional Analysis per Serving: Glycemic Index 49   •   Glycemic Load 17   •   Calories 166
•   Protein in grams 1   •   Animal Protein 0   •   Vegetable Protein 1   •   Carbohydrates
34 grams   •   Dietary Fiber 3 grams   •   Net Carbohydrate 31 grams   •   Fat 7½ grams   •
Saturated Fat 3 grams   •   Cholesterol 1 mg   •   Sodium 42 mg   •   Exchanges 2 fruit,
1½ fat

Apples:

4 medium (6-oz.) apples

4 tsp. brown sugar

2 TB. unsalted butter

Spice Mix:

1 tsp. ground mace

1 tsp. grated nutmeg

1 tsp. ground cardamom

1 tsp. crushed or ground coriander seeds

1 tsp. ground cinnamon

Wash and core apples. Arrange in a circle in a
microwave-safe baking dish or place in individual
microwave-safe custard dishes. Place 1 teaspoon brown
sugar and 1 teaspoon butter in each apple. Sprinkle
top with Spice Mix.

Microwave on high power for 6 to 8 minutes or until
just tender. Let stand 10 to 15 minutes. Serve. If you
are cooking just one apple, microwave for 3 minutes;
cook two apples for 4 minutes.

Palate Preview
Make quick baked
apples in the microwave. You can
make the full recipe of four apples,
or cook only one apple. Just be
sure to reduce the cooking time in
the microwave if you cook less
than four.

Fresh Fruit Parfait

Prep time: 20 minutes • Cook time: none • Serves: 6 • Serving size: 1 cup

Nutritional Analysis per Serving: Glycemic Index 46 • Glycemic Load 11 • Calories 145 • Protein in grams 6 • Animal Protein 5 • Vegetable Protein 2 • Carbohydrates 24 grams • Dietary Fiber 3 grams • Net Carbohydrate 21 grams • Fat 3 grams • Saturated Fat 2 grams • Cholesterol 13 mg • Sodium 53 mg • Exchanges 1½ fruit, 1 medium-lean meat

1 cup part-skim milk ricotta cheese	1 cup sliced oranges
½ tsp. almond extract	1 cup seedless red grapes
½ tsp. stevia with FOS	1 medium apple
1 TB. skim milk	2 ripe bananas

Place ricotta cheese, almond extract, stevia, and milk in a blender. Blend. Cover and refrigerate.

Peel, cut and dice the apples and slice the bananas. Place them with the oranges and grapes, apples, into a bowl and toss gently.

Palate Preview These fruit parfait glasses look inviting and delicious. The rich cheese mixture adds a tangy, cheesy taste to this sweetened fruit dish.

Prepare six parfait glasses, and place 2 tsp. cheese mixture in the bottom of each. Add a layer of fruit mixture to each glass. Top with 1 TB. cheese mixture; then add another layer of fruit mixture, and another 1 TB. cheese mixture. Continue with remaining fruit and cheese mixtures.

Delightfully Different For variety, use other fruits in place of those indicated. Try blueberries, peaches, mango, and melon.

Part 4

Lean Meat Entrées

Lean meat should be a regular part of your diet. Meat offers high-quality, complete protein. Cooked with a wide variety of seasonings and spices, these beef, pork, poultry, veal, and lamb dishes give you a fabulous repertoire to choose from.

You'll find recipes to suit your varied culinary preferences and recipes to suit the occasion—for everything from simple family meals to gala parties.

Chapter 12

Lean Beef Dishes

In This Chapter

◆ Eating lean beef for your health

◆ Cooking techniques that work best

◆ Familiar sauces and flavors

◆ Hearty meals for your heart and health

Beef endures. At one point beef had a bad reputation as the harbinger of chronic ills. Today beef's reputation as a good-for-you food has returned. It's about time.

Too much of any food, whether it's good for you or not, can turn into a health and weight menace. Eating a 16-ounce serving of prime rib is never a good idea. Eating a 3- to 4-ounce serving, though, is fine and can be wonderfully satisfying—both to your appetite and your spirit. A great beef dish can be good for your body and, shall we say, sumptuous.

An excellent-tasting beef meal doesn't need to be expensive, though. The recipes in this chapter are made with a wide variety of beef cuts, from brisket and round steak to rib eyes. Select the recipe that works for your budget and your taste buds, because they'll all work well for your health.

Many of the recipes call for marinating the meats, which makes them more tender. Also, the acids, such as lemon juice and vinegar used in the marinades break down the tissue and proteins in the meat. Plus, acid foods are terrific for diabetes as they slow digestion in the stomach and help prevent a rise in blood glucose levels.

Beef Is Good for You

Beef's reputation has come full circle. Once a treasured food, beef fell into disfavor when some health practitioners tried to scare us away from any saturated fats as perilous to one's health. However, many of us kept right on eating beef anyway.

So let's set the record straight. Beef contains saturated fat and eating too much saturated fat isn't healthy. Ideally, a person with diabetes should eat 10 percent or less of daily calorie intake as saturated fat. This rule of thumb doesn't preclude you from eating beef, just limiting its consumption. So you can have beef. Not three times a day, but certainly several times a week.

Check out the nutritional analysis summaries for these recipes and you'll notice that most have only 3 to 5 grams of saturated fat per serving.

Surprise! Beef contains an abundance of vitamins and minerals needed for health. Red meat contains the highest concentration of B vitamins in any foods. One B vitamin that's quite hard to get in your diet is B_{12}. Beef has plenty of it. Beef also includes high concentrations of the trace minerals we need for optimal health. You can almost think of beef as a vitamin tablet. Only it's better! It's the real thing in a chewable, tasty form.

Just in case you're wondering, beef has plenty of complete protein, too.

You'll find little salt, if any, added to these recipes because they naturally contain sodium in amounts you need, and not in amounts greater than you need.

The Least You Need to Know

♦ These recipes feature preparation techniques that reduce the amount of saturated fat in beef.

♦ You can enjoy the taste pleasure of your favorite beef dishes with the recipes in this chapter.

♦ Marinate less tender cuts of beef to enhance flavor and tenderness.

♦ Beef contains plenty of good nutrition and essential nutrients.

Easy Grilled Beef Kabobs

Prep time: 15 minutes • Cook time: 10 minutes • Serves: 4 • Serving size: 3 ounces cooked sirloin steak with vegetables on skewer

Nutritional Analysis per Serving: Glycemic Index (not significant) • Glycemic Load (not significant) • Calories 192 • Protein in grams 22 • Animal Protein 21 • Vegetable Protein 1 • Carbohydrates 5 grams • Dietary Fiber 1 gram • Net Carbohydrate 4 grams • Fat 9 grams • Saturated Fat 3 grams • Cholesterol 76 mg • Sodium 252 mg • Exchanges 3 medium-lean meat, 1 vegetable

Vegetable oil cooking spray

1 lb. boneless beef sirloin, cut into 1-inch cubes

2 small zucchinis, each cut into 6 pieces

1 red bell pepper, cored, seeded, and cut into 12 pieces

½ cup bottled low-fat and low-sugar barbecue sauce

Spray a grill rack with cooking spray. Preheat a gas grill to medium or prepare a medium-hot fire in a charcoal grill, with the rack placed 4 to 6 inches above the heat. Alternately thread equal portions of beef, zucchini, and bell pepper onto four metal 12- to 14-inch skewers. Brush beef and vegetables with most of sauce.

When ready to cook, grill kabobs for 8 to 12 minutes or until desired doneness, turning once and brushing with remaining sauce.

Palate Preview You'll find these beef kabobs easy and quick to cook. The barbeque sauce gives a piquant flavor to the vegetables.

Note: To broil kabobs, preheat the broiler. Spray a broiler pan with cooking spray and place kabobs on it. Broil 4 to 6 inches from the heat. Cook 8 to 12 minutes or until desired doneness, turning once and brushing with remaining sauce.

Rustic Beef Brisket

Prep time: 20 minutes • Cook time: 2½ to 3 hours • Serves: 6 • Serving size: 5 ounces cooked beef brisket with ¼ cup vegetable sauce

Nutritional Analysis per Serving: Glycemic Index 42 • Glycemic Load 3 • Calories 312 • Protein in grams 36 • Animal Protein 35 • Vegetable Protein 1 • Carbohydrates 8 grams • Dietary Fiber <1 gram • Net Carbohydrate 8 grams • Fat 12 grams • Saturated Fat 4 grams • Cholesterol 93 mg • Sodium 172 mg • Exchanges 5 medium-lean meat, 1 fat

1 TB. olive or vegetable oil	1 small carrot, sliced
1 (2-lb.) boneless beef brisket, trimmed of all fat	3 large garlic cloves, minced
¼ tsp. salt	1 (14.5-oz.) can no-salt-added diced tomatoes, liquid reserved
¼ tsp. coarsely ground black pepper	2 tsp. unpacked brown sugar
2 large onions, sliced	

Palate Preview

Slow cooking the brisket makes it so tender that you can cut it with a fork. The onions, carrots, garlic, and tomatoes give this a down-home flavor.

Preheat the oven to 325°F. Heat oil in an ovenproof Dutch oven or large skillet over medium-high heat. Season brisket with salt and pepper and place it into the skillet and sear on all sides for 30 seconds to 1 minute per side or until browned.

In large bowl, combine onions, carrots, garlic, tomatoes and brown sugar. Mix well. Spoon over brisket.

Cover and bake for 2½ to 3 hours or until brisket is fork-tender.

Remove brisket from the pan and place on a serving platter, leaving vegetable mixture and juices in the pan for sauce. Let stand 10 minutes before cutting into thin slices. Return pan to the stovetop and bring mixture to a boil, stirring constantly. If sauce is too thick, add ¼ cup water. To serve, spoon sauce over sliced brisket.

Italian Beef Stew

Prep time: 30 minutes • Cook time: 1½ hours • Serves: 6 • Serving size: 3 ounces cooked beef, 1 cup with liquid

Nutritional Analysis per Serving: Glycemic Index 36 • Glycemic Load 1 • Calories 250 • Protein in grams 25 • Animal Protein 24 • Vegetable Protein 1 • Carbohydrates 5 grams • Dietary Fiber <1 gram • Net Carbohydrate 5 grams • Fat 7 grams • Saturated Fat 3 grams • Cholesterol 76 mg • Sodium 83 mg • Exchanges 3 medium-lean meat, 1 fat, 1 alcohol

2 TB. olive oil	3 to 4 bay leaves
1 lb. beef chuck, trimmed of all fat, cut into 2-inch pieces	¼ cup red wine vinegar
2 large onions, thinly sliced	2 cups dry red wine
¼ tsp. salt	2 (14.5-oz.) cans no-salt-added, chopped tomatoes
¼ tsp. freshly ground black pepper	1½ cups low-salt beef broth
½ tsp. paprika	

Heat oil in a large skillet over medium heat. Add beef and cook, stirring, for 4 to 5 minutes or until lightly browned on all sides. Add onions. Cook, stirring, for 4 to 5 minutes or onions are lightly golden.

Season with salt and pepper. Add paprika, bay leaves, vinegar, and stir once or twice. Add wine and cook, stirring, for 6 to 7 minutes, until liquid is reduced in volume by half.

Palate Preview

A very tender beef stew that's great to serve to families and friends. Be sure to cook up plenty so you have yummy leftovers for breakfast or lunch—or both.

Add tomatoes and 1 cup of beef broth and mix well with the other ingredients. Partially cover the skillet and reduce the heat to low. Simmer 1 to 1½ hours, stirring a few times. If sauce dries out too much during cooking, add some more beef broth. (At the end of the cooking time meat should be so tender that it can be cut with a fork). Remove bay leaves before serving.

Rib-Eye Steaks with Tomato Salsa

Prep time: 20 minutes • Cook time: 8 to 12 minutes • Serves: 4 • Serving size: 4 ounces cooked rib-eye steak with 4 tablespoons salsa

Nutritional Analysis per Serving: Glycemic Index 36 • Glycemic Load 1 • Calories 218 • Protein in grams 34 • Animal Protein 32 • Vegetable Protein 2 • Carbohydrates 3 grams • Dietary Fiber <1 gram • Net Carbohydrate 3 grams • Fat 7 grams • Saturated Fat 3 grams • Cholesterol 98 mg • Sodium 253 mg • Exchanges 4 medium-lean meat

Salsa:

2 tomatillos, husks removed, diced

½ cup chunky salsa

2 TB. cored, seeded and finely chopped yellow bell pepper

1 TB. chopped fresh chives

⅛ to ¼ tsp. Liquid Smoke Barbecue Marinade

Steaks:

Vegetable oil cooking spray

4 (5-oz.) boneless beef rib-eye steaks, trimmed of all fat

1 tsp. no-salt Southwestern seasoning blend or no-salt seasoning blend of your choice

Palate Preview

The tomatillos add a festive Southwestern flavor to this salsa. You may want to keep the salsa handy as a condiment for other dishes. Fabulous with rib-eye steaks.

Spray a grill rack with cooking spray. Preheat a gas grill to medium or prepare a medium-hot fire in a charcoal grill, with the rack placed 4 to 6 inches above the heat. In a small bowl, combine tomatillos, salsa, bell pepper, chives, and liquid smoke. Mix well.

When ready to grill, sprinkle steaks on both sides with seasoning blend. Place steaks on the grill and cook for 6 to 12 minutes or until desired doneness, turning once or twice. Serve salsa with steaks.

Note: To broil steaks, preheat the broiler. Spray a broiler pan with cooking spray. Place steaks on the pan. Broil 4 to 6 inches from the heat for 6 to 12 minutes or until desired doneness, turning once or twice.

Grilled, Seasoned Flank Steak

Prep time: 20 minutes plus at least 4 hours refrigeration   •   Cook time: 12 to 20 minutes   •
Serves: 6   •   Serving size: 5 ounces cooked flank steak with 1 tablespoon stuffing

Nutritional Analysis per Serving: Glycemic Index (not significant)   •   Glycemic Load (not
significant)   •   Calories 352   •   Protein in grams 38   •   Animal Protein 38   •   Vegetable Protein <1   •   Carbohydrates <1 gram   •   Dietary Fiber 0   •   Net Carbohydrate 0
•   Fat 13 grams   •   Saturated Fat 5 grams   •   Cholesterol 77 mg   •   Sodium 153 mg   •
Exchanges 5 medium-lean meat, 1½ fat

Marinade:

3 TB. dry red wine

3 TB. olive oil

1 TB. fresh lemon juice

1 tsp. low-salt beef-flavor instant bouillon

1 large garlic clove, minced

Steak:

1 (2-lb.) beef flank steak, trimmed of all fat

Vegetable oil cooking spray

Stuffing:

2 TB. unsalted butter

1 shallot, finely chopped

3 garlic cloves, thinly sliced

2 TB. chopped fresh parsley

1 TB. chopped fresh oregano

2 TB. bread crumbs

1 tsp. grated lemon zest

In a shallow glass or ceramic dish or self-closing plastic bag, combine wine, olive oil, lemon
juice, bouillon, and minced garlic. Mix well. With a very sharp knife, make a pocket in one side
of steak, cutting lengthwise almost but not completely through to the opposite side. Add steak
to marinade and turn to coat. Cover dish or seal bag and refrigerate for 4 hours or overnight.

When ready to cook, spray a grill rack with cooking
spray. Preheat a gas grill to medium or prepare a
medium-hot fire in a charcoal grill, with the rack
placed 4 to 6 inches above the heat. Prepare stuffing:
Melt butter in a medium skillet over medium heat. Add
shallot and cook, stirring occasionally, for 2 minutes or
until shallot is tender. Add sliced garlic, parsley,
oregano, bread crumbs, and lemon zest. Cook, stirring,
for 1 minute. Remove from heat.

Palate Preview
Flank steak gets extra
tender from marinating in this simple but flavorful sauce. The filling is
an added surprise. Add a tossed
green salad to balance your meal.

Remove steak from marinade and discard marinade. Fill the pocket in steak with stuffing. If
necessary, secure the opening with toothpicks. Place steak on grill and cook for 12 to 20 minutes or until desired doneness, turning once. Place steak on cutting board and let stand 5 minutes. Cut steak across grain into ½ inch thick slices.

Strip Steaks with Broiled Asparagus

Prep time: 15 minutes • Cook time: 10 minutes • Serves: 2 • Serving size: 3 ounces cooked beef top loin steak with 2 tablespoons sauce and four spears of asparagus

Nutritional Analysis per Serving: Glycemic Index (not significant) • Glycemic Load (not significant) • Calories 226 • Protein in grams 26 • Animal Protein 24 • Vegetable Protein 2 • Carbohydrates 3 grams • Dietary Fiber 1 gram • Net Carbohydrate 2 grams • Fat 11 grams • Saturated Fat 3 grams • Cholesterol 67 mg • Sodium 58 mg • Exchanges 3 medium-lean meat, 1 fat, ½ vegetable

Vegetable oil cooking spray	2 tsp. garlic-flavored olive oil or regular olive oil
1 (8-oz.) boneless beef top loin (strip) steak, cut about ¾-inch thick, trimmed of all fat	Sauce:
1 or 2 cloves of garlic, coarsely chopped	½ cup low-salt beef broth
½ tsp. cracked or coarsely ground black pepper	1 TB. dry white wine
8–10 (6 oz.) thin asparagus spears, trimmed	¼ tsp Dijon mustard

Rub steak on both sides with a mixture of garlic and pepper. Place asparagus in shallow dish and drizzle with oil.

For sauce, in a medium skillet stir together broth and wine. Cook over high heat for 4 to 5 minutes or until mixture is reduced in volume to ¼ cup. Whisk in mustard. Remove from heat and keep warm.

Palate Preview

A very elegant dish, yet it belongs on your easy-to-make list. In only 25 minutes you can have steak with broiled asparagus—a true feast.

Preheat the broiler. Spray an unheated broiler pan with cooking spray and place steak on it. Broil 3 to 4 inches from the heat for 8 to 10 minutes for medium rare or 10 to 12 minutes for medium, turning once and placing asparagus into the pan next to the steak for the last two minutes of broiling.

Spoon sauce onto a plate. Cut steak in half crosswise and place atop sauce. Top with asparagus spears.

Stuffed Beef Tenderloin

Prep time: 15 minutes • Cook time: 1 hour • Serves: 4 • Serving size: 4 ounces cooked beef tenderloin steak with 2 tablespoons stuffing

Nutritional Analysis per Serving: Glycemic Index (not significant) • Glycemic Load (not significant) • Calories 342 • Protein in grams 30 • Animal Protein 30 • Vegetable Protein <1 • Carbohydrates <1 gram • Dietary Fiber <1 gram • Net Carbohydrate 0 • Fat 21 grams • Saturated Fat 10 grams • Cholesterol 124 mg • Sodium 58 mg • Exchanges 1½ high-fat meat, 3 medium lean meat

1 (16-oz.) beef tenderloin or beef loin roast	2 garlic cloves, minced
5 ounces or ½ cup plus 1 TB. goat cheese	1 tsp. freshly ground black pepper (optional)
¾ cup packed fresh spinach leaves, washed and trimmed	2 TB. whole black peppercorns, coarsely crushed

Preheat the oven to 425°F.

Using a very sharp knife, cut a slit lengthwise in tenderloin to form a pocket. Combine goat cheese, spinach, garlic, and if desired, ground black pepper, in a bowl and mix well. Spoon goat cheese mixture into the pocket. Using a larding needle, secure at 1- to 2-inch intervals with kitchen twine. Pat crushed peppercorns over the surface of tenderloin and press lightly.

 **In the Danger Zone**
You'll need kitchen twine to tie the stuffing inside the tenderloin or else it might come out of the tenderloin while cooking.

Place tenderloin in a shallow roasting pan. Roast for 15 minutes. Reduce the oven temperature to 325°F. Roast for 45 minutes longer or until a meat thermometer registers 135°F. Let rest for 5 to 10 minutes. Discard the kitchen twine. Cut tenderloin into slices of desired thickness.

Palate Preview
What a wonderful way to enjoy lean beef. The tenderloin is tender and the stuffing makes for a memorable meal. Goat cheese is an excellent accent, because it is lower in sodium than other cheeses.

Pepper Steak with Mustard Sauce

Prep time: 10 minutes • Cook time: 10 minutes • Serves: 4 • Serving size: 3 ounces cooked tenderloin steak with 2 tablespoons sauce

Nutritional Analysis per Serving: Glycemic Index (not significant) • Glycemic Load (not significant) • Calories 207 • Protein in grams 23 • Animal Protein 23 • Vegetable Protein 0 • Carbohydrates 0 • Dietary Fiber 0 • Net Carbohydrate 0 • Fat 9 grams • Saturated Fat 3 grams • Cholesterol 73 mg • Sodium 92 mg • Exchanges 3 medium-lean meat

4 (4-oz.) beef tenderloin steaks (1-inch thick)

2 tsp. coarsely ground black pepper

Vegetable oil cooking spray

2 garlic cloves, minced

⅓ cup dry red wine

⅓ cup low-salt beef broth

1 TB. country style Dijon mustard

Palate Preview ___ A mustard, garlic, and red wine sauce brings out the hearty taste of steak in this recipe. Serve with steamed vegetables and a vegetable salad to complete your meal.

Coat both sides of steaks with pepper. Spray a medium nonstick skillet with cooking spray and heat over medium-high heat. Place steaks into the pan in a single layer and sear for about 1 minute or until the steak is browned. Turn and cook 5 to 12 minutes or until desired doneness, turning once. Drain liquid fat from pan, if any.

Add garlic, cook, stirring, for 1 minute or until golden brown. Add wine and broth and boil 1 minute. Remove steaks from the skillet and cover to keep warm. With a wire whisk, stir in mustard until sauce is well blended. Serve sauce over steaks.

Delightfully Different _____ In any recipe that calls for wine, you can make the following substitutions for the wine: an equal amount of water with 1 TB. lemon or lime juice, an equal amount of water with 1 TB. vinegar, low-salt beef, or chicken bouillon.

Green Chili Swiss Steak

Prep time: 25 minutes   •   Cook time: 2 hours   •   Serves: 6   •   Serving size: 4 ounces cooked round steak with 2 tablespoons sauce

Nutritional Analysis per Serving: Glycemic Index 31   •   Glycemic Load 1   •   Calories 240   •   Protein in grams 29   •   Animal Protein 28   •   Vegetable Protein 1   •   Carbohydrates 5 grams   •   Dietary Fiber 1 gram   •   Net Carbohydrate 4 grams   •   Fat 12 grams   •   Saturated Fat 3 grams   •   Cholesterol 65 mg   •   Sodium 103 mg   •   Exchanges 4 medium-lean meat, 1 vegetable

Vegetable oil cooking spray

1½ lb. boneless beef round steak trimmed of all fat, and cut into bite-size pieces

1 (14.5-oz.) can no-salt-added chopped tomatoes with juice

1 (4.5-oz.) can chopped green chilies

¼ cup taco sauce

1 tsp no-salt chili powder

½ tsp ground cumin

¼ cup sliced green onions

Spray a 12-inch nonstick skillet with cooking spray and set over medium heat. Add beef and cook, stirring occasionally until browned on both sides.

Add tomatoes, chilies, taco sauce, chili powder, and cumin, and stir to mix. Reduce the heat to low, cover and simmer for 1½ to 2 hours or until beef is tender, stirring and turning beef occasionally.

Stir in green onions. Cover and cook an additional 8 to 10 minutes.

Palate Preview _____
Whenever you read green chilies, or any chilies for that matter, rejoice. Chilies help reduce blood glucose levels. Not only that, they taste so good that they make any food zesty and spicy.

Rib-Eye Steaks with Caramelized Onions

Prep time: 25 minutes • Cook time: 11 minutes • Serves: 4 • Serving size: 4 ounces cooked steak and 2 tablespoons sauce

Nutritional Analysis per Serving: Glycemic Index (not significant) • Glycemic Load • Calories 284 • Protein in grams 28 • Animal Protein 28 • Vegetable Protein <1 • Carbohydrates 4 grams • Dietary Fiber <1 gram • Fat 10 grams • Saturated Fat 2 grams • Cholesterol 107 mg • Sodium 66 mg • Exchanges 4 lean meat, 1 fat, 1 vegetable

¾ tsp. cracked black pepper

½ tsp. coarsely ground mustard seeds

4 (5–6-oz.) boneless beef rib-eye steaks, cut 1-inch thick

1 TB. olive oil

1 medium sweet onion (Walla Walla or Vidalia), halved and thinly sliced

1 garlic clove, minced

¼ cup cored, seeded and chopped red bell pepper

1 jalapeño chili pepper, seeded and finely chopped

2 TB. balsamic vinegar

1 tsp. brown sugar

½ tsp. dried sage, crushed

In a small bowl combine black pepper and mustard seeds and divide in half. Rub half of spice mixture onto one side of steaks. Set aside. Spray a grill rack with cooking spray. Preheat a gas grill to medium or prepare a medium-hot fire in a charcoal grill, with the rack placed 4 to 6 inches above the heat.

Palate Preview

Caramelizing onions brings out their sweetness. Add to this the spicy-hot taste of jalapeño chili pepper and you'll love these steaks.

In a large skillet heat olive oil over medium heat, and add onion and garlic. Cook, stirring, for about 5 minutes or until onion is tender. Add bell pepper and jalapeño chili pepper, and cook, stirring, for 1 minute. Add balsamic vinegar, brown sugar, sage, and remaining spice mixture. Cook, stirring and stir for 1 minute more. Remove from the heat, cover, and keep warm.

When you are ready to cook, place steaks on the grill directly over the coals and grill until desired doneness, turning once halfway through grilling. Allow 11 to 15 minutes for medium rare and 14 to 18 minutes for medium. If you are using a charcoal grill, grill the steaks uncovered. If you are using a gas grill, cover them. Serve with onion mixture.

Beef Tenderloin with Marsala Sauce

Prep time: 10 minutes • Cook time: 10 minutes • Serves: 4 • Serving size: 4 ounces cooked beef tenderloin steak with 2 tablespoons sauce

Nutritional Analysis per Serving: Glycemic Index (not significant) • Glycemic Load (not significant) • Calories 272 • Protein in grams 28 • Animal Protein 28 • Vegetable Protein 0 • Carbohydrates <1 gram • Dietary Fiber 0 • Net Carbohydrate 0 • Fat 13 grams • Saturated Fat 4 grams • Cholesterol 76 mg • Sodium 18 mg • Exchanges 4 medium-lean meat, 1 alcohol

1 tsp. vegetable oil	1 cup finely chopped onions
2 TB. fresh lemon juice	1 cup dry Marsala wine
4 (4-oz.) beef tenderloin steaks	2 TB. chopped fresh Italian parsley

Heat oil in a large skillet over medium-high heat. Add steaks to pan and drizzle with lemon juice. Cook 8 to 10 minutes or until desired doneness, turning once. Remove steaks from skillet and cover to keep warm.

Add onions and wine to juice mixture in skillet. Cook, stirring, for 4 minutes or until liquid is reduced in volume to about ½ cup.

To serve, spoon onion mixture over steaks and sprinkle with parsley.

Palate Preview

By reducing the volume of Marsala from 1 cup to ½ cup, you evaporate the alcohol, yet the lovely flavor of this wine remains.

Barbecue Beef

Prep time: • Cook time: 3 to 3½ hours • Serves: 5 per pound of beef • Serving size: 3 ounces cooked beef

Nutritional Analysis per Serving: Glycemic Index (not significant) • Glycemic Load (not significant) • Calories 180 • Protein in grams 22 • Animal Protein • Vegetable Protein 1 • Carbohydrates 4 grams • Dietary Fiber 1 gram • Net Carbohydrate 3 grams • Fat 9 grams • Saturated Fat 3 grams • Cholesterol 74 mg • Sodium 56 mg • Exchanges 3 medium lean meat

Barbecue Sauce:

1 cup finely chopped onion

2 cloves garlic, finely chopped

1½ cup finely chopped tomatoes

½ cup water

1 TB. Worcestershire sauce

¼ cup cider vinegar

2 tsp. salt

2 tsp. no-salt chili powder

2 tsp. brown sugar

2 tsp. dry mustard

Beef:

3 to 5 lb. brisket of beef

Combine onion, garlic, tomatoes, water, Worcestershire sauce, vinegar, salt, chili powder, brown sugar, and mustard in a Dutch oven or kettle big enough to hold beef. Add brisket of beef; turn to coat all sides. Cover, set over low heat and simmer for 3 to 3½ hours, or until fork-tender for slicing. (Cook longer to use for chopped beef sandwiches.) Turn several times during cooking. If necessary, add water while cooking to keep sauce from drying out. When done, remove meat to a cutting board and let cool 15 minutes before slicing or chopping.

Palate Preview

Barbecued meat is an all-time favorite. With this recipe, barbecue easily fits into your meal plans.

Chapter 13

Lean Ground-Meat Dishes

In This Chapter

- ◆ Ground meat favorites for you and your family
- ◆ Meats include beef, lamb, pork, and turkey
- ◆ Lean cooking techniques
- ◆ Versatility and your favorite flavors

Most likely, you've eaten some form of ground meat in the past week. You may have eaten hamburgers, Salisbury steak, or spaghetti with meat sauce. Perhaps you satisfied your taste buds with meatballs or a beef burrito. Ground meat shows up in every international and American regional cuisine. It's the all-around, all-purpose, blue-ribbon meat.

Ground meat is the "go-to" meat for all seasons and eating occasions. It's relatively inexpensive. It freezes well and defrosts quickly in the microwave. It cooks quickly and can save you cooking time over other cuts of meat. And it can be molded into meatballs and meat loaf.

You can serve ground meat differently every night of the week and never get bored. Ground meat blends with virtually every seasoning, cooking method, and vegetable imaginable. The recipes in this chapter offer you a wide range of your favorite ground-meat dishes.

Ground Meat Varieties

When you think of ground meat, are you just naturally thinking of ground beef? Many people do. You could use ground beef to prepare every recipe in this chapter. But not all the recipes call for beef. Some call for pork, lamb, or turkey. For the recipes in this chapter, the various ground meats are all interchangeable.

You can also blend ground meats within a recipe. For example, combine both turkey and beef for meat loaf, or vary your tastes even more by adding in some lamb or pork. Mixing ground meats gives your dishes varying flavors and textures.

All of the varieties of ground meat contain about the same amount of complete protein, approximately 20 grams per 3 ounce serving of cooked meat. But not all packages of ground meat contain the same amount of fat.

Healthy Notes

To defrost one pound of frozen ground meat quickly, place the meat in a microwave-safe dish or bowl, and set it into the microwave. Cook on defrost for 3 minutes. Remove and scrape off the softened meat. Return to the microwave for 3 more minutes. Scrape off the softened meat and break up the remaining block. Microwave on defrost for 5 to 6 more minutes. The meat is ready to be cooked.

Watch the Fat

You know that lean meats are much better for your health than fattier meats. So watch out! The amount of fat in any variety of ground meat—turkey, beef, pork, lamb—can vary greatly.

Don't assume that turkey always has the lowest percentage of fat. Sometimes it does and sometimes it doesn't. Don't be fooled and end up at home with a package of high-fat meat. Be sure to read the labels and comparison-shop.

It's a good idea to always keep a pound or two of ground meat in your freezer. That way, you'll have it on hand when you need a quick meal or when you don't want to go out to the grocery store before you prepare dinner.

The Least You Need to Know

◆ Ground meat is versatile and economical.

◆ Always choose the cut with lowest percentage of fat when purchasing ground meats. The percentage is listed on the label.

◆ Mix and match ground meats—beef, pork, turkey, and lamb.

◆ Keep ground meat on hand in your freezer for quick meals and unexpected guests.

Mom's Meat Loaf

Prep time: 25 minutes   •   Cook time: 60 to 70 minutes   •   Serves: 8   •   Serving size: 4-ounce slice

Nutritional Analysis per Serving: Glycemic Index 56   •   Glycemic Load 5   •   Calories 187   •   Protein in grams 20   •   Animal Protein 19   •   Vegetable Protein 1   •   Carbohydrates 9 grams   •   Dietary Fiber <1 gram   •   Net Carbohydrate 9 grams   •   Fat 5 grams   •   Saturated Fat 2 grams   •   Cholesterol 59 mg   •   Sodium 187 mg   •   Exchanges 3 medium-lean meat, ½ starch

Vegetable oil cooking spray	2 tsp. Worcestershire sauce
¾ lb. extra-lean ground beef	1 (8-oz.) can no-salt-added tomato sauce
¾ lb. lean ground turkey	2 eggs, beaten
1 cup shredded carrots	¼ cup homemade barbecue sauce (see the Barbecue Beef recipe in Chapter 12)
½ cup plain bread crumbs	
¼ cup finely chopped onion	

Preheat the oven to 350°F. Spray a 9×5-inch loaf pan with cooking spray. In a large bowl combine beef, turkey, carrots, bread crumbs, onion, Worcestershire sauce, tomato sauce, and eggs, and mix well. Press mixture into the pan. Brush the top with barbecue sauce.

Bake for 60 to 70 minutes or until a thermometer inserted into the center registers 170°F. Let stand 10 minutes before serving.

Palate Preview

Meat loaf is one of the best uses for ground beef. It slices up nicely and can easily be served hot or cold. It's loaded with flavor, and it's quite economical. Mom's Meat Loaf is filled with succulent ground beef and turkey, plus carrots, and is topped with barbecue sauce. Imagine having this even for breakfast!

Greek Meatball Kabobs

Prep time: 35 minutes • Cook time: 12 to 15 minutes • Serves: 4 • Serving size: Four 1-ounce meatballs and vegetables

Nutritional Analysis per Serving: Glycemic Index 42 • Glycemic Load 3 • Calories 274 • Protein in grams 26 • Animal Protein 25 • Vegetable Protein 1 • Carbohydrates 8 grams • Dietary Fiber 0 • Net Carbohydrate 8 grams • Fat 14 grams • Saturated Fat 4 grams • Cholesterol 76 mg • Sodium 135 mg • Exchanges 3 medium-lean meat, 1 vegetable, 2 fat

Meatballs:

Vegetable oil cooking spray

1 lb. extra-lean ground beef

¼ cup plain bread crumbs

2 TB. (1-oz.) crumbled feta cheese

2 TB. sliced green onions

½ tsp. garlic powder

Vegetables:

1 medium red bell pepper, cored, seeded, and cut into chunks

1 medium green bell pepper, cored, seeded, and cut into chunks

1 medium zucchini, halved, cut into ½ inch slices

Greek Seasoning:

2 TB. olive oil

½ tsp. dried oregano

½ tsp. grated lemon zest

Preheat the broiler. Spray a broiler pan with cooking spray. In large bowl, combine beef, bread crumbs, cheese, green onions, and garlic powder, and mix well. Shape mixture into 16 meatballs.

Palate Preview

A wonderful blending of feta cheese, oregano, and lemon peel gives these kabobs a mild Greek flavor. Plus, you get a serving of vegetables—red and green bell peppers and zucchini—on the kabobs.

Thread meatballs, red and green bell peppers, and zucchini alternately on four 14-inch or eight 7-inch metal skewers. Place kabobs on the broiler rack.

In a small bowl, combine oil, oregano, and lemon zest. Mix well. Brush mixture over kabobs.

Broil kabobs 4 to 6 inches from the heat for 12 to 15 minutes or until meatballs are thoroughly cooked and vegetables are crisp-tender, turning kabobs 2 or 3 times and brushing occasionally with remaining oil mixture.

Classic Salisbury Steak

Prep time: 5 minutes   •   Cook time: 10 minutes   •   Serves: 2   •   Serving size: 4-ounce beef patty with 3 tablespoons sauce

Nutritional Analysis per Serving: Glycemic Index 61   •   Glycemic Load 4   •   Calories 210   •   Protein in grams 25   •   Animal Protein 24   •   Vegetable Protein 1   •   Carbohydrates 7 grams   •   Dietary Fiber 0   •   Net Carbohydrate 7 grams   •   Fat 6 grams   •   Saturated Fat 2 grams   •   Cholesterol 70 mg   •   Sodium 332 mg   •   Exchanges 3 medium-lean meat, ½ starch

Patties:

½ lb. extra-lean ground beef

⅛ tsp. dried marjoram

2 TB. seasoned bread crumbs

Sauce:

¼ cup bottled home-style mushroom gravy

2 TB. red wine

1 TB. ketchup

⅛ tsp dried thyme

In a medium bowl, combine beef, marjoram, and bread crumbs. Mix well. Shape mixture into two oval patties, about ½-inch thick.

Heat a medium nonstick skillet over medium-high heat. Place beef patties into it and cook 5 to 7 minutes or until thoroughly cooked, turning twice. Remove patties from the skillet and place on a serving platter. Cover to keep warm.

Wipe the skillet clean with a paper towel. Return to the heat, add gravy, wine, ketchup, and thyme and mix to combine. Cook, stirring, over medium-high heat until bubbly. Serve sauce over beef patties.

Palate Preview

Salisbury steak is a time-honored favorite. The sauce includes red wine, which imparts a slightly more sophisticated taste. Don't be concerned about this small amount of alcohol because it evaporates during heating.

Beef Chow Mein

Prep time: 10 minutes • Cook time: 20 minutes • Serves: 4 • Serving size: ½ cup cooked basmati brown rice and 1 cup chow mein

Nutritional Analysis per Serving: Glycemic Index 45 • Glycemic Load 13 • Calories 312 • Protein in grams 28 • Animal Protein 24 • Vegetable Protein 4 • Carbohydrates 32 grams • Dietary Fiber 4 grams • Net Carbohydrate 28 grams • Fat 6 grams • Saturated Fat 2 grams • Cholesterol 70 mg • Sodium 124 mg • Exchanges 4 medium-lean meat, 2 starch

1 lb. extra-lean ground beef	1 (2-oz.) jar diced pimientos, drained
1 (8-oz.) pkg. fresh sliced mushrooms	1 tsp. low-sodium soy sauce
1½ cups sliced celery	½ tsp. ground ginger
1 (16-oz.) can bean sprouts, drained and rinsed	2 TB. cornstarch
1 (8-oz.) can sliced water chestnuts, drained and rinsed	3 TB. water
1 (14-oz.) can low-salt beef broth	2 cups hot cooked long-grain basmati brown rice

Palate Preview
A perfect blend of ground beef and oriental-type vegetables gives you Chinese cuisine the whole family can savor.

Place ground beef and mushrooms in a large skillet and set over medium–high heat. Cook, stirring frequently, for 5 minutes or until thoroughly cooked. Carefully drain fat from beef mixture in the pan and return it to the heat.

Add celery, bean sprouts, water chestnuts, broth, pimientos, soy sauce, and ginger. Mix well. Reduce heat to medium, cover and simmer, stirring occasionally, for 15 minutes.

Meanwhile, in a small bowl, blend cornstarch and water until smooth.

Stir cornstarch mixture into beef mixture. Cook until mixture is bubbly and slightly thickened. Serve over basmati brown rice.

Hamburger Florentine Soup

Prep time: 15 minutes • Cook time: 1 hour • Serves: 11 • Serving size: 1⅓ cups soup

Nutritional Analysis per Serving: Glycemic Index 25 • Glycemic Load 2 • Calories 115 • Protein in grams 11 • Animal Protein 9 • Vegetable Protein 2 • Carbohydrates 13 grams • Dietary Fiber 3 grams • Net Carbohydrate 10 grams • Fat 2 grams • Saturated Fat 1 gram • Cholesterol 26 mg • Sodium 259 mg • Exchanges 1 medium-lean meat, 1 vegetable, ½ starch

1 lb. extra-lean ground beef	½ tsp. dried basil
6 cups water	½ tsp. dried thyme
2 cups cubed sweet potatoes	¼ tsp. freshly ground black pepper
1 cup shredded cabbage	1 bay leaf
1 cup chopped onions	1 (28-oz.) can no-salt-added, chopped tomatoes
1 cup sliced celery	2 cups frozen green beans, thawed
⅓ cup uncooked barley	1 (9-oz.) pkg. frozen chopped spinach, thawed
1 tsp. salt	

Place ground beef in a 5-quart saucepan or Dutch oven set over medium-high heat and cook, stirring, until evenly browned. Carefully drain fat from beef in the pan and return it to the heat.

Stir in water, sweet potatoes, cabbage, onions, celery, barley, salt, basil, thyme, pepper, bay leaf, tomatoes and juice, and green beans. Bring to a boil. Reduce the heat to medium, cover and simmer 25 minutes. Add spinach. Cover and simmer an additional 15 minutes. Stir to blend spinach into soup. Remove bay leaf and serve hot.

Palate Preview

You are going to love this unusual soup. It's filled with healthy vegetables, barley, and sweet potatoes. Great for a cold day and hearty enough to be a whole meal in a bowl.

White Bean Turkey Chili

Prep time: 30 minutes • Cook time: 20 minutes • Serves: 10 • Serving size: 6 ounces or ¾ cup chili

Nutritional Analysis per Serving: Glycemic Index 31 • Glycemic Load 8 • Calories 274 • Protein in grams 20 • Animal Protein 9 • Vegetable Protein 11 • Carbohydrates 28 grams • Dietary Fiber 8 grams • Net Carbohydrate 20 grams • Fat 4 grams • Saturated Fat 1 gram • Cholesterol 56 mg • Sodium 73 mg • Exchanges 2 lean meat, 2 starch

Meatballs:

1 lb. lean ground turkey

¼ dry plain bread crumbs

¼ cup chopped onion

1 egg

Vegetable oil cooking spray

Chili:

1 medium zucchini, cut into 1-inch strips

2 garlic cloves, minced

1 (28-oz.) can no-salt-added, chopped tomatoes, liquid reserved

1 (55½-oz.) can Great Northern beans, drained and rinsed

1 (14½-oz.) can low-salt chicken broth

1 tsp. granulated sugar

1 tsp. ground cumin

3 tsp. no-salt chili powder

¼ tsp. freshly ground black pepper

Palate Preview _____ Chili is always a favorite. And with this lean turkey recipe, you can count on the great chili taste in a health-minded dish.

In a medium bowl, combine turkey, bread crumbs, onion, and egg, and mix well. Shape into 24 (1½-inch) balls.

Spray a large skillet with cooking spray and set over medium heat. Add meatballs and cook 8 to 10 minutes or until browned on all sides and no longer pink in the center.

In a Dutch oven or large saucepan, combine zucchini, garlic, tomatoes and juice, beans, broth, sugar, cumin, chili powder, and pepper, and mix well. Bring to a boil. Reduce the heat and add meatballs. Simmer 10 to 15 minutes or until thoroughly heated. Serve hot.

Ground Beef and Vegetable Stew

Prep time: 15 minutes   •   Cook time: 30 minutes   •   Serves: 5   •   Serving size: 1½ cups stew

Nutritional Analysis per Serving: Glycemic Index 28   •   Glycemic Load 5   •   Calories 210   •   Protein in grams 21   •   Animal Protein 19   •   Vegetable Protein 2   •   Carbohydrates 18 grams   •   Dietary Fiber 3 grams   •   Net Carbohydrate 15 grams   •   Fat 4 grams   •   Saturated Fat 2 grams   •   Cholesterol 56 mg   •   Sodium 96 mg   •   Exchanges 3 lean meat, 1 starch, 1 vegetable

1 lb. extra-lean ground beef	1 (14.5-oz.) can no-salt-added, chopped tomatoes, liquid reserved
¼ tsp. freshly ground black pepper	1 (8-oz.) pkg. sliced fresh mushrooms
3 carrots, cut into ½-inch pieces	½ tsp. dried thyme
1 medium potato, cut into ¾-inch chunks	1 TB. Worcestershire sauce
1 medium onion, cut into 8 wedges	¼ cup water
1 (14½-oz.) can low-salt beef broth	2 TB. all-purpose flour
1 medium zucchini, sliced	

Place ground beef into a Dutch oven or large saucepan, season with pepper and mix to combine. Set over medium-high heat, and cook, stirring occasionally, until beef is no longer pink. Carefully drain fat from beef in the pan and return it to the heat.

Add carrots, potato, onion, and broth. Bring to a boil. Reduce the heat to medium, cover, and simmer 15 to 20 minutes or until vegetables are almost tender.

Stir in zucchini, tomatoes and their juice, mushrooms, thyme, and Worcestershire sauce. Cook 5 to 10 minutes or until zucchini is tender.

Palate Preview

Cook up plenty of this simply delicious stew, because we know you'll want to have some left over. With plenty of vegetables and light seasoning, this stew is sure to please everyone.

In a small jar with a tight-fitting lid, combine water and flour, and shake well to blend. Gradually add flour mixture to stew, stirring constantly. Cook, stirring, until bubbly and thickened. Serve hot.

Gyro (Greek Pita Sandwiches)

Prep time: 10 minutes • Cook time: 6 to 8 minutes • Serves: 4 • Serving size: 3-ounce burger with ½ whole-wheat pita pocket, vegetables and ¼ cup yogurt sauce

Nutritional Analysis per Serving: Glycemic Index 45 • Glycemic Load 9 • Calories 348 • Protein in grams 30 • Animal Protein 27 • Vegetable Protein 3 • Carbohydrates 23 grams • Dietary Fiber 3 grams • Net Carbohydrate 20 grams • Fat 13 grams • Saturated Fat 4 grams • Cholesterol 95 mg • Sodium 242 mg • Exchanges 4 medium-lean meat, 1 starch, 1 vegetable

Dressing:

1 cup non-fat plain yogurt

1 TB. fresh lemon juice

¼ tsp. dried dill weed

1 garlic clove, minced, or ½ tsp. chopped garlic in oil

Sandwich:

½ lb. lean ground lamb

½ lb. ground beef

⅛ tsp. salt

¼ tsp. ground allspice

1 garlic clove, minced, or ½ tsp. chopped garlic in oil

2 whole-wheat pita pockets

1 cup shredded lettuce

1 medium onion, thinly sliced

1 medium tomato, thinly sliced

In a small bowl, combine yogurt, lemon juice, dill weed, and garlic. Blend well. Set aside.

In large bowl, combine lamb, beef, salt, allspice, and garlic. Mix well. Shape mixture into four patties. Place patties into a large skillet in a single layer and set over medium heat. Cook patties 3 to 4 minutes on each side or until browned on both sides and no longer pink in center.

Palate Preview _____
This interesting combination of meats—lamb and beef—makes a great combination for gyros. Try it as an interesting alternative to hamburgers.

Preheat toaster oven or regular oven to 350°F. Wrap pita pockets in aluminum foil and warm for 7 to 10 minutes in oven.

To assemble sandwiches, cut each warm pita pocket in half, forming two pockets. Place shredded lettuce in the bottom of each pocket. Layer with meat patty, onion, and tomato slices in each. Drizzle dressing inside pita over patties and vegetables.

Shepherd's Meat-and-Sweet-Potato Cups

Prep time: 25 minutes • Cook time: 20 minutes • Serves: 4 • Serving size: 3-ounces ground beef with ½ cup sweet potatoes

Nutritional Analysis per Serving: Glycemic Index 54 • Glycemic Load 11 • Calories 307 • Protein in grams 25 • Animal Protein 24 • Vegetable Protein 1 • Carbohydrates 21 grams • Dietary Fiber 2 grams • Net carbohydrate 19 grams • Fat 9 grams • Saturated Fat 3 grams • Cholesterol 122 mg • Sodium 481 mg • Exchanges 3 medium-lean meat, 1 starch, 1 vegetable

1 lb. lean ground beef	1 egg
¼ cup plain bread crumbs	3 cups peeled sweet potatoes, cut in 1-inch chunks
1 to 2 garlic cloves, minced	
1 tsp. dried oregano	¼ cup pitted kalamata olives, rinsed and sliced
¼ tsp salt	⅓ cup chopped seeded tomato
	¼ cup finely chopped green onions

Cook the sweet potato chunks in boiling water until very soft. Remove from heat and drain well. Mash well with electric beater on low speed.

Preheat the oven to 375°F. In a large bowl, combine ground beef, bread crumbs, garlic, oregano, salt, and egg, and mix well. Divide mixture evenly into an ungreased eight-cup muffin pan. Press mixture into the bottom and up the sides of each cup to form a crust.

Fill beef-lined cups with mashed sweet potato.

Place the muffin tin on a baking sheet in case of spillover and place both into the oven. Bake for 15 to 20 minutes or until beef is thoroughly cooked. Remove meat and sweet potato cups from the muffin pan and place two each on individual serving plates. Sprinkle with olives, tomato, and onions.

Palate Preview

This recipe calls for cooking the mashed sweet potatoes in the ground beef "cups" for an interesting twist on the traditional Shepherd's pie. Sweet potatoes add a sweet taste you'll appreciate.

Zucchini Meat Loaf

Prep time: 20 minutes • Cook time: 45 minutes • Serves: 8 • Serving size: 4-ounce slice of meat loaf

Nutritional Analysis per Serving: Glycemic Index 52 • Glycemic Load 3 • Calories 160 • Protein in grams 21 • Animal Protein 20 • Vegetable Protein 1 • Carbohydrate 5 grams • Dietary Fiber <1 gram • Net Carbohydrate 5 grams • Fat 5 grams • Saturated Fat 2 grams • Cholesterol 132 mg • Sodium 170 mg • Exchanges 3 medium-lean meat, 1 vegetable

Meat Loaf:

2 eggs, lightly beaten

2 cups shredded zucchini (1 large or 2 small)

⅓ cup plain bread crumbs

⅓ cup chopped onion

⅛ tsp. salt

½ tsp. dried oregano

¼ tsp. freshly ground black pepper

1½ lb. lean ground beef

Topping:

2 TB. ketchup

1 tsp. mustard

Palate Preview

You'll love this idea: combining lean ground beef with shredded zucchini. You get the value of a vegetable serving with your meat loaf. The loaf is extra tender and the zucchini nicely picks up the flavors of the beef, oregano, and ground black pepper.

Preheat the oven to 350°F. In a large bowl, combine eggs, zucchini, bread crumbs, onion, salt, oregano, pepper, and beef, and mix well. Press mixture into an ungreased 9½-inch deep-dish glass pie plate. Bake for 35 minutes.

Meanwhile, in a small bowl, combine ketchup and mustard, and mix well.

Remove meat loaf from the oven. Carefully pour any drippings off meat loaf in the pan. Spread topping over loaf. Return loaf to the oven and bake an additional 10 to 15 minutes or until a meat thermometer inserted into the center registers 160°F. Let stand 5 minutes. To serve, cut into wedges.

Chapter 14

Lean Pork, Veal, and Lamb Dishes

In This Chapter

◆ Adding a variety of meats to your meals

◆ Lean-cooking methods

◆ Purchasing pork, veal, and lamb

◆ Eating barbecue and ribs

Sometimes eating the same meats—beef and poultry—day after day, can just get plain old boring no matter how good they taste. You want a different flavor, but don't want to go so far out that you prepare foods that turn out too odd or unusual to enjoy.

Pork, veal, and lamb to the rescue! Perhaps you already vary your food intake with these meats. They are readily available and add variety to your eating plan. Prepare them with lean-cooking techniques and add your favorite seasonings.

The recipes in this chapter give you a wide variety of familiar recipes, all designed to meet your nutritional needs. You'll find pork tenderloin, pork chops, and even baby back ribs with barbecue sauce. You'll find veal scaloppini and roast lamb, plus lamb shanks. The recipes provide you with gustatory delights for all seasons.

Pork

Pork is a highly versatile meat. Pork contains complete protein, about 20 grams for a 3- to 4- ounce serving. While many people think of pork as full of fat, that isn't correct. Some cuts of pork are quite low in fat; others are high.

Pork is a mild-tasting, sweetish meat, so it readily picks up the flavors of the seasonings and vegetables in each recipe. The pork recipes in this book include mildly seasoned recipes, and also some with Southwestern chili and strong flavors.

Veal

Most likely, veal is an infrequent treat for you and your family. It can be quite pricey, but if you shop carefully, you can occasionally find veal on sale. When you do, you may want to purchase several packages and freeze some for later.

Favorite veal cuts are veal chops, usually cooked with the bone on, and boneless cutlets, which are often pounded very thin for such dishes as veal piccata and veal scallopini.

Lamb

Lamb is a stronger-tasting meat than pork and veal. So it can easily handle stronger flavors. Think garlic, Italian spices, chilies, cinnamon, and mint. For recipes, we've given you a traditional lamb roast as well as lamb chops and a very tender version of lamb shanks.

The Least You Need to Know

- ◆ Pork, lamb, and veal add complete protein and variety to your meal plans.
- ◆ Make your meat lean by trimming off all visible fat and using the lean-cooking techniques in this chapter.
- ◆ You can have pork ribs and enjoy barbecue, too, with the recipes in this book.
- ◆ Lamb has a strong flavor and takes well to strong seasonings.

Herb-Breaded Pork Chops

Prep time: 15 minutes • Cook time: 35 minutes • Serves: 4 • Serving size: 3-ounce pork loin chop with 1½ tablespoons stuffing

Nutritional Analysis per Serving: Glycemic Index 61 • Glycemic Load 4 • Calories 273 • Protein in grams 24 • Animal Protein 23 • Vegetable Protein 1 • Carbohydrates 7 grams • Dietary Fiber 0 • Net Carbohydrate 7 grams • Fat 15 grams • Saturated Fat 5 grams • Cholesterol 76 mg • Sodium 351 mg • Exchanges 3½ medium-lean meat, ½ starch, 1 fat

Vegetable oil cooking spray	2 TB. low-fat or nonfat mayonnaise
¼ cup garlic-herb bread crumbs	1 egg white
2 TB. grated Parmesan cheese	4 (3–4-oz.) boneless pork loin chops
1 tsp. dried sage	1 TB. all-purpose flour

Preheat the oven to 375°F. Spray a 12×8-inch (2-quart) glass baking dish or shallow pan with cooking spray. In a shallow bowl, combine bread crumbs, cheese, and sage. Mix well. In another shallow bowl, combine mayonnaise and egg white and beat until smooth. Pour the flour into a shallow bowl and dip each pork chop into it, tapping off any excess. Dip each chop in mayonnaise mixture, coating both sides. Dip each chop into breadcrumb mixture, coating both sides. Place chops in the baking dish in a single layer. Spray each chop lightly with cooking spray.

Bake for 35 to 40 minutes or until pork is no longer pink in center.

Palate Preview _____
The herb sage is terrific for bringing out the flavor of pork. Try this basic pork chop recipe for a simple family dinner.

Lamb Chops with Sugar Snap Peas

Prep time: 5 minutes • Cook time: 20 minutes • Serves: 4 • Serving size: 4-ounce lamb chop with vegetables

Nutritional Analysis per Serving: Glycemic Index 53 • Glycemic Load 10 • Calories 295 • Protein in grams 29 • Animal Protein 28 • Vegetable Protein 1 • Carbohydrates 19 grams • Dietary Fiber 1 gram • Net Carbohydrate 18 grams • Fat 13 grams • Saturated Fat 3 • Cholesterol 88 mg • Sodium 194 mg • Exchanges 4 medium-lean meat, 1 fruit, 1 vegetable

4 (4–5-oz.) lamb chops, trimmed of all fat	¼ cup mint jelly
2 cups frozen sugar snap peas, thawed	1 tsp. vegetable oil
1 red bell pepper, cored, seeded, and cut into 2-inch pieces	¼ tsp. salt
	¼ tsp. dried marjoram

Preheat the oven to 450°F. Line a 15×10×1-inch baking pan with foil and place lamb chops into it. Arrange sugar snap peas and bell pepper around chops. Bake for 10 minutes.

Palate Preview _____ Lamb and mint are favorite partners. Mint adds sparkle to this recipe. Sugar snap peas and red bell pepper add a rainbow of color to your meal.

Meanwhile, in small saucepan, combine mint jelly, oil, salt and marjoram. Cook over low heat, stirring constantly, until jelly is melted.

Remove chops and vegetables from the oven, brush each with one-quarter of jelly mixture. Return to the oven and bake an additional 10 minutes or until chops are of desired doneness and vegetables are tender, brushing with remaining jelly mixture once or twice.

Veal Scaloppini with Balsamic Glaze

Prep time: 10 minutes   •   Cook time: 10 minutes   •   Serves: 6   •   Serving size: 4-ounce veal scaloppini

Nutritional Analysis per Serving: Glycemic Index (not significant)   •   Glycemic Load   •   Calories 242   •   Protein in grams 28   •   Animal Protein 28   •   Vegetable Protein 0   •   Carbohydrates <1 gram   •   Dietary Fiber 0   •   Net Carbohydrate 0   •   Fat 10 grams   •   Saturated Fat 4 grams   •   Cholesterol 125 mg   •   Sodium 112 mg   •   Exchanges 4 medium-lean meat, ½ fat

1 TB. unsalted butter	1 cup dry white wine
1½ lb. veal scaloppini from top round, thinly sliced and pounded	¼ cup balsamic vinegar

Heat butter in a large, heavy skillet over medium heat. When butter foams, add veal in a single layer, making sure not to crowd the skillet. Cook for about 2 minutes, or until veal is lightly golden on both sides. Transfer veal to a plate.

Add wine and balsamic vinegar to the skillet. Cook over high heat, stirring quickly to dissolve any browned meat deposits attached to the bottom of the skillet. Cook for 3 to 4 minutes or until sauce is reduced in volume by half and return veal to the skillet. Reduce the heat to medium and cook for 30 to 40 seconds, stirring to coat the veal with sauce. Arrange equal portions of veal to six serving plates, spoon 1½ TB. sauce over each and serve at once.

Palate Preview

Veal scaloppini is quick to cook and adds nice variety to your food plan. Sautéing in butter adds wonderful flavor to food; just be careful not to burn it. The acidic balsamic vinegar adds tang.

Roast Leg of Lamb

Prep time: 30 minutes plus 12 hours refrigeration • Cook time: 1¾ hours • Serves: 12 • Serving size: 3-ounce slice

Nutritional Analysis per Serving: Glycemic Index (not significant) • Glycemic Load • Calories 175 • Protein in grams 21 • Animal Protein 21 • Vegetable Protein 0 • Carbohydrates 0 • Dietary Fiber 0 • Net Carbohydrate 0Fat 10 grams • Saturated Fat 4 grams • Cholesterol 55 mg • Sodium 72 mg • Exchanges 3 medium-lean meat, ½ fat

1 (5–7-lb.) whole lamb leg roast (bone in), trimmed of all fat	1 TB. olive oil
6 cloves garlic, cut into thin slices	1 TB. dried Italian seasoning or dried oregano, crushed
2–3 TB. fresh lemon juice	1 tsp. freshly ground black pepper
3 TB. snipped fresh parsley	

With a knife, cut ½-inch-wide slits into lamb at 1-inch intervals (approximately 36 holes) inserting a thin slice of garlic in each. Brush with lemon juice. In a small bowl, stir together parsley, oil, Italian seasoning or oregano, and pepper and brush or rub mixture all over lamb. Wrap in plastic wrap and refrigerate for 12 hours or overnight.

When you are ready to cook, preheat the oven to 325°F. Place lamb leg on a rack in a shallow roasting pan. Roast, uncovered for 1¾ to 2¼ hours or until a meat thermometer inserted into the thickest part registers 140°F for rare. For medium, roast for 2 to 2½ hours or until the meat thermometer registers 155°F. Cover with foil and let stand 15 minutes. (The temperature of meat will rise 5 to 10°F during standing.)

To carve, cut the large, round side off the bone. The opposite side will also come off in a single piece. Cut off the two smaller pieces on either side of the bone. Slice larger pieces into serving-size slices.

Palate Preview
Serve leg of lamb for a Sunday family dinner accompanied with green vegetables and a tossed salad. Great served cold the next day for breakfast or lunch.

Braised Lamb Shanks

Prep time: 20 minutes • Cook time: 3 hours • Serves: 4 • Serving size: 1½ cups stew (4 ounces meat)

Nutritional Analysis per Serving: Glycemic Index (not significant) • Glycemic Load • Calories 345 • Protein in grams 29 • Animal Protein 28 • Vegetable Protein 1 • Carbohydrates <1 gram • Dietary Fiber 0 • Net Carbohydrate 0 • Fat 16 grams • Saturated Fat 3 grams • Cholesterol 70 mg • Sodium 342 mg • Exchanges 4 medium-lean meat, 1 fat, 1 alcohol

1 TB. olive oil	1⅔ cups red wine
4 (½ lb.) lamb shanks	2 cups low-salt beef broth
1 onion, chopped	1 cup water
5 cloves garlic, coarsely chopped	4 sticks cinnamon
5 TB. canned Mexican red chili sauce	3 sprigs fresh rosemary or 2 tsp. dried

In a large stew pot, heat oil over medium heat. Add shanks, onion, and garlic to oil, stirring to keep onion and garlic from burning. Sear shanks for 3 to 4 minutes on each side or until browned.

When shanks are browned, add chili sauce and cook for another 2 minutes. Add red wine, water, beef stock, cinnamon, and rosemary. Bring to a boil, lower the heat to simmer and cook shanks, covered, for 3 hours, turning them occasionally.

Delightfully Different
Don't have time to stay at home while the lamb shanks simmer? Transfer them to a slow cooker and when you return, dinner will be waiting for you.

Meat should be extremely tender, but still attached to the bone. Remove shanks and strain fat and spices from cooking liquid. Return to pot. Cook over high heat until cooking liquid is reduced in volume by one quarter. Remove meat from shanks and trim away all fat and discard. Add trimmed lamb to cooking liquid and reheat. Serve in bowls.

Palate Preview
Cinnamon gives a spicy taste to this lamb recipe—plus, cinnamon helps you manage blood glucose levels. Let the lamb shanks simmer for the afternoon and the aromatic spices will fill your home with good cheer.

Southwestern Pork Stir-Fry

Prep time: 15 minutes • Cook time: 15 minutes • Serves: 4 • Serving size: 1½ cups stir-fry

Nutritional Analysis per Serving: Glycemic Index 20 • Glycemic Load 2 • Calories 330 • Protein in grams 35 • Animal Protein 27 • Vegetable Protein 8 • Carbohydrates 19 grams • Dietary Fiber 8 • Net carbohydrate 11 grams • Fat 11 grams • Saturated Fat 3 grams • Cholesterol 89 mg • Sodium 62 mg • Exchanges 4 medium-lean meat, 1 starch, 1 vegetable

1 TB. peanut or olive oil

1 lb. pork tenderloin, cut into 2×½×¼-inch strips

1 medium onion, cut into thin wedges

1 small red bell pepper, cored, seeded, and cut into strips

2 garlic cloves, minced

2 cups chopped zucchini

1 (15-oz.) can black beans, drained and rinsed

¼ cup chunky salsa

Palate Preview ___ Not your everyday stir-fry. This has Southwestern spices and vegetables that add zest to your meal. Serve with sliced avocado to complete your Southwestern meal.

Heat oil in a large nonstick skillet or wok over medium-high heat. Add pork, onion, bell pepper, and garlic. Cook, stirring, for 6 to 8 minutes or until pork is no longer pink and vegetables are crisp-tender.

Stir in zucchini, beans, and salsa. Cover and simmer 5 minutes or until zucchini is crisp-tender and flavors are blended.

Orange Marinated Pork Roast

Prep time: 25 minutes • Cook time: 1 hour • Serves: 8 • Serving size: 6 ounces vegetables and one 4-ounce pork slice

Nutritional Analysis per Serving: Glycemic Index 34 • Glycemic Load 9 • Calories 376 • Protein in grams 31 • Animal Protein 28 • Vegetable Protein 3 • Carbohydrates 30 grams • Dietary Fiber 4 grams • Net Carbohydrate 26 grams • Fat 16 grams • Saturated Fat 4 grams • Cholesterol 105 mg • Sodium 110 mg • Exchanges 4 medium-lean meat, 1 starch, 1 fruit, ½ fat

1 (2-lb.) boneless center-cut pork loin roast, trimmed of all fat	1 lb. Brussels sprouts, trimmed, cut in half if large
½ cup orange marmalade fruit spread	2 large leeks, washed well, trimmed of hard outer leaves and cut into ½ inch slices
3 TB. orange juice	2 TB. olive oil
2 tsp. fennel seed, crushed	¼ tsp. salt
1 tsp. dried thyme	¼ tsp. freshly ground black pepper
1 tsp. dried sage, crushed	
2 medium, dark-orange sweet potatoes, peeled, and cut into 1½-inch pieces	

Preheat the oven to 375°F. Place pork roast in an ungreased shallow roasting pan. In a small bowl, combine marmalade, orange juice, fennel seed, thyme, and sage. Mix well. Brush pork with half of marmalade mixture.

In a large bowl, combine sweet potatoes, Brussels sprouts, leeks, oil, salt and pepper, and toss gently to coat. Arrange vegetables around pork.

Bake for 45 minutes. Brush pork with remaining marmalade mixture, and gently stir vegetables to coat with pan juices. Bake an additional 15 minutes or until vegetables are tender, and pork is no longer pink in the center and a meat thermometer inserted into the center registers 160°F.

Palate Preview
Fruit greatly complements the taste of pork. Add some aromatic spices, sweet potatoes, and Brussels sprouts, and cook slowly—you have a complete meal.

In the Danger Zone
Leeks are grown in sandy soil, as you'll discover when you first wash one. It's not a lot of work to clean them, but you must be very thorough. Cut off the dark green tops and the root end. Cut each one in half lengthwise. Rinse under cold water, separating the leaves with your fingers to remove any excess sand. Shake off water and pat dry.

Grilled Mesquite Pork Chops

Prep time: 35 minutes plus 30 minutes refrigeration • Cook time: 15 minutes • Serves: 4 • Serving size: 6-ounce pork chop

Nutritional Analysis per Serving: Glycemic Index (not significant) • Glycemic Load (not significant) • Calories 205 • Protein in grams 22 • Animal Protein 21 • Vegetable Protein 1 • Carbohydrates 1 gram • Dietary Fiber 0 • Net Carbohydrate 1 gram • Fat 7 grams • Saturated Fat 1 gram • Cholesterol 75 mg • Sodium 256 mg • Exchanges 3 medium-lean meat, 1 fat

½ (1.1-oz.) pkg. mesquite marinade mix for the grill	4 (6-oz.) bone-in or boneless pork chops, trimmed of all fat
⅔ cup water	1 large sweet onion (Walla Walla or Vidalia), cut into ¼-inch-thick slices
1 TB. vegetable oil	Vegetable oil cooking spray

In a shallow glass or ceramic dish, combine marinade mix, water, and oil, and mix well with a fork. Add pork chops and onion rings. Turn to coat, cover and refrigerate for 30 minutes.

Palate Preview _____ Grilled pork chops marinated in with mesquite flavors make a simple and quick dinner. Add vegetables and salad to complete your meal.

When you are ready to cook, spray a grill rack with cooking spray. Preheat a gas grill to medium or prepare a medium-hot fire in a charcoal grill, with the rack placed 4 to 6 inches above the heat. Remove pork chops and onion rings from marinade, reserving the marinade. Pour marinade into a small saucepan and bring to a boil. Place pork chops and onion rings on the grill rack and grill for 10 to 15 minutes or until pork is no longer pink in the center, turning once and brushing frequently with marinade. Discard any remaining marinade.

Delightfully Different _____ You can also marinate the pork chops in a self-closing plastic bag. Put the meat, onions, and marinade in the bag, seal, and refrigerate. Turn several times during marinating.

Herb-Glazed Pork Tenderloin

Prep time: 10 minutes   •   Cook time: 20 minutes   •   Serves: 4   •   Serving size: 4-ounce pork tenderloin

Nutritional Analysis per Serving: Glycemic Index 54   •   Glycemic Load 5   •   Calories 267   •   Protein in grams 32   •   Animal Protein 32   •   Vegetable Protein 0   •   Carbohydrates 10 grams   •   Dietary Fiber 0   •   Net Carbohydrate 10 grams   •   Fat 9 grams   •   Saturated Fat 3 grams   •   Cholesterol 97 mg   •   Sodium 64 mg   •   Exchanges 4 medium-lean meat, ½ fruit, ½ fat

Herb Glaze:	¼ tsp. onion powder
1 TB. unsalted butter, melted	¼ tsp. garlic powder
¼ cup pure maple syrup	Pork:
1 tsp. dried thyme, crushed	Vegetable oil cooking spray
1 tsp. dried marjoram, crushed	1 (1-lb.) pork tenderloin, trimmed of all fat

Spray a grill rack with cooking spray. Preheat a gas grill to medium or prepare a medium-hot fire in a charcoal grill, with the rack placed 4 to 6 inches above the heat. In a small bowl, combine butter, maple syrup, thyme, marjoram, onion powder, and garlic powder. Mix well and set aside.

When ready to grill, place pork tenderloin on the grill rack and grill for 20 to 22 minutes or until pork is no longer pink in the center, turning frequently and brushing with glaze during the last 10 minutes of cooking time. Let stand 5 minutes. Cut pork into slices. Discard any remaining glaze.

Palate Preview _____
Pork tenderloin is an exceedingly tender and succulent meat. The glaze has the warming taste of real maple syrup with herbs and garlic.

Note: To broil pork tenderloin, preheat the broiler, spray a broiler pan with cooking spray, and place pork tenderloin on it. Broil 4 to 6 inches from the heat. Cook for 20 to 22 minutes or until pork is no longer pink in the center, turning once and brushing with glaze during the last 10 minutes of cooking time.

Oven-Baked Pork Chops and Vegetables

Prep time: 15 minutes • Cook time: 55 minutes • Serves: 4 • Serving size: 4-ounce pork chop and 1 cup vegetables

Nutritional Analysis per Serving: Glycemic Index 28 • Glycemic Load 3 • Calories 272 • Protein in grams 30 • Animal Protein 28 • Vegetable Protein 2 • Carbohydrates 12 grams • Dietary Fiber 2 grams • Net Carbohydrate 10 grams • Fat 12 grams • Saturated Fat 5 grams • Cholesterol 95 mg • Sodium 116 mg • Exchanges 4 medium-lean meat, 2 vegetable

Vegetable oil cooking spray	½ tsp. no-salt garlic-pepper blend
2 TB. frozen apple juice concentrate	4 (4-oz.) bone-in center-cut pork chops (½ inch thick), trimmed of all fat
1 tsp. olive oil	
1 TB. Dijon mustard	1½ cups fresh baby carrots
⅛ tsp. salt	1 medium red onion, cut into 8 wedges
½ tsp dried marjoram	2 cups frozen green beans, thawed

Preheat the oven to 425°F. Spray a 15×10×1-inch baking pan with cooking spray. In large bowl, combine apple juice concentrate, oil, mustard, salt, marjoram, and garlic-pepper blend. Mix well.

Brush pork chops with about half of oil mixture and set aside. Add carrots and onion to remaining oil mixture and toss to coat.

Palate Preview

These pork chops are baked in the oven on a bed of vegetables with Dijon mustard, marjoram, and some apple juice concentrate, making your meal heart-warming and cozy.

Arrange carrots and onion in the prepared pan. Bake for 15 minutes.

Remove vegetables from the oven. Add green beans, and stir gently to combine. Arrange pork chops on vegetable mixture.

Return the pan to the oven and bake an additional 30 to 40 minutes or until pork chops are no longer pink in the center and vegetables are fork-tender. Serve pork and vegetables with pan drippings.

Pork Tenderloin with Sweet Onions

Prep time: 25 minutes   •   Cook time: 40 minutes   •   Serves: 4   •   Serving size: 4-ounces pork tenderloin and 2 tablespoons onions

Nutritional Analysis per Serving: Glycemic Index 42   •   Glycemic Load 1   •   Calories 218   •   Protein in grams 32   •   Animal Protein 32   •   Vegetable Protein 0   •   Carbohydrates 4   •   Dietary Fiber 0   •   Net carbohydrate 4 grams   •   Fat 10 grams   •   Saturated Fat 3 grams   •   Cholesterol 89 mg   •   Sodium 145 mg   •   Exchanges 4 medium-lean meat, 1 vegetable, 1 fat

2 tsp. vegetable oil	Vegetable oil cooking spray
1 large sweet onion (Walla Walla or Vidalia) thinly sliced	1 (1-lb.) pork tenderloin, trimmed of all fat
	¼ tsp. salt
1 tsp. granulated sugar	⅛ tsp. freshly ground black pepper

Preheat the oven to 350°F. Heal oil in large skillet over medium-high heat until hot. Add onion and sprinkle with sugar. Cook, stirring frequently, for 12 to 15 minutes or until onion is soft and golden brown.

Spray a 13×9-inch pan with cooking spray and place pork tenderloin into it. Sprinkle with salt and pepper. Top with onion mixture.

Bake for 40 to 50 minutes or until no longer pink in center and thermometer inserted in the center registers 160°F.

Palate Preview

This pork tenderloin is baked in the oven with sweet onions. The sweet onions have a soft onion flavor and they will also caramelize lightly when baked and impart a sweet taste to the pork.

Stuffed Pork Tenderloin with Fruit Glaze

Prep time: 20 minutes • Cook time: 20 minutes • Serves: 4 • Serving size: 5-ounces stuffed pork tenderloin

Nutritional Analysis per Serving: Glycemic Index 35 • Glycemic Load 6 • Calories 283 • Protein in grams 35 • Animal Protein 33 • Vegetable Protein 2 • Carbohydrates 16 grams • Dietary Fiber 1 gram • Net carbohydrate 15 grams • Fat 9 grams • Saturated Fat 3 grams • Cholesterol 91 mg • Sodium 229 mg • Exchanges 4 medium-lean meat, 1 fruit,

Stuffing:

2 cups washed, trimmed and torn spinach

½ cup frozen artichoke hearts, thawed and chopped

¼ cup finely grated Parmesan cheese

1 tsp. snipped fresh rosemary or ¼ tsp. dried rosemary, crushed

Pork:

1 (1-lb.) pork tenderloin

Glaze:

½ cup frozen apple-cranberry juice concentrate, thawed

¼ cup balsamic vinegar

Palate Preview
This pork tenderloin is stuffed with spinach, artichoke hearts, and Parmesan cheese, with the added aromatic herb, rosemary. The meat is tender and flavorful, plus you get one serving of vegetables with the meat.

Preheat the oven to 425°F. For stuffing, in a large skillet cook spinach in a small amount of water until just wilted, and drain well. In a small bowl combine spinach, artichoke hearts, cheese, and rosemary.

With a very sharp knife, make a pocket in the tenderloin: starting an inch from one end, make an incision in the tenderloin lengthwise to within one inch of the other end, almost all the way through. Spoon stuffing into the pocket (stuffing will be exposed). Place in a shallow roasting pan, stuffing side up. Roast, uncovered, for 20 to 25 minutes or until a thermometer inserted into it registers 160°F. (The temperature of meat will rise 5 to 10°F during standing.)

Meanwhile, for glaze, in a small saucepan combine apple-cranberry juice concentrate and balsamic vinegar. Bring to a boil. Simmer, uncovered, for about 15 minutes or until mixture is reduced in volume to ⅓ cup. Spoon over pork during the last 10 minutes of roasting.

Veal Cutlets with Fresh Tomato Sauce

Prep time: 5 minutes prep plus 30 min refrig.   •   Cook time: 5 minutes   •   Serves: 4   •
Serving size: 4-ounce veal cutlet with ¼ cup sauce

Nutritional Analysis per Serving: Glycemic Index 54   •   Glycemic Load 9   •   Calories 371
•   Protein in grams 33   •   Animal Protein 30   •   Vegetable Protein 3   •   Carbohydrates
16 grams   •   Dietary Fiber 1   •   Net carbohydrate 15 grams   •   Fat 20 grams   •
Saturated Fat 5 grams   •   Cholesterol 175 mg   •   Sodium 210 mg   •   Exchanges
4 medium-lean meat, 1 starch, 2 fat

Tomato Sauce:

4 medium tomatoes, diced about the size of
large peas

1 medium stalk celery, finely sliced

4 scallions, white and green parts, finely sliced

8 to 10 large fresh basil, finely shredded, or
1 TB. finely chopped fresh parsley

1 TB. olive oil

1 TB. red wine vinegar

Veal Cutlets:

½ cup plain bread crumbs

1 TB. freshly grated Parmesan cheese

1 large egg, lightly beaten

1 lb. veal cutlets, sliced ¼-inch thick

1 TB. unsalted butter

In a medium bowl, combine tomatoes, celery, scallions, basil or parsley, oil, and vinegar, and
mix well. Set aside.

Combine bread crumbs and cheese and place in a shallow bowl. In a medium bowl, beat egg.
Dip one veal cutlet into egg, and then into bread crumbs and coat well. Lightly press crumbs
onto meat with the palm of your hand. Repeat with each cutlet. Place cutlets on a large plate,
cover and refrigerate for 30 minutes, so the coating settles and dries, which keeps it attached to
meat during cooking.

In a large, heavy skillet, heat butter over medium-high
heat. When the butter foams, add cutlets in a single
layer, making sure not to crowd the skillet. Cook for
about 2 minutes on each side, or until cutlets are
golden brown, working in batches if necessary. Transfer
cutlets to paper towels and pat dry to remove excess fat.
Place cutlets on individual serving dishes, top each with
a ¼ cup tomato sauce, and serve.

Palate Preview

Veal smothered in a
tomato and basil sauce that resembles salsa. The sauce is acidic,
and gives a slightly tart zest to this
veal recipe.

Barbecued Baby Back Pork Ribs

Prep time: 10 minutes • Cook time: 2½ hours • Serves: 8 • Serving size: 8 ounces baby back pork ribs

Nutritional Analysis per Serving: Glycemic Index (not significant) • Glycemic Load • Calories 245 • Protein in grams 21 • Animal Protein 21 • Vegetable Protein 0 • Carbohydrates 3 grams • Dietary Fiber 0 • Net Carbohydrate 3 grams • Fat 15 grams • Saturated Fat 5 grams • Cholesterol 80 mg • Sodium 278 mg • Exchanges 3 medium-lean meat, 2 fat

4 lb. baby back pork ribs, trimmed of all fat

1 cup homemade barbecue sauce (see the Barbecue Beef recipe in Chapter 12)

½ cup water

Vegetable oil cooking spray

Palate Preview
Yes, you can eat ribs. Baking the ribs in the oven first not only cuts down on the grilling time, but also helps make the ribs more tender and removes some of the fat.

Preheat the oven to 300 ° F. Arrange ribs in a 9×12-inch baking pan. Baste both sides with barbecue sauce. Pour ½ cup water into the bottom of pan. Bake, covered, for 2 hours or until almost cooked through. Remove ribs from the baking pan.

Spray a grill rack with cooking spray. Preheat a gas grill to medium/medium-high or prepare a medium-hot fire in a charcoal grill, with the rack placed 4 to 6 inches above the heat. Grill ribs for 15 to 30 minutes or until browned and cooked through, turning and basting frequently with additional sauce.

Chapter 15

Poultry Dishes

In This Chapter

♦ Cooking with poultry can be quite varied

♦ Poultry is an excellent choice for diabetic cooking

♦ High-quality protein with lower fat

♦ Tasty and varied meals

Just about everyone loves poultry, such as chicken, turkey, and Cornish game hens. Spouses, dinner guests, and even picky children enjoy poultry's mild taste and familiar texture. You can serve poultry often with confidence, knowing that everyone will enjoy it and that it's great for you to eat. Poultry is naturally healthy—low in fat, low in calories, and high in protein.

Poultry is also adaptable. It can be cooked in a variety of ways—baked, broiled, stewed, grilled, and others. It readily picks up the flavors of the spices and vegetables in a recipe and delivers wonderful taste-bud satisfaction. Oh, in addition, ounce for ounce, it's often quite economical, too.

In short, poultry is a cooking winner! Lots of varied flavors. Great recipes. Economical. And definitely *not* boring when you use the recipes in this chapter.

Poultry in Your Meal Plan

Poultry probably should be one of the mainstays of your diabetic diet. It's easy to prepare, convenient, and readily available. Poultry can be high fat or low fat depending upon how you cook and serve it. If you eat the dark meat and the skin, then poultry becomes high fat really fast. If the poultry has also been fried in a vat of fat, then it truly becomes bad for a diabetic's health. In fact, it becomes bad for anyone's health! However, if you bake or grill it with delicious seasoning, then eat the white meat with the skin removed, you have a low-fat entrée that satisfies.

Today, you can purchase chicken and turkey packaged as just the parts you want at the grocery store. Buy your poultry with the skin removed, if possible. Purchase just the breasts and, when you get them home, they're ready to be cooked according to the recipes in this chapter.

The one exception is Cornish game hens. They come in the store as a complete bird with the skins still attached. In the recipe in this chapter, cook them with the skins on, and discard the skins before you take them to the table to serve.

Chicken needs to be cooked until it is well done to avoid the possibility of food-borne diseases. When pricked with a fork, juices need to run clear and not pink. White meat needs to be white and not even slightly pink when you cut into it.

Healthy Notes

The chicken recipes in this chapter call for 3-ounce chicken breast halves. Three ounces is an ideal size for a serving. But you will find that boneless chicken breast halves in the store vary in weight from about 2.5 ounces to over 4 ounces. Don't worry, cook and serve them anyway. The size of the breast doesn't change the glycemic index or glycemic load of the recipe very much, but it does change the calories, protein, and fat in the nutritional analysis, though probably not enough to worry about.

The Least You Need to Know

- The familiar taste of poultry will please you and your family.
- Make poultry low in fat by eating the white meat and skipping the skin.
- The glycemic load of poultry recipes is quite low.
- These recipes offer you everyday tastes you love.

Garlic Chicken Breasts

Prep time: 15 minutes   •   Cook time: 10 to 15 minutes   •   Serves: 4   •   Serving size:
3-ounce half chicken breast

Nutritional Analysis per Serving: Glycemic Index 4   •   Glycemic Load 3   •   Calories 253
•   Protein in grams 25   •   Animal Protein 25   •   Vegetable Protein 0   •   Carbohydrates
5 grams   •   Dietary Fiber 0   •   Net Carbohydrate 5 grams   •   Fat 7 grams   •
Saturated Fat 2 grams   •   Cholesterol 129 mg   •   Sodium 5 mg   •   Exchanges 6 lean
meat, 1 fat, ½ fruit

Vegetable oil cooking spray

2 tsp. olive oil

4 garlic cloves, minced

4 tsp. brown sugar

4 (3-oz.) boneless, skinless chicken breast
halves

Preheat the oven to 500°F. Line a shallow roasting pan
with foil; spray the foil with cooking spray.

Heat oil in a small nonstick skillet over medium-low
heat. Add garlic and cook, stirring frequently, for
1 to 2 minutes or until it begins to soften. Remove
from heat and stir in brown sugar until well mixed.

Place chicken breast halves in the prepared pan. Spread
garlic mixture evenly over chicken.

Bake for 10 to 15 minutes or until chicken is cooked
through, no longer pink, and its juices run clear.

Palate Preview
Garlic added to this
chicken dish makes it delicious and
good for you. The small amount of
brown sugar enhances the chicken
taste. Perfect served hot or cold for
any meal or snack.

Grilled Cornish Hens

Prep time: 30 minutes • Cook time: 45 to 60 minutes • Serves: 8 • Serving size: ½ Cornish hen (4½ ounces)

Nutritional Analysis per Serving: Glycemic Index 0 • Glycemic Load 0 • Calories 150 no skin • Protein in grams 26 no skin • Animal Protein 26 no skin • Vegetable Protein 0 • Carbohydrates 0 • Dietary Fiber 0 • Net Carbohydrate 0 • Fat 5 grams (no skin) • Saturated Fat 1 grams (no skin) • Cholesterol 69 mg (no skin) • Sodium 82 mg • Exchanges 4 lean meat

Vegetable oil cooking spray	1 TB. olive oil
4 (4½-oz.) Cornish game hens	½ tsp. salt
2 TB. chopped fresh thyme	½ tsp. pepper
2 TB. chopped fresh rosemary	

Spray a grill rack with cooking spray. Preheat a gas grill to medium/medium-high or prepare a medium-hot fire in a charcoal grill, with the rack placed 4 to 6 inches above the heat.

Remove and discard neck and giblets from game hens. With kitchen scissors, cut each game hen along both sides of backbone. Remove backbone and discard. Rinse game hens with cold water and pat dry. Open game hens and flatten.

In small bowl, combine thyme, rosemary, olive oil, salt, and pepper. Mix well. Rub over outer surface of game hens.

Palate Preview
Whether you choose to grill or bake these hens, you'll love their basic taste. They go well with simple or fancy vegetables and salads. Be sure to remove and discard the skin before eating.

When ready to grill, place game hens on grill rack and grill for 10 minutes, turning once.

Stand game hens up on the grill and lean them against each other for support, cooking an additional 35 to 50 minutes or until fork-tender, cooked through and no longer pink, and juices run clear. To serve, cut game hens in half. Remove and discard skin before eating.

Note: To bake game hens in the oven, arrange in ungreased 15×10×1-inch baking pan. Bake at 350°F for 45 to 60 minutes.

Honey-Mustard Turkey Tenderloins

Prep time: 15 minutes • Cook time: 20 to 25 minutes • Serves: 6 • Serving size: 4 ounces

Nutritional Analysis per Serving: Glycemic Index 5 • Glycemic Load 3 • Calories 237 • Protein in grams 33 grams • Animal Protein 33 grams • Vegetable Protein 0 • Carbohydrates 5 grams • Dietary Fiber 0 • Net Carbohydrate 5 grams • Fat 8 ½ grams • Saturated Fat 1 ½ grams • Cholesterol 78 mg • Sodium 220 mg • Exchanges 4 lean meat, 2 fat

Honey-Mustard Dressing:

⅓ cup bottled tangy tomato-bacon salad dressing

2 tsp. honey mustard

Turkey:

Vegetable oil cooking spray

2 (¾-lb.) turkey tenderloins

Spray a grill rack with cooking spray. Preheat a gas grill to medium/medium-high or prepare a medium-hot fire in a charcoal grill, with the rack placed 4 to 6 inches above the heat

In a small bowl, combine salad dressing and mustard; mix well. Set aside.

Place turkey on grill rack and grill for 20 to 25 minutes or until turkey is no longer pink in the center. Turning and brushing several times with dressing mixture during last 10 minutes of cooking time. Discard any remaining dressing mixture. To serve, cut tenderloins into ¼-inch-thick slices.

Palate Preview
Turkey is an all-around winner. The soothing taste works well year round and the low-fat meat is sure to help your health. This tangy recipe is acidic, which benefits your blood sugar levels. Serve with a side salad and vegetable any time of day.

Note: To broil turkey tenderloins, place on a broiler pan; broil 4 to 6 inches from the heat for 20 to 25 minutes or until turkey is cooked through and no longer pink, turning once and brushing with dressing mixture during last 2 minutes of cooking on each side.

Delightfully Different
Do you prefer to bake chicken in the oven rather than use the grill? If so, here's what to do. Preheat the oven to 400°F. Place the chicken in a foil-lined shallow baking pan. Spray the foil lightly with cooking spray. Arrange chicken on the foil. Bake for 25 to 30 minutes or until chicken is cooked through and no longer pink, and its juices run clear when the meat is pricked with a fork.

Nutty Crusted Chicken

Prep time: 10 minutes   •   Cook time: 25 to 30 minutes   •   Serves: 4   •   Serving size: 3-ounce half chicken breast

Nutritional Analysis per Serving: Glycemic Index 10   •   Glycemic Load 2   •   Calories 390   •   Protein in grams 31   •   Animal Protein 24   •   Vegetable Protein 7   •   Carbohydrates 10 grams   •   Dietary Fiber 2 grams   •   Net Carbohydrate 8 grams   •   Fat 15 grams   •   Saturated Fat 3 grams   •   Cholesterol 65 mg   •   Sodium 562 mg   •   Exchanges 6 lean meat, 2 fats, ½ starch

Olive oil cooking spray

¾ cup dry-roasted peanuts

¾ cup Special K cereal

2 TB. low-salt soy sauce

½ tsp. garlic powder

¼ tsp. hot sauce such as Tabasco

4 (3-oz.) boneless, skinless chicken breast halves

Palate Preview Adding a crunchy-textured topping to this chicken makes it irresistible. The topping has lots of fiber and the nuts contain good-for-you oils. Great eaten hot or cold.

Delightfully Different You can substitute other nuts such as raw pecans, pine nuts, or almonds for the peanuts in this recipe.

Preheat the oven to 400°F. Line a shallow baking pan with foil; spray the foil with cooking spray. In the bowl of a food processor fitted with a metal blade, process peanuts and cereal until finely ground. Place mixture in a shallow bowl.

In a separate shallow bowl, combine soy sauce, garlic powder, and hot sauce; mix well. Dip a chicken breast half in soy-sauce mixture, turning to coat, and then into peanut-cereal mixture, turning to coat. Place in the prepared pan. Repeat for remaining chicken breast halves. Press any remaining peanut-cereal mixture onto chicken breast halves. Spray chicken with olive oil cooking spray.

Bake for 25 to 30 minutes or until chicken is cooked through and no longer pink, and its juices run clear.

Chicken Cordon Bleu

Prep time: 30 minutes • Cook time: 30 to 35 minutes • Serves: 4 • Serving size: 3-ounce half chicken breast

Nutritional Analysis per Serving: Glycemic Index 15 • Glycemic Load 8 • Calories 239 • Protein in grams 35 • Animal Protein 31 • Vegetable Protein 4 • Carbohydrates 10 grams • Dietary Fiber <1 gram • Net Carbohydrate 10 grams • Fat 4½ grams • Saturated Fat 1½grams • Cholesterol 131 mg • Sodium 383 mg • Exchanges 4 lean meat, 1 fat, ½ starch

4 (3-oz.) boneless, skinless chicken breast halves

2 (1-oz.) slices fat-free ham, halved

2 (¾-oz.) slices low-fat Swiss cheese, halved

¼ cup all-purpose flour

¼ cup plain bread crumbs

1 egg

Vegetable oil cooking spray

Preheat the oven to 350°F. Place one chicken breast half, boned side up, between two pieces of plastic wrap or waxed paper. Working from the center, gently pound chicken with the flat side of a meat mallet or rolling pin until chicken is ⅛ to ¼ inch thick; remove wrap. Repeat with remaining chicken breast halves.

Place ½ slice each of ham and cheese on each chicken breast half. Fold in sides; roll up jellyroll fashion, pressing ends to seal. If necessary, secure with toothpicks.

Palate Preview

Enjoy this all-time favorite updated to meet your nutritional needs. The combination of Swiss cheese, ham, and chicken is irresistible.

Place flour and bread crumbs in separate shallow bowls. Lightly beat egg in another shallow bowl. Dip one chicken roll into flour and tap off any excess. Then roll it into breadcrumbs to coat. Dip it into beaten egg. Place in ungreased 8-inch-square (1½-quart) baking dish. Repeat with remaining chicken rolls. Spray chicken rolls with cooking spray.

Bake for 30 to 35 minutes or until chicken is cooked through and no longer pink, and its juices run clear.

Grilled Chicken with Mango Salsa

Prep time: 15 minutes plus up to 2 hours refrigeration • Cook time: 8 to 10 minutes • Serves: 12 • Serving size: 3-ounce half chicken breast with ⅜ cup salsa

Nutritional Analysis per Serving: Glycemic Index:49 • Glycemic Load 2 • Calories 360 • Protein in grams 43 • Animal Protein 42 • Vegetable Protein 1 • Carbohydrates 5 grams • Dietary Fiber 1 gram • Net Carbohydrate 4 grams • Fat 15 grams • Saturated Fat 2 grams • Cholesterol 129 mg • Sodium 103 mg • Exchanges 6 lean meat, 2 fat

Chicken:

12 (3-oz.) boneless, skinless chicken breast halves

Vegetable oil cooking spray

Sprigs of cilantro for garnish

Marinade:

½ cup olive oil

½ cup white wine vinegar

3 TB. coarsely minced fresh gingerroot

3 TB. Dijon mustard

1 TB. ground coriander

1 TB. ground cumin

Freshly ground black pepper to taste

Mango Salsa:

3 cups pitted, peeled and chopped ripe mangos

½ cup finely chopped red onion

½ cup chopped fresh cilantro

3 TB. fresh lime juice

1 large garlic clove, minced

1 jalapeño chili pepper, seeded and minced

¼ tsp. crushed red pepper flakes or more to taste

Arrange chicken breast halves in a large glass or ceramic dish. Whisk oil, vinegar, gingerroot, mustard, coriander, cumin, and pepper in a bowl. Reserve ¼ cup marinade; cover and refrigerate. Pour remaining marinade over chicken, turning to coat. Cover and refrigerate chicken for up to 2 hours, turning occasionally.

Delightfully Different

You can substitute other fruits for the mangoes in the salsa. Try peaches, papaya, pineapple, avocado, and even tomatoes.

For Mango Salsa: Combine mangoes, onion, chopped cilantro, lime juice, garlic, jalapeño chili, red pepper flakes, and salt in a bowl and mix well. Cover and refrigerate. Bring to room temperature before serving.

When you are ready to cook, spray a grill rack with cooking spray. Preheat a gas grill to medium/medium-high or prepare a medium-hot fire in a charcoal grill, with the rack placed 4 to 6 inches above the heat.

Remove chicken from marinade and discard marinade. Place chicken on the grill and cook, basting with reserved chilled marinade frequently, for 6 to 10 minutes or until chicken is cooked through and no longer pink, and juices run clear. Spread salsa on a serving platter. Top with chicken and sprigs of cilantro.

Palate Preview

With this grilled chicken recipe, the mango salsa topping is optional, so family members can opt out and choose another dressing. Yet you can enjoy the wonderful tangy sweet-tasting salsa with confidence that this meets your nutritional needs and satisfies your palate. The recipe serves 12, so you can refrigerate leftovers and eat for breakfasts and lunches.

Note: To broil chicken, preheat the broiler. Spray an unheated broiler pan with cooking spray and place chicken on it. Broil 4 to 6 inches from heat for 6 to 10 minutes, turning once until chicken is cooked through and no longer pink, and juices run clear.

Cheese-Stuffed Chicken Breasts

Prep time: 10 minutes • Cook time: 35 to 40 minutes • Serves: 2 • Serving size: 3-ounce half chicken breast

Nutritional Analysis per Serving: Glycemic Index 5 • Glycemic Load 2 • Calories 372 • Protein in grams 36 • Animal Protein 35 • Vegetable Protein 1 • Carbohydrates 7 grams • Dietary Fiber 1 gram • Net Carbohydrate 6 grams • Fat 20 grams • Saturated Fat 8 grams • Cholesterol 103 mg • Sodium 243 mg • Exchanges 4 lean meat, 1 high fat meat, 3 fats

2 (3-oz.) boneless, skinless chicken breast halves

4 TB. or 2 ounces crumbled goat cheese, such as Montrachet

2 TB. chopped fresh parsley

1 tsp. chopped fresh oregano or ¼ tsp. dried oregano

1 TB. olive or canola oil

1 (14.5-oz) can no–salt-added, diced tomatoes, liquid reserved

2 TB. sliced, pitted black olives2 tsp. cornstarch

Palate Preview This dish is a little bit showy and a lot delicious! Goat cheese (called chevre in French), is way lower in sodium than many cheeses. This recipe works well with Montrachet, a popular regional variety from France that is widely available in the United State. If you and your family are cheese lovers, you'll love this recipe.

Preheat the oven to 350°F. Using a very sharp knife, cut a 3-inch slit into the thickest side of each chicken breast half to form pocket.

In a small bowl, combine cheese, parsley, oregano, and oil; mix well. Gently spoon half of filling into each breast half. Place chicken in an ungreased 8-inch-square (1½-quart) baking dish.

In another small bowl, combine tomatoes and their juice, olives, and cornstarch; mix well. Pour over chicken.

Bake for 35 to 40 minutes or until chicken is cooked through and no longer pink, and its juices run clear.

Herb Oven-Fried Chicken

Prep time: 15 minutes • Cook time: 30 to 40 minutes • Serves: 6 • Serving size: 3-ounce half chicken breast

Nutritional Analysis per Serving: Glycemic Index 30 • Glycemic Load 10 • Calories 228 • Protein in grams 30 • Animal Protein 28 • Vegetable Protein 2 • Carbohydrates 15 grams • Dietary Fiber <1 gram • Net Carbohydrate 15 grams • Fat 4 grams • Saturated Fat 1 grams • Cholesterol 75 mg • Sodium 238 mg • Exchanges 4 lean meat, 1 starch

1 cup plain bread crumbs	1 cup low-fat buttermilk
¼ cup finely chopped fresh parsley	6 (3-oz.) boneless, skinless chicken breast halves
1 TB no-salt garlic-herb seasoning	Olive oil cooking spray

Preheat the oven to 400°F. In a medium bowl combine bread crumbs, parsley, and garlic-herb seasoning; mix well.

Pour buttermilk into a shallow bowl. Dip one chicken breast half in buttermilk; then dip it into crumb mixture and turn to coat. Place chicken, boned side up, in an ungreased 13×9-inch pan. Repeat for remaining chicken breast halves, arranging them in the pan in a single layer. Spray chicken lightly with olive oil spray.

Bake for 30 to 40 minutes or until chicken is cooked through and no longer pink, and its juices run clear.

Palate Preview

Wonderfully simple ingredients create a down-home flavor with a slightly tangy taste. Use homemade bread crumbs. If you purchase the bread crumbs, be sure they don't have added salt. Serve with a side salad and a more elaborate vegetable dish.

Chicken and Broccoli Stir-Fry

Prep time: 10 minutes • Cook time: 10 minutes • Serves: 4 • Serving size: 1 cup

Nutritional Analysis per Serving: Glycemic Index (not significant) • Glycemic Load (not significant) • Calories 189 • Protein in grams 29 • Animal Protein 27 • Vegetable Protein 2 • Carbohydrates 5 grams • Dietary Fiber 2 grams • Net Carbohydrate 3 grams • Fat 4 grams • Saturated Fat 1 gram • Cholesterol 68 mg • Sodium 210 mg • Exchanges 4 lean meat, 1 fat

2 tsp. olive or canola oil

4 (3-oz.) boneless, skinless chicken breast halves, cut into thin strips

2 cloves garlic, minced

3 cups chopped broccoli florets

1 medium red bell pepper, cored, seeded, and cut into 2½-inch pieces

2 tsp. cornstarch

½ tsp. ground ginger

½ cup low-salt chicken broth

3 TB. Lea & Perrins White Wine Worcestershire Sauce

Palate Preview

Here's a quick stir-fry to please the whole family. The broccoli and red bell pepper make for a colorful dish and the white wine Worcestershire sauce makes for a harmonious taste. You can use regular Worcestershire sauce if you like. Be sure to use the full amount of garlic, both for flavor and because garlic helps lower blood glucose levels.

Heat oil in a large skillet over medium heat. Add chicken and garlic. Cook, stirring, for 3 to 5 minutes or until chicken is no longer pink. Reduce heat. Remove chicken to a plate and cover to keep warm.

Add broccoli and bell pepper to the same skillet; cover and cook for 3 to 5 minutes or until vegetables are crisp-tender.

Meanwhile, in a small bowl, combine cornstarch, ginger, chicken broth, and Worcestershire sauce, and blend well. Return chicken to skillet. Add cornstarch mixture. Bring to a boil, stirring constantly, about 5 minutes, until bubbly and thickened.

Lime-Grilled Chicken with Tropical Fruit Salsa

Prep time: 10 minutes plus 20 minutes to marinate • Cook time: 10 to 15 minutes • Serves: 4 • Serving size: 3-ounce half chicken breast plus ½ cup salsa

Nutritional Analysis per Serving: Glycemic Index 10 • Glycemic Load 2 • Calories 225 • Protein in grams 28 • Animal Protein 27 • Vegetable Protein 1 • Carbohydrates 15 grams • Dietary Fiber 1 gram • Net Carbohydrate 14 grams • Fat 5 grams • Saturated Fat 1 gram • Cholesterol 68 mg • Sodium 222 mg • Exchanges 4 lean meat, 1 fruit, 1 fat

Vegetable oil cooking spray

2 tsp. fresh or dried grated lime zest

¼ tsp. salt

¼ tsp. freshly ground black pepper

1 TB. olive oil

¼ cup fresh lime juice

2 TB. fructose

4 (3-oz.) boneless, skinless chicken breast halves

Salsa:

2 kiwi fruits, peeled and diced

1 small papaya, peeled, seeded and diced

¼ cup diced red onion

1 TB. chopped fresh cilantro (optional)

1 jalapeño chili pepper, seeded if desired and chopped

Spray a grill rack with cooking spray. Preheat a gas grill to medium/medium-high or prepare a medium-hot fire in a charcoal grill, with the rack placed 4 to 6 inches above the heat.

In a shallow glass or ceramic dish, combine lime zest, salt, pepper and oil; mix well. In a medium bowl, combine lime juice and fructose; mix well with a wire whisk. Pour half of lime-juice mixture into oil mixture in the shallow dish; stir to blend. Reserve remaining lime-juice mixture in the medium bowl and set aside.

Add chicken breast halves to lime juice-oil mixture in the shallow dish and turn to coat; let stand at room temperature for 20 minutes to marinate, turning once.

For salsa, add kiwi fruit, papaya, onion, cilantro (if desired), chili, reserved lime-juice mixture in the medium bowl; stir to combine and set aside.

When you are ready to cook, remove chicken from marinade and discard marinade. Place chicken the grill and cook for 10 to 15 minutes or until chicken is cooked through and no longer pink, and its juices run clear, turning once. Serve salsa with chicken.

Palate Preview

The salsa combination of lime, kiwi fruit, and papaya makes this dish tops in fresh-fruit Southwestern flavor. The salsa gives you healthful antioxidants, plus it's acidic, which can help lower blood glucose levels.

Note: To broil chicken, preheat the broiler. Spray an unheated broiler pan with cooking spray and place chicken on it. Broil 4 to 6 inches from the heat for 10 to 15 minutes or until chicken is cooked through and no longer pink, and its juices run clear, turning once.

Caesar Baked Chicken

Prep time: 10 minutes • Cook time: 50 minutes • Serves: 4 • Serving size: 3-ounce half chicken breast

Nutritional Analysis per Serving: Glycemic Index (not significant) • Glycemic Load (not significant) • Calories 243 • Protein in grams 29 • Animal Protein 29 • Vegetable Protein 0 • Carbohydrates <1 gram • Dietary Fiber 0 • Net Carbohydrate 0 • Fat 13 grams • Saturated Fat 3½ grams • Cholesterol 81 mg • Sodium 391 mg • Exchanges 4 lean meat, 2 fat

¼ cup bottled, low-fat creamy Caesar salad dressing

2 tsp. dried oregano

½ tsp. no-salt lemon-pepper seasoning or fresh ground pepper

4 (3-oz.) boneless, skinless chicken breast halves

2 oz. crumbled feta cheese (¼ cup)

Palate Preview

The Italian flavorings and spices give this chicken dish a familiar taste. Add a salad tossed with oil-and-vinegar dressing and a green vegetable to complement the Italian theme.

Preheat the oven to 400°F. Line a shallow pan with foil. In a small bowl, combine dressing, 1 teaspoon oregano, and lemon-pepper seasoning; mix well.

Place chicken breast halves in the prepared pan in a single layer. Brush dressing mixture over chicken.

Bake for 25 minutes. Remove from oven and sprinkle cheese over chicken; press lightly so cheese adheres to chicken. Bake an additional 10 to 15 minutes or until chicken is cooked through and no longer pink, its juices run clear, and cheese has begun to brown. Sprinkle remaining teaspoon oregano over chicken before serving.

Grilled Chicken with Sweet Onions

Prep time: 25 minutes plus 30 to 60 minutes refrigeration   •   Cook time: 10 to 15 minutes
•   Serves: 4   •   Serving size: 3-ounce half chicken breast plus ⅜ cup sauce

Nutritional Analysis per Serving: Glycemic Index 12   •   Glycemic Load 8   •   Calories 316
•   Protein in grams 28 ½   •   Animal Protein 28   •   Vegetable Protein ½   •
Carbohydrates 12   •   Dietary Fiber <1 gram   •   Net Carbohydrate 12 grams   •   Fat
1 ½ grams   •   Saturated Fat <1 gram   •   Cholesterol 68 mg   •   Sodium 373 mg   •
Exchanges 4 lean meat, 1 fruit

Marinade and Sauce:

½ cup bottled nonfat tomato French dressing

¼ cup chopped sweet onion (such as Vidalia,
Maui, or Texas Sweet)

1 TB. Worcestershire sauce

2 small Italian plum tomatoes, coarsely
chopped

Grilled Chicken and Onions:

4 (3-oz.) boneless, skinless chicken breast
halves

Vegetable oil cooking spray

4 (¼-inch thick) slices sweet onion (such as
Vidalia, Maui or Texas Sweet)

In a blender, combine dressing, onions,
Worcestershire sauce, and tomatoes. Blend until
smooth and creamy. Pour ½ cup tomato mixture in a
1-quart self-closing plastic bag; pour remaining mixture in a saucepan for sauce. Place chicken breast halves
in the plastic bag, seal, and turn the bag to coat
chicken. Refrigerate 30 to 60 minutes, turning once.

When you are ready to cook, spray a grill rack with
cooking spray. Preheat a gas grill to medium/medium-
high or prepare a medium-hot fire in a charcoal grill,
with the rack placed 4 to 6 inches above the heat.

 **Palate Preview**

If you love onions, this
dish is for you. The sweet onions
add a gentle onion taste to the
grilled chicken. The sauce with its
tomato French dressing, plum tomatoes, Worcestershire sauce, and
sweet onions is delightfully tangy.

Transfer reserved tomato sauce mixture to a saucepan and cook over low heat for 3 to 4 minutes, stirring occasionally. Cover and keep warm.

Remove chicken from marinade, reserving the marinade. Pour marinade into a small saucepan
and bring to a boil. Place chicken and onion slices on the grill. Brush onion slices with reserved
boiled marinade. Cook 10 to 15 minutes or until chicken is cooked through and no longer pink,
and its juices run clear, turning onions and chicken once. Discard any remaining marinade.
Serve chicken and onion slices with warm tomato sauce.

Note: To broil chicken, preheat the broiler. Spray an unheated broiler pan with cooking spray
and place chicken on it. Broil 4 to 6 inches from heat for 10 to 15 minutes or until chicken is
cooked through and no longer pink, and its juices run clear, turning onions and chicken once.

Lemon Herb Chicken

Prep time: 10 minutes plus 30 to 60 minutes to marinate • Cook time: 10 to 15 minutes •
Serves: 6 • Serving size: 3-ounce half chicken breast

Nutritional Analysis per Serving: Glycemic Index (not significant) • Glycemic Load (not
significant) • Calories 175 • Protein in grams 21 • Animal Protein 21 •
Vegetable Protein 0 • Carbohydrates < 1 gram • Dietary Fiber 0 • Net
Carbohydrate 0 • Fat 13 • Saturated Fat 2 • Cholesterol 68 mg • Sodium
76 mg • Exchanges 3 lean meat, 2 fat

¼ cup olive oil

¼ cup fresh lemon juice

2 TB. *herbes de Provence*

¼ tsp. freshly ground black pepper

6 (3-oz.) boneless, skinless chicken breast halves

Vegetable oil cooking spray

In a 1-gallon self-closing plastic bag, combine oil, lemon juice, *herbes de Provence*, black pepper,
and chicken; seal the bag and shake to coat. Refrigerate 30 to 60 minutes.

Palate Preview _____
The lemon-juice-and-oil
marinade makes this chicken particularly tender. You can grill the
marinated chicken or bake it at
350°F for 35 to 40 minutes.

When you are ready to cook, spray a grill rack with
cooking spray. Preheat a gas grill to medium/medium-
high or prepare a medium-hot fire in a charcoal grill,
with the rack placed 4 to 6 inches above the heat.

Remove chicken from marinade and discard marinade.
Place chicken on the grill and cook for 10 to 15 minutes or until chicken is cooked through and no longer
pink, and its juices run clear, turning once.

Words for Well-Being _____
Herbes de Provence is an herbal mixture of thyme, basil, savory, fennel seeds, and
lavender flowers that's widely available at regular grocery stores. Just look in the spice
section, and you'll be able to savor this wonderful blend of herbs from southern France.

Chicken Breasts *Piccata*

Prep time: 10 minutes • Cook time: 12 to 15 minutes • Serves: 4 • Serving size: 3-ounce half chicken breast plus 2 tablespoons sauce

Nutritional Analysis per Serving: Glycemic Index (not significant) • Glycemic Load (not significant) • Calories 211 • Protein in grams 28 • Animal Protein 21 • Vegetable Protein 0 • Carbohydrates 1 gram • Dietary Fiber 0 gram • Net Carbohydrate 1 Fat 7 grams • Saturated Fat 3 grams • Cholesterol 83 mg • Sodium 243 mg • Exchanges 3 lean meat, 1 fat

Vegetable oil cooking spray

4 (3-oz.) boneless, skinless chicken breast halves

½ tsp. no-salt lemon-pepper seasoning

2 TB. unsalted butter

1 TB. all-purpose flour

½ cup dry white wine

2 TB. drained capers

Spray a grill rack with cooking spray. Preheat a gas grill to medium/medium-high or prepare a medium-hot fire in a charcoal grill, with the rack placed 4 to 6 inches above the heat. Sprinkle chicken with lemon-pepper seasoning.

Place chicken on the grill and cook 12 to 15 minutes or until chicken is cooked through and no longer pink, and its juices run clear, turning once. Keep warm.

Melt 1 tablespoon butter in a small saucepan over medium heat. Stir in flour; cook, stirring to dissolve any lumps, for 1 minute. Stir in wine and capers; cook, stirring constantly for 2 minutes or until mixture is slightly thickened. Remove from the heat and stir in remaining 1 tablespoon butter. Serve sauce over chicken.

Words for Well-Being

Piccata is a Northern Italian method for preparing light meats, such as chicken or veal. Be prepared for a delicious, tangy sauce as the lemon-pepper seasoning, the capers, and the cooked wine join together to make a memorable meal.

Tandoori Chicken Breasts

Prep time: 5 minutes plus 30 to 60 minutes refrigeration   •   Cook time: 8 to 10 minutes   •
Serves: 2   •   Serving size: 3-ounce half chicken breast

Nutritional Analysis per Serving: Glycemic Index 14   •   Glycemic Load 2   •   Calories 329
•   Protein in grams 25 grams   •   Animal Protein 25 grams   •   Vegetable Protein 0   •
Carbohydrates 9 grams   •   Dietary Fiber 0 Net Carbohydrate 9 grams   •   Fat 10 grams   •
Saturated Fat 2.5 grams   •   Cholesterol 130 mg   •   Sodium 150 mg   •   Exchanges
½ milk, 3 lean meat, 1 fat

½ cup nonfat plain yogurt

2 tsp. fresh lemon juice

2 tsp. olive oil

1 tsp. curry powder

¾ tsp. paprika

½ tsp. ground cumin

⅛ tsp. salt

¼ tsp. ground ginger

⅛ tsp. ground cinnamon

⅛ tsp. crushed red pepper flakes or cayenne

2 (3-oz.) boneless, skinless chicken breast halves

Vegetable oil cooking spray

Delightfully Different

This roasted chicken dish combines several exotic spices to give you a tasty and simple main course. One of the spices is cinnamon, which aids the body with the uptake of glucose. It's wonderful hot, but also consider eating Tandoori Chicken cold for breakfasts, packed lunches, or picnics.

In a shallow glass or ceramic dish, combine yogurt, lemon juice, and oil; blend well. Add curry powder, paprika, cumin, salt, ginger, cinnamon, and red pepper flakes or cayenne; blend well. Add chicken and turn to coat. Cover and refrigerate 30 to 60 minutes. Preheat the oven to broil. Line a 15×10×1-inch baking pan with foil and spray with cooking spray. Remove chicken from marinade and discard marinade. Place chicken in the prepared pan in a single layer.

Broil 4 to 6 inches from the heat for 8 to 10 minutes or until chicken is cooked through and no longer pink, and its juices run clear, turning once.

Part 5

Shellfish and Fish Entrées

Vary your day-to-day meals with fish and shellfish dishes. Many such choices, such as salmon, contain important nutritional fats, especially the omega-3 essential fatty acids.

But it's quite all right to simply prepare and eat the fish and shellfish dishes for the sheer joy of their flavors and tastes.

Chapter 16

Shellfish Dishes

In This Chapter

◆ Favorite shellfish meals
◆ Nutritional gifts from the sea
◆ Purchasing fresh shellfish
◆ Lean cooking techniques for shellfish

Shellfish is a special gift from the sea. Most everyone loves shellfish and, if you live inland, you most likely consider it a special treat. If you live near the coast where it's readily available, shellfish may seem ordinary, but almost everyone from coastal areas still appreciates how delicious it is.

Shellfish fits well into food plans for persons with diabetes. It contains healthy, complete protein, and a very small serving—just three to four ounces—contains loads of energy-giving nutrients. Three to four ounces is about the size of a deck of cards. You should vary the protein you consume to increase the range of nutrients you ingest, so plan on having seafood no more than three or so times a week.

The recipes in this chapter are for the most commonly eaten shellfish—shrimp, crab, clams, mussels, and scallops. Fish dishes appear in Chapter 17. You are sure to find familiar favorites, such as Maryland Crab Cakes and Shrimp Scampi, as well as some new recipes to try. You'll be pleased with the results.

Seafood Cuisine

Shellfish delights our taste buds as virtually no other protein source does. It requires a light touch when cooking because overcooking seafood produces tough and very chewy food. Delicate yet hardy, seafood holds taste sensations that leave you satisfied.

Shellfish is low in carbohydrates and low in fat. It is classified as a very lean meat exchange for diabetic meal planning. Combining it with suitable sauces and seasonings, you can enjoy seafood frequently.

Delightfully Different
In these recipes, you can substitute shrimp for the scallops and vice versa. You can also mix shrimp and scallops in the same recipe.

Flavorful Shellfish

Bring on the sauces and condiments. Shellfish takes wonderfully to a wide variety of flavors. Garlic, hot or mild peppers, vegetables, mustard, lemon or lime juice, spices such as oregano, rosemary, basil, and tarragon are all good.

Shellfish has a richness that contrasts well with acid tastes, such as lemon and lime juice, or tomatoes.

Serve virtually any vegetable or salad with seafood. They all go well.

The Least You Need to Know

◆ Shellfish is a delectable form of complete protein.

◆ A good serving size is about 3 to 4 ounces.

◆ Shellfish is delicious with acid foods, such as lemon or lime juice, or tomatoes.

◆ Shellfish is great with garlic, hot or mild spices, and virtually every vegetable.

Cajun Shrimp with Rice

Prep time: 10 minutes • Cook time: 15 minutes • Serves: 4 • Serving size: 1¼ cups shrimp and sauce

Nutritional Analysis per Serving: Glycemic Index 40 • Glycemic Load 8 • Calories 382 • Protein in grams 50 • Animal Protein 48 • Vegetable Protein 2 • Carbohydrates 20 grams • Dietary Fiber 1 gram • Net Carbohydrate 19 grams • Fat 10 grams • Saturated Fat 2 grams • Cholesterol 439 mg • Sodium 122 mg • Exchanges 6 lean meat, 2 fat, 1½ starch

1 (3½-oz.) boil-in-bag long-grain white or brown rice	½ cup chopped green onions
2 TB. olive oil	¼ tsp. dried thyme
2 lb. large shrimp, shelled and deveined	½ cup canned, no-salt-added, chopped tomatoes
1 TB. no-salt Cajun seasoning	⅛ tsp. salt
1 TB. minced garlic	⅛ tsp. freshly ground black pepper
1 cup frozen bell pepper stir-fry, thawed	

Cook rice according to package directions, omitting salt and fat. Keep warm.

While rice cooks, heat 1 tablespoon oil in a large nonstick skillet over medium-high heat. Sprinkle shrimp with Cajun seasoning and toss to coat. Add shrimp to the pan and sauté, stirring and shaking the pan, for about 4 minutes or until shrimp is cooked through and opaque-pink. Remove from pan and keep warm.

Heat 1 tablespoon oil in the same pan over medium-high heat. Add garlic and sauté, stirring, for 30 seconds. Add bell pepper stir-fry, green onions, and thyme. Sauté, stirring, for 3 minutes or until tender. Stir in cooked rice, shrimp, tomatoes, salt, and pepper, and cook 1 minute or until thoroughly heated.

Palate Preview

This spicy Cajun-style shrimp is reminiscent of traditional Shrimp Creole. You'll enjoy the rice mixed with shrimp, tomatoes, and bell pepper.

Quick Cioppino (Stew)

Prep time: 10 minutes • Cook time: 20 minutes • Serves: 4 • Serving size: 5 ounces seafood in 1¼ cups broth

Nutritional Analysis per Serving: Glycemic Index 31 • Glycemic Load 4 • Calories 253 • Protein in grams 29 • Animal Protein 28 • Vegetable Protein 1 • Carbohydrates 14 grams • Dietary Fiber 3 grams • Net Carbohydrate 11 grams • Fat 6 ½ grams • Saturated Fat 1 gram • Cholesterol 126 mg • Sodium 313 mg • Exchanges 4 lean meat, 2 vegetable, 1 fat

8 oz. fresh or frozen cod fillets	1 cup chopped onion
8 oz. fresh or frozen shrimp, shelled and deveined	2 cloves garlic, minced
8 oz. mussels	2 cans no-salt-added chopped tomatoes, liquid reserved
1 TB. olive or vegetable oil	½ cup water
1 medium green bell pepper, cored, seeded, and cut into thin strips	3 TB. chopped fresh basil

Thaw cod and shrimp, if frozen. Discard mussels with broken shells. Pull off the "beards." Using a stiff brush, scrub mussels under cold running water.

Palate Preview

A San Francisco-style fish and seafood stew that's ready in only 30 minutes. Serve with crunchy stone-ground, low-glycemic bread and a fresh tossed vegetable salad with a simple oil-and-vinegar dressing.

Rinse cod and shrimp and pat dry. Cut cod into 1-inch pieces.

In a Dutch oven heat oil over medium-high heat. Add bell pepper, onion, and garlic, and cook, stirring, until tender. Stir in tomatoes and their juice and water. Bring to a boil. Stir in cod, shrimp, and mussels. Return to a boil and reduce heat to medium. Cover and simmer for 3 to 4 minutes or until cod flakes easily when tested with a fork, shrimp turn opaque-pink, and mussel shells open. Discard any unopened mussels. Stir in basil and serve.

Kung Pao Shrimp

Prep time: 10 minutes • Cook time: 7 minutes • Serves: 4 • Serving size: 4 ounces shrimp with 1 tablespoon peanuts

Nutritional Analysis per Serving: Glycemic Index 28 • Glycemic Load 1 • Calories 236 • Protein in grams 25 • Animal Protein 23 • Vegetable Protein 2 • Carbohydrates 5 grams • Dietary Fiber 1 gram • Net Carbohydrate 4 grams • Fat 10 grams • Saturated Fat 1 gram • Cholesterol 172 mg • Sodium 223 mg • Exchanges 3 lean meat, 2 fat, ½ fruit

1½ TB. hoisin sauce	1 lb. medium shrimp, shelled and deveined
1 TB. dry sherry	1 TB. vegetable oil
1 tsp. granulated sugar	½ tsp. fresh grated gingerroot
½ to 1 tsp. chili paste	1 garlic clove, minced
1 egg white	¼ cup unsalted, dry-roasted peanuts
1 TB. cornstarch	

In a small bowl, combine hoisin sauce, sherry, sugar, and chili paste. Mix well and set aside.

In a medium bowl, combine egg white and cornstarch. Beat well. Add shrimp and mix well to coat. Set aside.

Heat oil in large skillet or wok over medium-high heat. Add shrimp, ginger, and garlic. Cook, stirring, for 2 to 3 minutes or until shrimp are opaque-pink. Add hoisin-sauce mixture. Cook, stirring, for 1 to 2 minutes or until shrimp are well coated. Stir in peanuts and serve.

Palate Preview

A Chinese stir-fry that combines shrimp with peanuts and ginger in a mild hot sauce. Sure to satisfy your cravings for Chinese food.

Shrimp Scampi

Prep time: 5 minutes • Cook time: 5 minutes • Serves: 4 • Serving size: 6 ounces shrimp with 1½ tablespoons sauce

Nutritional Analysis per Serving: Glycemic Index (not significant) • Glycemic Load (not significant) • Calories 215 • Protein in grams 34 • Animal Protein 34 • Vegetable Protein 0 • Carbohydrates <1 gram • Dietary Fiber 0 • Net Carbohydrate 0 • Fat 8 grams • Saturated Fat 1 gram • Cholesterol 258 mg • Sodium 322 mg • Exchanges 5 lean meat, 1 fat

2 tsp. olive oil	⅛ tsp. salt
1½ lb. large shrimp, shelled and deveined	¼ tsp. freshly ground black pepper
3 garlic cloves, minced	¼ cup chopped fresh parsley
⅓ cup dry white wine	1 TB. fresh lemon juice

Palate Preview _____ This is a classic Italian dish with the delectable taste of garlic, white wine, parsley, and lemon juice. Add a fresh vegetable salad with Italian dressing.

Heat olive oil in a large skillet over medium-high heat. Add shrimp and sauté, stirring, for 1 minute. Add garlic and sauté, stirring, for 1 minute. Stir in wine, salt, and pepper. Bring mixture to a boil. Reduce heat to medium and cook 30 seconds. Add parsley and lemon juice and toss to coat. Cook 1 minute or until shrimp are opaque-pink.

Delightfully Different _____ You can adjust the amount of minced garlic based on your personal preference. If you love garlic, add more. If not, you can cook with less garlic and still have a terrifically tasty meal. Garlic helps lower blood glucose levels, so in this case, the more, the merrier—and healthier.

Steamed Mussels in Mustard-Herb Sauce

Prep time: 10 minutes   •   Cook time: 10 minutes   •   Serves: 2   •   Serving size: 6 ounces mustard with ¼ cup sauce

Nutritional Analysis per Serving: Glycemic Index 42   •   Glycemic Load 5   •   Calories 440 • Protein in grams 42   •   Animal Protein 41   •   Vegetable Protein 1   •   Carbohydrates 13 grams   •   Dietary Fiber < 1 Net Carbohydrate 13 grams   •   Fat 15 grams   • Saturated Fat 2 grams   •   Cholesterol 102 mg   •   Sodium 527 mg   •   Exchanges 6 lean meat, 2 fat, 1 milk

1½ lb. mussels

1 medium onion, chopped

1 TB. olive oil

2 garlic cloves, minced

2 TB. dry white wine

½ cup nonfat sour cream

2 TB. homemade bread crumbs

1 to 2 TB. Dijon mustard or to taste

2 TB. minced fresh parsley

Discard mussels with broken shells. Pull off the "beards." Using a stiff brush, scrub mussels under cold running water. Heat the oil in a stockpot over medium-low heat. Add the onion, and cook, stirring, until softened. Add garlic, mussels, and wine. Cover and steam mussels for 3 to 5 minutes, or until mussels are opened. Using a slotted spoon, transfer mussels as they open to a heated dish and keep covered. Discard any unopened mussels. When all mussels are removed from pot, add sour cream and bread crumbs and bring to a boil. Boil mixture over high heat for 3 to 5 minutes, or until sauce is thickened. Stir mustard and parsley into sauce. Add mussels, stirring to coat them with sauce.

Palate Preview

Start with fresh mussels. Add a tangy mustard sauce. What you get is a wonderful meal. Serve with a slice of crunchy stone-ground low-glycemic bread to dip in the sauce, or simply eat the sauce with a spoon.

Scallops with Tomato-Garlic Sauce

Prep time: 5 minutes • Cook time: 15 minutes • Serves: 2 • Serving size: 6 ounces scallops with ½ cup sauce

Nutritional Analysis per Serving: Glycemic Index (not significant) • Glycemic Load (not significant) • Calories 240 • Protein in grams 29 • Animal Protein 28 • Vegetable Protein 1 • Carbohydrates 3 grams • Dietary Fiber 1 gram • Net Carbohydrate 2 grams • Fat 9 grams • Saturated Fat 3 grams • Cholesterol 71 mg • Sodium 217 mg • Exchanges 4 lean meat, 1 vegetable, 1½ fat

1 TB. unsalted butter	2 plum tomatoes, seeded and chopped
1 garlic clove, minced	½ tsp. dried tarragon
¾ lb. bay scallops, patted dry	2 TB. minced fresh parsley
¼ cup dry white wine	⅛ tsp. freshly grated lemon zest, or to taste

Melt butter in a heavy skillet over medium-low heat. Add garlic and cook, stirring occasionally, for 1 minute; increase the heat to high and cook, stirring, until garlic is a pale golden color.

Delightfully Different
Vary this recipe by substituting large peeled, deveined shrimp for the scallops.

Add scallops and cook, stirring occasionally, for 1½ to 2 minutes, or until scallops are just firm; transfer them with a slotted spoon to a platter, reserving their cooking liquid in the skillet. Add wine, tomatoes, and tarragon to the skillet. Boil mixture, stirring, until it is reduced in volume to about ¼ cup. Remove the pan from the heat, stir in parsley, scallops, and lemon zest. Serve scallops in warmed soup bowls, with sauce spooned over them.

Palate Preview
A fantastic blend of flavors. Tarragon adds an aromatic and slightly peppery taste to this scallops recipe. If you like the taste of tarragon, you can also use it over vegetables and in salad dressings. And even in baked desserts.

Spicy Steamed Clams

Prep time: 10 minutes • Cook time: 15 minutes • Serves: 2 • Serving size: 12 clams and 1½ cups vegetable broth

Nutritional Analysis per Serving: Glycemic Index 28 • Glycemic Load 5 • Calories 239 • Protein in grams 15 • Animal Protein 14 • Vegetable Protein 1 • Carbohydrates 18 grams • Dietary Fiber 2 grams • Net Carbohydrate 16 grams • Fat 8 grams • Saturated Fat 1 gram • Cholesterol 37 mg • Sodium 60 mg • Exchanges 2 lean meat, 1 fat, 3 vegetable

1 large garlic clove, minced

¼ tsp. crushed red pepper flakes

½ tsp. dried oregano

½ cup finely chopped onion

1¼ cups thinly sliced, cored fennel bulb

1 (14.-oz.) can no-salt-added chopped tomatoes, liquid reserved

½ cup dry white wine

24 small hard-shelled clams, scrubbed well

2 TB. minced fresh parsley

Heat oil in a heavy saucepan over medium-low heat. Add garlic, pepper flakes, and oregano and cook, stirring, for 1 minute. Add onion and fennel, and cook mixture over medium heat, stirring until fennel is softened. Add tomatoes and wine, and simmer uncovered, stirring occasionally, for 5 minutes. Add clams and cover. Steam for 5 to 7 minutes, or until clams are open. Discard any unopened clams. Add parsley and stir just to wilt. Spoon equal portions of clams and sauce to serving dishes and divide any sauce remaining in the pot between them. Serve hot.

Delightfully Different
If you want to soften the taste and make the intensity of the heat milder, omit the hot red pepper flakes.

Palate Preview
Fennel with tomatoes makes any meal a feast. This clam recipe is no exception. The dish is highly spiced and highly nutritious, with plenty of vegetables to give you three servings for the day.

Maryland Crab Cakes

Prep time: 20 minutes • Cook time: 6 to 8 minutes • Serves: 2 • Serving size: Two 4-ounce crab cakes

Nutritional Analysis per Serving: Glycemic Index 65 • Glycemic Load 15 • Calories 400 • Protein in grams 28 • Animal Protein 27 • Vegetable Protein 1 • Carbohydrates 23 grams • Dietary Fiber <1 gram • Net Carbohydrate 23 grams • Fat 20 grams • Saturated Fat 5 grams • Cholesterol 220 mg • Sodium 403 mg • Exchanges 1 starch, 4 lean meat, 4 fats

1 TB. unsalted butter

1 small garlic clove, minced

¼ cup finely chopped green bell pepper

¼ cup finely chopped red bell pepper

¼ cup plus 2 TB. unsalted, crushed saltine crackers

1 large egg, beaten lightly

2 TB. minced green onions

2 tsp. fresh lemon juice

1 tsp. Worcestershire sauce

Pinch cayenne

1 TB. nonfat mayonnaise

½ lb. lump crabmeat, picked over for bits of shell

All-purpose flour for coating the crab cakes

1 TB. vegetable oil

Lemon wedges for garnish

Palate Preview

Even though they seem exotic, crab cakes can become a regular quick meal. You can prepare the cooking mixture in advance, refrigerate, and then sauté at the last minute, right before you're ready to sit down to eat.

Melt butter in a small skillet over low heat. Add garlic and bell peppers and stir while cooking for 2 minutes or until softened. Transfer mixture to a bowl, add cracker crumbs, egg, green onions, lemon juice, Worcestershire sauce, cayenne, and mayonnaise, and mix well. Add crabmeat, stirring gently until mixture is just combined. Let stand for 10 minutes. Form crab mixture into four patties ½-inch thick and coat with flour.

In a large, heavy skillet heat oil over medium-high heat. Add crab cakes in a single layer and cook for 3 to 4 minutes on each side, or until they are golden brown, watching them carefully so they do not burn. Serve crab cakes with the lemon wedges.

Chapter 17

Fish Dishes

In This Chapter

- Fish dishes for everyday eating
- Naturally low-fat heart-healthy fish
- Best lean cooking methods for fish
- EFAs—essential fatty acids in salmon and other fish

The value of fish in our diets becomes more apparent almost daily. News releases about scientific research praise the health values of eating fish. For example, one study shows that men who eat at least one serving of fish a week have fewer heart attacks than those who don't eat fish. That's significant.

Most likely, you're aware that fish is a terrific food for persons with diabetes. Fish provides you a low-fat complete protein source with very little saturated fat. Plus, and this is a big plus, much of the fat in fish is comprised of the all-important omega-3 essential fatty acids.

The recipes in this chapter make fish eating a delicious experience. Whether you have eaten fish most of your life or are relatively new to its taste and goodness, you'll find recipes that you'll cook over and over again.

Oils from the Sea

By "oils from the sea" we're not referring to crude oil from offshore oil rigs. That's a different kind of oil. This chapter covers the wonderful and life-giving oils in fish.

Fish tastes good and is an enjoyable food all by itself, but it's also vitally nutritious. That's because it has omega-3 essential fatty acids—EFAs. Omega-3s are the least commonly available of all EFAs in our day-to-day diets. By contrast, the equally valuable omega-6s are present in most vegetable oils.

Omega-3s consist of docosahexaenoic, eicosapentaenoic, and alpha-linolenic acids. The first two are considered to be the most important omega-3 essential fatty acids and are found only in fish. Salmon and sardines are the fish with the highest amounts of these EFAs. Alpha-linolenic acid is found in fish, emu oil, and some vegetable-based oils, including flaxseed oil and walnut oil.

Even if you are faithfully taking flaxseed oil daily to get your EFAs, your body still needs omega-3s from fish. The scientific research studies that show positive impacts of EFAs on longevity, heart disease, aches and pains, and mood disorders were all based on consuming EFAs from fish and fish oil, not from vegetables.

Purchasing Fish

When purchasing fish, seek out wild fish. Farmed fish has been shown to be contaminated with toxins. Canned tuna, salmon, and sardines are wild. Some tuna, including albacore, contains high levels of mercury and should be avoided.

Avoid purchasing fish that has been frozen and then thawed—you'll lose taste and texture. You can't freeze it again when you get home. Instead, select the freshest and best-looking fish at the market.

The Least You Need to Know

- Fish, especially salmon and sardines, give you omega-3 essential fatty acids that your body needs for health and longevity.
- The proteins in fish cook quickly, usually within 5 to 20 minutes.
- Purchase fresh fish whenever possible for the best flavor.
- Avoid purchasing fish that has been frozen and then thawed.
- Fish lends itself to being baked, broiled, grilled, and marinated.

Grilled Fish with Curry Sauce

Prep time: 10 minutes plus 1 hour refrigeration • Cook time: 6 to 10 minutes •
Serves: 6 • Serving size: 4 ounces fish with ⅓ cup sauce

Nutritional Analysis per Serving: Glycemic Index 14 • Glycemic Load 1 • Calories 200
• Protein in grams 27 • Animal Protein 27 • Vegetable Protein <1 • Carbohydrates
6 grams • Dietary Fiber 0 • Net Carbohydrate 6 grams • Fat 3 grams •
Saturated Fat <1 gram • Cholesterol 73 mg • Sodium 188 mg • Exchanges
4 very lean meat, ½ fat, ½ milk

Fish:

Vegetable oil cooking spray

2 TB. fresh lemon juice

1 TB. olive oil

1 garlic clove, minced

6 (4-oz.) fish steaks, such as cod, haddock, or
swordfish

Sauce:

6 TB. fresh lemon juice

1½ tsp. mild curry powder

½ to ¼ tsp. ground cumin, or to taste

1 tsp. crushed coriander seeds

1 tsp. grated fresh gingerroot

2 cups nonfat plain yogurt

⅛ tsp. salt

⅛ tsp. freshly ground black pepper

Cilantro sprigs for garnish

Combine lemon juice, olive oil, and garlic. Pour into a
shallow glass or ceramic baking dishes large enough to
accommodate all fish steaks. (If necessary, use two baking dishes and divide the mixture between them.) Add
fish steaks, turn to coat, cover and refrigerate for 1
hour, turning steaks once halfway through.

Palate Preview _____
The mild curry sauce
dresses up this grilled-fish entrée.
Serve with steamed vegetables
and a tossed salad on the side.

For sauce, combine lemon juice, curry powder, cumin,
coriander, gingerroot, yogurt, cilantro, salt, and pepper
in a glass or ceramic container. Taste and adjust seasonings if necessary. Set aside.

When you are ready to cook, spray a grill rack or broiler pan with cooking spray. Preheat a gas
grill to medium or prepare a medium-hot fire in a charcoal grill, with the rack placed 4 to 6
inches above heat or preheat the broiler.

Remove fish steaks from marinade and brush them on both sides with marinade. Discard
remaining marinade. Place fish steaks on the grill or broiler pan and cook for 3 minutes on
each side or until fish is opaque and flakes easily with a fork. Remove from the heat and place
one fish steak on each plate. Spoon sauce over each, garnish with cilantro sprigs and serve.

Salmon with Fresh Fruit Salsa

Prep time: 20 minutes • Cook time: 35 minutes • Serves: 4 • Serving size: 4 ounces salmon with ½ cup salsa

Nutritional Analysis per Serving: Glycemic Index 50 • Glycemic Load 5 • Calories 260 • Protein in grams 28 • Animal Protein 27 • Vegetable Protein 1 • Carbohydrates 10 • Dietary Fiber < 1 • Net Carbohydrate 11 grams • Fat 13 grams • Saturated Fat 4 grams • Cholesterol 96 mg • Sodium 68 mg • Exchanges 4 lean meat, 1 fruit

Fish:

1 lb. salmon fillet, cut into 4 portions

½ tsp. no-salt chili powder

Salsa:

1 cup diced fresh pineapple

1 cup diced fresh cantaloupe

½ cup diced red bell pepper

¼ cup seasoned rice wine vinegar

2 TB. finely chopped fresh cilantro

¼ tsp. crushed red pepper flakes

Palate Preview You'll love the combination of salmon and fruit. In addition, this salsa adds a spicy zing for your taste buds.

Preheat the oven to 350°F. Spray a 9×9-inch baking pan with olive oil cooking spray. Place salmon fillets in the pan in a single layer and sprinkle with chili powder. Spray fillets lightly with cooking spray and bake, uncovered, for 35 minutes or the thickest part of fillet is translucent. Meanwhile, mix pineapple, cantaloupe, red bell pepper, vinegar, cilantro, and red pepper flakes together in a small bowl. Set aside.

Top each fillet with ½ cup salsa and serve.

Sesame Crusted Halibut

Prep time: 10 minutes plus 15 minutes refrigeration   •   Cook time: 10 minutes   •
Serves: 4   •   Serving size: 4 ounces fish

Nutritional Analysis per Serving: Glycemic Index (not significant)   •   Glycemic Load (not
significant)   •   Calories 238   •   Protein in grams 30   •   Animal Protein 29   •
Vegetable Protein 1   •   Carbohydrates <1 gram   •   Dietary Fiber 0   •   Net
Carbohydrate 0   •   Fat 11 grams   •   Saturated Fat 2 grams   •   Cholesterol 54 mg   •
Sodium 93 mg   •   Exchanges 4 very lean meat, 2 fat

2 TB. fresh lemon juice	1 (1-lb.) halibut fillet, cut into four portions
2 TB. extra-virgin olive oil	2 TB. sesame seeds
1 clove minced garlic	1½ to 2 tsp. dried thyme
½ tsp. freshly ground black pepper	Lemon wedges for garnish

Preheat the oven to 450°F. Line a baking sheet with foil.

Mix lemon juice, oil, garlic, and pepper in a shallow glass or ceramic dish. Add halibut fillets
and turn to coat. Cover and refrigerate for 15 minutes.

Meanwhile, toast sesame seeds in a small dry skillet
over medium-low heat, stirring constantly, for 2 to
3 minutes or until golden and fragrant. Transfer to a
small bowl to cool. Mix in thyme.

Palate Preview
Sesame seeds contain
good-for-you monounsaturated fats.
They add a crunchy and slightly
exotic flavor to the baked halibut.

When you are ready to cook, remove halibut from
marinade and discard marinade. Coat fish evenly with
sesame seed mixture and arrange it on the prepared
baking sheet in a single layer. Roast for 10 to 14 minutes or until just opaque in the center. Serve with
lemon wedges.

Lemon-Thyme Grilled Tuna

Prep time: 5 minutes plus 30 minutes refrigeration • Cook time: 8 minutes • Serves: 4 • Serving size: 4 ounces fish

Nutritional Analysis per Serving: Glycemic Index (not significant) • Glycemic Load (not significant) • Calories 186 • Protein in grams 28 • Animal Protein 28 • Vegetable Protein <1 • Carbohydrates <1 gram • Dietary Fiber 0 • Net Carbohydrate 0 • Fat 9 grams • Saturated Fat 1 gram • Cholesterol 52 mg • Sodium 318 mg • Exchanges 4 very lean meat, 1½ fat

4 (4-oz.) yellow fin tuna steaks (1½-inch thick)	1 tsp. fresh or dried grated lemon zest
2 TB olive oil	½ tsp. freshly ground black pepper
2 tsp. finely chopped fresh thyme	¼ cup fresh lemon juice
½ tsp. salt	

Palate Preview You'll appreciate the simple, delicious taste of fresh tuna that's been marinated in lemon juice seasoned with the garden herb thyme.

Place tuna steaks in a large self-closing plastic bag. Add oil, thyme, salt, lemon zest, pepper, and lemon juice and seal the bag. Turn the bag to coat fish. Refrigerate at least 30 minutes.

When you are ready to cook, spray a grill rack with cooking spray. Preheat a gas grill to medium or prepare a medium-hot fire in a charcoal grill, with the rack placed 4 to 6 inches above the heat. Remove tuna steaks from marinade and discard marinade. Place tuna on the grill and cook 6 to 7 minutes or until tuna is firm but still pink inside and flakes easily with fork, turning once.

Creole Catfish Cakes

Prep time: 15 minutes   •   Cook time: 12 minutes   •   Serves: 4   •   Serving size: 3-ounce cake

Nutritional Analysis per Serving: Glycemic Index 52   •   Glycemic Load 8   •   Calories 217   •   Protein in grams 20   •   Animal Protein 18   •   Vegetable Protein 2   •   Carbohydrates 18 grams   •   Dietary Fiber 2 grams   •   Net Carbohydrate 16 grams   •   Fat 10 grams   •   Saturated Fat 2 grams   •   Cholesterol 79 mg   •   Sodium 158 mg   •   Exchanges 2½ lean meat, 1 starch, 1 fat

½ lb. skinless catfish fillets	¼ cup chopped green onions
⅛ tsp. salt	¼ cup finely chopped red or green bell pepper
⅛ tsp. freshly ground black pepper	1 tsp. dried no-salt Creole seasoning
¾ cup whole-grain cornmeal	¼ cup low-fat buttermilk
1 tsp. baking powder	1 egg
	1 TB. olive oil

Sprinkle catfish fillets with salt and pepper. Place in a 13×9-inch (3 quart) microwave-safe baking dish. Cover and microwave on high power for 5 to 8 minutes or until catfish flakes easily with a fork.

With a slotted spoon, remove fish from the baking dish and place it in a large bowl. With a fork, break fish into small pieces. Add cornmeal, baking powder, green onions, bell pepper, and Creole seasoning, and mix well. In a small bowl combine buttermilk and egg, and blend well. Add catfish mixture and mix well.

Heat 1 tablespoon oil on a griddle or in a large skillet, over medium-high heat. Drop catfish mixture by ¼ cupfuls onto the hot griddle, for a total of eight fish cakes. Flatten to form patties. Cook 2 to 4 minutes or until lightly browned, turning once.

Palate Preview

If you love cornmeal-crusted fried fish, you'll love Creole catfish cakes. The cakes have that wonderful crunch and Southern-style seasoning. They are pan-fried in just the slightest amount of olive oil to keep your meal healthy.

Primavera Fish Fillets

Prep time: 15 minutes • Cook time: 15 minutes • Serves: 4 • Serving size: 4 ounces fish with 1¼ cups vegetables

Nutritional Analysis per Serving: Glycemic Index 13 • Glycemic Load 1 • Calories 177 • Protein in grams 28 • Animal Protein 26 • Vegetable Protein 2 • Carbohydrates 7 grams • Dietary Fiber 2 ½ grams • Net Carbohydrate 5 grams • Fat 11 grams • Saturated Fat 3 grams • Cholesterol 38 mg • Sodium 216 mg • Exchanges 4 very lean meat, 1 fat, 1 vegetable

4 (4-oz.) fresh or frozen orange roughy fillets	1 cup julienne-cut (2½ × ⅛ × ⅛-inch) carrots
2 TB. unsalted butter	1 cup sliced fresh white mushrooms
1 TB. fresh lemon juice	½ cup diagonally sliced celery
¼ tsp. freshly ground black pepper	⅛ tsp. salt
1 garlic clove, minced	¼ tsp. dried basil
1½ cups fresh broccoli florets	2 TB. grated Parmesan cheese
1 cup fresh cauliflower florets	

Palate Preview

Orange roughy is served on a bed of sautéed vegetables: broccoli, cauliflower, mushrooms, and celery, seasoned with basil, then sprinkled with Parmesan cheese. Makes for an interesting and healthy fish dish.

Delightfully Different

Substitute other firm-bodied fish for the orange roughy. You can use salmon, trout, snapper, and any other you may prefer.

Heat the oven to 450°F. Thaw roughy if frozen. Place 1 tablespoon butter into a 13×9-inch glass or ceramic baking dish and melt in the oven. Place roughy fillets in melted butter and turn to coat, arranging fillets in a single layer. Sprinkle with lemon juice and pepper. Bake for 5 minutes. Remove from the oven.

While fish is baking, melt remaining 1 tablespoon butter in large skillet over medium-high heat. Add garlic and cook until lightly browned. Add broccoli, cauliflower, carrots, mushrooms, celery, salt, and basil. Cook, stirring, for 5 to 6 minutes or until vegetables are crisp-tender.

Spoon hot vegetables into the center of the baking dish, moving fish to the sides of the dish. Sprinkle vegetables and fish with Parmesan cheese.

Return the dish to the oven and bake an additional 3 to 5 minutes or until fish flakes easily with a fork.

Baked Salmon with Cilantro Pesto

Prep time: 10 minutes   •   Cook time: 35 minutes   •   Serves: 4   •   Serving size: 4 ounces

Nutritional Analysis per Serving: Glycemic Index (not significant)   •   Glycemic Load (not significant)   •   Calories 231   •   Protein in grams 27   •   Animal Protein 27   •   Vegetable Protein 0   •   Carbohydrates < 1 gram   •   Dietary Fiber 0   •   Net Carbohydrate 0   •   Fat 14 grams   •   Saturated Fat 4 grams   •   Cholesterol 96 mg   •   Sodium 89 mg   •   Exchanges 4 lean meat, ½ fat

1 (1-lb.) salmon fillet, cut into 4 portions	1 tsp. finely chopped pickled jalapeño chili peppers
Olive oil cooking spray	2 TB. low-salt chicken broth
⅛ cup fresh lime juice	1 TB. olive oil
⅓ cup thinly sliced green onions	¾ cup minced fresh cilantro

Preheat the oven to 350°F.

Using a sharp knife, score skin side of salmon fillets lightly to prevent curling. Place fillets, skin side down, in a 9×9-inch baking dish. Spray fillets lightly with olive oil cooking spray.

For sauce, in a small bowl, combine lime juice, green onions, jalapeño chili, chicken broth, olive oil, and cilantro. Spread ½ of cilantro sauce evenly over fillets.

Bake fillets, uncovered, for about 35 minutes or until thickest part of fillet is slightly translucent for medium-rare. Continue cooking for 5 minutes for medium. Spoon remaining sauce over fillets and serve.

Palate Preview _____

The cilantro pesto gives the salmon a fresh, light, and spicy taste yet it's richness will satisfy your hunger for a substantial meal.

Red Snapper with Fennel and Bell Peppers

Prep time: 10 minutes • Cook time: 20 minutes • Serves: 4 • Serving size: 4 ounces fish

Nutritional Analysis per Serving: Glycemic Index (not significant) • Glycemic Load (not significant) • Calories 176 • Protein in grams 26 • Animal Protein 25 • Vegetable Protein 1 • Carbohydrates 8 grams • Dietary Fiber 2 grams • Net Carbohydrate 6 grams • Fat 5 grams • Saturated Fat 1 gram • Cholesterol 41 mg • Sodium 244 mg • Exchanges 4 very lean meat, 1 fat, 1 vegetable

1 fennel bulb with stalks, cored, and cut into ½ inch slices, reserving leaves	1 small onion, cut into ½-inch-thick wedges
1 red bell pepper, cored, seeded, and cut into ½-inch-wide strips	1 TB. olive oil
	1 lb. red snapper fillets, in 4 portions
1 yellow bell pepper, cored, seeded, and cut into ½-inch-wide strips	¼ tsp. salt
	¼ tsp. coarsely ground black pepper

Preheat the oven to 425°F. In large bowl toss fennel slices, bell peppers, and onion with oil. Place in an ungreased 15×10×1-inch baking pan. Bake for 5 minutes.

Palate Preview _____ Fennel adds an aromatic taste and crunchy texture to fish. Adding the yellow and red bell peppers gives color to the baked snapper.

Remove the pan from the oven. Push aside vegetables, and add snapper fillets to the pan in a single layer; sprinkle with salt and pepper. Surround fillets with partially baked vegetables.

Return the pan to the oven and bake an additional 10 to 15 minutes or until fish flakes easily with a fork. Serve snapper and vegetables garnished with fennel leaves.

Pecan-Crusted Catfish

Prep time: 10 minutes   •   Cook time: 15 to 20 minutes   •   Serves: 4   •   Serving size: 4 ounces catfish fillet with 2 teaspoons topping

Nutritional Analysis per Serving: Glycemic Index (not significant)   •   Glycemic Load (not significant)   •   Calories 205   •   Protein in grams 26   •   Animal Protein 15   •   Vegetable Protein 1   •   Carbohydrates < 1 gram   •   Dietary Fiber < 1 gram   •   Net Carbohydrate 0   •   Fat 14 grams   •   Saturated Fat 2 grams   •   Cholesterol 53 mg   •   Sodium 131 mg   •   Exchanges 4 lean meat, 1½ fat

1 shallot, chopped	1 tsp. grated lemon zest
2 TB. finely chopped pecans	1 TB. fresh lemon juice
1 tsp. chopped fresh marjoram or ¼ tsp. dried marjoram	⅛ tsp. salt
	¼ tsp. cracked black pepper
1 tsp. chopped fresh parsley or ¼ tsp. dried parsley	4 (4-oz.) catfish fillets
	1 TB. olive oil

Spray a grill rack with cooking spray. Preheat a gas grill to medium or prepare a medium-hot fire in a charcoal grill, with the rack placed 4 to 6 inches above the heat.

In a small bowl, combine shallot, pecans, marjoram, parsley, lemon zest, lemon juice, salt, and pepper. Place catfish fillets in large shallow glass or ceramic dish in a single layer. Brush one side with oil. Top each fillet evenly with pecan mixture and press into the surface of fillets.

Carefully place catfish, coated side up, on the grill and cover the grill, or make a tent of foil and place it over catfish. Cook 15 to 20 minutes or until thickest part of catfish flakes easily with a fork.

Note: Preheat oven to 350°F. Spray an unheated baking dish with cooking spray and place catfish fillets in a single layer. Brush one side with oil. Top each fillet evenly with pecan mixture and press into the surface of the fillets. Cover dish with foil and bake for 15 to 20 minutes.

Palate Preview

Pecans with marjoram, parsley, and lemon make a delicious baked topping for catfish. Pecans contain plenty of monounsaturated fats—the good-for-you kind.

Citrus Dill Salmon

Prep time: 10 minutes • Cook time: 10 to 12 minutes • Serves: 2 • Serving size
4 ounces salmon

Nutritional Analysis per Serving: Glycemic Index (not significant) • Glycemic Load (not
significant) • Calories 236 • Protein in grams 25 • Animal Protein 25 •
Vegetable Protein <1 • Carbohydrates <1 gram • Dietary Fiber <1 gram • Net
Carbohydrate 0 • Fat 10 grams • Saturated Fat 4 grams • Cholesterol 72 mg •
Sodium 238 mg • Exchanges 4 lean meat, 1½ fat

Vegetable oil cooking spray	¼ tsp. grated lemon zest
1 TB. unsalted butter, softened	1 tsp. fresh lemon juice
1 tsp. chopped fresh chives or ¼ tsp. dried chives	⅛ tsp. salt
1 tsp. chopped fresh dill or ¼ tsp. dried dill	2 (4-oz.) salmon fillets
	2 sprigs fresh dill

Spray a grill rack with cooking spray. Preheat a gas grill to medium or prepare a medium-hot
fire in a charcoal grill, with the rack placed 4 to 6 inches above the heat.

In a small bowl, combine butter, chives, dill, lemon zest, lemon juice, and salt. Mix until well
blended.

With salmon fillets skin side up, spread ½ teaspoon butter mixture over each fillet. Place fillets,
skin side up on the grill and cook 3 minutes. Turn skin side down and spread ½ tsp butter over
each fillet. Cook 8 to 10 minutes or until fish flakes easily with a fork.

Palate Preview
This grilled salmon
recipe brings you two big rewards.
First, it tastes great because of the
citrus and dill. Second, salmon
contains high amounts of essential
fatty acids—EFAs—that your body
requires for overall strength and
health.

Note: To broil fish, preheat the broiler. Spray an
unheated broiler pan with cooking spray and place fish
on it. Broil 4 to 6 inches from heat according to above
instructions.

Place fillets, skin side up, on the grill and cook 3 minutes. Turn skin side down and spread ½ tsp butter over
the top of fillets. Cook 8 to 10 minutes or until fish
flakes easily with a fork.

To serve, spread remaining butter mixture over salmon
fillets. Garnish with dill sprigs.

Lime-Marinated Swordfish with Pineapple Salsa

Prep time: 5 minutes plus 30 minutes refrigeration • Cook time: 12 to 15 minutes •
Serves: 4 • Serving size: 4 ounces fish with 3 tablespoons salsa

Nutritional Analysis per Serving: Glycemic Index 51 • Glycemic Load 4 • Calories 168
• Protein in grams 25 • Animal Protein 25 • Vegetable Protein < 1 •
Carbohydrates 8 grams • Dietary Fiber < 1 gram • Net Carbohydrate 8 grams • Fat
4 grams • Saturated Fat 1 gram • Cholesterol 44 mg • Sodium 166 mg •
Exchanges 4 very lean meat, ½ fruit

Swordfish:

3 garlic cloves, minced

2 tsp. grated lime zest

⅛ tsp. salt

4 (4-oz.) swordfish steaks

Pineapple salsa:

1 (8-oz.) can pineapple tidbits in unsweetened juice, liquid reserved

¼ cup chopped red bell pepper

2 TB. chopped red onion

1 TB. chopped fresh cilantro

1 jalapeño chili pepper, finely chopped

Finely chop garlic, lime zest, and salt together. Rub onto the surface of swordfish steaks.

Cut four 15 × 12-inch pieces of foil. Place one swordfish steak in the center of each piece of foil. Wrap securely using double-fold seals. Place the folded packets on a baking sheet. Refrigerate 30 minutes.

Meanwhile, in medium bowl, combine pineapple, red bell pepper, onion, cilantro, and jalapeño chili with 2 tablespoons of reserved pineapple juice. Mix well. Set aside.

Preheat the oven to 450°F. Place the fish packets, on the baking sheet into the oven and bake for 10 to 12 minutes or until fish flakes easily with a fork.

To serve, place each steak on a serving dish and spoon salsa over it. Or for a dramatic presentation, place each foil pouch on a serving dish and slit open the foil to make "petals." Spoon salsa over each swordfish steak in its foil pouch and serve.

 **Palate Preview**
Pineapple salsa adds a festive note to this swordfish recipe. Salsa always seems festive with its unusual blending of flavors: sweet, tangy, and chili hot.

Red Snapper Fillets in Champagne Sauce

Prep time: 10 minutes • Cook time: 15 to 20 minutes • Serves: 4 • Serving size: 4 ounces fish with 2 tablespoons stuffing

Nutritional Analysis per Serving: Glycemic Index (not significant) • Glycemic Load (not significant) • Calories 175 • Protein in grams 26 • Animal Protein 26 • Vegetable Protein < 1 • Carbohydrates 1 gram • Dietary Fiber 0 • Net Carbohydrate 1 gram • Fat 2 grams • Saturated Fat ½ gram • Cholesterol 41 mg • Sodium 208 mg • Exchanges 4 lean meat, ½ alcohol

1 lb. fresh or frozen skinless red snapper fillets or any other delicate- to moderate-flavored fillet, in 4 portions

1 (3-oz.) pkg. nonfat cream cheese

1 tsp. crumbled blue cheese

1 TB. minced shallot or mild onion

1 TB. chopped, drained canned pimiento

1 cup Champagne or sparkling wine

Vegetable oil cooking spray

Lemon wedges for garnish

Parsley sprigs for garnish

Thaw fish if frozen. Cut into eight pieces.

Preheat the oven to 375°F.

In a small bowl, combine cheeses, shallots, and chopped pimiento. Mash together into a paste. Add enough Champagne to produce the consistency of a spread. Spread equal portions of cheese mixture over four fillet pieces. Top with remaining pieces of fillet.

Palate Preview — The cheeses are sandwiched between two layers of fish fillets and baked, making for a sparkling fish entrée.

Spray a baking pan with cooking spray and place fillet sandwiches into it in a single layer. Pour remaining champagne over and around them. Bake for 15 to 20 minutes, or until fish flakes easily with a fork. Remove sandwiches to a heated serving platter, reserving Champagne sauce in a small bowl. Garnish the platter with lemon wedges and parsley. Serve at once, passing Champagne sauce separately.

Fish Veracruz

Prep time: 10 minutes   •   Cook time: 8 to 10 minutes   •   Serves: 6   •   Serving size: 4 ounces fish with 2½ tablespoons sauce

Nutritional Analysis per Serving: Glycemic Index 33   •   Glycemic Load 4   •   Calories 210   •   Protein in grams 28   •   Animal Protein 26   •   Vegetable Protein 2   •   Carbohydrates 9 grams   •   Dietary Fiber 3 grams   •   Net Carbohydrate 6 grams   •   Fat 5 grams   •   Saturated Fat 1 gram   •   Cholesterol 41 mg   •   Sodium 380 mg   •   Exchanges 4 very lean meat, 1 vegetable, 1 fat

Fish:

1 lb. red snapper fillets, in 6 portions

Juice of 1½ lemons

Freshly ground black pepper to taste

Sauce:

1 TB. olive oil

1½ medium onions, sliced into thin strips

3 large garlic cloves, minced

2¼ lb. (about 12 medium) tomatoes, chopped

3 TB. sliced, pitted green olives

2 TB. drained capers

1 can jalapeño pepper, seeded and sliced

Freshly ground pepper to taste

Sprinkle fish with lemon juice and pepper. Set aside.

For sauce, heat olive oil in a heavy-bottom saucepan over medium heat, and add onions and garlic. Sauté, stirring, until onions are tender. Add tomatoes, olives, capers, and jalapeño, and bring to a simmer, stirring occasionally, for 30 minutes. Add pepper to taste and remove from the heat.

Preheat the oven to 450°F. Cut six double thicknesses of aluminum foil, large enough to accommodate fillets. Brush fillets with olive oil and place them on the foil squares. Spoon about 2 heaping tablespoons of sauce over each portion. Fold the foil loosely over fish and crimp the edges together tightly. Place on a baking sheet.

Bake for 8 to 10 minutes. Place each foil pouch on a serving dish and have guests open them at the table.

Palate Preview

The red snapper is smothered with a sauce of tomatoes, olives, capers, and jalapeño. Then it's cooked in aluminum-foil "bags" to hold in the moisture. Serve fish in the foil on individual plates and everyone can open their fish package. Similar to fish preparation style in Veracruz, Mexico.

Sea Bass Habanero

Prep time: 10 minutes • Cook time: 20 minutes • Serves: 4 • Serving size: 4 to 5 ounces fish with vegetable broth

Nutritional Analysis per Serving: Glycemic Index 43 • Glycemic Load 4 • Calories 247 • Protein in grams 27 • Animal Protein 26 • Vegetable Protein 1 • Carbohydrates 9 grams • Dietary Fiber 1 gram • Net Carbohydrate 8 grams • Fat 5 grams • Saturated Fat 1 gram • Cholesterol 70 mg • Sodium 188 mg • Exchanges 4 very lean meat, ½ fruit, 1 fat, ½ alcohol

1 TB. olive oil	⅛ tsp. salt
4 (4–5-oz.) sea bass fillets with skin	⅛ tsp. freshly ground black pepper
1 small onion, thinly sliced	1 cup dry white wine
1 large tomato, seeded, cut into thick strips	¼ cup water
1 small mango, peeled, pitted and chopped	Juice of 1 lime
4 garlic cloves, minced	¼ cup chopped fresh cilantro
1 habanero chili, seeded, and sliced	

Heat olive oil in a skillet over medium-high heat. Place sea bass fillets into it, skin side up, in a single layer, and cook for 1 minute per side or until brown and slightly opaque. Remove to a platter, reserving the pan drippings in the pan. Add onion to the pan and cook for 3 minutes or until browned. Increase the heat to high. Add tomato, mango, garlic, habanero chili, salt, and pepper and cook, stirring constantly, for 2 minutes or until fragrant. Stir in wine. Cook, stirring constantly, for 2 minutes or until reduced in volume by half. Stir in water. Bring to a boil and reduce heat to medium-low. Simmer, stirring constantly, for 2 minutes.

Squeeze lime juice into spicy vegetable broth, stir once, and carefully place fillets into it. Cook, covered, for 1 to 3 minutes or until fish flakes easily with a fork. Carefully transfer fillets and equal portions of spicy vegetable broth into four shallow soup bowls, garnish each with cilantro and serve.

Delightfully Different

If you prefer a milder taste, omit the habanero chili. Or substitute a pinch of chili powder for just a little heat.

Palate Preview

Sea bass prepared this way is essentially poached in a sauce of onion, mango, tomato, garlic, habanero chili, and white wine. Habanero chilies are among the hottest, so adjust the amount to suit your taste. The sea bass is utterly delicious, and *very* spicy. You can temper the "heat" to suit your taste buds.

Part 6 Combination Main Dishes

The combination of ingredients—lean proteins, healthy fats, and vegetables—prepared and cooked together delivers great health and eating value. Here are recipes for timesaving one-pot meals, plus soups and stews.

The main-dish salads meet your highest expectations for interesting tastes and textures. The recipes feature many of your favorite tastes, all designed with a focus on eating for health and pleasure.

Chapter 18

One-Pot Meals

In This Chapter

- ◆ Complete meals cooked in one pot
- ◆ Traditional favorites for diabetic meals
- ◆ Spending less time in the kitchen
- ◆ Using the best ingredients

One-pot meals are now a solid American tradition. They offer time savings and convenience. No longer must you slave over a hot stove all day to prepare delicious and healthful meals. With one-pot meals, your time is freed up for other fun or important activities.

Many popular one-pot meals aren't suitable for persons with diabetes. Often the recipes call for canned soups, which are high in salt, or for a high proportion of noodles or rice, which make the meal high glycemic, thus, giving the meals high-glycemic loads.

In this chapter, you'll find recipes for one-pot meals with familiar tastes, such as Pot Roast and Gravy, Burgundy Beef, and Family Hamburger Casserole. Included are recipes for Turkey Pasta Casserole, Chicken à la King, and more. All of them are low salt and low fat. Each serving has a low glycemic load that fits beautifully into your meal plans.

Appeal of One-Pot Meals

One-pot meals are becoming more and more popular. Our busy lifestyles make for less time to spend in the kitchen cooking. Yet we all want to eat delicious and healthy home cooking. One-pot meals are a great solution. We spend less time in the kitchen and still enjoy nutritious food.

By making one-pot meals, a family can avoid the temptation of going out for fast food when they're pressed for time. A one-pot meal often takes less prep time than the time it takes to drive to a fast-food joint. Needless to say, these one-pot meals are more likely better for you than standard fast food.

Using Low-Salt Liquids

The recipes in this chapter work well for persons with diabetes because they are designed to meet your nutritional needs. Here are a few critical do's and don'ts:

- Do use low-salt soups. Don't substitute regular soups because they have high-salt counts.
- Do use low-salt broths and bouillons. Don't use regular bouillon or broth. They are way too high in salt.
- Do use low-salt canned goods, such as low-salt tomatoes. Regular canned vegetables are high in salt.

Seasonings, such as herbs, spices, garlic, onions, freshly ground black pepper and condiments, lend great taste and satisfaction to these recipes.

The Least You Need to Know

- One-pot meals save you time and add convenience to your daily routine.
- One-pot meals combine meat or poultry with vegetables and seasonings and perhaps starches, such as pasta or rice.
- Most of the cooking time for one-pot meals is for baking in the oven or simmering on the stove or in the slow cooker.
- Use low-salt canned products and low-salt broths and bouillons to keep the sodium levels in these recipes low.

Pot Roast and Gravy

Prep time: 20 minutes   •   Cook time: 2 hours 15 minutes   •   Serves: 6   •   Serving size: 4 ounces pot roast with 1 cup vegetables

Nutritional Analysis per Serving: Glycemic Index 34   •   Glycemic Load 5   •   Calories 325   •   Protein in grams 29   •   Animal Protein 27   •   Vegetable Protein 2   •   Carbohydrates 15 grams   •   Dietary Fiber 2 grams   •   Net Carbohydrate 13 grams   •   Fat 17 grams   •   Saturated Fat 3 grams   •   Cholesterol 72 mg   •   Sodium 86 mg   •   Exchanges 4 medium-lean meat, 1 fat, ½ starch, 1 vegetable

2 TB. olive oil	2 bay leaves
1 (1½-lb.) beef chuck arm, blade, or seven bone chuck roast, trimmed of all fat	2 tsp. low-salt instant beef-flavor bouillon
½ tsp. freshly ground black pepper	1½ cups boiling water
5 medium onions, quartered	2 TB. chopped garlic
6 stalks celery, cut into ½ inch pieces, leaves removed	8 medium carrots, cut into ½ inch pieces
	¼ cup cold water
	3 TB. all-purpose flour

Preheat the oven to 325°F. In a 5-quart Dutch oven or ovenproof skillet, heat oil over medium-high heat, add beef and cook about 5 minutes on each side or until browned. Drain off excess fat.

Sprinkle pepper on all sides of beef. Add 1 onion (in pieces), 1 stalk celery (in pieces) and bay leaves to beef. Dissolve bouillon in boiling water, reserving ¾ cup. Pour remaining ¾ cup bouillon around beef. Bring to a boil and cover.

Bake for 1 hour. Add garlic, carrots, and remaining onions, and celery. Cover and bake an additional 1 to 1¼ hours or until beef and vegetables are tender.

To prepare gravy, place beef and vegetables on a warm platter, and cover loosely to keep warm. Remove and discard bay leaves. Transfer cooking liquid from the Dutch oven to a heat-proof measuring container and skim off fat. Add enough reserved bouillon to make 3 cups. Return liquid to the Dutch oven.

In small a jar with a tight-fitting lid, combine cold water and flour, and shake well. Gradually stir flour mixture into liquid in the Dutch oven. Cook over medium heat, stirring constantly, until mixture boils and thickens. Serve gravy with beef and vegetables.

Palate Preview
An all-time classic pot roast with gravy included. This dish is just right, with very tender meat and simple seasonings of black pepper, garlic, onions, and bay leaf.

Burgundy Beef

Prep time: 15 minutes • Cook time: 3 hours • Serves: 10 • Serving size: 1 cup

Nutritional Analysis per Serving: Glycemic Index 34 • Glycemic Load 4 • Calories 243 • Protein in grams 19 • Animal Protein 17 • Vegetable Protein 2 • Carbohydrates 11 grams • Dietary Fiber 2 grams • Net Carbohydrate 9 grams • Fat 10 grams • Saturated Fat 2 grams • Cholesterol 63 mg • Sodium 156 mg • Exchanges 2½ lean meat, ½ starch, 1 vegetable, 1 fat

2 TB. olive oil

2½ lb. beef round steak, cut into cubes, trimmed of all fat

2 cups burgundy wine or other dry red wine

½ cup water

1 (10½-oz.) can low-salt condensed beef broth

½ tsp. dried thyme

4 garlic cloves, minced

1 bay leaf

16 small onions, or 1 (16-oz.) package frozen small onions, thawed

16 baby carrots or 5 carrots, cut into 2-inch pieces

3 TB. water

3 TB. all-purpose flour

1 cup frozen peas, thawed

2 TB. chopped fresh parsley (optional)

Palate Preview

A one-pot meal with the classic taste of the French country-side. Serve with steamed vegetables or a fresh garden salad with vinaigrette dressing.

Delightfully Different

If using wine in cooking doesn't appeal to you, you can substitute water or water with 1 or 2 tablespoon lemon juice or vinegar.

Preheat oven to 350°F. In a 5-quart Dutch oven or ovenproof skillet, heat oil over medium-high heat, add beef and cook, stirring, until browned. Stir in wine, water, beef broth, thyme, garlic, and bay leaf. Cover and bake for 2 hours, stirring occasionally. Add onions and carrots, and bake, covered, for an additional 1 to 1½ hours or until meat and vegetables are tender, stirring occasionally.

Remove the pot from oven, and discard bay leaf. Remove meat and vegetables from the pot and keep warm. To make gravy, in a small bowl combine water and flour, and gradually add about ½ cup cooking liquid, stirring until smooth. Stir flour mixture into remaining liquid in the pot. Cook over medium heat, stirring constantly, until mixture thickens. Add meat, cooked vegetables and peas. Heat thoroughly. Sprinkle with parsley, if desired. Remove bay leaf before serving.

Family Hamburger Casserole

Prep time: 15 minutes • Cook time: 45 minutes • Serves: 6 • Serving size: 1¼ cups casserole

Nutritional Analysis per Serving: Glycemic Index 46 • Glycemic Load 11 • Calories 277 • Protein in grams 18 • Animal Protein 16 • Vegetable Protein 2 • Carbohydrates 26 grams • Dietary Fiber 2 grams • Net Carbohydrate 24 grams • Fat 8 grams • Saturated Fat 3 grams • Cholesterol 46 mg • Sodium 191 mg • Exchanges 2½ medium-lean meat, 1½ starch, 1 vegetable

1 lb. lean ground beef	½ tsp. freshly ground black pepper
1 large onion, chopped	1 can (10¾-oz.) low-salt, condensed tomato soup
2 TB. chopped garlic	
2 cups cooked long-grain brown rice	¼ cup water
	4 cups coleslaw mix or shredded cabbage

Preheat the oven to 400°F.

Cook beef, garlic, and onion in 10-inch skillet over medium heat, stirring occasionally, for 8 to 10 minutes or until beef is browned. Drain. Stir in rice, pepper, soup, and water.

Place coleslaw mix or shredded cabbage in an ungreased 2-quart casserole. Spoon beef mixture over coleslaw mix or shredded cabbage. Cover and bake about 45 minutes or until hot and bubbly.

Palate Preview

Ground beef combined with cabbage makes a nutritious and interesting casserole meal. Easy to prepare—just put the ingredients together in a casserole dish and bake for 45 minutes. A great meal for a busy day.

Turkey-Pasta Casserole

Prep time: 25 minutes • Cook time: 40 minutes • Serves: 6 • Serving size: 1½ cups casserole

Nutritional Analysis per Serving: Glycemic Index 43 • Glycemic Load 16 • Calories 351 • Protein in grams 21 • Animal Protein 19 • Vegetable Protein 2 • Carbohydrates 37 grams • Dietary Fiber 3 grams • Net Carbohydrate 34 grams • Fat 16 grams • Saturated Fat 2 grams • Cholesterol 38 mg • Sodium 167 mg • Exchanges 2½ lean meat, 2 starch, 1 vegetable, 2 fat

Casserole:

Vegetable oil cooking spray

1 cup uncooked whole-grain elbow macaroni

1 lb. ground turkey breast

¾ tsp. no-salt garlic-pepper blend

3 medium zucchinis, chopped

2 TB. chopped fresh basil or 2 tsp. dried basil

1 cup sliced white mushrooms

1 (10-oz.) container light Alfredo sauce (from the supermarket refrigerator aisle

Topping:

¼ cup bread crumbs

1 tsp. unsalted butter

Preheat the oven to 350°F. Spray a 2½-quart casserole with cooking spray. Bring a pot of water to a boil according to package directions and cook macaroni for about 6 minutes or until al dente (firm to the bite).

Palate Preview This recipe is an everyday turkey one-pot meal with an Italian flavor. The Alfredo sauce adds a rich, creamy taste.

Spray a large nonstick skillet with cooking spray and add turkey. Season with garlic-pepper blend and mix to work seasoning into meat. Cook over medium-high heat for 6 to 8 minutes or until turkey is no longer pink.

Add cooked macaroni, zucchinis, basil, mushrooms, and Alfredo sauce to turkey mixture. Mix well. Spoon mixture into the prepared casserole. In small bowl, combine bread crumbs and butter, and mix well. Sprinkle over casserole. Bake for 40 minutes or until hot and lightly bubbling.

Stewed Chicken with Mushrooms and Onions

Prep time: 20 minutes • Cook time: 30 minutes • Serves: 4 • Serving size: 4 ounces chicken and 1 cup vegetables

Nutritional Analysis per Serving: Glycemic Index 31 • Glycemic Load 4 • Calories 242 • Protein in grams 28 • Animal Protein 27 • Vegetable Protein 1 • Carbohydrates 14 grams • Dietary Fiber 2 grams • Net Carbohydrate 12 grams • Fat 8 grams • Saturated Fat 2 grams • Cholesterol 31 mg • Sodium 122 mg • Exchanges 4 lean meat, 1 vegetable, ½ starch, 1 fat

¼ cup whole-wheat flour	½ cup dry white wine
3 tsp. paprika	1 TB. tomato paste
⅛ tsp. salt	1 tsp. dried *herbs de Provence*
4 (4-oz.) skinless, boneless chicken breast halves	2 (8-oz.) pkg. sliced fresh white mushrooms
1 TB. vegetable oil	3 TB. chopped garlic
	1 cup frozen small whole onions, thawed

In a large self-closing plastic bag, combine flour, paprika, and salt. Mix well. Add chicken to bag and seal. Shake to coat chicken with flour mixture.

Heat oil in a 12-inch nonstick skillet over medium heat until hot. Remove chicken from flour mixture. Place chicken in skillet in a single layer and cook about 9 minutes, turning once.

Add wine, tomato paste, and *herbs de Provence*, blending well, so that paste dissolves. Stir in mushrooms, garlic, and onions. Reduce heat, cover, and simmer 20 to 25 minutes or until chicken is cooked through and no longer pink, and its juices run clear, stirring once. Uncover and cook 3 to 5 minutes or until sauce is slightly thickened.

Palate Preview

Cook this one-pot meal on your stove in a heavy skillet. You'll be delighted with the flavor of *herbs de Provence*, a combination of herbs from the south of France, which includes thyme, basil, savory, fennel seeds, and lavender flowers.

Rump Roast with Roasted Vegetables

Prep time: 30 minutes • Cook time: 1 hour and 45 minutes • Serves: 8 • Serving size: 4 ounces roast with 1½ cups vegetable

Nutritional Analysis per Serving: Glycemic Index 38 • Glycemic Load 6 • Calories 294 • Protein in grams 29 grams • Animal Protein 26 grams • Vegetable Protein 3 grams • Carbohydrates 16 grams • Dietary Fiber 3 grams • Net Carbohydrate 13 grams • Fat 13 grams • Saturated Fat 4 grams • Cholesterol 56 mg • Sodium 60 mg • Exchanges 4 medium-lean meat, 3 vegetable

Roast and Vegetables:

6 cups water

5 cups rutabagas, parsnips, or carrots, peeled, and cut into 1-inch pieces, or a combination of these

1 (2-lb.) boneless beef rump roast, trimmed of all fat

1 medium head cabbage, cut into 8 wedges

10 cloves garlic, chopped

1 medium red onion, cut into wedges

1 TB. olive oil

½ tsp. dried thyme

½ tsp. dried marjoram

½ tsp. coarsely ground black pepper

Vegetable oil cooking spray

Gravy:

1 (14½-oz.) can low-salt beef broth

2 TB. cornstarch

1 TB. Dijon mustard

1 TB. currant jelly

Preheat the oven to 375°F. In a large saucepan, bring water to a boil. Add rutabagas, parsnips, or carrots, and return to a boil. Cook 2 minutes. Drain thoroughly.

Place beef roast in an ungreased shallow roasting pan. Arrange rutabagas, parsnips, or carrots, cabbage, garlic, and onion around roast. Brush roast and vegetables with olive oil. Sprinkle with thyme, marjoram, and pepper. Spray a sheet of foil with cooking spray. Cover the pan tightly with the sprayed foil. Bake for 1 hour.

Palate Preview

A traditional rump roast and vegetables served with a special gravy made from beef broth, Dijon mustard, and currant jelly. Choose your vegetables from these root vegetables: rutabagas, parsnips, or carrots. All are excellent for low cooking.

Uncover the pan and bake uncovered for an additional 30 to 45 minutes or until a meat thermometer registers 145 to 165°F, (depending on desired doneness) and vegetables are tender. Remove roast and vegetables from the pan. Place on a serving platter and cover to keep warm.

In a medium saucepan, combine broth and cornstarch. Mix until smooth. Add drippings from the roasting pan, scraping up any browned meat deposits attached to the bottom of the pan. Add mustard and jelly. Cook over medium heat, stirring constantly, until mixture boils and thickens. Serve gravy with roast and vegetables.

Turkey Pot Roast with Sweet Potatoes and Cranberries

Prep time: 20 minutes • Cook time: 1 hour and 30 minutes • Serves: 8 • Serving size: 4 ounces turkey with ¾ cup vegetables

Nutritional Analysis per Serving: Glycemic Index 52 • Glycemic Load 18 • Calories 290 • Protein in grams 29 • Animal Protein 26 • Vegetable Protein 3 • Carbohydrates 34 grams • Dietary Fiber 3 grams • Net Carbohydrate 31 grams • Fat 7 ½ grams • Saturated Fat 2 ½ grams • Cholesterol 41 mg • Sodium 132 mg • Exchanges 3½ lean meat, 1 starch, 1 fruit, 1 vegetable, ½ fat

1 (2-lb.) boneless-skinless turkey breast,	¾ cup orange juice
5 cups sweet potatoes, peeled and cubed	½ tsp. dried marjoram
½ cup sweetened dried cranberries	½ tsp. ground cinnamon
1 bunch Swiss chard	¼ tsp. salt
6 green onions, cut into ½-inch pieces	2 TB. unsalted butter, melted

Preheat the oven to 350°F. Place turkey breast in an ungreased 13×9-inch (3-quart) baking dish. Arrange sweet potatoes, cranberries, Swiss chard, and green onions around turkey. Pour orange juice over top. Sprinkle with marjoram, cinnamon, and salt. Cover with foil.

Bake for 1 hour. Uncover and brush with melted butter. Bake an additional 30 minutes or until turkey is cooked through and no longer pink, and its juices run clear. Spooning pan juices over turkey and vegetables once during roasting. Serve turkey and vegetables with pan juices.

Delightfully Different

You can use sweet potatoes and yams interchangeably, because they have virtually identical tastes. Yams are lower glycemic at about 25 and sweet potatoes are about 50, but both are in the low-glycemic range.

Palate Preview

Turkey combined with sweet vegetables and fruit is a favorite, whether you serve it for a holiday meal or anytime during the year. This recipe combines turkey breast with sweet potatoes, cranberries, orange juice, and cinnamon, plus Swiss chard and onions.

Chicken à la King

Prep time: 20 minutes • Cook time: 30 minutes • Serves: 8 • Serving size: 1 cup chicken à la king

Nutritional Analysis per Serving: Glycemic Index 48 • Glycemic Load 5 • Calories 173 • Protein in grams 21 • Animal Protein 19 • Vegetable Protein 2 • Carbohydrates 10 grams • Dietary Fiber 2 grams • Net Carbohydrate 8 grams • Fat 4 grams • Saturated Fat 1 ½ grams • Cholesterol 36 mg • Sodium 134 mg • Exchanges 3 lean meat, 2 vegetable, ½ fat

1 TB. unsalted butter

1½ lb. boneless, skinless chicken breast halves, cut into bite-size pieces

1½ cups carrots strips (1½×¼×¼ inches)

1½ cups cut fresh green beans or frozen green beans, thawed

1 medium red bell pepper, cored, seeded, and cut into thin strips

½ cup sliced green onions

¼ cup all-purpose flour

½ tsp. dried Italian seasoning

⅛ tsp. freshly ground black pepper

1 (14½-oz.) can low-salt chicken broth

¾ cup skim milk

2 TB. grated Parmesan cheese

Palate Preview
Chicken morsels in a white sauce with carrots, green beans, and red bell pepper, flavored with green onions, Italian seasoning, and topped with Parmesan cheese. A creamy taste you'll love.

In a large skillet, melt butter over medium-high heat. Add chicken and cook, stirring, for 3 minutes. Add carrots, green beans, bell pepper, and green onions. Cover and cook, stirring occasionally, until chicken is no longer pink and vegetables are crisp-tender.

Lightly spoon flour into a measuring cup, and level off. Add flour, Italian seasoning, and pepper to the skillet. Stir in broth and milk. Bring to a boil, stirring constantly to dissolve any lumps. Stir in Parmesan cheese. Turn heat to low, simmer for 5 minutes and serve.

Wild Rice-Turkey Casserole

Prep time: 15 minutes • Cook time: 2 hours 15 minutes • Serves: 6 • Serving size: 4 ounces turkey on ¾ cup rice and vegetables

Nutritional Analysis per Serving: Glycemic Index 49 • Glycemic Load 14 • Calories 295 • Protein in grams 31 • Animal Protein 26 • Vegetable Protein 5 • Carbohydrates 28 grams • Dietary Fiber 3 grams • Net Carbohydrate 25 grams • Fat 5 grams • Saturated Fat 1 gram • Cholesterol 26 mg • Sodium 69 mg • Exchanges 4 lean meat, 2 starch, 1 vegetable

Rice:	½ cup skim milk
1 cup uncooked wild rice, rinsed	⅛ tsp. freshly ground black pepper
2 TB. chopped garlic	Casserole:
½ cup chopped onion	1 cup chopped carrots
3 cups water	1 cup chopped celery
Sauce:	½ tsp. dried sage
3 TB. water	2 (¾-lb.) fresh turkey breast tenderloins
3 TB. all-purpose flour	1 tsp. dried parsley flakes
¾ cup low-salt chicken broth	⅛ tsp. paprika

In a medium saucepan, combine wild rice, garlic, onion, and water. Bring to a boil. Reduce heat to low. Cover and simmer 50 to 60 minutes or until rice is tender and water is absorbed.

For sauce, in a small jar with a tight-fitting lid, combine water and flour, and shake well. Pour broth and milk into a small saucepan set over medium heat, and gradually stir in flour mixture; add pepper. Cook, stirring constantly, until mixture boils and thickens. Remove from heat.

Preheat the oven to 350°F. In an ungreased 12×8-inch (2-quart) baking dish, combine cooked rice mixture, sauce, carrots, celery, and sage. Mix well. Place turkey breast tenderloins over rice mixture. Sprinkle with parsley and paprika. Cover with foil.

Bake for 1 to 1¼ hours or until turkey is cooked through and no longer pink, and its juices run clear. To serve, cut turkey breast tenderloins crosswise into ½-inch thick slices and serve on top of rice mixture.

Palate Preview

Turkey breast tenderloins on a bed of seasoned wild rice. Add carrots and celery in a white sauce, and you have a great one-pot meal for guests or family.

Easy Mexican Chicken Lasagna

Prep time: 20 minutes • Cook time: 30 minutes • Serves: 6 • Serving size: 3×4-inch portion

Nutritional Analysis per Serving: Glycemic Index 48 • Glycemic Load 11 • Calories 380 • Protein in grams 38 • Animal Protein 35 • Vegetable Protein 3 • Carbohydrates 28 grams • Dietary Fiber 2 • Net Carbohydrate 26 grams • Fat 10 grams • Saturated Fat 2 grams • Cholesterol 78 mg • Sodium 237 mg • Exchanges 4 lean meat, 1½ starch, 1 vegetable, 1 fat

4 (4-oz.) boneless, skinless chicken breast halves	1 can (8-oz.) tomato sauce
1 TB. olive oil	1 tsp. hot sauce, (optional)
2 tsp. no-salt chili powder	1 cup low-fat ricotta cheese
1 tsp. ground cumin	1 can (4-oz.) diced green chili peppers
1 can (14½-oz.) no-salt-added, diced tomatoes with garlic, drained	¼ cup chopped fresh cilantro
	8 (6-inch) corn tortillas
	4-oz. shredded low-fat cheddar cheese

Preheat the oven to 375°F. Cut chicken into ½-inch pieces. Heat oil in a large skillet over medium heat. Add chicken, chili powder, and cumin. Cook, stirring occasionally, for about 4 minutes or until browned. Stir in tomatoes, tomato sauce, and hot pepper sauce, if desired. Bring to a boil. Reduce the heat and simmer 2 minutes.

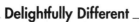

Delightfully Different
Substitute one pound of ground beef for the chicken. Brown the ground beef in the heated oil, and follow the recipe directions.

Combine ricotta cheese, chilies, and 2 tablespoons cilantro in a small bowl. Mix until well blended.

Spoon half of chicken mixture into the bottom of a 12×9-inch baking dish. Top with 4 tortillas, ricotta cheese mixture, remaining tortillas, remaining chicken mixture, cheddar cheese, and remaining cilantro. Bake 25 minutes or until heated through.

Palate Preview
A lasagna made with layered corn tortillas instead of noodles. A zesty flavor comes from the Mexican seasonings of chili powder, cumin, and diced green chilies. An excellent variation on traditional lasagna and great for persons with diabetes.

Chapter 19

Soups and Stews

In This Chapter

- ◆ Soups and stews for everyday meals
- ◆ Healthy, lean cooking techniques
- ◆ Nature's bounty in a bowl

What is it about a hot bowl of soup or stew that warms the heart and keeps the body energized, too? Soups and stews are one-bowl miracles. They remind us of our childhoods, comforting moments, and delectable aromas stirred up by Mom as she cooked.

We love their savory tastes and their liquid warmth in our mouths. That we eat soups and stews with a spoon gives them a sort of comforting, home-style feel—even if we are spooning in vichyssoise at an elegant restaurant. (You'll find a variation on vichyssoise included in this chapter.)

Soups and stews are excellent to include in a food plan for persons with diabetes. Healthy soups and stews are loaded with vegetables and complete protein. The ones we've included here are low in carbohydrates, and we've also made them low in fat.

Oh yes, we've also included some cold soups for you to prepare during the warm-weather months!

Anytime Meals

Soups and stews are amazingly easy and quick to prepare. They just "look" as if they require lots of cooking time. Soups and stews are great for stretching your food budget. Cook plenty and you'll have food enough for several meals. They reheat quickly, taste fabulous, and give you plenty of nutrient value. Many of the recipes can be frozen.

Don't overlook their value as food for any meal—breakfast, lunch, or dinner. We even believe soups and stews have great morning appeal. They can certainly hold their own against any other quick breakfast. Reheat in a serving-size bowl in the microwave, and a nutritious breakfast is ready. If you're accustomed to eating sweet-tasting foods for breakfast, you can add a serving of fruit as an accompaniment. That way you get a sweet taste and also some down-home nutrition.

Saving Those Water-Soluble Vitamins

One of the great things about soups and stews is that the cooking methods keep the liquid or broth teeming with a veritable "soup" of vitamins and minerals. Be sure to use only low-sodium canned vegetables and broths to keep the sodium count within your daily recommended amounts.

Other cooking methods for most vegetables, such as steaming or boiling, have you discard the cooking water. Water-soluble vitamins and minerals that are dissolved into the cooking water go down the drain. Not so with soups and stews. The cooking water becomes the broth and you receive as much nutrient value as possible from the vegetables.

The Least You Need to Know

- ◆ Soups and stews are highly nutritious, economical, and complete meals.
- ◆ Soups and stews are good eating anytime of the day or night.
- ◆ Use only low-salt canned tomatoes and broths ingredients for soups and stews.
- ◆ Many of your favorite soup recipes are included in this chapter.

Vegetable-Beef Soup

Prep time: 15 minutes　•　Cook time: 20 minutes　•　Serves: 6　•　Serving size: 1½ cups with 2 ½ ounces ground beef

Nutritional Analysis per Serving: Glycemic Index 49　•　Glycemic Load 11　•　Calories 220 • Protein in grams 22　•　Animal Protein 17　•　Vegetable Protein 5　•　Carbohydrates 25 grams　•　Dietary Fiber 6 grams　•　Net Carbohydrate 19 grams　•　Fat 4 grams　• Saturated Fat 1½ grams　•　Cholesterol 47 mg　•　Sodium 148 mg　•　Exchanges 2½ lean meat, 1 starch, 1 vegetable

1 lb. lean ground beef	2 (14.5-oz.) cans low-salt beef broth
¼ cup chopped onion	1 (14.5-oz.) can no-salt-added, diced tomatoes, liquid reserved
1 cup chopped celery	
2 (1 lb.) pkg. frozen mixed vegetables, thawed	1 TB. Worcestershire sauce

In a large saucepan or Dutch oven, cook ground beef and onion over medium-high heat, stirring frequently until beef is no longer pink and onion is tender. Drain.

Add celery, mixed vegetables, beef broth, tomatoes and their juice, and Worcestershire sauce. Mix well. Bring to a boil. Reduce heat to low. Cover and simmer, stirring occasionally, for 18 to 20 minutes or until vegetables are tender.

Palate Preview _____
Reminiscent of Grandmother's vegetable soup. Great for cold days or anytime you want some down-home comfort soup. It's hearty with plenty of vegetables.

Delightfully Different _____
Substitute your favorite frozen vegetables for the frozen mixed vegetables. Choose from the wide variety offered at the grocery store: green beans, artichokes, spinach, Asian-style vegetables, and more.

Wild Rice and Chicken Soup

Prep time: 15 minutes • Cook time: 20 minutes • Serves: 6 • Serving size: 1⅓ cups and ¼ cup meat

Nutritional Analysis per Serving: Glycemic Index 51 • Glycemic Load 7 • Calories 140 • Protein in grams 13 • Animal Protein 10 • Vegetable Protein 3 • Carbohydrates 13 grams • Dietary Fiber 2 grams • Net Carbohydrate 11 grams • Fat 5 grams • Saturated Fat 1 gram • Cholesterol 26 mg • Sodium 51 mg • Exchanges 1½ lean meat, 1 starch

1 TB. unsalted butter	1½ cups cubed cooked chicken or turkey
2 cups sliced fresh mushrooms (about 5 oz.)	½ cup coarsely shredded carrots
½ cup chopped green onions	½ tsp. poultry seasoning
3 (14.5-oz.) cans low-salt chicken broth	¼ tsp. dried marjoram, crushed
2 cups cooked wild rice	1 to 2 TB. dry sherry (optional)

Palate Preview

Wild rice gives this chicken soup a rustic, though elegant, taste. It will both warm and satisfy you. Serve as a main course in a bowl, or in a cup before dinner as the first course.

Melt butter in a 4-quart saucepan or Dutch oven over medium heat. Add mushrooms and green onions. Cover and cook 2 to 3 minutes or until mushrooms release their juices. Stir in broth, wild rice, chicken or turkey, carrots, poultry seasoning, and marjoram. Simmer uncovered 10 minutes, stirring occasionally. Stir in sherry, if desired.

Quick Sweet Potato Soup

Prep time: 20 minutes • Cook time: 10 minutes • Serves: 4 • Serving size: 1½ cups

Nutritional Analysis per Serving: Glycemic Index 46 • Glycemic Load 14 • Calories 180 • Protein in grams 5 • Animal Protein 3 • Vegetable Protein 2 • Carbohydrates 30 grams • Dietary Fiber 4 grams • Net Carbohydrate 26 grams • Fat 4 grams • Saturated Fat 2 grams • Cholesterol 11 mg • Sodium 26 mg • Exchanges 2 starch, 1 fat

3 cups cooked sweet potatoes

¼ cup chopped green onions

2 (14.5-oz.) cans low-salt chicken broth

⅛ tsp. freshly ground black pepper

⅔ cup skim milk

½ cup low-fat sour cream

1 TB. chopped fresh chives or 1 tsp. dried chives

In the bowl of a food processor fitted with a metal blade, combine sweet potatoes, green onions, and 1 can broth, and process until smooth. Pour mixture into a medium saucepan.

Stir in remaining can broth and season with pepper. Cook over medium heat until thoroughly heated, stirring frequently. Add milk, sour cream, and chives. Stir to blend. Reduce heat to low and cook until thoroughly heated, watching it carefully so milk doesn't scorch.

Palate Preview

A delectable, creamy, rich sweet potato soup seasoned with green onions and low-fat sour cream. It's tangy and reminiscent of the French potato soup with leeks known as vichyssoise.

Swiss Onion Soup

Prep time: 20 minutes • Cook time: 1 hour 15 minutes • Serves: 4 • Serving size: 1½ cups

Nutritional Analysis per Serving: Glycemic Index 42 • Glycemic Load 10 • Calories 290 • Protein in grams 8 • Animal Protein 6 • Vegetable Protein 2 • Carbohydrates 30 grams • Dietary Fiber 5 grams • Net Carbohydrate 25 grams • Fat 5 grams • Saturated Fat 2 grams • Cholesterol 11 mg • Sodium 325 mg • Exchanges 1 starch, 2 vegetable, 1 medium-fat meat, 1 alcohol

1 TB. unsalted butter	Big pinch of freshly grated nutmeg
6 medium onions, thinly sliced	4 TB. low-fat shredded Swiss cheese
1½ cups white wine	4 slices dense, stone-ground, whole-grain bread, toasted
3½ cups low-salt chicken broth	
¼ tsp. freshly ground white pepper	

In a large skillet, heat butter over medium-high heat until it foams. Add onions and sauté, tossing constantly, for 2 to 3 minutes.

Reduce the heat to low, and cook slowly, stirring occasionally, until onions are very tender and golden, about 1 hour.

Palate Preview _____ Yes, even persons with diabetes can enjoy the taste of onion soup. Go ahead and prepare this onion soup with cheese floating on the top and crusty bread underneath. You'll love this treat served with a meal.

Scrape onions into a 3-quart saucepan. Add white wine and bring to a boil.

Add broth to boiling onions and wine. Add pepper and nutmeg. Simmer very gently, uncovered, stirring occasionally, for 15 minutes.

Preheat the oven to 400°F. Place one slice toast each in four ovenproof soup bowls. Pour equal portions soup over toast; then sprinkle cheese over the top of each. Place the bowls in the oven and heat until cheese melts. Serve immediately.

Winter Squash and Ginger Soup

Prep time: 20 minutes • Cook time: 50 minutes • Serves: 6 • Serving size: 1½ cups

Nutritional Analysis per Serving: Glycemic Index 41 • Glycemic Load 10 • Calories 135 • Protein in grams 4 • Animal Protein 2 • Vegetable Protein 2 • Carbohydrates 28 grams • Dietary Fiber 4 grams • Net Carbohydrate 24 grams • Fat 2½ grams • Saturated Fat ½ gram • Cholesterol <1 mg • Sodium 203 mg • Exchanges 1 starch, ½ fruit, ½ fat

1 TB. olive oil	2 tart apples, peeled and sliced
1 leek, white part only, washed well and sliced	4 cups water
1 medium onion, chopped	½ tsp. salt
3 garlic cloves, minced or put through a press	1 cup skim milk
2 tsp. chopped fresh gingerroot	Lots of freshly ground black pepper, to taste
2 lb. winter squash or pumpkin, peeled, seeded and chopped	Fresh lime juice
	½ cup nonfat plain yogurt

Heat olive oil in a large heavy-bottom soup pot or casserole and add leek and onion. Sauté, stirring often, over low heat until vegetables begin to soften. Add garlic and ginger, and continue to sauté, stirring, for another 5 minutes or until garlic begins to color.

Add squash or pumpkin, apples, and water, and bring to a boil. Add salt, reduce the heat, cover, and simmer 45 minutes until all vegetables are thoroughly tender and aromatic.

Palate Preview

This soup will heat you up on a cold day. The ginger is a warming spice and blends well with the taste of winter squash. Adding fresh lime juice and yogurt to the soup right before serving adds an acidic and tangy touch.

Transfer soup in batches to a blender or a food processor fitted with the metal blade, and process until smooth and creamy. Return to the pot. Thin out as desired with milk. Add lots of freshly ground black pepper.

Heat through and serve, garnishing each bowlful with a squeeze of fresh lime juice, and 1 tablespoon yogurt.

Scotch Soup with Lamb, Barley, and Split Peas

Prep time: 15 minutes • Cook time: 45 minutes • Serves: 10 • Serving size: 1½ cups (including 3 ounces meat)

Nutritional Analysis per Serving: Glycemic Index 18 • Glycemic Load 1 • Calories 265 • Protein in grams 22 • Animal Protein 20 • Vegetable Protein 2 • Carbohydrates 10 grams • Dietary Fiber 3 grams • Net Carbohydrate 7 grams • Fat 15 grams • Saturated Fat 6½ grams • Cholesterol 69 mg • Sodium 269 mg • Exchanges 3 medium-fat meat, 2 vegetable

2 lb. cubed lamb, trimmed of all fat	¼ cup yellow split peas
1 tsp. dried thyme	3 medium carrots, cut into ¼-inch slices
½ tsp. dried crushed rosemary	2 large stalks celery, cut into ½-inch slices
3 quarts water	1 large white turnip, peeled and cut into ½-inch cubes
1 tsp. coarse sea salt	
½ tsp. freshly ground black pepper	2 large leeks (white only), halved, washed well, and sliced
¼ cup uncooked medium-pearl barley	¼ cup finely chopped fresh parsley

In a 6-quart pot, combine lamb cubes, rosemary, thyme, and water. Bring to a boil over high heat. Immediately reduce heat and skim off the foam that comes to the top. When the dark foam stops rising and only specks of meat are rising, add salt, pepper, barley, and split peas.

Palate Preview

A flavorful meal in a dish. You'll enjoy this interesting combination of ingredients: lamb, barley, split peas, and vegetables. This recipe serves 10, so invite a crowd or have some left over for breakfasts and lunches.

Simmer gently, partially covered, for about 30 minutes, until meat is tender.

Add carrots, celery, turnip, and leeks. Simmer steadily for 10 to 15 minutes more or until vegetables are tender.

Just before serving, while soup is simmering, stir in parsley and remove from heat.

Minestrone

Prep time: 20 minutes • Cook time: 2 hours • Serves: 10 • Serving size: 1½ cups

Nutritional Analysis per Serving: Glycemic Index 32 • Glycemic Load 7 • Calories 156 • Protein in grams 5 • Animal Protein 0 • Vegetable Protein 5 • Carbohydrates 30 grams • Dietary Fiber 8 grams • Net Carbohydrate 22 grams • Fat 3 grams • Saturated Fat ½ gram • Cholesterol 0 • Sodium 122 mg • Exchanges 1 starch, 2 vegetable, ½ fat

2 TB. extra-virgin olive oil	1 lb. Savoy cabbage, finely shredded (½ average-size head)
2 medium onions	
3 medium carrots	10 cups water
2 large celery stalks	5 tsp. low-salt, granulated chicken bouillon
10 oz. frozen green beans, thawed and cut into ½-inch pieces	½ tsp. coarse sea salt
2 medium sweet potatoes, diced	½ tsp. pepper
1 lb. zucchini, diced)	½ tsp. chopped fresh basil or parsley
4 cups chopped fresh tomatoes, cut into roughly 1-inch pieces, or 4 cups no-salt-added, canned chopped tomatoes	8 oz. dried kidney beans rinsed and picked over, soaked overnight in several inches of water to cover, then drained

In an 8- to 10-quart pot, heat olive oil over medium heat. Dice onions and sauté, stirring, until golden. While onions are cooking, dice carrots and add them to the pot, stirring to coat with oil and continuing to stir occasionally while you dice celery. Add it to the pot and stir occasionally while you cut green beans. Add them, continuing to stir while you cut sweet potatoes. Add them and stir occasionally while you dice zucchini. Add zucchini and chop tomatoes. Add them and shred cabbage. Add it. Cover the pot and let steam for about 10 minutes, until cabbage has wilted.

Add water, chicken bouillon, salt, pepper, basil or parsley, and beans. Cover and bring to a boil over high heat. Reduce heat, partially cover, and simmer gently, stirring occasionally for 2 hours, or until beans are fully tender and soup is thickened.

Palate Preview

An Italian vegetable soup made hearty with kidney beans and sweet potatoes. Soak the beans overnight so they're ready for cooking. When you are ready to cook, chop the other vegetables as you go, adding each to the pot as you finish prepping it.

Beef and Barley Soup

Prep time: 25 minutes • Cook time: 1 hour 15 minutes • Serves: 6 • Serving size: 1½ cups

Nutritional Analysis per Serving: Glycemic Index 27 • Glycemic Load 4 • Calories 413 • Protein in grams 31 • Animal Protein 28 • Vegetable Protein 3 • Carbohydrates 21 grams • Dietary Fiber 5 grams • Net Carbohydrate 16 grams • Fat 22 grams • Saturated Fat 7 grams • Cholesterol 88 mg • Sodium 95 mg • Exchanges 4 medium-lean meat, 1 starch, 1½ vegetable, 1 fat

1 TB. olive oil

1½ lb. beef stew meat, cut into 1-inch cubes, trimmed of all fat

1 cup sliced carrots

½ cup uncooked medium-pearl barley

2 TB. minced garlic

¼ tsp. freshly ground black pepper

1 medium onion, cut into thin wedges

1 cup water

2 (14.5-oz.) cans low-salt beef broth

1 (14.5-oz.) can no-salt-added, diced tomatoes, liquid reserved

2 cups frozen green beans, thawed

Palate Preview

Barley is a fabulous grain for your eating plan. It is high in fiber, and its glycemic index is low at 22. It's wonderfully satisfying. Beef and Barley Soup is an old-time classic, modified here to fit your eating needs.

Heat oil in a Dutch oven or large saucepan over medium-high heat. Add beef stew meat and cook until browned on all sides. Drain.

Add carrots, barley, garlic, pepper, onion, water, broth, and tomatoes and their juice. Mix well. Bring to a boil. Reduce heat to low. Cover and simmer 1 hour or until beef is tender.

Stir in green beans. Cook uncovered, over medium-high heat for an additional 15 minutes or until beans are tender.

Bouillabaisse

Prep time: 10 minutes • Cook time: 20 minutes • Serves: 8 • Serving size: 1½ cups

Nutritional Analysis per Serving: Glycemic Index 27 • Glycemic Load 2 • Calories 171 • Protein in grams 28 • Animal Protein 27 • Vegetable Protein 1 • Carbohydrates 5½ grams • Dietary Fiber 1 gram • Net Carbohydrate 5 grams • Fat 2½ grams • Saturated Fat ½ gram • Cholesterol 106 mg • Sodium 117 mg • Exchanges 4 very lean meat, 1 vegetable, ½ fat

1 TB. olive oil	¼ tsp. saffron threads
1 large onion, chopped	1 tsp. fennel seeds
1 sweet green bell pepper, cored, seeded, and chopped	¼ tsp. dried thyme
3 garlic cloves, minced	Freshly ground black pepper to taste
1 cup low-salt canned chicken broth	1 bay leaf
3 cups water	2 lb. boneless fish fillets, cut into pieces
2 (8-oz.) bottles clam juice	½ to 1 lb. shrimp, scallops, crab meat, and lobster (use one or more)
3 ripe tomatoes cut into wedges	1 lb. small clams or mussels
1 (14.5-oz.) can no-salt-added, chopped tomatoes	

Heat oil in a large heavy pot. Add onion, green pepper, and garlic, and sauté, stirring, until softened. Add broth, water, clam juice, tomato wedges, canned tomatoes, saffron, fennel seeds, and thyme. Stir and add pepper to taste. Add bay leaf.

Bring to a boil and cook for 10 minutes, stirring occasionally.

Lower heat to simmer and add fish and shellfish, according to length of time it will take each kind to cook. Cook just until clams and mussels open (discard any that do not), lobster shells turn red, and fish separates easily when gently probed with a fork. Remove bay leaf before serving.

Palate Preview

A favorite soup filled with goodness from the sea. Prepare with your favorite fish, such as snapper or salmon, and your favorite seafood. Serve with a tossed green salad or steamed vegetable. Add a half slice of crusty stone-ground bread and you have a meal fit for family and guests.

Gazpacho with Kidney Beans

Prep time: 20 minutes plus 3 hours to marinate • Cook time: 0 • Serves: 6 • Serving size: 1½ cups

Nutritional Analysis per Serving: Glycemic Index 34 • Glycemic Load 5 • Calories 121 • Protein in grams 6 • Animal Protein 0 • Vegetable Protein 6 • Carbohydrates 20 grams • Dietary Fiber 4½ grams • Net Carbohydrate 16 grams • Fat 2 grams • Saturated Fat <1 gram • Cholesterol 0 • Sodium 36 mg • Exchanges 1 starch, 1 vegetable, ½ very lean meat

24 oz. tomato juice

1 medium onion, finely chopped

2 small green bell peppers, cored, seeded, and finely chopped

2 large garlic cloves, finely minced

2 small ripe tomatoes, diced

1 TB. extra-virgin olive oil

1 (14.5-oz.) can low-salt kidney beans, drained and rinsed

½ tsp. hot sauce, such as Tabasco

¼ tsp freshly ground black pepper

1 TB. balsamic vinegar

In a 3-quart ceramic or glass bowl, mix together tomato juice, onion, bell peppers, garlic, tomatoes, oil, beans, hot sauce, pepper, and vinegar.

Cover with plastic wrap and place in the refrigerator for 3 hours or overnight.

When thoroughly chilled, adjust seasonings and serve in deep or wide bowls.

Palate Preview _____

Totally refreshing on a summer day. Serve out of doors on the patio, or inside at the table. Either way, this soup is cool and light enough for a hot day.

Delightfully Different _____

You can modify this gazpacho recipe to suit your tastes. Spice it up by adding a finely diced hot chili pepper or more hot sauce. If you want to include more vegetables, add diced cucumber, grated carrots, or diced jicama.

Cauliflower-Squash Soup

Prep time: 10 minutes   •   Cook time: 20 to 30 minutes   •   Serves: 8   •   Serving size: 1½ cups

Nutritional Analysis per Serving: Glycemic Index 29   •   Glycemic Load 4   •   Calories 111   •   Protein in grams 3 grams   •   Animal Protein 1 gram   •   Vegetable Protein 2 grams   •   Carbohydrates 16 grams   •   Dietary Fiber 3½ grams   •   Net Carbohydrate 13 grams   •   Fat 2 grams   •   Saturated Fat <1 gram   •   Cholesterol 1 mg   •   Sodium 83 mg   •   Exchanges 1 starch, ½ vegetable

1 medium-sized onion, chopped	3½ chopped, peeled butternut squash
1 stalk celery, chopped	1 medium-size head cauliflower, florets only
1 Granny Smith apple, peeled and chopped	¼ cup fresh cilantro, chopped
1 tsp. curry powder, or to taste	Freshly ground black pepper to taste
½ tsp. ground coriander	½ cup nonfat sour cream
8 cups low-salt chicken broth	

Heat oil in a stockpot over medium-high heat. Add onion, celery, and apple, and cook, stirring, for 5 minutes. Stir in curry powder and coriander. Cook for several minutes, stirring occasionally, until curry and coriander are fragrant. Add broth and mix well.

Bring to a boil. Stir in squash and cauliflower. Reduce the heat and simmer for 20 minutes, stirring occasionally. Remove from the heat and process squash mixture in a blender or food processor fitted with a metal blade until smooth and creamy, working in batches if necessary. Return to pot and stir in cilantro and pepper.

Reheat if desired and serve warm, or serve at room temperature. Ladle into soup bowls. Top each serving with 1 TB. of sour cream.

Palate Preview

You can serve this creamy, thick soup cold or heated. It contains the spices of curry powder and coriander plus fresh cilantro. Add a dollop of sour cream for a slightly tart (and acid) taste.

Garden Vegetable Soup

Prep time: 10 minutes • Cook time: 30 to 40 minutes • Serves: 8 • Serving size: 1½ cups

Nutritional Analysis per Serving: Glycemic Index 28 • Glycemic Load 3 • Calories 85 • Protein in grams 4½ • Animal Protein 0 • Vegetable Protein 1½ • Carbohydrates 14½ grams • Dietary Fiber 4 grams • Net Carbohydrate 11 grams • Fat 0 • Saturated Fat 0 • Cholesterol 0 • Sodium 24 mg • Exchanges ½ starch, 2 vegetable

2 large tomatoes, diced	½ cup finely chopped fresh parsley
2 medium onions, thinly sliced	½ tsp. freshly ground black pepper
3 garlic cloves, minced	4 cups zucchini, sliced ¼-inch thick
1 (10-oz.) pkg. frozen peas, thawed	2 cups low-salt chicken broth
1 (10-oz.) pkg. frozen lima beans, thawed	½ tsp. dried oregano
2 TB. finely chopped fresh basil	

Layer tomatoes, onions, garlic, peas, lima beans, basil, oregano, parsley, pepper, and zucchini in a 6-quart pot. Add chicken broth. Cook, covered, over medium heat for 20 minutes. Stir, and cook an additional 10 to 15 minutes or until vegetables are tender.

Ladle hot soup into bowls.

Palate Preview

A fresh-tasting vegetable soup. It clocks in as low calorie at just 85 calories for 1½ cups of soup. Serve with lunch or dinner, and you have two servings of vegetables.

Chapter 20

Main-Dish Salads

In This Chapter

- ◆ Mouth-watering healthy main-dish salads
- ◆ Eating a rainbow of vegetables and fruits
- ◆ Delicious and healthful salad dressings
- ◆ Ingredients for salad mayonnaises and dressings

Main-dish salads are a simple and quick way to add plenty of health-giving vegetables to your daily food plan. These recipes offer you two, three, or even four servings of vegetables, and sometimes a serving of fruit, too.

Are you already a big salad eater? If you are, you'll love the new recipes in this chapter. If not, try to make these main-dish salads a normal part of your menu planning. Most are a snap to prepare. You can modify them to suit your taste. They're mouth-watering and refreshing. And of course, they're a great way to consume health-giving vegetables and fruits. Prepare main-dish salads for meals at home, and pack them with you for lunches and snacks. Be sure to pack the salad greens, vegetables, and meats separately from the dressing, so the greens don't wilt from overexposure.

The salad dressings in this chapter have plenty of good-for-you monounsaturated oils. As an added bonus, the vinegars and lemon or lime juices in the salad dressings add acidity, thus lowering the glycemic load of your meals and helping you regulate blood glucose levels.

You'll find main-dish salads with poultry, fish, seafood, and meat that add complete protein. You'll find diabetic-sensitive recipes for your favorite salads. And you'll find main-dish salads that will tantalize your taste buds with new flavors.

The Eating-a-Rainbow Benefit

Eating lots of vegetables and fruits is an excellent health strategy for everyone, including persons with diabetes. In a sense, vegetables and fruits seem almost too good to be true. But they really are! Yet most people underestimate their value and, as a result, skimp on eating them.

When you eat a "rainbow" of vegetables and fruits (which we describe in Chapter 3) your body benefits from the combination of different nutrients found in different vegetables. Red vegetables, green vegetables, yellow vegetables, orange fruits, and so on all have their nutritional "strengths." When you eat a wide variety of vegetables and fruits, your body benefits from the full range of vitamins, minerals, and antioxidants in them. These in turn promote a healthier heart, lower cholesterol, normalize blood pressure, and help regulate blood glucose levels. Not to mention add more fiber, satisfy you more when eating, and help you maintain your ideal weight.

Salad Dressings

The salad dressings in this chapter are made with good-for-you ingredients. Keep these ingredients on hand:

- Low-fat mayonnaise
- Fresh lemon juice and lime juice
- Red wine and white wine vinegars
- Cold-expeller pressed canola and peanut oils

- Low-fat yogurt
- Olive Oil
- Balsamic vinegar
- Lite soy sauce

You'll get the best taste by making your salad dressings fresh when you prepare your main dish salads.

The Least You Need to Know

- Main-dish salads are quick to prepare and give you great nutritional value.
- Main-dish salads are great for eating at home or for packed lunches or snacks.
- Eat a wide variety of vegetables to insure that your get optimal nutrition from varied vitamins, minerals, and antioxidants.

Turkey-Rice Salad

Prep time: 20 minutes   •   Cook time: none   •   Serves: 6   •   Serving size: 1½ cups greens with 1 cup turkey salad

Nutritional Analysis per Serving: Glycemic Index 37   •   Glycemic Load 11   •   Calories 305   •   Protein in grams 19   •   Animal Protein 15   •   Vegetable Protein 4   •   Carbohydrates 34 grams   •   Dietary Fiber 4 grams   •   Net Carbohydrate 30 grams   •   Fat 12 grams   •   Saturated Fat 2 grams   •   Cholesterol 42 mg   •   Sodium 195 mg   •   Exchanges 2½ lean meat, 1 starch, 1 fruit, 1 vegetable, 2 fat

2 cups cooked wild rice

2 cups cubed cooked turkey

1 cup red or green seedless grapes (halved if large)

1 red bell pepper, cored, seeded, and diced

2 celery stalks, diced

¼ cup chopped fresh parsley

2 large apples (do not peel), cored and chopped

¼ cup chopped walnuts

4 green onions, chopped

½ cup nonfat buttermilk

½ cup low-fat mayonnaise

2 TB. fresh lemon juice

1 TB. honey mustard

8 cups torn mixed greens

In a large mixing bowl, combine rice, turkey, grapes, bell pepper, celery, parsley, apples, walnuts, and green onions, and toss to mix.

In a small bowl, combine buttermilk, mayonnaise, lemon juice, and mustard. Blend well.

Pour dressing over rice and turkey mixture, and toss gently. When you are ready to serve, mound salad on greens and serve.

Delightfully Different
You can substitute cubed cooked chicken for the turkey in this recipe and you can substitute pecans for the walnuts.

Palate Preview
The combination of wild rice and turkey creates a true American taste, because both these foods are native to North America. The salad is crunchy with the addition of fresh apples and walnuts.

Tuna Nicoise Salad

Prep time: 20 minutes • Cook time: none • Serves: 6 • Serving size: 1½ cups tuna and vegetables plus 1 ½ cup greens

Nutritional Analysis per Serving: Glycemic Index 21 • Glycemic Load 3 • Calories 225 • Protein in grams 14 • Animal Protein 8 • Vegetable Protein 6 • Carbohydrates 22 grams • Dietary Fiber 7 grams • Net Carbohydrate 15 grams • Fat 9 grams • Saturated Fat 1½ grams • Cholesterol 14 mg • Sodium 258 mg • Exchanges 2 very lean meat, 1 starch, 1½ fat

1 cup cooked green beans, cut into 1½-inch pieces

1 (15-oz.) can chickpeas, rinsed and drained

1 (14 oz.) can artichoke hearts, rinsed, drained, and quartered

1 carrot, julienne-cut (2 × ⅛ × ⅛-inch)

½ green bell pepper, cored, seeded, and finely sliced

¼ cup Greek olives, rinsed and sliced

¼ cup diced red onion

1 TB. capers, drained and rinsed

¼ cup red wine vinegar

¼ cup chopped fresh basil

1 tsp. dried oregano

4 garlic cloves, minced

3 TB. extra-virgin olive oil

1 (6½- to 7-oz.) can water-packed, no-salt-added tuna, drained and flaked

4 plum tomatoes, diced

9 cups torn mixed salad greens

Palate Preview

A salad sure to please with its tangy taste and delicious vegetables. The Greek olives, capers, garlic, and red onion add plenty of pizzazz. The salad dressing is acidic, which is great for lowering the glycemic load of your meal.

In a large salad bowl, combine beans, chickpeas, artichoke hearts, carrots, bell pepper, olives, onion, and capers.

In a small bowl, whisk together vinegar, basil, oregano, garlic, and olive oil. Pour over vegetables. Set salad aside for at least 30 minutes at room temperature.

Just before serving, add tuna and tomatoes to bean mixture and toss well. Mound tuna-vegetable salad on top of greens.

Dilled Chicken Salad on Greens

Prep time: 30 minutes   •   Cook time: 15 minutes   •   Serves: 6   •   Serving size: 1½ cups salad greens and 6 ounces chicken salad

Nutritional Analysis per Serving: Glycemic Index 27   •   Glycemic Load 2   •   Calories 224   •   Protein in grams 33   •   Animal Protein 32   •   Vegetable Protein 1   •   Carbohydrates 10 grams   •   Dietary Fiber 2 grams   •   Net Carbohydrate 8 grams   •   Fat 6 grams   •   Saturated Fat 1 gram   •   Cholesterol 46 mg   •   Sodium 198 mg   •   Exchanges 4½ lean meat, 2 vegetable, ½ fat

1½ lb. boneless, skinless chicken breasts	2 TB. chopped fresh dill or 1 tsp. dried dill
Dilled Mayonnaise:	1 TB. extra-virgin olive oil
2 cups chopped watercress, tough stems removed	¼ cup low-fat mayonnaise
	¼ cup low-fat plain yogurt
1 TB. chopped garlic	1 red bell pepper, cored, seeded, and diced
2 TB. chopped onion	9 cups torn mixed salad greens
⅛ tsp. salt	2 large tomatoes, chopped
Juice of ½ lemon	

Place chicken in a medium saucepan and pour in just enough water to cover it. Bring just to a boil, reduce heat to low and poach chicken until white and firm throughout, about 15 minutes. Remove from pot and cool.

To make dilled mayonnaise, combine watercress, garlic, onion, salt, lemon juice, dill, and olive oil in a food processor and process until finely chopped. Transfer to a medium bowl and stir in mayonnaise and yogurt.

Cut cooled chicken into bite-size chunks and add to mayonnaise, along with bell pepper. Toss to mix well.

When you are ready to serve, arrange greens on plates. Top with chicken salad. Garnish with tomatoes and serve.

Palate Preview The dilled mayonnaise with watercress gives this chicken salad a refreshing flavor. Add a half slice of crunchy stone-ground bread as an accompaniment.

Salmon and Asparagus with Cucumber Sauce

Prep time: 20 minutes • Cook time: 8 minutes • Serves: 4 • Serving size: 4 ounces salmon fillet with ¾ cup cucumber sauce and 1½ cups salad greens

Nutritional Analysis per Serving: Glycemic Index 6 • Glycemic Load 1 • Calories 308 • Protein in grams 34 • Animal Protein 32 • Vegetable Protein 2 • Carbohydrates 14 grams • Dietary Fiber 4 grams • Net Carbphydrate 10 grams • Fat 10 grams • Saturated Fat 2 grams • Cholesterol 64 mg • Sodium 88 mg • Exchanges 4 medium-lean meat, 2 vegetable, ⅓ milk

4 (4-oz.) salmon fillets, skin and bones removed	1 small cucumber, peeled, seeded, and chopped
1½ qt. water	2 green onions, chopped
1 lb. asparagus, trimmed	½ tsp. ground cumin
Herbed Cucumber Sauce:	¼ cup chopped fresh parsley
1½ cups nonfat plain yogurt	1 TB. chopped fresh dill or 1 tsp. dried dill
1 TB. fresh lemon juice	6 cups salad greens

Place salmon fillets in a pot large enough to hold them and cover with cold water. Bring just to a boil. Turn off the heat and let fillets stand for about 8 minutes or until they are opaque and flake easily with a fork. Remove fillets from water and let cool to room temperature.

Boil a pot of water and prepare a bowl of cold water. Cook asparagus in boiling water for about 5 minutes or until barely tender. Plunge immediately into cold water for about 30 seconds to stop the cooking and set the color, and drain well.

Palate Preview

Enjoy this salmon main-dish salad knowing that you're getting plenty of essential fatty acids (EFAs). The combination of salmon, asparagus, and cucumber sauce is a classic.

In a small bowl, stir together yogurt, lemon juice, cucumber, green onions, cumin, parsley, and dill. Taste and adjust the seasonings.

When you are ready to serve, arrange salad greens on individual plates. Place salmon and asparagus on greens. Top each salmon fillet with about ¾ cup Herbed Cucumber Sauce and serve.

Turkey and Marinated Vegetable Salad

Prep time: 20 minutes • Cook time: 5 minutes • Serves: 6 • Serving size: 1½ cups greens with 1½ cups turkey and vegetables

Nutritional Analysis per Serving: Glycemic Index 10 • Glycemic Load 1 • Calories 250 • Protein in grams 24 • Animal Protein 18 • Vegetable Protein 6 • Carbohydrates 24 grams • Dietary Fiber 11 grams • Net Carbohydrate 13 grams • Fat 10 grams • Saturated Fat 2 grams • Cholesterol 18 mg • Sodium 218 mg • Exchanges 2½ lean meat, 1 starch, 2 vegetable, 1 fat

Marinated Vegetables:

2 cups small cauliflower florets

1 cup green beans, cut into 1-inch pieces

1 carrot, sliced

1 (14-oz.) can artichoke hearts, rinsed and drained

1 cup no-salt-added kidney beans, drained

¼ cup diced red onion

½ green bell pepper, cored, seeded, and thinly sliced

2 celery stalks, sliced

Dressing:

¾ cup low-salt chicken broth

¼ cup fresh lemon juice

2 TB. extra-virgin olive oil

4 garlic cloves, chopped

1 TB. chopped fresh oregano or 1½ tsp. dried oregano

¼ tsp. salt

¼ tsp. ground black pepper

Salad:

1 lb. cooked turkey breast, diced

4 plum tomatoes, diced

9 cups cut-up romaine lettuce

To make salad, bring a saucepan full of water to a boil. Prepare a bowl of cold water. Cook cauliflower, green beans, and carrot in boiling water for 5 minutes. Plunge vegetables into cold water for about 30 seconds to stop the cooking, and drain.

Place vegetables in a large bowl and add artichoke hearts, kidney beans, onion, bell pepper, and celery.

In a small bowl, whisk together chicken broth, lemon juice, olive oil, garlic, and oregano, salt, and pepper. Pour over salad. Cover and refrigerate for at least 4 hours or up to 8 hours, tossing occasionally.

Just before serving, add turkey and tomatoes to marinated vegetables. Toss well. Mound on lettuce and serve.

Palate Preview
The vegetables are cooked just until crisp-tender and then marinated in a lemon-and-olive oil dressing. Add the turkey and you have a great salad for any season of the year.

Asian Chicken Salad

Prep time: 30 minutes • Cook time: none • Serves: 4 • Serving size: 4½ cups salad with 2 tablespoons dressing

Nutritional Analysis per Serving: Glycemic Index 23 • Glycemic Load 3 • Calories 317 • Protein in grams 29 • Animal Protein 20 • Vegetable Protein 9 • Carbohydrates 20 grams • Dietary Fiber 7 grams • Net Carbohydrate 13 grams • Fat 15 grams • Saturated Fat 2 grams • Cholesterol 53 mg • Sodium 88 mg • Exchanges 3 lean meat, 3 vegetable, ½ fruit, 2 fat

8 cups baby spinach	2 cups cubed cooked chicken
4 cups sliced Napa cabbage	Asian Salad Dressing:
2 cups bean sprouts	1 TB. canola oil
1 cup julienne-cut jicama (2×⅛×⅛-inch)	1 tsp. sesame oil
1 cup julienne-cut carrot (2×⅛×⅛-inch)	2 TB. rice wine vinegar
6 green onions, chopped	1 tsp fructose
1 (8-oz.) can mandarin oranges, rinsed and drained	1 tsp. low-salt soy sauce
	½ cup toasted slivered almonds

Palate Preview

This all-time favorite salad made of mandarin oranges, toasted almonds, and chicken is revised for persons with diabetes. You'll appreciate the familiar taste and benefit from its healthfulness.

Preheat the oven to 350°F. Place nuts on a cookie sheet in a single layer. Bake for ten minutes or until lightly browned. Remove from oven and cool before using.

Combine spinach, cabbage, bean sprouts, jicama, carrot, green onions, mandarin oranges, almonds, and chicken in a large bowl and toss to mix.

In a small bowl, combine canola and sesame oils, vinegar, fructose, and soy sauce, and mix well. Just before serving, add dressing to chicken salad mixture, toss again, and serve.

Thai-Style Pork and Pineapple Salad

Prep time: 20 minutes • Cook time: 5 minutes • Serves: 6 • Serving size: 1½ cups spinach and 1 cup pork and vegetables (4 ounces pork)

Nutritional Analysis per Serving: Glycemic Index 46 • Glycemic Load 6 • Calories 266 • Protein in grams 34 • Animal Protein 31 • Vegetable Protein 3 • Carbohydrates 13 grams • Dietary Fiber 3 grams • Net Carbohydrate 10 grams • Fat 8 grams • Saturated Fat 2 grams • Cholesterol 88 mg • Sodium 111 mg • Exchanges 4 lean meat, 1 fruit, 1 fat, 1½ vegetables

1 (15¼-oz.) can unsweetened pineapple chunks in juice, juice reserved	½ cup chopped fresh basil
2 TB. fresh lime juice	1 tsp. low-salt soy sauce
1 TB. Thai fish sauce	1 tsp. minced fresh gingerroot
1 tsp. granulated or brown sugar	1½ lb. pork tenderloin, trimmed and cut into ¾-inch pieces
1 TB. minced garlic	1 TB. peanut oil
⅔ cup sliced red onion	9 cups washed and trimmed spinach

Drain pineapple, reserving 1 tablespoon juice. Discard remaining pineapple juice. Set pineapple chunks aside. Combine reserved pineapple juice, lime juice, fish sauce, sugar, and garlic.

Place pineapple chunks, onion, basil, soy sauce and ginger in a bowl. Drizzle 2 tablespoons lime juice mixture over pineapple and onion mixture. Toss gently. Pour remaining lime juice mixture with uncooked pork in a separate bowl, stirring well.

Heat oil in a large nonstick skillet over medium-high heat. Add pork to the skillet in a single layer and sauté, stirring, for 3 minutes or until browned on the outside and pale pink on the inside. Add pork to pineapple and onion mixture and toss well. Serve over spinach.

Palate Preview

Pork works well in salads, as in this Thai-Style Pork and Pineapple Salad. The taste is genuinely Thai and the pineapple adds a delightful sweetness, yet the glycemic load is quite low at 6.

Crab and Asparagus Salad

Prep time: 25 minutes • Cook time: 5 minute • Serves: 6 • Serving size: 6 asparagus spears with 4 ounces crab salad

Nutritional Analysis per Serving: Glycemic Index 7 • Glycemic Load 1 • Calories 185 • Protein in grams 26 • Animal Protein 24 • Vegetable Protein 2 • Carbohydrates 8 grams • Dietary Fiber 2 grams • Net Carbohydrate 6 grams • Fat 5 grams • Saturated Fat 1 gram • Cholesterol 99 mg • Sodium 195 mg • Exchanges 3 very lean meat, 1½ vegetable, 1 fat

1½ lb. (36 spears) asparagus, trimmed

1½ lb. cooked crabmeat, picked over for bits of shell

1 cup chopped celery

3 green onions, finely chopped

¼ tsp. Old Bay Seasoning or any no-salt seasoning

2 TB. chopped fresh parsley

½ cup chopped roasted red bell pepper

2 tsp. capers, rinsed and drained

¾ cup nonfat buttermilk

¼ cup low-fat mayonnaise

2 TB. fresh lemon juice

¼ tsp. freshly ground black pepper

Palate Preview

This salad combines crab, celery, green onions, parsley, and roasted bell pepper together in a light mayonnaise dressing. Add asparagus spears and you have a nutritious main-dish salad.

Boil a pot of water and prepare a bowl of cold water. Cook asparagus in boiling water for 3 to 4 minutes or until just tender. Drain and plunge immediately into cold water for 30 seconds to stop the cooking and set the color. Drain and set aside.

Combine crabmeat, celery, green onions, seasoning, parsley, bell pepper, capers, buttermilk, mayonnaise, lemon juice, and pepper in a medium bowl. Toss to combine.

Arrange six asparagus spears on each of six serving plates. Top with crab salad and serve.

Roasted Vegetable Salad

Prep time: 20 minutes • Cook time: 45 minutes • Serves: 6 • Serving size: 1½ cups salad greens with 1½ cups roasted vegetables

Nutritional Analysis per Serving: Glycemic Index 43 • Glycemic Load 17 • Calories 314 • Protein in grams 11 • Animal Protein 6 • Vegetable Protein 5 • Carbohydrates 44 grams • Dietary Fiber 11 grams • Net Carbohydrate 33 grams • Fat 12 grams Saturated Fat 5 grams • Cholesterol 20 mg • Sodium 75 mg • Exchanges 1 high-fat meat, 2 starch, 2 vegetable, 1 fat

1 lb. sweet potatoes, peeled and cut into wedges	2 red bell peppers, cored, seeded, and cut into strips
1 lb. beets, peeled and sliced	¾ cup low-salt chicken broth
½ lb. whole baby carrots	2 TB. olive oil
½ lb. green beans, chopped	9 cups torn mixed salad greens (include some radicchio for color)
1 small onion, slivered	1 large tomato, cut into wedges
½ cup peeled garlic cloves	2 tsp. balsamic vinegar
2 fennel bulbs, cored and sliced, Stalks and fronds discarded	½ cup crumbled goat cheese (4-oz.)

Preheat the oven to 450°F.

In large bowl, combine sweet potatoes, beets, carrots, green beans, onion, garlic, fennel, bell peppers, broth, and 1 tablespoon oil in a large roasting pan and toss well. Roast vegetables for about 45 minutes, stirring every 15 minutes or so, or until vegetables are tender and lightly browned. Remove from the oven and let cool to room temperature.

When you are ready to serve, combine salad greens and tomato in a bowl. Toss with remaining 1 tablespoon oil and vinegar. Sprinkle on goat cheese. Spoon vegetables on top. Serve.

Palate Preview

Roasted vegetables give you that familiar oven-toasted, crunchy flavor everyone seems to love. But the good news is that this recipe is low salt and low fat. The cheesy taste of goat cheese gives you a dish you'll want to cook often. Add a side dish of sliced meat to complete your meal.

Italian Shrimp and Cannellini (White) Bean Salad

Prep time: 15 minutes • Cook time: none • Serves: 4 • Serving size: 2 cups salad with 4 ounces shrimp and 3.5 ounces beans

Nutritional Analysis per Serving: Glycemic Index 15 • Glycemic Load 5 • Calories 362 • Protein in grams 35 • Animal Protein 24 • Vegetable Protein 11 • Carbohydrates 35 grams • Dietary Fiber 10 grams • Net Carbohydrate 25 grams • Fat 7.5 grams • Saturated Fat 1 grams • Cholesterol 221 mg • Sodium 378 mg • Exchanges 5 very lean meat, 1 starch, 2 vegetable, 1.5 fat

Roasted Garlic Vinaigrette:

20 cloves roasted garlic

2 TB. olive oil

2 TB. white wine vinegar

⅛ tsp. salt

⅛ tsp. freshly ground black pepper

Salad:

8 cups arugula or other salad greens

4 medium tomatoes, cut into wedges

1 (14.5-oz.) can cannellini beans, rinsed and drained

1 lb. cooked, peeled shrimp

½ cup thinly sliced sweet onion

2 TB. finely chopped red bell pepper

2 tsp. capers, rinsed and drained

Place roasted garlic, olive oil, vinegar, salt, and pepper in the bowl of a food processor fitted with a metal blade and process until smooth.

Just before serving, place a bed of arugula on individual plates. Arrange tomato wedges around the outside of arugula. Spoon beans onto the center of greens. Arrange shrimp on top of beans, and top with onion, bell pepper, and capers. Drizzle with Roasted Garlic Vinaigrette and serve.

Palate Preview

Don't let the 20 cloves of roasted garlic in the dressing scare you off. Roasted garlic is mellower and sweeter than raw garlic. And quite delectable. Plus, need we add, the garlic is really good for you. Roasting garlic takes over an hour, so you may want to prepare the night before. Add the dressing to the shrimp, cannellini beans, and vegetables and this salad offers you Italian zing and good eating.

Chicken, Avocado, and Wild Rice Salad

Prep time: 30 minutes plus 2 to 4 hours refrigeration   •   Cook time: none   •   Serves: 6   •
Serving size: 1½ cups salad

Nutritional Analysis per Serving: Glycemic Index 43   •   Glycemic Load 12   •   Calories 390
•   Protein in grams 21   •   Animal Protein 14   •   Vegetable Protein 7   •   Carbohydrates
30 grams   •   Dietary Fiber 4 grams   •   Net Carbohydrate 26 grams   •   Fat 23 grams   •
Saturated Fat 2 gram   •   Cholesterol 51 mg   •   Sodium 121 mg   •   Exchanges 2 lean
meat, 1½ starch, 1 vegetable, 4 fat

Dressing:

2 large cloves garlic, minced

1 TB. Dijon mustard

¼ tsp. salt

¼ tsp. fructose

¼ tsp. freshly ground black pepper

¼ cup rice wine vinegar

2 TB. olive oil

Salad:

4 cups cooked wild rice

Juice of ½ lemon or 2 TB. lemon juice

12 oz. skinless, boneless chicken breasts,
cooked and cubed

3 green onions including tops, sliced

½ red bell pepper, cored, seeded, and diced

2 oz. snow pea pods, cut into 1-inch pieces

1 medium avocado

1 cup lightly toasted pecan halves

Lettuce leaves for garnish

Combine garlic, mustard, salt, fructose, pepper, vinegar, and olive oil in a food processor fitted
with a metal blade and blend thoroughly. Toss warm rice with lemon juice and cool. After rice
is cool, add chicken, green onions, bell pepper, and pea pods to rice and toss with dressing.
Cover and refrigerate for 2 to 4 hours.

Just before serving, cut avocado in half. Carefully insert the widest part of a sharp knife blade
into pit and twist the knife slightly. Remove and discard the pit. Slice the flesh of 1 avocado half
into small dice while still in the shell by cutting several
times in one direction and then several times in the
other. Scoop out the flesh into a medium bowl. Repeat
with remaining avocado half. Add avocados and pecans
to chicken salad and toss gently, so that avocados are
well coated with dressing. Transfer chicken salad to a
salad bowl and garnish with lettuce leaves.

Palate Preview _____
This salad delivers a
powerhouse of delicious and
good-for-you foods.

Thai Beef Salad

Prep time: 30 minutes • Cook time: 15 minutes • Serves: 6 • Serving size: 1½ cups salad with 4 ounces beef

Nutritional Analysis per Serving: Glycemic Index 39 • Glycemic Load 5 • Calories 249 • Protein in grams 31 • Animal Protein 30 • Vegetable Protein 1 • Carbohydrates 12 grams • Dietary Fiber 2 gram • Net Carbohydrate 10 grams • Fat 8 grams • Saturated Fat 2 grams • Cholesterol 48 mg • Sodium 116 mg • Exchanges 4 medium-lean meat, 2 vegetable

Lime Marinade:	Vegetable oil cooking spray
½ cup fresh lime juice	1 (1½ lb.) flank steak, trimmed of all fat
¼ cup chopped fresh cilantro	1 cup sliced red onion
1 TB. brown sugar	4 plum tomatoes, each cut into 6 wedges
1 TB. Thai fish sauce	9 cups chopped romaine lettuce
1 TB. chili paste with garlic	1¼ cups thinly sliced cucumber
2 garlic cloves, minced	2 TB. chopped fresh mint
Salad:	2 TB. chopped unsalted peanuts

Combine lime juice, cilantro, brown sugar, fish sauce, chili paste, and garlic, stirring until sugar dissolves. Set half of lime marinade aside. Place steak in a large bowl and pour remaining marinade over it, turning to coat well. Cover and refrigerate for 10 minutes, turning once. Remove steak from marinade and discard marinade.

Palate Preview

Do you like Oriental spices? Then you'll love the terrific flavors of this salad and still eat healthy. The traditional Thai spices enhance the flavor of the flank steak. Combined with fresh vegetables, plus mint and peanuts, the result is irresistible.

Place steak on grill rack or broiler pan and cook for 6 minutes on each side or until desired degree of doneness. Let stand 5 minutes. Cut steak diagonally across grain into thin slices.

Spray a large nonstick skillet with cooking spray and heat over medium-high heat. Add onion, and sauté, stirring, for 3 minutes. Add tomatoes, and sauté 2 minutes. Place onion and tomato mixture, lettuce, cucumber, and mint in a large bowl, and toss gently to combine. Divide salad evenly among six plates. Top each serving with steak and drizzle each serving with 1 tablespoon reserved lime marinade and chopped peanuts.

Part 7

Favorite Cuisines

Yes, you can go ahead and eat your favorite ethnic cuisines, such as Italian, Mexican, and Asian, and do so confidently, knowing that these mouthwatering dishes are great for your health.

You'll find many of your favorite ethnic meals, such as lasagna, enchiladas, and beef lo mein, along with some new taste combinations.

Chapter 21

Mexican Cuisine

In This Chapter

- ◆ Enjoying beloved south-of-the-border cuisine
- ◆ Preparing traditional Mexican foods
- ◆ Adding fish to Mexican dishes
- ◆ Fajitas, tacos, and more

As odd it sounds, these days you just can't get much more American than Mexican food. Mexican cuisine has been fondly embraced and adopted in every corner of America. You can find Mexican restaurants in virtually every city in the United States. And every grocery store is stocked with Mexican food ingredients.

Why? Because we love its spicy hot flavors. And the combination of meats, cheeses, corn, and chili peppers is simply irresistible to most of us. Smothered with a red or green salsa, Mexican foods are yummy and satisfying.

The most familiar traditional Mexican foods include enchiladas, tacos, and burritos. But authentic Mexican cuisine, with recipes imported directly from Mexico, includes many fresh vegetables and both seafood and fish.

A Forbidden Cuisine?

Perhaps you've avoided eating Mexican food ever since you discovered you had diabetes. On the surface, there's not much about Mexican food that seems good for your health. It's often high in salt, high in saturated fat, and high in high-glycemic carbohydrates. The glycemic load can be, to say the least, stunningly high. In short, the nutritional stats for Mexican fare, as typically prepared in the United States, are downright alarming. The good news is that you can prepare traditional Mexican cuisine using low-fat, low-salt, and low-glycemic ingredients and the results are delicious.

The great news is that Mexican can be "good for you" depending upon how you cook it. Many of the authentic regional dishes of Mexico are made with fish and lots of fresh vegetables. You can prepare salsas using fresh vegetables and fruits and turn up or down the heat based on your personal taste. Mexican dishes can be good for persons with diabetes and yet these dishes retain the spicy, hot, and peppery tastes that Mexican cuisine is known for.

In this chapter, you'll find diabetes-friendly recipes that will delight your taste buds in ways you never imagined possible with Mexican cuisine.

Healthy Notes

Avocado figures prominently in Mexican cuisine. Here's an easy way to slice, dice, or cube an avocado right in its shell. Cut the avocado in half and carefully insert the widest part of a sharp knife blade into the pit and twist the knife slightly. Remove and discard the pit. Slice the flesh of the avocado half by cutting several times in one direction, and scoop out the flesh. If you want the avocado chopped or diced, slice the flesh in one direction and then in the other, making the slices as wide or thin as you need. Repeat with the remaining avocado half. Avocados will brown quickly when exposed to air, but this can be prevented by quickly applying a small amount of acid such as lemon juice, limejuice, or an acid-based salad dressing.

The Least You Need to Know

- Mexican foods can fit well into a food plan for persons with diabetes.
- Prepare traditional recipes using low-salt, low-fat, and low-glycemic ingredients.
- Make salsas and sauces using fresh vegetables.
- Modify the recipes to deliver the spicy heat you prefer.

Chili-Crusted Halibut with Black Bean Salsa

Prep time: 10 minutes plus 10 minutes to marinate • Cook time: 15 minutes • Serves: 6 • Serving size: 4 ounces fish with ⅓ cup salsa

Nutritional Analysis per Serving: Glycemic Index 20 • Glycemic Load 2 • Calories 175 • Protein in grams 31 • Animal Protein 27 • Vegetable Protein 4 • Carbohydrates 10 grams • Dietary Fiber 4 grams • Net Carbohydrate 6 grams • Fat 4 grams • Saturated Fat 1 gram • Cholesterol 55 mg • Sodium 62 mg • Exchanges 4 very lean meat, ½ starch, ½ vegetable

1½ tsp. no-salt chili powder blend	Salsa:
1 tsp. ground cumin	1 (15-oz.) can black beans, drained and rinsed
¼ tsp. cayenne	⅔ cup chunky tomato salsa
6 (4-oz.) halibut steaks (¾- to 1-inch thick)	2 TB. chopped green onion
1 TB. fresh lime juice	2 TB. chopped fresh cilantro
Vegetable oil cooking spray	

In a small bowl, combine chili powder, cumin, and cayenne. Mix well. Place halibut on a large plate. Brush both sides of fish with lime juice and sprinkle both sides with chili powder mixture. Let stand at room temperature for 10 minutes.

Meanwhile, spray a grill rack with cooking spray. Preheat a gas grill to medium or prepare a medium-hot fire in a charcoal grill, with the rack placed 4 to 6 inches above the heat.

Palate Preview
Fresh fish dishes are an important part of Mexican cuisine but are often overlooked north of the border. Fish takes well to salsas, chilies, and lime juice.

In a medium bowl, combine black beans, salsa, green onion, and cilantro, and mix well. Set aside.

Place fish on the grill, cover the grill and cook for 10 to 14 minutes or until fish is opaque and flakes easily with a fork, turning once. Serve bean salsa with fish. Garnish with fresh cilantro.

Note: To broil halibut, place on a broiler pan and broil 4- to 6-inches from heat 10 to 14 minutes or until fish flakes easily with a fork, turning once.

Taco Salad

Prep time: 20 minutes • Cook time: 15 minutes • Serves: 6 • Serving size: 1 cup chili with 2 cups salad

Nutritional Analysis per Serving: Glycemic Index 31 • Glycemic Load 9 • Calories 517 • Protein in grams 33 • Animal Protein 26 • Vegetable Protein 7 • Carbohydrates 38 grams • Dietary Fiber 8 grams • Net Carbohydrate 30 grams • Fat 26 grams • Saturated Fat 6 grams • Cholesterol 84 mg • Sodium 190 mg • Exchanges 4 medium-lean meat, 2 starch, 1½ vegetable, 2½ fat

Chili:

1 small onion, finely chopped

¾ pound lean ground beef

2 TB. chili powder blend

1½ tsp. ground cumin

1 (15-oz.) can kidney beans, rinsed and drained

1 (15-oz.) can no-salt-added, diced tomatoes

Salad:

8 cups chopped iceberg lettuce

½ cucumber, sliced

¼ cup chopped red onion

4 plum tomatoes, chopped

2 TB. fresh lemon juice

1 tsp. olive oil

6 TB. shredded low-fat cheddar or Monterey jack cheese

6 TB. nonfat sour cream

6 TB. chopped fresh or chopped canned green chili peppers, drained

2 avocados, pitted and sliced thinly

3 oz. baked tortilla chips (about 40) for garnish

Heat a large nonstick skillet over medium-high heat. Add chopped onion, ground beef, chili powder, and cumin, and cook, stirring frequently, until meat is browned and no pink remains. Drain mixture in a colander to remove excess fat. Return mixture to the skillet and add beans and tomatoes and their juice. Keep warm.

Palate Preview

A main-dish salad that offers you the spicy Mexican taste you love, and the fresh vegetables make it even more healthy.

In a large bowl, combine lettuce, cucumber, red onion, and tomatoes. Add lemon juice and oil. Toss well.

Place 1 cup chili mixture in each of six shallow serving bowls. Top with equal portions of cheese, salad, sour cream, green chili, and ⅓ avocado, sliced. Garnish with 6 or 7 baked tortilla chips.

Beef Fajitas

Prep time: 15 minutes • Cook time: 12 minutes • Serves: 4 • Serving size: 4 ounces beef and vegetables with 1 tortilla

Nutritional Analysis per Serving: Glycemic Index 37 • Glycemic Load 8 • Calories 439 • Protein in grams 28 • Animal Protein 24 • Vegetable Protein 4 • Carbohydrates 22 grams • Dietary Fiber 5 grams • Net carbohydrate 17 grams • Fat 22 grams • Saturated Fat 5 grams • Cholesterol 83 mg • Sodium 102 mg • Exchanges 4 medium-lean meat, 1 starch, 1½ vegetable, 2 fat

1 TB. vegetable oil

1 lb. boneless beef top sirloin, cut into 1×⅛-inch strips

1 tsp. ground cumin

1 small onion, thinly sliced

1 small red or green bell pepper, cored, seeded, and thinly sliced

1 garlic clove, minced

3 TB. fresh lime juice

2 tsp. Worcestershire sauce

4 (6-inch) whole-wheat tortillas, warmed

1 lime, cut into quarters

¼ cup thick and chunky tomato salsa

1 avocado, pitted and cut into 8 chunks

2 TB. nonfat sour cream (optional)

Heat oil in a medium skillet or wok over medium-high heat. Add beef and cumin. Cook, stirring for 2 to 3 minutes or until beef is browned and no pink remains and drain fat from mixture. Remove from the skillet. Cover to keep warm.

In the same skillet, combine onion, bell pepper, garlic, lime juice and Worcestershire sauce, and mix well. Cook, stirring, for 4 to 6 minutes or until vegetables are crisp-tender. Return beef to the skillet, and cook, stirring, until thoroughly heated.

 **Palate Preview**
These luscious fajitas are filled with steak, onions, and bell peppers, seasoned with lime juice, and then topped with salsa, avocado, and sour cream. Great for any time you want that south-of-the-border taste.

To serve, place tortillas on individual plates. Spoon ½ cup beef mixture onto each tortilla. Squeeze lime wedges over beef filling. Top with equal portions of salsa, avocado, and sour cream (if desired). Fold or roll up tortillas.

Margarita Shrimp for Two

Prep time: 5 minutes plus 30 minutes refrigeration   •   Cook time: 5 minutes   •   Serves: 2
•   Serving size: 4 ounces shrimp

Nutritional Analysis per Serving: Glycemic Index (not significant)   •   Glycemic Load (not
significant)   •   Calories 147   •   Protein in grams 25   •   Animal Protein 25   •
Vegetable Protein <1   •   Carbohydrates 2 grams   •   Dietary Fiber <1   •   Net
Carbohydrate 2 grams   •   Fat 2½ grams   •   Saturated Fat ½ gram   •   Cholesterol
212 mg   •   Sodium 69 mg   •   Exchanges 4 very lean meat, ½ alcohol

1 TB. chopped green onion	2 TB. tequila
1 TB. chopped fresh cilantro	12 large shrimp, shelled and deveined
1 TB. minced garlic	4 bamboo skewers, soaked in water for 1 hour.
¼ cup margarita mix	

Palate Preview
A fabulous main dish for a special dinner. You can double or triple the recipe to serve a family or guests. Add a vegetable salad or steamed vegetables to complete your meal.

Delightfully Different
You can omit the tequila and substitute 2 tablespoons lemon or lime juice in the marinade.

In a 1-quart self-closing plastic bag, combine green onion, cilantro, garlic, margarita mix, and tequila. Add shrimp, and seal bag and shake to coat. Refrigerate 30 minutes.

Meanwhile, spray a grill rack with cooking spray. Preheat a gas grill to medium or prepare a medium-hot fire in a charcoal grill, with the rack placed 4 to 6 inches above the heat. When ready to grill, thread shrimp on the skewers and discard marinade. Place shrimp on the grill and cook for 5 to 7 minutes or until shrimp is opaque-pink, turning several times.

Note: To broil shrimp, preheat the broiler. Spray an unheated broiler pan with cooking spray and place shrimp skewers on it. Broil 4 to 6 inches from heat for 5 to 7 minutes or until shrimp is opaque-pink, turning several times. Watch carefully.

Shrimp and Avocado Salsa

Prep time: 20 minutes   •   Cook time: none   •   Serves: 6   •   Serving size: 1½ cups salad

Nutritional Analysis per Serving: Glycemic Index 22   •   Glycemic Load 2   •   Calories 360   •   Protein in grams 36   •   Animal Protein 32   •   Vegetable Protein 4   •   Carbohydrates 19 grams   •   Dietary Fiber 8 grams   •   Net Carbohydrate 11 grams   •   Fat 21   •   Saturated Fat 3 grams   •   Cholesterol 108 mg   •   Sodium 171 mg   •   Exchanges 5 very lean meat, ½ fruit, 2 vegetable, 3 fat

2 pounds cooked shrimp, peeled and deveined	½ cup diced bell pepper
4 avocados, pitted and chopped	Juice of 2 limes
8 small tomatoes, chopped	1 (12 oz.) jar seafood cocktail sauce
½ cup chopped fresh cilantro	2 jalapeño chili pepper for garnish
¼ cup diced red onion	Lettuce leaves
2 jalapeño chili peppers, seeded and chopped	

Combine shrimp, avocados, tomatoes, cilantro, red onion, jalapeño chilies, bell pepper, and lime juice in a bowl and mix gently. Stir in cocktail sauce. Serve immediately or refrigerate, covered, until serving time. Serve mounded on lettuce leaves on individual plates.

Palate Preview

This shrimp salsa combines the tastes of Mexico and a classic shrimp cocktail into a healthful and delicious treat. The avocados give you plenty of the all-important monounsaturated fats that help modulate blood glucose levels. Serve as an appetizer, as a luncheon salad, or as a main dish.

Chicken Chiles Rellenos

Prep time: 20 minutes • Cook time: 30 minutes • Serves: 4 • Serving size: 1 poblano pepper with filling

Nutritional Analysis per Serving: Glycemic Index 24 • Glycemic Load 1 • Calories 261 • Protein in grams 31 • Animal Protein 30 • Vegetable Protein 1 • Carbohydrates 6 grams • Dietary Fiber 1 gram • Net Carbohydrate 5 grams • Fat 12 grams • Saturated Fat 2½ grams • Cholesterol 73 mg • Sodium 245 mg • Exchanges 4 lean meat, 1 vegetable, 2 fat

1 lb. cooked boneless, skinless chicken breast	4 large poblano peppers
1 (14.5-oz.) can no-salt-added, diced tomatoes, liquid reserved	Olive oil cooking spray
½ cup red chili sauce or taco sauce	½ cup shredded low-fat Monterey jack or low-fat cheddar cheese
Freshly ground black pepper to taste	¼ cup crumbled goat cheese (about 2 oz.)
Vegetable oil cooking spray	

Coarsely chop chicken, and put in a medium-size bowl. Add tomatoes, chili sauce, and black pepper. Mix gently.

Preheat the oven to 350°F. Spray a sheet pan with cooking spray. Slit peppers lengthwise and carefully remove seeds. Spoon ¼ of chicken mixture in each pepper, with the cut side facing up. Place poblano peppers on the prepared pan. Mix together Monterey jack (or cheddar) and goat cheeses, and spoon equal portions of cheeses on top of chicken mixture in each pepper. Bake 30 minutes or until filling is heated through and cheese is melted and bubbling. Serve at once.

Delightfully Different

You can substitute any kind of leftover meat, poultry, fish, or seafood for the chicken in this recipe.

Palate Preview

Everyone loves Chiles Rellenos. This version offers you chilies stuffed with chicken and two kinds of cheeses. Wonderfully rich and cheesy.

Cumin-Crusted Pork with Spicy Garden Salad

Prep time: 30 minutes plus 1 hour refrigeration • Cook time: 20 minutes • Serves: 4 • Serving size: 3 ounces pork tenderloin with 1½ cups salad

Nutritional Analysis per Serving: Glycemic Index 13 • Glycemic Load 1 • Calories 220 • Protein in grams 21 • Animal Protein 19 • Vegetable Protein 2 • Carbohydrates 10 grams • Dietary Fiber 1½ gram • Net carbohydrate 9 grams • Fat 11 grams • Saturated Fat 2 grams • Cholesterol 54 mg • Sodium 27 mg • Exchanges 3 medium-lean meat, 1½ vegetable, ½ fat

Pork:

1 tsp. ground cumin

½ tsp. granulated sugar

½ tsp. no-salt chili powder blend

¼ tsp. ground allspice

1 (¾ lb.) pork tenderloin

Spicy Garden Salad:

3 large vine-ripened tomatoes, cubed

½ red bell pepper, cored, seeded, and diced

½ green bell pepper, cored, seeded, and diced

½ yellow bell pepper, cored, seeded, and diced

1 cucumber, peeled, seeded and sliced

½ red onion, diced

2 celery stalks, diced

¼ cup chopped fresh parsley

2 TB. red wine vinegar

1 TB. olive oil

½ tsp. dried oregano

¼ tsp. freshly ground black pepper

Romaine lettuce

Combine cumin, sugar, chili powder, and allspice in a small bowl. Place pork in shallow baking dish and rub spice mixture into it on all sides. Cover and refrigerate for at least 1 hour.

Combine tomatoes, bell peppers, cucumber, onion, celery, and parsley in a large bowl. Add vinegar, oil, oregano, and black pepper, and toss to coat. Set aside for at least 1 hour.

Preheat the oven to 375°F. Place pork into a baking dish and roast for 20 minutes. Cut pork into 8 slices. Line 4 serving plates with lettuce. Spoon 1½ cups spicy garden salad on each. Arrange 2 pork slices over each salad. Serve at once.

Palate Preview

Be sure not to pass up this recipe because of the long list of ingredients. The spicy garden salad gives the pork a fresh and interesting taste. As a plus, the vegetables in the salad are all free foods!

Delightfully Different

If you love the flavors of spicy garden salad, make extra helpings and serve as an appetizer before meals. All of the vegetable ingredients are free foods and the vinegar makes this spicy salad acidic, so it's great for lowering the glycemic load of a meal.

Turkey Picadillo-Stuffed Peppers

Prep time: 10 minutes • Cook time: 20 to 30 minutes • Serves: 4 • Serving size: 1 bell pepper with 1 cup filling

Nutritional Analysis per Serving: Glycemic Index 36 • Glycemic Load 8 • Calories 298 • Protein in grams 29 • Animal Protein 27 • Vegetable Protein 2 • Carbohydrates 22 grams • Dietary Fiber 4 grams • Net Carbohydrate 18 grams • Fat 12 grams • Saturated Fat 3 grams • Cholesterol 89 mg • Sodium 106 mg • Exchanges 4 lean meat, 1 fruit, 1½ vegetable, 1 fat

1 TB. olive oil	½ cup sliced pitted green olives
1 cup chopped onions	⅓ cup raisins
1 medium green bell pepper, cored, seeded, and chopped	½ tsp. dried oregano
	¼ tsp. freshly ground black pepper
1 lb. extra-lean ground turkey	4 large yellow, red, or green bell peppers
1 (14.5-oz.) can no-salt-added, diced tomatoes, liquid reserved	

Heat oil in a large nonstick skillet over medium heat.

Add onions and chopped green bell pepper. Cook, stirring occasionally, for 3 to 4 minutes or until just tender. Add ground turkey and cook 4 to 5 minutes, stirring frequently, or until turkey is cooked through and no longer pink..

Palate Preview

Stuffed bell peppers with a spicy Mexican flavor. Raisins are the special ingredient that add sweetness to this recipe. If you prepare the peppers in the oven rather than the microwave, do that step first, because it will take 30 minutes for them to bake sufficiently.

Add tomatoes and their juice, olives, raisins, oregano, and pepper. Mix well. Cook, stirring occasionally, for 7 to 10 minutes or until most of liquid has evaporated.

Meanwhile, cut bell peppers in half lengthwise, remove seeds and membrane. Place peppers on a microwave-safe plate, and cover with plastic wrap. Microwave on high power for 4 to 6 minutes or until tender, rotating the plate halfway through the cooking time.

To prepare bell peppers in the oven, preheat it to 350°F, place peppers a 9×12-inch pan, cover, and bake for 30 minutes.

Fill cooked bell pepper halves with hot turkey mixture. Serve.

Grilled Salmon Tacos with Mexican Coleslaw

Prep time: 15 minutes • Cook time: 15 to 20 minutes • Serves: 6 • Serving size: 2 tacos with 4 ounces fish and ½ cup salad

Nutritional Analysis per Serving: Glycemic Index 48 • Glycemic Load 17 • Calories 427 • Protein in grams 30 • Animal Protein 26 • Vegetable Protein 4 • Carbohydrates 35 grams • Dietary Fiber 3 grams • Net Carbohydrate 32 grams • Fat 15 grams • Saturated Fat 3 grams • Cholesterol 84 mg • Sodium 370 mg • Exchanges 4 medium-lean meat, 2 starch, 1 vegetable, 1 fat

Salmon:

Vegetable oil cooking spray

1½ lb. salmon fillets with skin

1 TB. olive oil

2 tsp. no-salt-added chili powder blend

Mexican Coleslaw:

3 cups shredded coleslaw blend (without dressing)

¼ cup chopped fresh cilantro

1 fresh jalapeño chili pepper, seeded and finely chopped

½ cup nonfat mayonnaise

12 corn taco shells

Spray a grill rack with cooking spray. Preheat a gas grill to medium-low or prepare a medium-low fire in a charcoal grill, with the rack placed 4 to 6 inches above the heat. Brush salmon with oil and coat with chili powder.

Place salmon, skin side down, on the grill and cover the grill, or make tent of foil for each fillet and cover. Cook 15 to 20 minutes or until thickest part of fish flakes easily with fork.

While fish is cooking, combine coleslaw blend, cilantro, jalapeño chili, mayonnaise, and chili powder.

To serve, carefully remove skin from salmon. Break up salmon with a fork. Fill each taco shell with equal portions of salmon. Spoon equal portions of coleslaw over salmon.

Palate Preview _____
A healthful variation on traditional tacos cooked on the grill. Salmon gives you Essential Fatty Acids, and the coleslaw topping adds a spicy and refreshing taste.

Delightfully Different _____
To broil salmon, spray a broiler pan with cooking spray and place salmon, skin side down, on it. Broil 4- to 6-inches from heat 15 to 20 minutes or until thickest part of fish flakes easily with fork.

Layered Enchilada Pie

Prep time: 20 minutes • Cook time: 20 minutes plus 10 minutes hold time • Serves: 6
• Serving size: ⅙ casserole

Nutritional Analysis per Serving: Glycemic Index 49 • Glycemic Load 7 • Calories 265
• Protein in grams 24 • Animal Protein 22 • Vegetable Protein 2 • Carbohydrates
17 grams • Dietary Fiber 2 grams • Net Carbohydrate 15 grams • Fat 10 grams •
Saturated Fat 3 grams • Cholesterol 52 mg- • Sodium 376 mg- • Exchanges
3 medium-lean meat, 1 starch, ½ vegetable

1 lb. extra-lean ground beef	1 (8-oz.) can low-salt tomato sauce
1 medium-size onion, chopped	6 (6-inch) corn tortillas
¼ tsp. salt	1 (4½-oz.) can black ripe olives, rinsed and drained
¼ tsp. freshly ground black pepper	1 cup shredded low-fat cheddar cheese
1 TB. chili powder	

Palate Preview _____ A family favorite. Enchiladas with beef and cheese baked in a casserole. You'll love the meaty-cheesy combo.

Brown beef and onion in a medium-size skillet. Drain on paper towels. Return to skillet. Combine salt, pepper, chili powder, and tomato sauce in a small bowl and add to meat. Rinse tomato sauce can with water and add ¼ can water to meat mixture. Stir. In a casserole, alternate layers of tortillas, chili-tomato sauce, olives, and cheese. Cover and bake at 400°F for 20 minutes. Let sit 10 minutes, then cut into six sections and serve.

Tortilla Soup

Prep time: 15 minutes   •   Cook time: 65 minutes   •   Serves:10   •   Serving size: 1 cup

Nutritional Analysis per Serving: Glycemic Index 49   •   Glycemic Load 7   •   Calories 146   •   Protein in grams 5   •   Animal Protein 3   •   Vegetable Protein 2   •   Carbohydrates 15 grams   •   Dietary Fiber 1½ grams   •   Net Carbohydrate 14 grams   •   Fat 7 grams   •   Saturated Fat 1½ grams   •   Cholesterol 3 mg   •   Sodium 98 mg   •   Exchanges ½ starch, ½ medium-lean meat, 1 vegetable, 1 fat

¼ cup olive oil

1 cup chopped onion

2 jalapeño peppers, seeded and chopped

4 cloves garlic, minced

1 (14½-oz.) cans low-salt stewed tomatoes, drained

2 (10 oz.) cans tomatoes with green chilies, like Rotel brand

2 (10½-oz.) cans condensed low-salt beef broth

2 (10¾-oz.) cans condensed, low-salt chicken broth, undiluted

2 (10¾-oz.) cans low-salt tomato soup, undiluted

3 cup water

2 tsp. ground cumin

½ to 1 tsp. dried ground mild red chili powder, like Hatch chili

2 TB. chopped fresh cilantro

1 cup shredded low-fat cheddar cheese

6 flour tortillas, cut into ½-inch strips

Heat oil in a large Dutch oven over medium-high heat. Add onion, jalapeño peppers, and garlic, and cook, stirring, until tender. Add stewed tomatoes, tomatoes and green chilies, beef broth, chicken broth, tomato soup, water, cumin, red chilies, and cilantro, bring to a boil, reduce heat, and simmer 1 hour. Add ¾ of tortilla strips and shredded cheese. Simmer 5 minutes. Garnish with remaining tortilla strips, equally divided among 10 bowls.

Delightfully Different

Add a cup of diced, cooked chicken to this soup and you have complete protein and a main-dish soup.

Palate Preview

A light Mexican-flavored broth-type soup that is warm, comforting, and spicy hot. Enjoy with meat, fish, or chicken main dish entrée and vegetables.

Beefy Mexican Soup

Prep time: 15 minutes • Cook time: 20 minutes • Serves: 9 • Serving size: 1 cup

Nutritional Analysis per Serving: Glycemic Index 46 • Glycemic Load 3 • Calories 117 • Protein in grams 13 • Animal Protein 12 • Vegetable Protein 1 • Carbohydrates 6 grams • Dietary Fiber 1 gram • Net Carbohydrate 5 grams • Fat 4½ grams • Saturated Fat 1½ gram • Cholesterol 32 mg • Sodium 120 mg • Exchanges 2 medium-lean meat, 1 vegetable

1 lb. extra-lean ground beef

½ cup chopped onion

¼ cup chopped green bell pepper

½ tsp. ground cumin

5 cups water

1 tsp. chili powder

½ tsp. minced garlic

¼ tsp. salt

1 (16-oz.) can no-salt whole tomatoes, liquid reserved

1 (8-oz.) can low-salt, whole-kernel corn, liquid reserved

2 TB. sliced black olives

Palate Preview
Savor the taste of Old Mexico in this meaty soup filled with vegetables and spices. A warming soup great for cooler weather.

Cook ground beef, onion, and green pepper in a Dutch oven set over medium-high heat, stirring frequently, until beef is no longer pink and vegetables are tender; drain. Stir in cumin, water, chili powder, minced garlic, salt, and tomatoes and their juice.

Break up tomatoes with a fork. Heat to boiling, stirring constantly; reduce heat. Cover and simmer, stirring occasionally, for 10 minutes. Stir in corn and olives. Cover and cook 10 minutes longer.

Italian Cuisine

In This Chapter

- Italian dishes to suit diabetic food plans
- Healthful Italian ingredients
- Cooking methods for pasta
- Accompaniments and side dishes

Great Italian food is loved by us all. From childhood on we've eaten spaghetti with meat sauce or meatballs, and almost as many pizza slices as hamburgers. Even better, you can have pizza delivered! (In our yellow pages phone book, "pizza" even warrants a separate listing from restaurants.)

Italian food is so integrated into our day-to-day eating that it's often offered in many different kinds of restaurants—not just Italian eateries.

Italian cuisine can also be healthy. The health benefits of many Mediterranean ingredients, such as tomato sauce and olive oil, make the news often because they've give you powerful health benefits. Tomatoes and tomato sauce contain the antioxidant, lycopene, thought to prevent prostrate and other cancers. Garlic boosts the power of your immune system. Olive oil contains monounsaturated fats that help prevent heart disease. The herbs and spices contain antioxidants that neutralize free radicals and boost your health. You can count on the recipes in this chapter being healthy and delicious.

A Taste of Italy

The special tastes of Italian foods have become an established part of our American eating heritage. Just think of the mouth-watering ingredients: tomato sauce seasoned with garlic, onions, oregano, and olive oil. Pizza with mushrooms and black olives. A wide range of cheeses from Parmesan to ricotta to mozzarella.

Perhaps you've thought of Italian food as way too heavy on the breads and pastas and too high in salt and fat to fit your nutritional requirements. You're partially right. Many pizzas and some pasta dishes are overloaded with carbohydrates. They won't work for your food plan.

But, a plethora of Italian dishes do work. They're made with meats and vegetables that give you maximum nutrition without losing that saucy Italian flavor, but don't overload you with fat, salt, and carbohydrates. Plus, we offer some of your favorite Italian recipes modified to meet the needs of persons with diabetes.

Spaghetti squash is a vegetable substitute for wheat pasta that some people prefer. The taste of spaghetti squash is very mild and it picks up the complex flavors of Italian cuisine well. Your cooking method for wheat pastas can make it low-glycemic. Add the pasta to boiling water. Boil for only 5-6 minutes, then drain. The longer you boil pasta, the higher the glycemic index value. If your meal includes wheat or grain pasta, take a pass on bread. Otherwise, you'll glycemic load for the meal will be too high.

You'll find recipes for Pizza Rustica, Make-Ahead Meatballs, Spaghetti Sauce, and Lasagna along with fancier fare such as Osso Buco, Stuffed Pasta Shells Florentine, and Puttanesca Pasta Sauce.

The Least You Need to Know

- Many ingredients in Italian cooking are great for your health.
- Cook pasta for a short amount of time to keep it in the low- to moderate-glycemic range.
- If your Italian meal includes pasta, pass on adding bread to your menu.
- The recipes in this chapter offer you all-time favorites as well as some specialty Italian meals.

Vegetable Pizza with Polenta Crust

Prep time: 20 minutes • Cook time: 20 minutes • Serves: 6 • Serving size: 1 (4-inch) slice

Nutritional Analysis per Serving not including crust: Glycemic Index (not significant) • Glycemic Load (not significant) • Calories 123 • Protein in grams 10 • Animal Protein 9 • Vegetable Protein 1 • Carbohydrates 5 grams • Dietary Fiber 2 grams • Net Carbohydrate 3 grams • Fat 6½ grams • Saturated Fat 1½ gram • Cholesterol 13 mg • Sodium 62 mg • Exchanges 1 vegetable, 1 medium-fat meat, ½ fat

1 TB. olive oil	1 (16-oz.) pkg. frozen broccoli, red peppers, onions, and mushrooms, thawed
1 clove garlic, finely chopped	
1 tsp. dried basil	2 cups shredded low-fat mozzarella cheese

Prepare polenta crust (see recipe that follows).

Preheat the oven to 425°F. Mix oil, garlic, and basil in a small bowl. Spread vegetables over baked polenta crust. Sprinkle with cheese. Drizzle with oil mixture.

Bake pizza for 15 to 20 minutes or until cheese is melted and vegetables are hot.

Palate Preview

This recipe uses a unique crust for pizza. Polenta is cooked cornmeal and has a moderate glycemic index of 68. Top with vegetables and you have a modern-style "white" pizza.

Delightfully Different

You can substitute other vegetables for the broccoli, red peppers, onions, and mushrooms in this recipe. Select the ones you enjoy the most. You can also add leftover sliced or shredded meat to the vegetables, then add the cheese and bake.

Polenta Crust

Prep time: 10 minutes • Cook time: 7 minutes • Serves: 6 • Serving size: 1 (4-inch) slice

Nutritional Analysis per Serving: Glycemic Index 68 • Glycemic Load 12 • Calories 103 • Protein in grams 2 • Animal Protein 0 • Vegetable Protein 2 • Carbohydrates 17 grams • Dietary Fiber 2 grams • Net Carbohydrate 15 grams • Fat 3 grams • Saturated Fat 1 gram • Cholesterol 2 mg • Sodium 43 mg • Exchanges 1 starch, ½ fat

Vegetable oil cooking spray	⅛ tsp. salt
2⅓ cups water	⅛ tsp. cayenne
1 TB. unsalted butter	1 cup yellow cornmeal

Preheat the oven to 425°F. Spray a 12-inch pizza pan with cooking spray.

Heat water, butter, salt, and cayenne to boiling in a 2-quart saucepan over medium-high heat. Slowly stir in cornmeal with a wire whisk, and continue whisking until mixture is smooth and thickened, breaking up any lumps.

Spoon cornmeal mixture onto the prepared pizza pan and spread evenly, mounding the edge slightly.

Bake 5 to 7 minutes or until crust is set and lightly browned.

Italian Meatballs

Prep time: 20 minutes • Cook time: 22 minutes • Serves: 9 • Serving size: 4 meatballs

Nutritional Analysis per Serving: Glycemic Index 46 • Glycemic Load 1 • Calories 173 • Protein in grams 23½ • Animal Protein 23 • Vegetable Protein ½ • Carbohydrates 3 grams • Dietary Fiber 0 • Net Carbohydrate 3 grams • Fat 6 grams • Saturated Fat 3½ grams • Cholesterol 109 mg • Sodium 84 mg • Exchanges 3 medium-lean meat, ¼ starch

2 eggs	¼ cup plain bread crumbs
½ cup skim milk	¼ tsp. freshly ground black pepper
2 lb. lean ground beef	1 tsp. Worcestershire sauce
1 cup chopped onions	

Preheat the oven to 400°F.

In a large bowl, combine eggs and milk, blending well. Stir in ground beef, onions, bread crumbs, pepper, and Worcestershire sauce. Mix well. Shape into 36 meatballs, 1¼ to 1½ inches in diameter. Place in an ungreased 15×10×1-inch pan.

Bake for 17 to 22 minutes or until lightly browned and thoroughly cooked. Cool 5 minutes.

To freeze: Place meatballs in an ungreased 13×9-inch pan. Freeze uncovered for 45 minutes. Place 12 partially frozen meatballs in each of three freezer-proof containers or freezer bags. Label and date. Freeze for up to 90 days.

Palate Preview

These meatballs go well with spaghetti squash and an Italian tomato sauce, or with any Italian-style meal, such as lasagna or stew. Make them ahead and freeze for later or cook and serve right now.

Puttanesca Pasta Sauce

Prep time: 10 minutes • Cook time: 52 minutes • Serves: 6 • Serving size: ¾ cup

Nutritional Analysis per Serving: Glycemic Index 32 • Glycemic Load 3 • Calories 71 • Protein in grams 2 • Animal Protein 0 • Vegetable Protein 2 • Carbohydrates 8 grams • Dietary Fiber 1 gram • Net Carbohydrate 7 grams • Fat 4 grams • Saturated Fat ½ gram • Cholesterol 0 • Sodium 216 mg • Exchanges 1½ vegetable, 1 fat

1 medium onion, cut into thin rings

12 large cloves garlic, halved

2 (14.5-oz.) cans no-salt-added, chopped tomatoes, liquid reserved

¼ cup pitted nicoise or small black olives, rinsed, drained, and chopped

¼ cup capers, rinsed and drained

3 TB. coarsely chopped, oil-packed sun-dried tomatoes, drained

1 TB. mixed Italian seasoning

1 TB. balsamic vinegar

Pinch crushed red pepper flakes

Palate Preview

An Italian sauce that has plenty of zing with the addition of olives, capers, and sun-dried tomatoes. Serve with al dente pasta or over spaghetti squash.

Heat oil in a large skillet over medium-high heat. Add onion and garlic and sauté, stirring, for 5 to 7 minutes, until onion is soft and translucent.

Stir in tomatoes and their juice. One at a time, stir in olives, capers, sun-dried tomatoes, herbs, vinegar, and red pepper flakes.

Reduce the heat, cover the pan and simmer about 45 minutes. This recipe freezes nicely and can easily be doubled. Serve with al dente pasta or spaghetti squash.

Stuffed Pasta Shells Florentine

Prep time: 20 minutes • Cook time: 45 minutes • Serves: 8 • Serving size: 2 stuffed shells

Nutritional Analysis per Serving: Glycemic Index 44 • Glycemic Load 12 • Calories 260 • Protein in grams 26 • Animal Protein 20 • Vegetable Protein 6 • Carbohydrates 28 grams • Dietary Fiber 1 gram • Net Carbohydrate 27 grams • Fat 4½ grams • Saturated Fat 1½ grams • Cholesterol 46 mg • Sodium 215 mg • Exchanges 1½ starch, 3 lean meat, 1 vegetable, ½ fat

16 jumbo pasta shells (al denté)

1 TB. unsalted butter

1 lb. lean ground beef

1 cup coarsely chopped mushrooms (about 4 oz.)

½ cup chopped onion

1 clove garlic, minced

1 tsp. Italian seasoning

¼ tsp. freshly ground black pepper

1 TB. butter

1 (16-oz.) container non-fat cottage cheese

1 (10-oz.) package frozen chopped spinach, thawed and well drained

½ cup liquid egg substitute

2 cups homemade Spaghetti Sauce (see next recipe) or Puttanesca sauce

Preheat the oven to 350°F. Cook pasta shells according to package directions in unsalted water. Drain and keep warm.

Meanwhile, melt butter in a large skillet over medium-high heat. Add beef, mushrooms, onion, garlic, Italian seasoning, and pepper and cook, stirring, until vegetables are tender and beef is thoroughly cooked. Remove from the heat and stir in cottage cheese, spinach, and egg substitute. Spoon equal portions of mixture into shells.

Spread ½ cup spaghetti sauce in the bottom of a 13×9×2-inch baking dish. Arrange shells over sauce. Top with remaining sauce. Cover and bake for 35 minutes or until hot.

Palate Preview

A delicious version of stuffed pasta shells. They're filled with ground beef, mushrooms, cottage cheese, and spinach. Top them with the homemade Spaghetti Sauce found in the next recipe and you have a satisfying Italian dish. Also excellent with Puttanesca Sauce.

Spaghetti Sauce

Prep time: 15 minutes   •   Cook time: 40 minutes   •   Serves: 6   •   Serving size: ¾ cup

Nutritional Analysis per Serving: Glycemic Index 35   •   Glycemic Load 5   •   Calories 64
•   Protein in grams 1   •   Animal Protein 0   •   Vegetable Protein 1   •   Carbohydrates
13 grams   •   Dietary Fiber 2 grams   •   Net Carbohydrate 11 grams   •   Fat 0   •
Saturated Fat 0   •   Cholesterol 0   •   Sodium 132 mg   •   Exchanges 2½ vegetable

Vegetable oil cooking spray

1 medium onion, chopped

1 large carrot, grated

2 TB. chopped garlic

½ cup chopped green bell pepper

3 tsp. Italian seasoning

2 (14.5-oz.) no-salt-added, chopped tomatoes, liquid reserved

1 (8-oz.) can low-salt tomato sauce

½ tsp. freshly ground black pepper

1 TB. balsamic vinegar

¼ tsp. salt

Spray a medium saucepan with cooking spray and place over medium heat. Add onion, carrot, garlic, bell pepper, and Italian seasoning.

Simmer until soft, stirring occasionally.

Add chopped tomatoes, tomato sauce, balsamic vinegar and salt. Return to a simmer. Cook 30 minutes or until of desired consistency.

Palate Preview

A meatless spaghetti sauce you can serve with your Italian dishes. Try over al dente pasta or cooked spaghetti squash. You may want to make extra and freeze for later use.

Delightfully Different

Add 1 pound of browned ground beef or pork to the sauce and you have spaghetti sauce with meat. Be sure to drain the fat from the meat before adding to the sauce. By adding meat, the protein and fat counts in the nutritional analysis increase.

Osso Buco

Prep time: 30 minutes • Cook time: 1½ hours • Serves: 8 • Serving size: 1 (3 to 4 ounces) shank with ½ cup sauce

Nutritional Analysis per Serving: Glycemic Index 54 • Glycemic Load 6 • Calories 226 • Protein in grams 22 • Animal Protein 21 • Vegetable Protein 1 • Carbohydrates 11 grams • Dietary Fiber 1 gram • Net Carbohydrate 10 grams • Fat 9 grams • Saturated Fat 2 grams • Cholesterol 91 mg • Sodium 249 mg • Exchanges 2 vegetable, 3 lean meat, ½ fat

8 medium veal shanks (2 to 2½ lb. total) cut about 2 inches thick

½ cup all-purpose flour

2 TB. unsalted butter

1 TB. olive oil

1 large carrot, grated

2 stalks celery, diced

1 cup dry Marsala wine, preferably imported Florio Marsala, or one cup water with 2 TB. lemon juice

1 cup low-salt beef broth

1 (14.5-oz.) can no-salt-added, chopped tomatoes, liquid reserved

⅛ tsp. salt

⅛ tsp. freshly ground black pepper

2 TB. finely chopped fresh parsley

Dredge veal shanks in flour and shake off any excess. Heat butter and oil in a large, heavy skillet over medium heat. When butter foams, add veal and cook for 6 to 7 minutes or until golden on both sides.

Transfer meat to a dish and keep warm. Add carrots and celery to the skillet. Cook, stirring, for 5 to 6 minutes, or until vegetables are lightly golden. Return meat to the skillet, raise the heat to high, and add Marsala wine or lemon water. Cook for 5 to 6 minutes or until liquid is almost completely evaporated. Add broth and tomatoes, and bring to a boil. Season with salt and pepper. Reduce the heat to low, partially cover the skillet, and cook for 1 to 1½ hours or until meat begins to fall away from the bone. Stir in parsley and serve.

Palate Preview

A traditional Italian delicacy, osso buco is veal shanks cooked until the meat is exceedingly tender and delectable. Serve with a tossed salad, vinaigrette dressing, and steamed vegetables.

Lasagna

Prep time: 20 minutes • Cook time: 45 minutes • Serves: 12 • Serving size: 1 square, 3 × 3 inches

Nutritional Analysis per Serving: Glycemic Index 41 • Glycemic Load 14 • Calories 450 • Protein in grams 39 • Animal Protein 35 • Vegetable Protein 4 • Carbohydrates 35 grams • Dietary Fiber 3 grams • Net Carbohydrate 32 grams • Fat 16½ grams • Saturated Fat 7 grams • Cholesterol 82 mg • Sodium 317 mg • Exchanges 4 medium-lean meat, ½ high-fat meat, 2 starch, 1 vegetable

2 lb. ground beef	1 tsp. dried basil
½ lb. ground pork	2 cups creamed low-fat, low-salt cottage cheese
1 (28-oz.) can whole tomatoes, liquid reserved	3 (4-oz.) pkg. shredded low-fat mozzarella cheese
1 (12-oz.) can tomato paste	½ cup. grated Parmesan cheese
2 tsp. minced garlic	
1½ tsp. dried oregano	

Palate Preview

Lasagna is versatile and easily portable. You can prepare ahead and freeze, serve a whole houseful of guests as well as a family, take to a potluck dinner, or serve by candlelight for a romantic dinner for two.

Preheat the oven to 350°F. Cook lasagna noodles according to package directions. Drain and keep warm.

Meanwhile, cook ground beef and pork in a large skillet until meat is no longer pink, and drain. Add tomatoes to the skillet, and break apart with a fork. Stir in tomato paste, garlic, oregano, and basil. Heat to boiling, lower the heat, and simmer 20 minutes.

Set aside 1 cup meat sauce and ½ cup mozzarella. In a 13×9-inch ungreased pan, alternate layers of noodles, meat sauce, and cheese mixture. Spread reserved sauce and cheese mixture on top layer and sprinkle with Parmesan. Bake, uncovered, for 45 minutes. Let stand 15minutes before cutting into squares.

Zucchini Ripieni

Prep time: • Cook time: 30 to 40 minutes • Serves: 8 • Serving size: ½ stuffed zucchini

Nutritional Analysis per Serving: Glycemic Index 42 • Glycemic Load 4 • Calories 268 • Protein in grams 19 • Animal Protein 16 • Vegetable Protein 2 • Carbohydrates 10 grams • Dietary Fiber 1 gram • Net Carbohydrate 9 grams • Fat 20 grams • Saturated Fat 5 grams • Cholesterol 106 mg • Sodium 432 mg • Exchanges 2 medium-lean meat, ½ high-fat meat, ⅓ starch, 1 vegetable, 1½ fat

4 medium zucchinis, scrubbed but not peeled	2 oz. finely chopped prosciutto (or smoked sausage)
1 lb. lean ground beef (chuck)	½ tsp. salt
½ cup finely chopped onion	¼ tsp. freshly ground black pepper
½ tsp. finely chopped garlic	½ tsp. dried oregano
½ cup plus 2 TB. grated Parmesan cheese	Olive or vegetable oil cooking spray
1 egg, beaten	1½ cups low-salt tomato sauce
½ cup plain bread crumbs	Few drops olive oil

Preheat the oven to 375°F.

Cut zucchinis in half lengthwise, and spoon out most of pulp, leaving hollow boatlike shells about ¼ inch thick. Set shells aside and chop pulp.

In a large skillet, heat oil over medium-high heat. Add ground beef and onion until beef is no longer pink and onion is tender. Drain well and add zucchini pulp and garlic. Cook 5 to 10 minutes longer. Drain entire contents in a colander.

Palate Preview

Ripieni is Italian for "stuffed" and these stuffed zucchini are filled with ground meat, prosciutto, tomatoes, Parmesan, and Italian herbs. A taste treat you'll love.

In a large mixing bowl, combine meat mixture with 6 tablespoons Parmesan, beaten egg, bread crumbs, prosciutto or sausage, salt, pepper, and oregano. Mix well and spoon stuffing into zucchini shells, mounding the tops slightly.

Spray a 13×9×2-inch baking dish with cooking spray and cover it with a small amount of tomato sauce. Place stuffed zucchinis into dish in a single layer. Sprinkle tops with Parmesan. Drizzle a few drops of olive oil and remaining tomato sauce. Cover with aluminum foil and cook 30 to 40 minutes or until tender. Serve warm.

Pizza Rustica

Prep time: • Cook time: 50 to 60 minutes • Serves: 8 • Serving size: 1 slice-8 slices to pizza

Pizza dough: Prep time: • Cook time: 30 to 40 minutes • Serves: 8 • Serving size: ½ stuffed zucchini

Nutritional Analysis per Serving: Glycemic Index 71 • Glycemic Load 11 • Calories 290 • Protein in grams 21 • Animal Protein 17 • Vegetable Protein 4 • Carbohydrates 16 grams • Dietary Fiber 2 grams • Net Carbohydrate 14 grams • Fat 15 grams • Saturated Fat 6 grams • Cholesterol 68 mg • Sodium 467 mg • Exchanges 2 medium-fat meat, ½ high fat meat, 1 starch

Vegetable oil cooking spray

¼ lb. Italian sausage

½ lb. lean ground pork or beef

¾ lb. mozzarella cheese, sliced

½ c. tomato sauce

½ tsp. dried oregano

1 (10-oz.) pkg. frozen spinach, thawed and well drained

1 egg, beaten

12 large pimiento-stuffed green olives, cut in half lengthwise

1 (7-oz.) jar whole pimientos

¼ lb. pepperoni, thinly sliced

Palate Preview

Here's a traditional pizza recipe that fits into your meal plan. Enjoy a slice for dinner or lunch along with a side salad and a vegetable serving. The taste is traditional – so your family will love it, too.

Preheat the oven to 400°F. Spray 8½×4½×2½ loaf pan with cooking spray. Lightly flour a cutting board or work surface.

Prepare pizza dough as presented in Chapter 24. While dough is rising, cook sausages thoroughly in a skillet over medium-high heat. Remove from skillet and cut into thick slices. Brown ground pork or beef in the same skillet, stirring often until meat is lightly browned. Drain fat.

Reserve ¼ of dough and roll out remaining dough on the prepared board. Carefully lift dough and line prepared pan with it, moistening dough at seams to seal.

Arrange ⅓ mozzarella cheese on top of dough and top with sausage slices and browned beef or pork. Spoon tomato sauce over sausages and sprinkle with oregano.

Combine spinach with beaten egg; and spread in an even layer over the sausages. Sprinkle pimientos evenly over spinach and top with remaining cheese. Roll out remaining dough and carefully place it on top of pizza; crimp edges to seal. Cut a few slits in top crust to allow steam to escape. Bake for 50 to 60 minutes or until crust is well browned.

Chapter 23

Asian Cuisine

In This Chapter

- ◆ Recipes from Asia
- ◆ Preparing a healthy stir-fry
- ◆ Steaming vegetables in low-salt broth
- ◆ Making take-in Asian meals

Preparing and eating Asian food at home has become a special—and healthy—treat. With its fresh vegetables, interesting spices, and quickly cooked meats, Asian dishes are a total delight to savor and enjoy.

Although Asian cooking is often associated with for massively high-salt content, with home preparation you are in charge of the amount of salt you eat. In particular, home preparation of Asian foods lets you avoid eating the MSG—*monosodium glutamate*—that's often used as a flavor enhancer in restaurants and is actually a form of sodium. For many people MSG seems to be a sure way to a throbbing headache. (Your food should not hurt!)

In this chapter, you'll find a wide variety of healthy stir-fry meals—from mild to quite hot and spicy. Be sure to cook the Tandoori Chicken to sample the marvelous Indian spices of this baked chicken-breast dish.

The Secret to Diabetic-Friendly Stir-Fry

You may think that a stir-fried meal is off limits for persons with diabetes. That certainly would be true if you used lots of hot oil and actually fried all the foods, as you may have done in the past.

Words for Well-Being

MSG, also known as **monosodium glutamate** is a food additive that has the taste of protein on the tongue. Used to intensify existing meat flavors in soups,

The good news is that you can eat stir-fry dishes provided that you use a slightly different preparation technique. The stir-fry recipes in this chapter use only 1 to 2 tablespoons of fat for the entire recipe, usually to brown the meat or seafood. The vegetables are then cooked in a savory broth and added to the meat. The result is that you get the wonderful taste of stir-fry and use very little oil.

Plus, the liquid that the vegetables are cooked in is loaded with many of the vegetables' vitamins and minerals. Since the liquid is used to make the sauce, you get added nutritional value in every bite.

Adding a Side Dish

If your glycemic load allotment allows, you can serve a small amount of brown rice—about ⅓ cup—with your stir-fry. If not, top your meal with alfalfa or mung bean sprouts for added vegetables and nutrition.

A side salad of tossed greens works great, too.

The Least You Need to Know

◆ Asian cooking works well in a diabetic meal plan when prepared with less oil and salt than in restaurants.

◆ Stir-frying offers you quick and varied meals.

◆ Eat stir-fry alone as a meal or add a small amount of brown rice if your daily meal plan allows.

◆ Alfalfa or mung bean sprouts complement Asian meals.

Chicken and Pea Pod Stir-Fry

Prep time: 20 minutes • Cook time: 10 minutes • Serves: 4 • Serving size: 1½ cups stir-fry includes ⅝ cup chicken

Nutritional Analysis per Serving: Glycemic Index 44 • Glycemic Load 5 • Calories 257 • Protein in grams 28 • Animal Protein 26 • Vegetable Protein 2 • Carbohydrates 14 grams • Dietary Fiber 2½ grams • Net Carbohydrate 12 grams • Fat 7 grams • Saturated Fat 2 grams • Cholesterol 63 mg • Sodium 211 mg • Exchanges 4 very lean meat, 1 vegetable, ½ starch, ½ fat

2 TB. cornstarch	2 cups fresh snow pea pods or sugar snap peas, or 1 (6-oz.) pkg. frozen pea pods, thawed and drained
1 tsp. granulated sugar	
1 cup water	¾ cup sliced green onions
1 TB. low-salt soy sauce	2 TB. grated fresh gingerroot
1 TB. peanut oil	2½ cups cubed (¾-inch), cooked chicken breast
1½ cups julienne-cut carrot (2×¼×¼-inch)	

In a small bowl, combine cornstarch and sugar, and blend well. Add water and soy sauce, blending until smooth. Set aside.

Heat oil in a large skillet or wok over medium-high heat. Add carrots and stir to coat. Cover and cook 3 minutes. Add snow pea pods or snap peas, green onions, and gingerroot, and cook, stirring, for 3 to 4 minutes or until vegetables are crisp tender.

Stir in chicken and cornstarch mixture. Cook, stirring, until mixture thickens and is thoroughly heated.

Palate Preview

This stir-fry offers a taste of Asian cuisine with very little fat and carbohydrates. The secret is to fry in a small amount of oil.

Vegetable and Beef Stir-Fry

Prep time: 30 minutes refrigeration   •   Cook time: 12 minutes   •   Serves: 6   •
Serving size: 3 ounces beef with ¾ cup vegetables

Nutritional Analysis per Serving: Glycemic Index 31   •   Glycemic Load 2   •   Calories 237
•   Protein in grams 24   •   Animal Protein 22   •   Vegetable Protein 2   •   Carbohydrates
8 grams   •   Dietary Fiber 2½ grams   •   Net Carbohydrate 6 grams   •   Fat 10 grams   •
Saturated Fat 3   •   Cholesterol 80 mg   •   Sodium 185 mg   •   Exchanges 3 medium-lean
meat, 1 vegetable, ¼ starch, 1 fat

1¼ lb. boneless beef round steak, trimmed of all fat

⅔ cup plus ¾ cup water

¾ cup broccoli florets, thinly sliced

¾ cup cauliflower florets, thinly sliced

¾ cup carrots, thinly sliced

¾ cup Chinese cabbage, diagonally sliced

¾ cup green beans, diagonally sliced

1 (8-oz.) can bamboo shoots, drained and rinsed

2 TB. cornstarch

½ tsp. ground ginger

¼ tsp. freshly ground black pepper

¼ tsp. minced garlic

3 TB. dry sherry or rice wine

1½ TB. low-salt soy sauce

1 TB. vegetable oil

Chill beef in the freezer 20 to 30 minutes. Cut partially frozen beef across the grain into thin strips. Set aside.

Meanwhile, in a medium saucepan, bring ⅔ cup water to a boil. Add broccoli, cauliflower, carrots, Chinese cabbage, and green beans. Cover and cook for about 5 minutes or until crisp-tender. Add bamboo shoots and heat thoroughly. Drain and keep warm.

 **Palate Preview**
Thinly sliced beef stir-fried with broccoli, cauliflower, carrots, Chinese cabbage, and green beans adds up to a wonderfully healthy and tasty entrée.

In a small bowl, combine cornstarch, ginger, pepper, garlic, ¾ cup water, sherry, and soy sauce. In a large skillet or wok, heat oil over medium-high heat and stir-fry beef for 2 to 3 minutes or until it is cooked through to desired doneness. Pour soy sauce mixture over beef. Heat until sauce is thick and bubbly, stirring constantly. Arrange hot vegetables on a serving platter. Spoon meat and sauce over vegetables.

Tandoori Chicken Breasts

Prep time: 5 minutes plus 30 minutes refrigeration • Cook time: 10 minutes • Serves: 2 • Serving size: 4 ounces chicken

Nutritional Analysis per Serving: Glycemic Index 14 • Glycemic Load 1 • Calories 290 • Protein in grams 31 • Animal Protein 31 • Vegetable Protein 0 • Carbohydrates 4 grams • Dietary Fiber 0 • Net Carbohydrate 4 grams • Fat 11 grams • Saturated Fat 2½ grams • Cholesterol 94 mg • Sodium 210 mg • Exchanges 4 very lean meat, 1 fat, ⅓ skim milk

½ cup nonfat plain yogurt	⅛ tsp. salt
2 tsp. fresh lemon juice	¼ tsp. ground ginger
2 tsp. vegetable oil	⅛ tsp. ground cinnamon
1 tsp. curry powder	⅛ tsp. cayenne
¾ tsp. paprika	2 (4-oz.) boneless, skinless chicken breast halves
½ tsp. ground cumin	Vegetable oil cooking spray

In shallow glass or ceramic dish, combine yogurt, lemon juice, and oil. Blend well. Add curry powder, paprika, cumin, salt, ginger, cinnamon, and cayenne. Blend well. Add chicken, turning to coat. Cover and refrigerate 30 to 60 minutes.

Preheat the broiler. Line a 15×10×1-inch baking dish with foil. Spray the foil with cooking spray. Remove chicken from marinade and discard marinade. Place chicken in foil-lined pan.

Broil 4 to 6 inches from heat for 8 to 10 minutes or until chicken is cooked through and no longer pink and its juices run clear, turning once.

Palate Preview

The exotic taste of Indian cooking in baked chicken. The meat is tender and spicy—just right for picnics, parties, and every-day dinners.

Chicken with Oyster Sauce

Prep time: 15 minutes • Cook time: 15 minutes • Serves: 4 • Serving size: 3 ounces chicken with ½ cup vegetables

Nutritional Analysis per Serving: Glycemic Index 41 • Glycemic Load 2 • Calories 157 • Protein in grams 20 • Animal Protein 19 • Vegetable Protein 1 • Carbohydrates 6 grams • Dietary Fiber 1 gram • Net Carbohydrate 5 grams • Fat 8 grams • Saturated Fat 2 grams • Cholesterol 52 mg • Sodium 125 mg • Exchanges 3 very lean meat, 1 vegetable, ½ fat

1 cup low-salt chicken broth	½ tsp. ground ginger
2 tsp. oyster sauce	1 TB. peanut oil
½ tsp. granulated sugar	1 cup fresh snow pea pods
3 tsp. cornstarch	1 cup sliced mushrooms (3-oz.)
¾ lb. skinless chicken breast strips for stir-frying	½ medium red bell pepper, cored, seeded, and cut into 2 × ¼-inch strips
	2 garlic cloves, minced

In a small bowl, combine broth, oyster sauce, sugar, and 2 teaspoons cornstarch. Blend well and set aside.

In a medium bowl, combine chicken, ginger, and remaining teaspoon cornstarch. Mix gently to coat and set aside.

Palate Preview _____ The oyster sauce gives this chicken stir-fry the delectable taste of Asian cooking. Serve with ⅓ cup of cooked brown basmati rice and an additional vegetable to complete your meal.

Heat oil in a wok or a large nonstick skillet over medium-high heat. Add chicken mixture, and cook, stirring, for 3 minutes. Add snow pea pods, mushrooms, bell pepper, and garlic. Cook, stirring, for 3 minutes or until chicken is cooked through and no longer pink, and any juices run clear.

Add broth mixture and cook an additional 1 to 2 minutes or until sauce is slightly thickened and vegetables are crisp-tender.

Asian Pork with Peppers and Pineapple

Prep time: 10 minutes plus 15 minutes refrigeration • Cook time: 15 minutes •
Serves: 4 • Serving size: 1 cup stir-fry including 4 ounces pork.

Nutritional Analysis per Serving: Glycemic Index 11 • Glycemic Load 2 • Calories 264
• Protein in grams 25 • Animal Protein 23 • Vegetable Protein 2 • Carbohydrates
23 grams • Dietary Fiber 2 grams • Net Carbohydrate 21 grams • Fat 10 grams •
Saturated Fat 2½ grams • Cholesterol 75 mg • Sodium 255 mg • Exchanges 3 lean
meat, 1 fruit, 1 vegetable, ¼ starch, 1 fat

1 lb. pork tenderloin, cut into thin strips

2 tsp. plus ½ tsp. fructose

1 TB. plus 1 tsp. low-salt soy sauce

1 TB. fresh gingerroot, minced, or 1½ tsp. ground ginger

2 cloves garlic minced

1 TB. peanut oil

1 medium green bell pepper, cored, seeded, and cut into ¼-inch strips

1 medium red bell pepper, cored, seeded, and cut into ¼-inch strips

1 medium yellow bell pepper, cored, seeded, and cut into ¼-inch strips

1 green onion, sliced

1 (8-oz.) can pineapple chunks in its own juice, liquid reserved

1 TB. cornstarch

In medium glass or ceramic bowl, combine pork, 2
teaspoons fructose, 1 tablespoon soy sauce, ginger,
and garlic. Mix well. Cover and refrigerate for 15
minutes to blend flavors. Heat a 12-inch skillet or
wok over medium-high heat. Add oil and heat. Add
pork mixture and stir-fry for 3 minutes or until pork is
no longer pink. Remove pork from skillet and stir-fry
bell peppers and green onion for 3 minutes or until
crisp-tender.

Palate Preview _____
The pork tenderloin is
complemented with three colors of
bell peppers and pineapple. You'll
savor the sweet and tangy taste of
this stir-fry.

In small bowl, combine reserved pineapple liquid, cornstarch, ½ tsp. fructose, and 1 teaspoon
soy sauce, blending well. Add cooked pork and pineapple chunks to the skillet. Stir in cornstarch mixture. Cook until sauce is thickened and pineapple is thoroughly heated, stirring
constantly.

Asian-Style Vegetables

Prep time: 10 minutes • Cook time: 8 minutes • Serves: 6 • Serving size: ¾ cup vegetables

Nutritional Analysis per Serving: Glycemic Index 24 • Glycemic Load 1 • Calories 41 • Protein in grams 2 • Animal Protein 0 • Vegetable Protein 2 • Carbohydrates 7 grams • Dietary Fiber 2 grams • Net Carbohydrate 5 grams • Fat <1 gram • Saturated Fat 0 • Cholesterol 0 • Sodium 41 mg • Exchanges 1½ vegetable

Vegetable oil cooking spray

2 tsp. finely chopped fresh gingerroot

1 clove garlic, finely chopped

1½ cups small broccoli florets

2 medium carrots, thinly sliced

1 small onion, sliced and separated into rings

¾ cup low-salt chicken broth

1 TB. cornstarch

1 TB. cold water

1 (8-oz.) can sliced water chestnuts, rinsed and drained

1 cup sliced mushrooms (3-oz.)

1 TB. oyster sauce

Palate Preview _____ A distinctive blend of Asian vegetables. Use as a vegetable side dish to complement any meat, seafood, or poultry main dish.

Spray a wok or a 12-inch skillet with cooking spray and heat over medium heat. Add ginger and garlic, and stir-fry about 1 minute or until lightly browned. Add broccoli, carrots, and onion, and stir-fry 1 minute. Stir in broth, cover and cook about 3 minutes or until carrots are crisp-tender.

Mix cornstarch and water. Stir into cooked vegetable mixture. Cook, stirring, for about 10 seconds or until thickened. Add water chestnuts, mushrooms, and oyster sauce, and cook 30 seconds. Serve hot.

Stir-Fried Szechwan Vegetables

Prep time: 10 minutes • Cook time: 8 minutes • Serves: 6 • Serving size: ¾ cup vegetables

Nutritional Analysis per Serving: Glycemic Index 7 • Glycemic Load 1 • Calories 52 • Protein in grams 2 • Animal Protein 0 • Vegetable Protein 2 • Carbohydrates 8 grams • Dietary Fiber 2 grams • Net Carbohydrate 6 grams • Fat 2½ grams • Saturated Fat ½ gram • Cholesterol 0 • Sodium 103 mg • Exchanges 1½ vegetable, ½ fat

Szechwan Sauce:

1 TB. low-salt soy sauce

1 tsp. cider vinegar

½ tsp. cornstarch

½ tsp fructose

¼ to ½ tsp. crushed red pepper flakes

¼ tsp. ground ginger

Vegetables:

2 tsp. vegetable oil

1 cup sliced mushrooms (3-oz.)

½ cup sliced green onions, in 1-inch pieces

6 large stalks bok choy (with leaves), chopped (4 cups)

1 medium red bell pepper, cored, seeded, and thinly sliced

3 cloves garlic, finely chopped

2 TB. chopped unsalted peanuts

In a small bowl, prepare Szechwan Sauce by combining soy sauce, vinegar, cornstarch, fructose, red pepper flakes, and ginger; set aside.

Heat a wok or a 10-inch skillet over medium-high heat. Add oil and rotate the wok or skillet to coat sides. Add mushrooms, green onions, bok choy, bell pepper, and garlic, and stir-fry 2 minutes. Stir in reserved Szechwan Sauce, and cook, stirring until thickened. Sprinkle with peanuts and serve.

Palate Preview
A hot and spicy vegetable medley from the Szechwan province of China. Chopped peanuts garnish the vegetables.

Spicy Hot Chicken and Vegetables

Prep time: 10 minutes plus 20 minutes refrigeration • Cook time: 10 minutes • Serves: 4 • Serving size: 1¼ cups stir-fry includes 4 ounces chicken

Nutritional Analysis per Serving: Glycemic Index 31 • Glycemic Load 2 • Calories 220 • Protein in grams 30 • Animal Protein 27 • Vegetable Protein 3 • Carbohydrates 6 grams • Dietary Fiber 1 gram • Net Carbohydrate 5 grams • Fat 10 grams • Saturated Fat 1½ grams • Cholesterol 90 mg • Sodium 198 mg • Exchanges 4 very lean meat, 1 vegetable, 1 fat

Chicken:

1 lb. boneless, skinless chicken breast halves, cut into bite-size pieces

1 egg white

1 tsp. cornstarch

1 tsp. low-salt soy sauce

1 tsp. vegetable oil

Vegetables:

2 tsp. vegetable oil

1 medium onion, cut into 1-inch pieces

2 cloves garlic, finely chopped

1 large green bell pepper, cored, seeded, and cut into 1-inch pieces

1 (8-oz.) can sliced bamboo shoots, drained and rinsed

1 TB. Asian chili sauce

1 tsp. finely chopped dried chili pepper or ¼ tsp. crushed red pepper flakes

¼ cup low-salt chicken broth

Cornstarch Mixture:

1 TB. cornstarch

1 TB. cold water

1 tsp. low-salt soy sauce

Palate Preview _____ Make this dish as hot or mellow as you like by varying the amounts of red pepper and Asian chili sauce. No matter what degree of heat you like, this chicken stir-fry is fantastic.

Mix chicken, egg white, cornstarch, and soy sauce in a glass or ceramic bowl. Cover and refrigerate 20 minutes.

Heat a wok or a 12-inch skillet over medium-high heat until hot. Add oil and rotate the wok or skillet to coat sides. Remove chicken from marinade and discard marinade. Add chicken to the wok and stir-fry about 2 minutes or until cooked through and no longer pink. Remove chicken from wok.

Add 2 teaspoons oil to the wok or skillet and rotate to coat sides. Add onion and garlic and stir-fry until garlic is lightly browned. Return chicken to the wok and add bell pepper, bamboo shoots, chili sauce, and dried chili or red pepper flakes. Stir-fry 1 minute. Stir in broth and heat to boiling.

Combine cornstarch, cold water, and soy sauce. Add cornstarch mixture, and cook, stirring for 30 seconds or until thickened.

Beef Lo Mein

Prep time: 10 minutes   •   Cook time: 10 minutes   •   Serves: 6   •   Serving size: 1½ cups including 2.6 ounces beef

Nutritional Analysis per Serving: Glycemic Index 39   •   Glycemic Load 14   •   Calories 356   •   Protein in grams 25   •   Animal Protein 18   •   Vegetable Protein 7   •   Carbohydrates 39 grams   •   Dietary Fiber 2½ grams   •   Net Carbohydrate 37 grams   •   Fat 12 grams   •   Saturated Fat 3 grams   •   Cholesterol 78 mg   •   Sodium 386 mg   •   Exchanges 3 lean meat, 2 starch, 1 vegetable

4 cups cooked linguini, boiled only 6 minutes (about 8-oz. uncooked pasta)	1½ cups sliced onion
1 tsp. dark sesame oil	1 (1-lb.) flank steak, trimmed and cut across the grain into long, thin strips
1 TB. peanut oil	1½ TB. low-salt soy sauce
1 TB. minced, fresh gingerroot	1 TB. brown sugar
6 garlic cloves, minced	1 TB. oyster sauce
4 cups chopped broccoli	1 TB. chili paste with garlic

Combine cooked linguini and sesame oil, tossing well to coat.

Heat peanut oil in a large nonstick skillet or wok over medium-high heat. Add ginger and garlic and sauté, stirring, for 30 seconds. Add broccoli and onion, and sauté, stirring, for 3 minutes. Add steak and sauté, stirring, for 5 minutes or until desired doneness. Add linguini mixture, soy sauce, brown sugar, oyster sauce, and chili paste, and cook 1 minute or until lo mein is thoroughly heated, stirring constantly.

Palate Preview Cook the noodles only until al dente, about 6 minutes, and this Beef Lo Mein will give you a satisfying meal with a light glycemic load. Add one more vegetable with your meal for the best nutrition.

Egg Rolls

Prep time: 15 minutes • Cook time: 20 minutes • Serves: 12 • Serving size: 1 egg roll

Nutritional Analysis per Serving: Glycemic Index 48 • Glycemic Load2 • Calories 45 • Protein in grams1 ½ • Animal Protein ½ • Vegetable Protein 1 • Carbohydrates 6 grams • Dietary Fiber 1 gram • Net Carbohydrate 5 gram • Fat 1 ½ grams • Saturated Fat ½ gram • Cholesterol 18 mg • Sodium 65 mg • Exchanges ½ starch

1 cup chopped cooked chicken or shrimp

½ cup chopped bean sprouts

½ cup chopped water chestnuts

½ cup chopped bamboo shoots

¼ cup chopped green onions, including green part

¼ cup chopped green bell pepper

1 tsp. chopped fresh gingerroot

¼ cup ground almonds

1 TB. low-salt soy sauce

12 egg roll wrappers (3½-inch square size)

1 egg, lightly beaten

Olive oil cooking spray

Preheat the oven to 350°F. Mix together chicken or shrimp, bean sprouts, water chestnuts, bamboo shoots, green onions, bell pepper, gingerroot, almonds, and soy sauce.

Palate Preview ____ These egg rolls are baked, not fried, yet they're great tasting. They're filled with Asian vegetables and seasonings. You can prepare them with either chicken or shrimp.

Spoon a small amount of filling in the center of each egg roll wrapper. Working first from top and bottom and then from right and left, fold opposite edges of the wrapper into center and fold over filling. Cut off any excess wrapper so that there isn't much overlap. Seal egg rolls by brushing them lightly with beaten egg.

Spray a baking sheet with olive oil spray. Place egg rolls on the cookie sheet, about 1-inch apart, folded side down. Bake for 20 minutes or until golden and crisp on the outside.

Thai Shrimp

Prep Time: 15 minutes   •   Cook Time: 10 minutes   •   Serves: 4   •   Serving Size: ¼ lb. shrimp with 2 TB. sauce

Nutritional Analysis: Glycemic Index: 62   •   Glycemic Load 2   •   Calories 170   •   Protein in grams 24   •   Animal Protein 24   •   Vegetable Protein 0   •   Carbohydrate 4 grams   •   Fiber 0   •   Net Carbohydrate 4 grams   •   Fat 5 grams   •   Saturated Fat 2 grams   •   Cholesterol 220 mg   •   Sodium 253 mg   •   Exchanges 4 very lean meat, 1 fat

1 TB. lime juice	4 cloves garlic minced
1 tsp. Thai fish sauce	2 small, fresh, hot chilies, minced (optional)
2 tsp. brown sugar	1 lb. large, peeled and deveined, raw shrimp
1 tsp. cornstarch	¼ cup chopped fresh basil
1 Tb. cooking oil	¼ cup chopped fresh mint

In a small bowl, combine the lime juice, fish sauce, brown sugar, and cornstarch. Set aside.

Place a skillet or wok over medium-high heat and add the oil, garlic and chili. Sauté for 2 minutes and add the shrimp, sautéing for 3 to 5 minutes or until shrimp turn white. Add the basil and mint and stir in the lime juice mixture. Cook for 2 more minutes and serve.

Palate Preview

An unusual blending of flavors—basil, mint, lime, garlic, and hot chilies—gives the shrimp an exotic and refreshing taste. Plus, it's easy and quick to prepare.

Vietnamese Chicken with Lemongrass

Prep Time: 20 minutes • Cook Time: 15 to 20 minute • Serves: 4 • Serving Size: ¼ lb. chicken with ¼ cup sauce

Nutritional Analysis: Glycemic Index: 68 • Glycemic Load 1 • Calories 210 • Protein in grams 28 • Animal Protein 28 • Vegetable Protein 0 • Carbohydrate 2 grams • Fiber 0 • Net Carbohydrate 2 grams • Fat 7 grams • Saturated Fat 2 grams • Cholesterol 87 mg • Sodium 300 mg • Exchanges 4 very lean meat, 1 fat

2 TB. minced fresh gingerroot

2 TB. white or Chinese vinegar

1 lb. boneless, skinless chicken breasts, cut into ¼ inch chunks

2 tsp. fish sauce

¼ tsp. black pepper

2 TB. minced lemongrass stem (optional)

1 tsp. cornstarch

6 TB. water

½ tsp. sugar

1 TB. canola oil

1 medium onion, cut in wedges

3 cloves garlic, finely minced

3 scallions chopped in 1-inch pieces

Palate Preview

Just one whiff of the lemongrass aroma will whet your appetite. And one taste will inspire you to prepare this dish frequently. The lemongrass imparts an earthy lemon flavor that blends well with chicken.

Combine ginger and vinegar, set aside. Combine chicken, fish sauce, pepper, and the lemongrass. Combine the cornstarch, water, and sugar.

Heat a skillet or wok over high heat and add the oil. Fry the onion, garlic, chicken, and scallion pieces for about 5 minutes. Reduce heat to medium, cover and cook for 5 more minutes. Uncover and add ginger mixture and the cornstarch mixture and stir well. Cook for an additional 5 minutes or until slightly thickened and hot.

Part  Extras: Starches, Desserts, and Beverages

The rich and satisfying tastes and textures of these low-glycemic breads and grains will amaze you. They're great. Plus you'll find a couple of great recipes for baked beans, seasoned just as you like them.

These desserts with low-glycemic loads are just plain delicious! Your sweet tooth will definitely be satisfied eating these healthier cheesecakes, brownies, cookies, and puddings.

Chapter 24

Breads

In This Chapter

- ◆ Low-glycemic breads
- ◆ Baking breads at home
- ◆ Ingredients for low-glycemic breads
- ◆ A wide variety of muffins

Basic bread has lost some of its popular nutritional appeal. While bread has for centuries been considered the "staff of life," that notion derived in part from bread's low-cost, filling nature. Bread offered an inexpensive way to fuel the body and sustain life.

But modern research has shown that the nutritional value of many breads isn't very healthy and doesn't meet humankind's dietary needs of nutrient-dense foods. Most regular store-bought breads are full of high-glycemic carbohydrates, a small, usually insignificant, amount of dietary fiber and enriched flours that contain some B vitamins. But overall, eating store-bought breads is risky for persons with diabetes.

Most everyday breads are high glycemic. The glycemic index values of both regular store-bought white bread and whole-wheat bread are 70. Eating even one slice can put you at risk for elevated blood glucose levels.

The bread recipes in this chapter are different. Each recipe was developed to be low glycemic and high in fiber, and to fulfill your desire for a tasty and satisfying bread, cracker, or muffin. As a bonus, there's even a recipe for pizza crust.

Of course, persons with diabetes must consume any breads cautiously, including the ones here. You need to limit your consumption to the recommended serving size to keep your overall glycemic load within an acceptable range.

Baking Bread

Bread can be low glycemic and also delicious. In fact, low-glycemic breads are more delicious because they contain added ingredients such as wheat bran, rolled oats, or oat bran. This added fiber increases your daily fiber intake and makes the bread more filling—so you can eat less and yet feel satisfied. Here are some of the ingredients you'll need:

- **Wheat bran**. It enhances the wheat taste of the bread. Recipes here call for unprocessed wheat bran.
- **Rolled oats.** Use the slow cooking kind and avoid using the quick (instant) oats. Quick oats have less fiber and is higher glycemic. You can also use steel-cut oats, which are low glycemic.
- **Stone-ground whole-wheat flour.** This has more fiber and better taste than regular whole-wheat flour. The flour is somewhat grainy with partially intact wheat kernels. This imparts a nut-like flavor to the flour. Plus, stone ground wheat flour make lower-glycemic bread.
- **Stevia with FOS.** This is a powdered sweetener made from a South American herb, combined with fruit ogliosaccharides (FOS).
- **Fructose.** Fructose is sweeter than table sugar and is low glycemic. Fructose is the natural sugar present in fruit. Bulk fructose is extracted from fruit.
- **Yeast**. Used to add air bubbles to the dough, causing bread to rise.
- **Psyllium**. A grain with a very high fiber content and no net carbohydrates. Used as a health supplement to promote regularity.

For more about whole-grain flours, alternative sweeteners, and other ingredients used in the recipes in this book, please read Chapter 3.

The Least You Need to Know

◆ Research has shown that many store-bought breads offer low nutritional value while being high-glycemic—not a good health value for persons with diabetes.

◆ The bread recipes in this chapter are low glycemic and high in fiber, so you can eat them with confidence.

◆ Eat only the amount of bread suggested in the serving size listed in the recipe to assure that you don't eat too high a glycemic load.

Oat and Whole-Wheat Yeast Bread

Prep time: 15 minutes • Cook time: 30 to 40 minutes • Serves: 2 loaves (20 slices per loaf) • Serving size: 1 slice

Nutritional Analysis per Serving: Glycemic Index 50 • Glycemic Load 7 • Calories 82 • Protein in gram 4 • Animal Protein 1 • Vegetable Protein 3 • Carbohydrates 17 grams • Dietary Fiber 3 grams • Net Carbohydrate 14 grams • Fat 1 gram • Saturated Fat <1 gram • Cholesterol 11 mg • Sodium 122 mg • Exchanges 1 starch

Vegetable oil cooking spray

3 TB. canola oil

3 cups sour milk, or skim milk with 1 tsp. lemon juice added

¼ cup pure honey

2 tsp. salt

2 cups unprocessed wheat bran

2 cups slow-cooking rolled oats

3 ½ to 4 cups stone-ground whole-wheat flour

2 pkg. active dry yeast (2 TB.)

2 eggs

Palate Preview _____ This recipe makes a versatile, everyday bread. Honey adds a slightly sweet taste. Serve as toast or use for sandwiches.

Delightfully Different _ You can make dinner rolls from this recipe. Simply mold the dough into dinner-roll size after the first rising and put on a baking sheet sprayed with cooking spray. Let rise until doubled in size and place in preheated oven. Check rolls after 20 minutes to test for doneness.

Spray two 3×9×5-inch loaf pans with cooking spray.

Pour 1 TB. oil, sour milk, honey, and salt into a saucepan set over medium heat and heat until warm. Pour mixture into a 3- to 4-quart bowl. Add bran, oats, 2 cups whole-wheat flour, yeast, 1 tablespoon oil, and eggs. Mix well. Gradually stir in 1½ to 2 cups whole-wheat flour, until dough is fairly stiff and can be pulled away from the side of the bowl. (If dough is too sticky, add the extra ½ cup flour.) Brush top of dough with remaining oil.

Cover and let dough rise until doubled in size. Punch down dough and shape it into two loaves. Place them into the prepared pans. Cover loaves and let rise in a warm place until doubled in size.

During the last 10 minutes of the rising time, preheat the oven to 375°F. Bake loaves for 30 to 40 minutes or until the bread is crisp and brown. The bread is done when bottom is tapped and you hear a hollow sound.

Bran Bread

Prep time: 20 minutes   •   Cook time: 40 minutes   •   Serves: 2 loaves (20 slices per loaf)   •   Serving size: 1 slice

Nutritional Analysis per Serving: Glycemic Index 44   •   Glycemic Load 7   •   Calories 70   •   Protein in grams 3   •   Animal Protein <1   •   Vegetable Protein 3   •   Carbohydrates 20 grams   •   Dietary Fiber 4 grams   •   Net Carbohydrate 16 grams   •   Fat 1 gram   •   Saturated Fat <1 gram   •   Cholesterol <1 gram   •   Sodium 63 mg   •   Exchanges 1 starch, ¼ fruit

1 pkg. active dry yeast (1 TB.)	1 TB. olive oil or canola oil
¾ cup warm water	1 tsp. salt
1 cup warm skim milk	2 cups unprocessed wheat bran
¼ cup fructose	1½ to 2 cups stone-ground whole-wheat flour

Spray a bowl and two 9×5-inch loaf pans with cooking spray.

In another bowl, dissolve yeast in warm water. Add warm milk, fructose, oil, and salt. Mix in bran and 1 cup flour. Gradually stir in flour, ½ cup at a time, until dough is soft. (If dough is too sticky, add more flour.)

Knead until smooth. Place dough into the prepared bowl. Cover and let dough rise for about two hours or until doubled in size.

Punch down dough and shape it into two loaves. Place them into the prepared pans. Cover loaves, and let rise in a warm place for about 1½ hours or until doubled in size. During the last 10 minutes of the rising time, preheat the oven to 375°F. Bake loaves for 40 minutes.

Palate Preview _____
Wheat bran adds healthful fiber and lowers the glycemic load for this delicious bread.

High-Fiber Pizza Crust

Prep time: 20 minutes • Cook time: 35 minutes • Serves: 6 • Serving size: 1 slice of pie cut into sixths

Nutritional Analysis per Serving: Glycemic Index 53 • Glycemic Load 6 • Calories 88 • Protein in grams 4 • Animal Protein 0 • Vegetable Protein 4 • Carbohydrates 18 grams • Dietary Fiber 6 grams • Net Carbohydrate 12 grams • Fat 1 gram • Saturated Fat <1 gram • Cholesterol 0 • Sodium 93 mg • Exchanges 1 starch

1 pkg. active dry yeast (1 TB.)	¾ cup stone-ground whole-wheat flour
1 teaspoon fructose	¼ teaspoon salt
½ to ⅔ cup warm water	1 TB. vegetable oil
1 cup unprocessed wheat bran	

Palate Preview

Yes, you can eat pizza when you use this high-fiber pizza crust as a base. Add the meat and vegetable toppings that work best for your food plan.

Preheat the oven to 450°F. Spray a 12-inch pizza pan with cooking spray.

In a small bowl, combine yeast, fructose, and warm water. Let stand 5 minutes. Stir in bran and let stand for 5 minutes longer. In a medium bowl, mix flour, salt, and oil. Add bran and yeast mixture to flour mixture. Combine and form into dough.

On a lightly floured surface, knead for 5 minutes or until smooth. Place dough on the prepared pizza pan, cover, and let rest for 10 minutes.

Uncover and press dough to edge of pan to form a crust. Arrange topping ingredients of your choice evenly on top. Bake for 35 minutes or until crispy and golden.

Note: For crispier crust, arrange only ¼ of toppings and bake pizza for 8 minutes; then add remaining amount of toppings and bake for 8 more minutes.

High-Fiber Flat Bread

Prep time: 20 minutes • Cook time: 30 to 45 minutes • Serves: 8 • Serving size: ⅛ section of cracker

Nutritional Analysis per Serving: Glycemic Index 45 • Glycemic Load 5 • Calories 84 • Protein in grams 4½ • Animal Protein 1½ • Vegetable Protein 3 • Carbohydrates 16 grams • Dietary Fiber 4 grams • Net Carbohydrate 12 grams • Fat 1½ grams • Saturated Fat <1 gram • Cholesterol 26 mg • Sodium 71 mg • Exchanges 1 starch

Vegetable oil cooking spray

1 cup steel-cut oats

½ cup unprocessed wheat bran

½ cup stone-ground whole-wheat flour

2 tsp. ground cinnamon

¼ tsp. salt

1 egg plus 1 egg white

1 to 1½ cups water

2 teaspoons fructose

Preheat the oven to 325°F. Spray a round pizza pan or a baking sheet with cooking spray.

Mix oats, bran, flour, cinnamon, salt, egg, and egg white. Add 1 cup water. Mix and form into a ball of dough. Add additional water if the consistency is too dry to be spread out on a pan.

Place dough onto the prepared pan or sheet and press until the bottom of the pan is covered. Score the bread into 8 pieces. Sprinkle dough with fructose. Bake for 30 to 45 minutes, until crispy and golden in color.

Palate Preview

This flatbread recipe produces a sweet, crispy cracker seasoned with cinnamon and dusted with fructose. Use this flatbread as you would crackers or regular yeast bread.

Delightfully Different

For a flatbread that's more like a water biscuit, omit the cinnamon and fructose. You can also sprinkle with two teaspoons sesame seeds before baking for a different flavor. The sesame seeds won't significantly change the nutritional analysis per serving.

Cranberry Muffins

Prep time: 20 minutes • Cook time: 25 minutes • Serves: 12 • Serving size: one muffin

Nutritional Analysis per Serving: Glycemic Index 42 • Glycemic Load 11 • Calories 121 • Protein in grams 5 • Animal Protein 2 • Vegetable Protein 3 • Carbohydrates 33 grams • Dietary Fiber 6 grams • Net Carbohydrate 27 grams • Fat <1 gram • Saturated Fat 0 • Cholesterol 0 • Sodium 56 mg • Exchanges 1½ starch, ½ fruit

1¼ cup stone-ground whole-wheat flour

1 TB low-salt baking powder

⅛ tsp. salt

1 tsp. pumpkin pie spice of spices of your choice

3 teaspoons powdered stevia with FOS

¼ cup fructose

1½ cup 100% bran cereal

1¼ cup skim milk

3 egg whites

½ cup unsweetened applesauce

1 cup coarsely chopped frozen or fresh cranberries, unsweetened

½ cup raisins

1 tsp. grated orange zest, fresh or dried

Preheat the oven to 375°F. Spray a 12-cup (12×2½-inch) muffin pan with cooking spray.

In a small bowl, mix together flour, baking powder, salt, pumpkin pie spice, stevia, and fructose.

Palate Preview Along with cranberries, these muffins contain applesauce, raisins, and orange peel. You'll love these fruit-filled treats.

In a large mixing bowl, combine bran cereal with milk until softened. Add egg whites and applesauce and beat well with a large spoon. Stir in cranberries, raisins, and orange zest. Add flour mixture, and stir until combined.

Spoon batter evenly into the prepared pan. Bake for 25 minutes or until lightly browned and toothpick inserted into muffin comes out clean.

Oatmeal-Apple Muffins

Prep time: 15 minutes   •   Cook time: 20 minutes   •   Serves: 12   •   Serving size: 1 muffin

Nutritional Analysis per Serving: Glycemic Index 54   •   Glycemic Load 10   •   Calories 105   •   Protein in grams 3½   •   Animal Protein 1   •   Vegetable Protein 2½   •   Carbohydrates 20 grams   •   Dietary Fiber 2½ grams   •   Net Carbohydrate 18 grams   •   Fat 1½ gram   •   Saturated Fat <1 gram   •   Cholesterol 18 mg   •   Sodium 94 mg   •   Exchanges 1 starch, ⅓ fruit

Vegetable oil cooking spray	1 TB. stevia with FOS
¾ cup stone-ground whole-wheat flour	1 egg
1¼ cup slow cooking rolled oats	¾ cup skim milk
½ tsp. salt	½ cup unsweetened applesauce
3 tsp. low-salt baking powder	1 large apple, cored, chopped
½ tsp. ground nutmeg	½ cup raisins
2 tsp. ground cinnamon	

Preheat the oven to 375°F. Spray a 12-cup (12×2½-inch) muffin pan with cooking spray.

In a medium bowl, combine flour, oats, salt, baking powder, nutmeg, cinnamon, and stevia, and mix thoroughly. Combine egg, milk, applesauce, apple, and raisins in a large bowl. Add flour mixture to apple mixture and mix well. Spoon batter evenly into the prepared pan. Bake for 15 to 20 minutes or until a toothpick inserted into muffin comes out clean.

Palate Preview ___ The wholesome goodness of oatmeal and apples make these hearty and delicious muffins. They also contain raisins.

High-Fiber Cornbread

Prep time: 15 minutes • Cook time: 25 minutes • Serves: 6 • Serving size: ⅙ portion

Nutritional Analysis per Serving: Glycemic Index 55 • Glycemic Load 8 • Calories 94 • Protein in grams 4½ • Animal Protein 2½ • Vegetable Protein 2 • Carbohydrates 18 grams • Dietary Fiber 3½ grams • Net Carbohydrate 15 grams • Fat 2 grams • Saturated Fat <1 gram • Cholesterol 36 mg • Sodium 138 mg • Exchanges 1 starch, ¼ skim milk

½ cup unprocessed wheat bran

½ cup yellow cornmeal

2 TB. stone-ground whole-wheat flour

1 tsp. low-salt baking powder

1 tsp. baking soda

1 cup buttermilk, or add 1 tsp. lemon juice to 1 cup skim milk

1 egg

½ cup frozen corn kernels, thawed

1 tsp. olive or canola oil

Palate Preview

This cornbread is a delicious version that includes actual kernels of corn. The cornbread meets your nutritional needs and satisfies any cornbread cravings.

Preheat the oven to 425°F. Spray an 8-inch glass pie dish or an 8-inch ovenproof skillet with cooking spray.

Combine bran, cornmeal, flour, baking powder, and baking soda in a large bowl. Add buttermilk or soured skim milk, egg, and corn. Mix all ingredients, and set aside to soften.

Pour batter into the prepared pie dish or skillet. Bake for 20 to 25 minutes or until the top is golden and a toothpick inserted into cornbread comes out clean.

Carrot-Raisin Muffins

Prep time: 20 minutes • Cook time: 25 minutes • Serves: 24 • Serving size: 1 muffin

Nutritional Analysis per Serving: Glycemic Index 53 • Glycemic Load 6 • Calories 71 • Protein in grams 4 • Animal Protein 1 • Vegetable Protein 3 • Carbohydrates 16 grams • Dietary Fiber 5 grams • Net Carbohydrate 11 grams • Fat 1 gram • Saturated Fat <1 gram • Cholesterol 17 mg • Sodium 24 mg • Exchanges ½ starch, ½ fruit

Vegetable oil cooking spray

3 cups unprocessed wheat bran

1 cup unprocessed oat bran

½ cup raisins

2 cups shredded carrots

1 (8-oz.) can unsweetened, crushed pineapple

2 TB. ground cinnamon

1 TB. ground ginger

¼ tsp. salt

1 TB. low-salt baking powder

3 cups warm water

3 TB. stevia with FOS

2 tsp. pure vanilla extract

½ cup liquid egg substitute, or 2 eggs and 1 egg white

1 cup stone-ground whole-wheat flour

Preheat the oven to 350°F. Spray two 12-cup medium (2¼-inches in diameter) muffin pans with cooking spray.

In a large bowl, mix together wheat bran, oat bran, raisins, carrots, pineapple, cinnamon, ginger, salt, baking powder, warm water, stevia, vanilla, and egg substitute or eggs.

Mixture should be fairly moist, so add a little extra water if needed. Add whole-wheat flour and mix to combine thoroughly. Spoon batter evenly into the prepard muffin pans. Bake for 25 minutes or until a toothpick inserted into muffin comes out clean.

Palate Preview
These muffins are reminiscent of carrot cake seasoned with ginger and cinnamon and blended with raisins and pineapple.

Orange-Bran Muffins

Prep time: 15 minutes • Cook time: 25 minutes • Serves: 12 • Serving size: 1 muffin

Nutritional Analysis per Serving: Glycemic Index 58 • Glycemic Load 7 • Calories 65 • Protein in grams 3 • Animal Protein 1 • Vegetable Protein 2 • Carbohydrates 16 grams • Dietary Fiber 4 grams • Net Carbohydrate 12 grams • Fat <1 gram • Saturated Fat <1 gram • Cholesterol 18 mg • Sodium 81 mg • Exchanges 1 starch

Vegetable oil cooking spray

1 egg, lightly beaten

2 TB. pure honey

1 cup low-fat buttermilk

¼ cup unsweetened applesauce

1 cup stone-ground whole-wheat flour

1 cup unprocessed wheat bran

1 tsp. baking soda

⅛ tsp. salt

¼ cup orange zest, fresh or dried

Palate Preview Rich-tasting bran muffins flavored with orange rind and applesauce.

Preheat the oven to 350°F, and spray a 12–cup medium muffin pan with cooking spray.

In a large bowl, beat together egg with honey, buttermilk, and applesauce. In a medium bowl, combine flour, bran, baking soda, salt, and orange zest. Add flour mixture to egg mixture and mix well. Spoon batter evenly into the prepared muffin pan. Bake for 25 minutes or until a toothpick inserted into the center of muffin comes out clean.

Angel Pecan Cupcakes

Prep time: 20 minutes • Cook time: 20 minutes • Serves: 12 • Serving size: 1 cupcake

Nutritional Analysis per Serving: Glycemic Index 30 • Glycemic Load 6 • Calories 112 • Protein in grams 3 • Animal Protein 1½ • Vegetable Protein 2 • Carbohydrates 20 grams • Dietary Fiber <½ gram • Net Carbohydrate 20 grams • Fat 4 grams • Saturated Fat <1 gram • Cholesterol 35 mg • Sodium 27 mg • Exchanges 1½ starch

2 eggs, separated	⅛ tsp. salt
¼ cup hot tap water	½ cup cake flour
1 tsp. pure vanilla extract	¾ tsp. low-salt baking powder
¾ cup fructose	½ cup chopped pecans

Preheat the oven to 325°F.

In a medium bowl, with an electric mixer, beat egg yolks, hot water, and vanilla together until very thick and pale. Slowly beat in ½ cup fructose and set aside. In a small bowl, beat egg whites until foamy. Add salt, and continue beating until whites hold soft peaks.

Gradually add remaining ¼ cup fructose to egg whites, beating until stiff but not dry. Stir ⅓ of whites into yolks, and sift flour and baking powder over egg mixture. Add pecans and remaining whites, and gently fold until blended.

Place 12 paper liners in a 12-cup muffin pan. Spoon batter evenly into cups, and bake for 20 minutes or until a toothpick inserted into a cupcake comes out clean.

Chapter 25

Grains and Beans

In This Chapter

- ◆ Satisfying your yen for stomach-pleasing grains and legumes
- ◆ Wholesome whole-grain side dishes
- ◆ Low-glycemic baked bean recipes
- ◆ Great fare for parties and at-home eating

Do you have a gustatory inclination for baked beans and rice pilaf? That's a fancy way of saying, do you like to eat them? If so, you've come to the right chapter. Yes, both grains and legumes—the formal term for these kinds of beans—are high in starch. Persons with diabetes must be careful consuming them. But in their natural state, as whole grains and dried beans, both contain plenty of healthy fiber and good nutrition.

Grains and beans are filling and can give your stomach a sense of satiety. Plus, they taste great. Grain and legume side dishes *can be* low glycemic and low in glycemic load, so they can fit perfectly into your daily food plan.

The recipes in this chapter offer you side dishes with delicious seasonings and vegetables that are great accompaniments to main dishes. You'll find yourself fixing them to go with meat, fish, and poultry dishes. There's even a special stuffed squash dish—Walnut-and-Rice-Stuffed Butternut Squash—that's wonderful for festive holiday occasions.

Making Friends with Grains

Perhaps you haven't eaten many forms of whole grains before. Of course you've eaten rice, but what about barley or bulgur? They're low glycemic and are actually quite delicious. You can find both in most large grocery stores, health food stores, and ethnic food stores.

Rice has many interesting variations, such as Basmati, brown, long-grain, short-grain, and white. The recipes in this chapter call for long-grain white or brown rice and wild rice. You can interchange them in the recipes because virtually all rice, including wild rice, is comparable on the glycemic index. Rice ranges from 52-58, which is at the upper end of low-glycemic, and the lower end of medium glycemic.

Brown rice and wild rice contain more fiber than white rice, but for the purpose of managing your blood glucose levels, choose the rice you like the best. The only rices that are high-glycemic are glutinous rice and jasmine rice from Thailand.

Healthy Notes _____
Wild rice, though called rice, is actually a grass indigenous to the north central United States. Wild rice is harvested in the swampy lake areas of Minnesota and is now grown commercially on farms in California. High in flavor, it adds wonderful crunch to your recipes. Mix with brown or white rice in recipes, as the cooking times are similar.

Barley is especially good in pilafs because it adds texture and taste, and readily picks up the flavors of the additional seasonings, such as garlic, onions, mushrooms, or bouillon. The most common form of barley sold today is pearl barley, from which the husk, bran and germ have been removed, leaving a soft kernel. Several forms of barley require longer cooking times; there's s whole barley and Scotch barley, which has some bran still attached and is higher in fiber and minerals. Manufacturers also process barley in several ways so that it cooks quickly (typically by pre-steaming it or rolling or cutting it.)

Bulgur is a form of wheat berry, or whole-kernel wheat, which has been steamed, dried and milled. The whole-wheat kernel is cracked in processing so that the wheat cooks faster. Bulgur is used in making tabouli, a traditional Middle Eastern dish that has become popular in the United States. As you'll see in the Tabouli recipe in this chapter, you don't cook bulgur, but rather pour boiling water over it and let it steep. We recommend using fine-grain bulgur because it works best for tabouli, but if you can't find it, any size bulgur is okay.

You'll also find lower-glycemic recipes for rice and wild rice in this chapter. Of course, persons with diabetes need to carefully watch the serving sizes they eat of any of these recipes.

Baking Beans

Baked beans have lots of fans. Maybe that's because they're a traditional part of fun outdoor-eating events like barbecues, picnics, and "chuck-wagon" dinners. Of course, they're just fine for your indoor meals, too.

If you have a fondness for baked beans, check out the recipes here. Texas Pinto Beans are extra spicy hot and Southwest Baked Beans are a combination of four different kinds of legumes slow cooked to perfection.

The Least You Need to Know

♦ Legumes and grains are filled with healthy fiber and good nutrition.

♦ Grains and beans are good at giving your stomach a sense of satiety.

♦ Serve grain side dishes with main-dish meat, seafood, and poultry.

♦ Baked bean side dishes are great for barbecues and summertime outdoors—and indoors—eating.

♦ Experiment with less familiar grains and get to know their wonderful flavors and textures.

Vegetable Confetti Rice

Prep time: 10 minutes • Cook time: 20 minutes • Serves: 6 • Serving size: ½ cup

Nutritional Analysis per Serving: Glycemic Index 50 • Glycemic Load 10 • Calories 142 • Protein in grams 3 • Animal Protein 0 • Vegetable Protein 3 • Carbohydrates 21 grams • Dietary Fiber 2 grams • Net Carbohydrate 19 grams • Fat 2½ grams • Saturated Fat <1 gram • Cholesterol 0 • Sodium 186 mg • Exchanges 1 starch, 1 vegetable, ½ fat

2 cups water	½ cup shredded carrot
1 TB. unsalted butter or olive oil	½ cup sliced celery
1 tsp. low-salt, powdered chicken bouillon	1 TB. finely chopped onion
¾ cup uncooked white or brown long-grain rice	½ cup frozen sweet peas, thawed

Palate Preview

The carrots, celery, onions, and peas give this rice dish great flavor. Serve with any meat, poultry, or seafood main dish.

In a medium saucepan, bring water, butter or oil, and bouillon to a boil. Stir to dissolve bouillon. Add rice, carrot, celery, and onion, and mix well. Bring to a boil and reduce heat to medium. Cover and simmer 20 minutes or until rice is tender and liquid is absorbed. Stir in peas and cook an additional 5 minutes.

Tabouli

Prep time: 15 minutes plus 45 minutes to soak   •   Cook time: none   •   Serves: 12   •
Serving size: ½ cup

Nutritional Analysis per Serving: Glycemic Index 28   •   Glycemic Load 3   •   Calories 57
•   Protein in grams 2   •   Animal Protein 0   •   Vegetable Protein 2   •   Carbohydrates
10 grams   •   Dietary Fiber 1½ gram   •   Net Carbohydrate 9 grams   •   Fat 1 gram   •
Saturated Fat <1 gram   •   Cholesterol 0   •   Sodium 186 mg   •   Exchanges ½ starch,
½ vegetable

¾ cup fine-grained bulgur wheat

3 cups boiling water

2 medium tomatoes

4 TB. very finely minced onion

1 cucumber, peeled and chopped

2 cups very finely chopped parsley, loosely
packed

3 TB. fresh lemon juice

1 tsp. salt

1 TB. olive oil

Pour bulgur into a glass or ceramic large bowl. Pour
boiling water over it and mix to moisten thoroughly.
Soak for 45 minutes.

Cut tomatoes in half crosswise. Core tomato halves
and cut into ¼-inch dice. Put diced tomato in a glass
or ceramic bowl and set aside for 45 minutes.

Line a fine sieve with several layers of paper toweling.
When bulgur wheat has finished soaking, transfer to
the prepared sieve and press to drain well. Return to
the bowl. Drain diced tomatoes. Add drained tomatoes,
onion, cucumber, parsley, lemon juice, salt, oil to bulgur, and mix well. Taste and adjust seasonings if you
need to.

Palate Preview
Tabouli is a vegetable
and grain dish from the Middle
East. The secret to its fresh taste is
the parsley and tomatoes. Can
keep for up to a week stored in
the refrigerator. Serve as a side
dish with a main dish for lunch or
dinner.

Walnut-and-Rice-Stuffed Butternut Squash

Prep time: 15 minutes • Cook time: 1 hour • Serves: 8 • Serving size: ¼ squash (¾ cup) with ⅓ cup filling

Nutritional Analysis per Serving: Glycemic Index 55 • Glycemic Load 14 • Calories 153 • Protein in grams 3½ • Animal Protein 0 • Vegetable Protein 3½ • Carbohydrates 29 grams • Dietary Fiber 4 grams • Net Carbohydrate 25 grams • Fat 3 grams • Saturated Fat <1 gram • Cholesterol 7 mg • Sodium 84 mg • Exchanges 1 starch, 1 fruit, ½ fat

Vegetable oil cooking spray	¼ cup chopped walnuts
2 medium butternut squash, halved lengthwise, seeds removed	½ tsp. dried marjoram
	¼ tsp. salt
2 cups cooked wild rice	2 TB. frozen apple juice concentrate, thawed
½ cup sweetened, dried cranberries	2 tsp. unsalted butter, melted

Preheat the oven to 375°F. Spray a 15×10-inch baking dish with cooking spray. Place squash, cut side down, into the prepared baking dish. Bake for 30 minutes.

Palate Preview ____ An excellent recipe for a cold winter's night, and festive enough for a holiday dinner. You'll love the combination of walnuts, cranberries, wild rice, and squash.

Meanwhile in medium bowl, combine wild rice, cranberries, walnuts, marjoram, and salt, mixing well. In a small bowl, combine apple juice concentrate and butter.

When squash has baked for 30 minutes, remove it from the oven and turn it cut side up. Brush each half with ¼ of the butter mixture. Spoon equal portions wild rice mixture into each half. Drizzle each with remaining butter mixture.

Return to the oven and bake for an additional 30 minutes or until squash is tender and filling is thoroughly heated, covering with foil during last 10 minutes of baking.

Barley Pilaf with Artichokes

Prep time: 10 minutes • Cook time: 40 minutes • Serves: 8 • Serving size: ½ cup

Nutritional Analysis per Serving: Glycemic Index 17 • Glycemic Load 3 • Calories 134 • Protein in grams 5 • Animal Protein 1 • Vegetable Protein 4 • Carbohydrates 22 grams • Dietary Fiber 6 grams • Net Carbohydrate 16 grams • Fat 3 grams • Saturated Fat 1 gram • Cholesterol <1 gram • Sodium 115 mg • Exchanges 1½ starch, ½ fat

2 cups low-salt chicken broth	2 cups sliced white mushrooms (16-oz.)
1 cup uncooked, quick-cooking barley	2 tsp. minced garlic
¼ tsp. salt	1 TB. fresh lemon juice
1 TB. olive oil	¼ cup grated Parmesan cheese
1 (14-oz.) can quartered artichoke hearts, drained and rinsed	

Combine broth, barley, and salt in a medium saucepan. Bring to a boil, reduce heat, and cook for about 30 minutes or until barley is tender and all liquid is absorbed.

While barley cooks, heat olive oil in a large nonstick skillet over medium-high heat. Add artichokes, mushrooms, and garlic. Sauté, stirring frequently, for 3 minutes.

Stir lemon juice and artichoke mixture into cooked barley. Sprinkle cheese evenly over top of barley mixture. Serve hot.

Palate Preview
You'll love this combination of mushrooms, artichokes, garlic, Parmesan cheese, and barley. The taste is rich and the dish is filling.

Southwest Baked Beans

Prep time: 15 minutes • Cook time: 5 hours • Serves: 30 • Serving size: ⅓ cup

Nutritional Analysis per Serving: Glycemic Index 37 • Glycemic Load 2 • Calories 75 • Protein in grams 8 • Animal Protein 3 • Vegetable Protein 5 • Carbohydrates 10 grams • Dietary Fiber 5 grams • Net Carbohydrate 5 grams • Fat 1 gram • Saturated Fat <½ gram • Cholesterol 11 mg • Sodium 114 mg • Exchanges ⅔ starch, ½ medium-lean meat

1 (12-oz.) pkg. spicy hot pork sausage	1 (9-oz.) package frozen baby lima beans, thawed
4 (15-oz.) cans baked beans, drained	1 cup thick and chunky tomato salsa
1 (15-oz.) can dark red kidney beans, drained and rinsed	2 TB. no-salt-added chili powder blend
1 (15.8-oz.) can black-eyed peas, drained and rinsed	1 cup water

Cook sausage in a medium skillet over medium heat until browned and no longer pink, stirring frequently. Drain. Chop the sausage into bite-sized chunks.

Delightfully Different

For the spicy pork sausage, you can substitute chorizo or andouille sausage.

In a 3½- to 4-quart slow cooker, combine cooked sausage, baked beans, kidney beans, black-eyed peas, lima beans, salsa, chili powder, and water, and gently stir to mix.

Cover and cook on the low setting for 5 hours.

Palate Preview

This baked bean dish is a combination of four kinds of beans cooked together in a slow cooker. This recipe serves 30. If you have leftovers, you can freeze for later use. The baked beans will make your mouth happy with its spicy and meaty flavors.

Wild Rice and Barley Pilaf

Prep time: 5 minutes   •   Cook time: 1 hour and 10 minutes   •   Serves: 6   •   Serving size: ⅔ cup

Nutritional Analysis per Serving: Glycemic Index 34   •   Glycemic Load 7   •   Calories 138   •   Protein in grams 4   •   Animal Protein 0   •   Vegetable Protein 4   •   Carbohydrates 23 grams   •   Dietary Fiber 3½ grams   •   Net Carbohydrate 20 grams   •   Fat 3 grams   •   Saturated Fat 2 grams   •   Cholesterol 10 mg   •   Sodium 50 mg   •   Exchanges 1½ starch, ½ fat

1 TB. unsalted butter	1 cup water
½ cup uncooked barley	½ cup uncooked wild rice, rinsed and drained
½ cup chopped onion	½ tsp. grated fresh lemon zest
1 garlic clove, minced	⅛ to ¼ tsp. freshly ground black pepper
1 (14½-oz.) can low-salt chicken broth	

In a medium saucepan, melt butter over medium heat. Add barley and cook, stirring occasionally, for 6 to 8 minutes or until lightly browned. Add onion and garlic. Cook, stirring, for 2 to 3 minutes or until crisp-tender. Add broth and water and bring to a boil. Stir in rice, lemon zest, and pepper, and return to a boil. Reduce heat to medium. Cover and simmer 50 to 60 minutes or until barley and rice are tender and liquid is absorbed.

Palate Preview

This recipe is an usual pilaf of barley and wild rice accented with the zing of lemon plus garlic and onions. You'll love the texture and nutty flavor.

Texas Pinto Beans

Prep time: ½ hour plus 6 hours to soak • Cook time: 2½ hours • Serves: 20 •
Serving size: ⅓ cup

Nutritional Analysis per Serving: Glycemic Index 37 • Glycemic Load 3 • Calories 70
• Protein in grams 4 • Animal Protein 0 • Vegetable Protein 4 • Carbohydrates
12 grams • Dietary Fiber 3½ grams • Net Carbohydrate 9 grams • Fat 1 gram •
Saturated Fat <1 gram • Cholesterol 0 • Sodium 349 mg • Exchanges ⅔ starch

2 cups dried pinto beans	2 cups diced onions
¼ cup no-salt-added chili powder blend	2 TB. chopped garlic
1 TB. salt	1 cup diced red bell pepper
½ bunch fresh cilantro, stemmed and chopped	1 cup diced green bell pepper
1 TB. olive oil	

Wash beans and sort through them to remove any foreign particles and broken beans.

In a stockpot, cover beans with cold water by 6 inches and soak 6 hours or overnight. Be sure
beans remain covered with water during the soaking process.

Drain beans and return them to the same pan. Cover with fresh water by 1½ inches. Add chili
powder, salt, and cilantro, and stir to blend. Bring beans to a boil over medium heat. Reduce
heat. Cover and cook for about 2½ hours or until beans
are tender. From time to time check and stir beans. If
the pot is too dry, water as needed. Near the end of
cooking time, liquid should be almost absorbed.

Close to serving time, heat olive oil in a large skillet.
When oil is hot, add garlic, diced onions and bell peppers, and cook, stirring and tossing for about 6 minutes,
or until crisp-tender. Stir bell pepper mixture into
beans. Serve at once.

Palate Preview

Make a pot of these
beans for summer barbecues and
picnics. They serve a large crowd
and you can freeze any leftovers.
The beans go well with hamburgers, steaks, and chicken.

Healthy Notes

Soaking the beans before cooking reduces cooking time and yields a softer cooked
bean. Soaking softens the bean and neutralizes the complex sugars that cause flatulence.
If you don't have the time to soak the pinto beans, you can use canned pinto beans without added sauces or flavorings.

Chapter 26

Desserts

In This Chapter

- ◆ Delicious low-glycemic desserts
- ◆ Cooking with fructose and stevia
- ◆ Eating desserts and staying healthy
- ◆ Sweets for you and the whole family

Sometimes a meal just doesn't seem complete without dessert. You want that sweet finish to a great dinner. And why not? Humankind has eaten dessert in some form or fashion for many thousands of years. While we probably started out eating fruits and nuts for dessert, with perhaps some honey mixed in, we now choose from an almost unlimited range of desserts—pastries, cakes, cookies, ices, pies, and more.

As you know, desserts are often filled with way too many starches, sugars, and fats to meet your dietary requirements. But plenty of desserts are acceptable and even good for you, depending on how they're made and what they're made of.

In this chapter, you'll find recipes tailored to your health that also satisfy your sweet tooth. All of them are low glycemic and have a low-glycemic load ranging from 2 to 14, with most under 8. So, by all means, eat dessert and stay healthy, too.

Sweet Things

A significant challenge in preparing desserts is figuring out how to sweeten them. Sugar is moderate glycemic at 68. A tablespoon contains 10 grams of carbohydrates and a glycemic load of 7, so a little sugar is fine, but sugar-laden desserts cause too big and swift a rise in blood glucose levels.

The recipes in this chapter call for such sweeteners as granulated table sugar, brown sugar, fructose, and stevia with fruit olgiosaccharides (FOS).

Stevia is an herb from South America that's four times as sweet as table sugar and has virtually no calories or carbohydrates. The native peoples of South America have used stevia for thousands of years. Fruit ogliosaccharides (FOS) contain nutritive fiber that supports the health of the intestinal tract by promoting the growth of good bacteria. FOS also mitigates the aftertaste of stevia that some people find disagreeable. The combination of stevia with FOS tastes sweet and holds up to both heat and cold. (For more about stevia and other sweeteners, please read Chapter 3.)

Artificial sweeteners are controversial. Sure, they make desserts sweet and don't cause a lift in blood glucose levels, but the downside is that no one is "100 percent" certain of their long-term safety. Besides, some do not hold up to heat during cooking. So, to be on the safe side, the recipes in this chapter use only natural sweeteners.

You can top all of the desserts in this chapter with frozen nondairy whipped topping. The brand name you're familiar with is Cool Whip. It's a free food for persons with diabetes and it tastes great. The recipes don't have a specific amount listed for this topping, so you can add a reasonable amount to your dessert.

The Least You Need to Know

◆ Desserts are an acceptable part of meals for persons with diabetes.

◆ The glycemic load of the desserts in this chapter range from 2 to 14, with most under 8.

◆ Natural sweeteners are used in these dessert recipes.

◆ Eating a sweet-tasting food after meals is an ancient human preference.

Apple Crisp

Prep time: 15 minutes • Cook time: 30 to 35 minutes • Serves: 12 • Serving size: ¹⁄₁₂ recipe

Nutritional Analysis per Serving: Glycemic Index 50 • Glycemic Load 10 • Calories 105 • Protein in grams 2 • Animal Protein <1 • Vegetable Protein 1½ • Carbohydrates 24 grams • Dietary Fiber 3½ grams • Net Carbohydrate 21 grams • Fat <1 gram • Saturated Fat 0 • Cholesterol <2 mg • Sodium 10 mg • Exchanges 1 fruit, ½ starch

Vegetable oil cooking spray

6 Granny Smith apples, peeled, cored, and sliced

⅓ cup fructose

¾ cup whole-wheat flour

¾ cup slow-cooking rolled oats

1 tsp. ground cinnamon

½ tsp. grated nutmeg

¼ cup nonfat plain yogurt

Frozen nondairy whipped topping

Preheat the oven to 375°F. Spray a 12×8×2-inch baking pan with cooking spray. Place apples in the pan. In a mixing bowl, combine fructose, flour, oats, cinnamon, nutmeg, and yogurt and mix until crumbly. Spread flour mixture over apples. Bake for 30 to 35 minutes or until topping is browned. Serve with frozen nondiary whipped topping.

Palate Preview ___ Just the aroma of the Apple Crisp while it's baking is enticing. Actually eating it is even better!

Apricot Cheesecake

Prep time: 15 minutes plus 2 hours or more refrigeration time • Cook time: 65 to 70 minutes • Serves: 16 • Serving size: 1/16 cheesecake

Nutritional Analysis per Serving: Glycemic Index 34 • Glycemic Load 5 • Calories 126 • Protein in grams 8 • Animal Protein 8 • Vegetable Protein 0 • Carbohydrates 14 grams • Dietary Fiber 0 • Net Carbohydrate 14 grams • Fat 3½ grams • Saturated Fat 2 grams • Cholesterol 49 mg • Sodium 230 mg • Exchanges 1 lean meat, 1 starch

1 (8-oz.) pkg. low-fat cream cheese	3 eggs, beaten
2 (8-oz.) pkg. nonfat cream cheese	¼ cup no sugar added apricot preserves without aspartame
1 (8-oz.) container nonfat sour cream	¼ cup orange juice
¼ cup all-purpose flour	1 TB. fresh lemon juice
½ cup fructose	2 tsp. grated fresh lemon zest
2 tsp. stevia with FOS	

Palate Preview

A rich and flavorful cheesecake. The apricots and sour cream lend a slightly tangy yet sweet taste.

Preheat the oven to 325°F. Combine cream cheeses and sour cream in a large mixing bowl. Using an electric mixer set on high speed, beat until fluffy.

Sprinkle flour, fructose, and stevia over cheese mixture and mix on low speed to combine. Add beaten eggs, apricot preserves, orange juice, lemon juice, and lemon zest, and mix. Pour mixture into a 9-inch glass pie dish. Bake for 65 to 70 minutes or until the center is just set. Spread top of cheesecake with apricot preserves. Refrigerate until chilled, about 2 hours.

Healthy Notes

Cheesecake tends to crack on top as it cooks. By spreading the preserves over top, you can hide the cracks and increase the visual appeal of this luscious dessert.

Baked Custard

Prep time: 15 minutes • Cook time: 45 minutes • Serves: 10 • Serving size: ¾ cup

Nutritional Analysis per Serving: Glycemic Index 32 • Glycemic Load 2 • Calories 86 • Protein in grams 10 • Animal Protein 10 • Vegetable Protein 0 • Carbohydrates 7 grams • Dietary Fiber 0 • Net Carbohydrate 7 grams • Fat 1 gram • Saturated Fat ½ gram • Cholesterol 42 mg • Sodium 142 mg • Exchanges 1 lean meat, ½ skim milk

6 cups skim milk	⅛ tsp. grated nutmeg
⅛ tsp. salt	10 large egg whites
2 TB. plus 2 tsp. stevia with FOS	2 large eggs
2 tsp. ground cinnamon	3 tsp. pure vanilla extract

Preheat the oven to 325°F.

Pour milk into an 8-quart saucepan. Add salt, 2 tablespoons stevia, cinnamon, and nutmeg. Cook on medium heat but do not boil. Remove from the heat. Slowly beat in egg whites and eggs with an electric mixer. Add vanilla.

Pour mixture into a 13×9-inch glass baking dish. Place dish into a 15×10-inch rectangular pan and fill the outer pan with water until the water level reaches ¼ to ½ up the sides of the inner pan. Carefully place the pans in the oven and bake for 45 minutes.

Cool at room temperature for about 1 hour before serving.

Palate Preview
A creamy baked custard flavored with nutmeg and cinnamon. Just right for those moments when you want a comfort food or a delicious dessert.

Berry Delight

Prep time: 5 to 10 minutes • Cook time: none • Serves: 4 • Serving size: 1 cup berries plus 2 tablespoons cream sauce

Nutritional Analysis per Serving: Glycemic Index 38 • Glycemic Load 11 • Calories 133 • Protein in grams 4 • Animal protein 4 • Vegetable protein <1 • Carbohydrates 32 grams • Dietary Fiber 2–4 grams • Net Carbphydrate 30 grams • Fat <1 gram • Saturated Fat <1 gram • Cholesterol 2 mg • Sodium 150 mg • Exchanges 2 fruit, ½ lean meat

4 cups fresh or unsweetened frozen berries (strawberries, blueberries, raspberries, etc.)

4 oz. non-fat cream cheese

1 TB. fructose

2 TB. frozen orange juice concentrate, thawed

2 TB. water

1 tsp. pure vanilla extract

¼ cup frozen nondairy whipped topping.

Place equal portions of berries into four parfait glasses. Place cream cheese, fructose, orange juice concentrate, water, and vanilla in a blender and process until smooth. Spoon 2 tablespoons sauce over each dish of berries. Top each with 1 tablespoon frozen nondairy whipped topping. Serve.

Palate Preview

Makes a quick and luscious dessert. Just spoon the berries into parfait glasses and top with cream cheese mixture. Sure to please.

Delicious Fudge Brownies

Prep time: 15 minutes • Cook time: 22 minutes • Serves: 16 • Serving size: One 2 × 2-inch square brownie

Nutrition Analysis per Serving: Glycemic Index 45 • Glycemic Load 8 • Calories 82 • Protein in grams 2 • Animal Protein 1½ • Vegetable Protein ½ • Carbohydrates 16 grams • Dietary Fiber 1 gram • Fat <1 gram • Saturated Fat <1 gram • Cholesterol 18 mg • Sodium 24 mg • Exchanges 1 starch

Vegetable oil cooking spray

¾ cup slow-cooking rolled oats

¼ cup plain non-fat yogurt

2 TB. water

2 TB. stevia with FOS

5 TB. fructose

¼ cup unsweetened cocoa powder

3 TB. non-sugar added apricot preserves without aspartame

2 egg whites plus 1 egg

1½ tsp. pure vanilla extract

¼ cup crushed pineapple, drained

½ tsp. baking powder

Pinch of salt (¹⁄₁₆ tsp.)

½ cup whole-wheat flour

Preheat the oven to 325°F. Spray an 8-inch square pan with cooking spray. In a large bowl, combine oats, yogurt, water, stevia, fructose, cocoa powder, apricot preserves, eggs, vanilla, pineapple, baking powder, and salt. Mix well. Add flour and mix again.

Pour batter into the prepared pan and spread in an even layer. Bake for 22 minutes. Cool to room temperature. Serve plain or with frozen nondairy whipped topping.

Palate Preview

A chocolaty, decadent fudge brownie. For when nothing less will satisfy.

Cheesecake with Cherry Topping

Prep time: 10 minutes plus overnight refrigeration • Cook time: 60 minutes • Serves: 12 • Serving size: ½₂ cheesecake

Nutritional Analysis per Serving: Glycemic Index 40 • Glycemic Load 7 • Calories 90 • Protein in grams 9 • Animal Protein 9 • Vegetable Protein 0 • Carbohydrates 17 grams • Dietary Fiber 0 • Net Carbohydrate 17 grams • Fat 1 gram • Saturated Fat ½ gram • Cholesterol 56 mg • Sodium 264 mg • Exchanges 1 lean meat, 1 starch

16 oz. nonfat cream cheese, softened

16 oz. nonfat sour cream

2 TB. stevia with FOS

½ cup fructose

3 eggs

2 TB. cornstarch

1 tsp. pure vanilla extract

Fresh fruit, cherry sauce (see recipe followings), and/or light whipped cream

Palate Preview

A serious cheesecake lover's cheesecake—rich, heavy, and creamy.

Preheat the oven to 300°F. Using an electric mixer set on high speed, beat cream cheese, sour cream, stevia, and fructose until fluffy. Add eggs, cornstarch, and vanilla, and beat on medium speed until thoroughly combined. Pour mixture into a pie plate (with no crust).

Bake for 60 minutes or until firm in the center. Turn off the oven and let cheesecake cool.

Refrigerate overnight. Serve with fresh fruit, cherry sauce (see the recipe that follows), and/or frozen nondairy whipped topping.

Cherry Sauce Topping for Cheesecake

Prep time: 15 minutes • Cook time: 2 minutes • Serves: 12 • Serving size: 3 tablespoons

Nutritional Analysis per Serving: Glycemic Index 36 • Glycemic Load 4 • Calories 43 • Protein in grams <1 • Animal Protein 0 • Vegetable Protein <1 • Carbohydrates 12 grams • Dietary Fiber <1 gram • Net Carbohydrate 12 grams • Fat 0 • Saturated Fat 0 • Cholesterol 0 • Sodium 20 mg • Exchanges 1 fruit

1 (16-oz.) can tart, pitted, red cherries packed in water, drained, liquid reserved

⅓ cup stevia

Pinch of ground cinnamon

1 TB. plus 1 tsp. cornstarch

½ tsp. fresh lemon juice (optional)

Combine cherries, ½ cup reserved cherry liquid, cinnamon, cornstarch, and stevia in a medium saucepan. Bring to a light boil, and cook until thickened. Add lemon juice if desired.

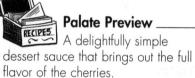

Palate Preview
A delightfully simple dessert sauce that brings out the full flavor of the cherries.

Chocolate Lemon Cream Pie

Prep time: 15 minutes plus hours refrigeration • Cook time: 5 minutes • Serves: 6 •
Serving size: ⅙ pie

Nutritional Analysis per Serving: Glycemic Index 42 • Glycemic Load 8 • Calories 136
• Protein in grams 8 • Animal Protein 7 • Vegetable Protein 1 • Carbohydrates
20 grams • Dietary Fiber 1 gram • Net Carbohydrate 19 grams • Fat 2 grams •
Saturated Fat 1 gram • Cholesterol 3 mg • Sodium 130 mg • Exchanges 1 skim
milk, ½ starch

2 TB. stevia with FOS

5 TB. unsweetened cocoa powder

4 TB. cornstarch

2 cups skim milk

½ cup egg whites

2 tsp. pure vanilla extract

2 (8-oz.) cartons of non-fat lemon yogurt

¼ cup nondairy whipped topping

¼ cup semisweet chocolate morsels

Palate Preview
This pie is a "wow!"
Chocolate filling topped with
lemon yogurt, light whipped topping, and chocolate morsels.
Beautiful to behold and wonderful
to taste.

In a large saucepan set on an unheated work surface,
combine stevia, cocoa, and cornstarch. Slowly add milk
and blend well with a whisk. Set over medium heat and
cook, stirring constantly, until liquid boils. Boil, still
stirring, for 1 minute. Remove from heat.

Slowly stir egg whites into boiling cocoa mixture. Mix
well. Stir in vanilla.

Pour cocoa mixture into a round 9-inch glass pie dish
(with no crust). Cool and refrigerate for 2 hours or
more. Spread yogurt on top of chocolate pie filling in
an even layer. Top with frozen nondairy whipped topping. Sprinkle with chocolate morsels.

Chocolate Pudding

Prep time: 15 minutes • Cook time: 5 minutes • Serves: 4 • Serving size: ½ cup

Nutritional Analysis per Serving: Glycemic Index 54 • Glycemic Load 7 • Calories 93 • Protein in grams 5½ • Animal Protein 4 • Vegetable Protein 1½ • Carbohydrates 12 grams • Dietary Fiber 0 • Net Carbohydrate 12 grams • Fat <1 gram • Saturated Fat < 1 gram • Cholesterol 55 mg • Sodium 156 mg • Exchanges ½ skim milk, ½ starch

3 TB. cornstarch	2 to 3 tsp. stevia with FOS
2 TB. unsweetened cocoa powder	1 tsp. butter-flavored granules, such as Butter Buds
⅛ tsp. salt	
2 cups plus 2 TB. 1% low-fat or skim milk	1 tsp. pure vanilla extract
1 egg, beaten	Frozen nondairy whipped topping

In a heavy-bottom saucepan, stir together, cornstarch, cocoa, and salt with milk. Set over medium heat, and cook, stirring constantly, until mixture simmers and begins to thicken. Add beaten egg. Simmer, stirring constantly, for about 1 minute.

Remove from the heat and add stevia, Butter Buds, and vanilla. Add more stevia if necessary, to taste. Serve warm or cold. Top with low-fat whipped cream.

Palate Preview

An all-time favorite dessert, both satisfying and healthy.

Key Lime Cheesecake

Prep time: 20 minutes • Cook time: 60 minutes plus overnight refrigeration • Serves: 12 • Serving size: $\frac{1}{12}$ pie

Nutritional Analysis per Serving: Glycemic Index 34 • Glycemic Load 5 • Calories 160 • Protein in grams 9 • Animal Protein 9 • Vegetable Protein 0 • Carbohydrates 14 grams • Dietary Fiber 0 • Net Carbohydrate 14 grams • Fat 7 grams • Saturated Fat 5 grams • Cholesterol 40 mg • Sodium 234 mg • Exchanges 1 lean meat, 1 fat, 1 starch

1 egg

4 egg whites

2 (8-oz.) pkg. low-fat cream cheese

1 (8-oz.) pkg. nonfat cream cheese

1 (8-oz.) container nonfat plain yogurt

$\frac{1}{2}$ cup fructose

2 tsp. stevia with FOS

$\frac{1}{4}$ cup fresh key lime juice if available, otherwise lime juice

2 tsp. grated fresh lime zest

1$\frac{1}{2}$ tsp. pure vanilla extract

2 TB. plus 1 tsp. cornstarch

frozen nondairy whipped topping

Lime wedges for garnish

Palate Preview _____
This cheesecake offers you a taste of the islands for your dessert. Rich, sensuous, and cooling.

Preheat the oven to 300°F.

Using an electric mixer set on high speed, beat egg, egg whites, cream cheeses, yogurt, fructose, stevia, lime juice, lime peel, and vanilla until thoroughly blended. Sprinkle in cornstarch and mix on low speed until combined. Pour into a 9-inch glass pie dish.

Bake for about 60 minutes or until firm in the center. Cool and refrigerate overnight. Serve with light whipped topping and garnish with lime wedges.

Mandarin Orange Whip

Prep time: 15 minutes • Cook time: 5 minutes plus at least 3 hours refrigeration • Serves: 7 • Serving size: ½ cup

Nutritional Analysis per Serving: Glycemic Index 51 • Glycemic Load 6 • Calories 63 • Protein in grams 1 • Animal protein ½ • Vegetable protein ½ • Carbohydrates 12 grams • Dietary Fiber <1 gram • Net Carbohydrate 12 grams • Fat <1 gram • Saturated Fat <1 gram • Cholesterol 0 • Sodium 19 mg • Exchanges 1 fruit

1 cup water

1 envelope unflavored gelatin

½ cup nonfat sour cream

¼ cup frozen orange juice concentrate, thawed

1 TB. plus ¼ tsp. stevia with FOS

⅓ cup orange juice

1 (11-oz.) can mandarin oranges, drained

½ cup frozen nondairy whipped topping for garnish

Orange zest curls for garnish

In a medium saucepan, bring water to a boil. Reduce the heat to medium-low add gelatin, and stir for about 5 minutes or until gelatin is dissolved. Add sour cream, orange juice concentrate, and stevia. Mix well. Pour mixture into a bowl, cover, and refrigerate for 3 hours or more until gelled.

Put orange juice into a blender. Add gelled mixture to orange juice, and blend until fluffy.

Pour blended mixture into a large bowl. Mix in drained mandarin oranges and whipped topping. Spoon equal portions into 7 dessert dishes. Serve with a dab of light whipped topping and an orange zest curl for garnish.

Palate Preview

A light dessert. Mandarin orange pieces folded into a fluffy whipped orange gelatin mixture and topped with whipped topping. For when you want a light sweet taste after dinner.

Peach Cobbler

Prep time: 20 minutes • Cook time: 45 to 50 minutes • Serves: 12 • Serving size: $\frac{1}{12}$ recipe

Nutritional Analysis per Serving: Glycemic Index 40 • Glycemic Load 12 • Calories 165 • Protein in grams 3 • Animal Protein 1 • Vegetable Protein 2 • Carbohydrates 33 grams • Dietary Fiber 3 grams • Net Carbohydrate 30 grams • Fat 2½ grams • Saturated Fat ½ gram • Cholesterol 18 mg • Sodium 66 mg • Exchanges 1 fruit, 1 starch, ½ fat

Vegetable oil cooking spray

6 cups pitted sliced fresh or frozen, thawed peaches (about 6 large peaches)

1 TB. fresh lemon juice

1 TB. whole-wheat flour

2 TB. fructose

1 tsp. ground cinnamon

Topping:

1½ cups whole-wheat flour

¼ cup plus 1 TB. fructose

1½ tsp. baking powder

½ cup skim milk

1 egg

2 TB. canola oil or unsalted butter, melted

½ tsp. ground cinnamon

Palate Preview

An old-fashioned peach cobbler made with some new-fashioned healthy ingredients, such as fresh peaches, whole-wheat flour, fructose, and skim milk. You'll love it.

Preheat the oven to 350°F. Spray a 9×9-inch pan with cooking spray. Set aside.

Combine peaches, lemon juice, flour, fructose, and cinnamon and toss gently. Pour peach mixture into the prepared pan.

For topping, mix flour, ¼ cup fructose, and baking powder in a medium bowl. Combine milk, egg, and oil or butter in a small bowl. Add milk mixture to flour mixture, and stir until blended.

Drop batter by tablespoonfuls on top of peach mixture. Combine 1 TB. and cinnamon in a small bowl and sprinkle on top. Bake for 45 to 50 minutes or until topping is crispy and golden.

Pineapple Upside Down Cake

Prep time: 25 minutes • Cook time: 35 minutes • Serves: 12 • Serving size: ¹⁄₁₂ cake

Nutritional Analysis per Serving: Glycemic Index 33 • Glycemic Load 8 • Calories 130 • Protein in grams 5 • Animal Protein 1 • Vegetable Protein 4 • Carbohydrates 27 • Dietary Fiber 4 • Net carbohydrate 23 grams • Fat 1½ grams • Saturated Fat ½ gram • Cholesterol 54 mg • Sodium 104 mg • Exchanges 1 fruit, ½ skim milk, ½ starch

Vegetable oil cooking spray

2 (8-oz.) cans pineapple slices in juice, drained, and liquid reserved

¼ cup raisins

1¼ cups 100% bran cereal

1 cup whole-wheat flour

2 tsp. baking powder

⅛ tsp. salt

1½ tsp. plus ½ tsp ground cinnamon.

½ cup unsweetened applesauce

¼ cup plus 1 tsp. fructose

3 eggs

1 cup nonfat plain yogurt

2 tsp. pure vanilla extract

Preheat the oven to 350°F. Spray a 9-inch round cake pan with cooking spray. Arrange pineapple slices on the bottom of the pan. Scatter raisins around pineapple slices and in the center of slices. In a medium bowl, mix together cereal, flour, baking powder, salt, and 1½ teaspoons cinnamon. Set aside.

Palate Preview

Here's a favorite pineapple upside down cake updated to meet your nutritional needs. Great for your family's dinner or for a potluck dinner.

In a large mixing bowl, beat together applesauce and fructose. Add eggs, yogurt, vanilla, and ¼ cup reserved pineapple liquid. Mix until blended.

Stir in cereal and flour mixture, mixing only until combined. Spread over pineapple slices and raisins.

Bake for about 35 to 40 minutes or until center is firm. Let stand for about 10 minutes.

When the pan is cool enough to handle, place a serving plate on top of it. With one hand holding the plate in place, lift and invert the pan with the other hand, so that the plate is on the bottom. Remove the pan from plated cake. Combine ½ teaspoon cinnamon and 1 teaspoon fructose in a small bowl, and sprinkle on top. Cool and cut into 12 wedges.

Tapioca Pudding

Prep time: 15 minutes • Cook time: 5 to 7 minutes • Serves: 12 • Serving size: ½ cup

Nutritional Analysis per Serving: Glycemic Index 51 • Glycemic Load 4 • Calories 62 • Protein in grams 5 • Animal Protein 5 • Vegetable Protein 0 • Carbohydrates 10 grams • Dietary Fiber 0 • Net Carbohydrate 10 grams • Fat 0 • Saturated Fat 0 • Cholesterol 3 mg • Sodium 100 mg • Exchanges ½ skim milk, ¼ starch

5½ cups skim milk	⅓ cup dry tapioca
2 TB. plus 2 tsp. stevia with FOS	½ cup egg whites
⅛ tsp. salt	2 tsp. pure vanilla extract

Mix milk, stevia, salt, and tapioca into a 2-quart saucepan. Stirring constantly, bring to a boil.

Reduce the heat to medium and beat in egg whites with a wire whisk. Simmer for about 2 minutes or until tapioca is translucent and pudding is thickened. Add vanilla and mix to combine. Cool.

Delightfully Different

Vary the seasonings for tapioca pudding to suit your taste. You can use cardamom, cinnamon, or nutmeg for variety.

Palate Preview

Only tapioca pudding gives you that delectable creamy and "bumpy" texture. This version is flavored with vanilla.

Vanilla-Cinnamon Pudding

Prep time: 15 minutes • Cook time: 5 minutes • Serves: 4 • Serving size: ½ cup

Nutritional Analysis per Serving: Glycemic Index 54 • Glycemic Load 6 • Calories 85 • Protein in grams 4½ • Animal Protein 4 • Vegetable Protein ½ • Carbohydrates 11 grams • Dietary Fiber 0 • Net Carbohydrate 11 grams • Fat 1 gram • Saturated Fat <1 gram • Cholesterol 55 mg • Sodium 53 mg • Exchanges ½ skim milk, ½ starch

3 TB. cornstarch

⅛ tsp salt

2 cups plus 2 TB. skim or 1% low-fat milk

1 egg, beaten

1½ tsp pure vanilla extract

½ tsp. ground cinnamon

Pinch of grated nutmeg, plus more for garnish

1 tsp. butter-flavored granules, or Butter Buds

1 to 2 tsp. stevia with FOS

Frozen nondairy whipped topping

In a medium heavy-bottom saucepan, stir together stevia, cornstarch, and salt with milk. Set over medium heat, and cook, stirring constantly, until mixture simmers and begins to thicken. Add beaten egg. Simmer, stirring constantly, for about 1 minute.

Remove from the heat and add vanilla, cinnamon, nutmeg, Butter Buds and stevia. Add more stevia if necessary, to taste.

Serve warm or cold. Top with a dab of light whipped cream and sprinkle with nutmeg.

Palate Preview _____
Cinnamon gives this vanilla pudding a spicy, old-fashioned taste and aroma.

Pumpkin Pie

Prep time: 15 minutes • Cook time: 45 minutes • Serves: 16 (two pies at 8 servings per pie) • Serving size: ⅛ pie

Nutritional Analysis per Serving: Glycemic Index 45 • Glycemic Load 9 • Calories 120 • Protein in grams 6 • Animal Protein 5 • Vegetable Protein 1 • Carbohydrates 22 grams • Dietary Fiber 2 grams • Net Carbohydrate 20 grams • Fat 1½ grams • Saturated Fat ½ gram • Cholesterol 54 mg • Sodium 63 mg • Exchanges 1 skim milk, ½ starch

1 cup fructose	1 (29-oz.) can pure pumpkin
3½ tsp. pumpkin pie spice	2 (12-oz.) cans evaporated skim milk
4 eggs	Frozen nondairy whipped topping

Preheat the oven to 375°F.

In a large bowl, combine fructose, pumpkin pie spice, eggs, and pumpkin, and mix well. Gradually add evaporated skim milk and blend well. Pour into two 9-inch pie plates (no crust).

Palate Preview _____ Serve this pumpkin pie at your holiday meals and you'll find that everyone loves its familiar taste.

Bake pies at 375°F for the first 15 minutes, then reduce the temperature to 345°F and bake 30 more minutes or until a toothpick or clean knife inserted into the middle of a pie comes out clean.

Serve warm or chilled with frozen nondairy whipped topping.

Golden Ginger Macaroons

Prep time: 10 minutes • Cook time: 20 minutes • Serves: 24 • Serving size: 1 macaroon

Nutritional Analysis per Serving: Glycemic Index 54 • Glycemic Load 7 • Calories 40 • Protein in grams 1 • Animal Protein <1 • Vegetable Protein 1 • Carbohydrates 13 grams • Dietary Fiber ½ gram • Net Carbohydrate 13 grams • Fat 2 grams • Saturated Fat 0 • Cholesterol 0 • Sodium 4 mg • Exchanges 1 fruit, ½ fat

1 egg white

Vegetable oil cooking spray

½ cup unpacked light-brown sugar

1 cup ground almonds, from ¾ cup whole almonds

1 tsp. ground ginger

Preheat the oven to 350°F. Spray 2 baking sheets with vegetable oil cooking spray.

In a large, grease-free bowl, beat egg white, with an electric mixer, until stiff and standing in peaks, but not dry and crumbly; then whisk in brown sugar.

In a food processor fitted with a metal blade, grind almonds until flourlike in texture. Sprinkle ground almonds and ginger over whisked egg white and gently fold together.

Measure about two teaspoons batter and drop it onto a baking sheet, repeating with remaining batter and leaving plenty of space between macaroons. Bake for about 20 minutes, until pale golden brown and just turning crisp.

Let cool slightly on the baking sheets before transferring to a wire rack to cool completely.

Palate Preview
A moist and irresistible macaroon cookie made with ground almonds and brown sugar.

Delightfully Different
You can substitute pecans for the almonds in this recipe. Use a food processor to grind the nuts into a flour consistency.

Chocolate–Hazelnut Macaroons

Prep time: 10 minutes • Cook time: 20 minutes • Serves: 24 • Serving size: 1 macaroon

Nutritional Analysis per Serving: Glycemic Index 53 • Glycemic Load 3 • Calories 40 • Protein in grams 1 • Animal Protein < 1 • Vegetable Protein < 1 • Carbohydrates 6 grams • Dietary Fiber ½ gram • Net Carbohydrate 6 grams • Fat grams 2 grams • Saturated Fat < 1 gram • Cholesterol 0 • Sodium 5 mg • Exchanges ½ fat, ½ fruit

½ oz. bittersweet baking chocolate	½ cup brown sugar
1 egg white	1 cup ground hazelnuts or ¾ cup whole

Palate Preview _____
You'll love tasting the chocolate bits in these hazelnut cookies.

Preheat the oven to 350°F. Prepare 2 baking sheets by spraying with nonstick vegetable oil.

With a chef's knife, carefully shave baking chocolate into very small bits and shavings.

In a large, grease-free bowl, whisk egg white until stiff and standing in peaks, but not dry and crumbly; then whisk in brown sugar.

In a food processor fitted with a metal blade, grind hazelnuts until flourlike in texture. Sprinkle ground hazelnuts over whisked egg white and gently fold them together. Then sprinkle shaved baking chocolate over mixture and gently fold together.

Measure about two teaspoons batter and drop it onto a baking sheet, repeating with remaining batter and leaving plenty of space between macaroons. Bake for about 20 minutes, until pale golden brown and just turning crisp.

Let cool slightly on the baking sheets before transferring to a wire rack to cool completely.

Beverages

In This Chapter

- ◆ Hot and cold low-glycemic beverages
- ◆ Party punches and festive drinks
- ◆ Hot chocolate with antioxidants
- ◆ Soothing teas

Now that you are on an eating plan for persons with diabetes, you may have given up some of your favorite libations—and we don't just mean the kinds with alcohol. Many commercial sodas are filled with high-fructose corn syrup and other high-glycemic ingredients that send your blood glucose levels soaring.

Even beverages with caffeine, such as coffee and black tea, can set off undesirable body reactions. Perhaps you're concerned about the long-term safety of drinking artificially sweetened commercial sodas and want to avoid them.

In this chapter, you'll find solutions—beverage recipes that are low-glycemic and noncaffeinated. Plus, many contain ingredients that are actually good for you, such as stevia with FOS, ginger, and cocoa. None contain artificial sweeteners.

Beverages for All Occasions

The recipes in this chapter offer you beverage choices for all the occasions in your life. Your family and guests will enjoy them—just as you will. The ingredients are healthy and the tastes are tantalizing. It's the combination of ingredients that gives these beverages and punches their "punch"—so to speak.

For quiet moments when you want something warm and soothing, try Hot Chocolate, Ginger Tea, or Spiced Tea. Serve to your friends for a morning or afternoon chat.

Red Tea with Mint Punch and Raspberry Ginger Ale are well-suited as refreshments for parties both in the summer and winter. You can also prepare a full recipe of these beverages and store the extra in the refrigerator for when you want a bright and cheerful pick-me-up.

There are recipes for Lemonade, with variations, and a Cranberry-Apple Drink that you can serve for breakfast in place of juice. Just reading these simple-to-make recipes will make you thirsty!

The Least You Need to Know

- ◆ Great-tasting beverages can be healthy and meet your food requirements.
- ◆ You can combine ingredients to give beverages wonderful flavors.
- ◆ The beverages in this chapter contain natural sweeteners and have no artificial sweeteners.
- ◆ Your entire family will enjoy these punches, sodas, and hot beverages.

Hot Chocolate

Prep time: 2 minutes • Cook time: 2½ minutes • Serves: 1 • Serving size: 1½ cups

Nutritional Analysis per Serving: Glycemic Index 32 • Glycemic Load 4 • Calories 84 • Protein in grams 8 • Animal Protein 0 • Vegetable Protein 0 • Carbohydrates 13 grams • Dietary Fiber <½ gram • Net Carbohydrate 13 grams • Fat <½ gram • Saturated Fat <½ gram • Cholesterol 4 mg • Sodium 124 mg • Exchanges 1 skim milk

1½ cups water	½ cup non-fat dry powdered milk
1 tsp. unsweetened cocoa powder	½ tsp. stevia with FOS

Pour water into a large, microwaveable mug. Add cocoa powder, powdered milk, and stevia, and stir to blend. Microwave on high power for 1½ minutes. Stir. Microwave on high power for 1½ minutes more.

Delightfully Different

Vary the taste of the cocoa by adding one or more of the following: ¼ teaspoon decaffeinated coffee granules, ¼ teaspoon ground cinnamon, or a pinch cayenne.

Palate Preview

This recipe is a hot chocolate for the times when only a steaming cup of cocoa will do. The antioxidant content in hot chocolate is four to five times greater than in black tea. Antioxidants have been shown to fight cancer, heart disease, and aging. So drink your hot chocolate.

Lemonade

Prep time: 3 minutes • Cook time: none • Serves: 1 • Serving size: 2 cups

Nutritional Analysis per Serving: Glycemic Index (not significant) • Glycemic Load (not significant) • Calories 10 • Protein in grams 0 • Animal Protein 0 • Vegetable Protein 0 • Carbohydrates 4 grams • Dietary Fiber 0 • Net Carbohydrate 4 grams • Fat 0 • Saturated Fat 0 • Cholesterol 0 • Sodium 0 • Exchanges free

3 TB. freshly squeezed lemon juice or freshly squeezed bottled lemon juice, found in health food stores

2 to 3 tsp. stevia with FOS, to taste

2 cups water

Mix lemon juice, stevia, and water together. Stir. Add ice, if desired.

Palate Preview

A long, tall glass of lemonade seems to hit the spot on a warm summer day. Garnish with mint sprigs, a strawberry, or a lemon or lime wedge to add color and interest.

Delightfully Different

Substitute sparkling water for the water in this lemonade recipe and you have lemon soda. You can also substitute limejuice for lemon juice in the recipe. Garnish with mint sprigs, a strawberry, or a lemon or lime wedge.

Healthy Notes

You can purchase fresh-squeezed bottled lemon or limejuice at health food stores. You can also find it in the frozen food section of the grocery store. Often you can find organic versions. Be sure not to use bottled lemon or lime juice that contains preservatives. If you do, the lemonade will taste odd, and preservatives certainly don't benefit your health.

Ginger Tea

Prep time: 5 minutes   •   Cook time: 10 minutes   •   Serves: 4   •   Serving size: 1½ cups

Nutritional Analysis per Serving: Glycemic Index 39   •   Glycemic Load 5   •   Calories 16 • Protein in grams 0   •   Animal Protein 0   •   Vegetable Protein 0   •   Carbohydrates 12 grams   •   Dietary Fiber 0   •   Net Carbohydrate 12 grams   •   Fat 0   •   Saturated Fat 0   •   Cholesterol 0   •   Sodium 0   •   Exchanges ¾ fruit

4 (¼-inch-thick) slices peeled fresh gingerroot	2 tsp. fructose
6 cups water	2 tsp. brown sugar

Bruise gingerroot slices slightly, by flattening with the broad side of a knife. Combine ginger, water, fructose, and brown sugar in a saucepan, and cook until boiling and sugar is dissolved. Strain and serve hot.

Palate Preview
If you love the taste of ginger ale, you'll love this hot ginger tea.

Spiced Tea

Prep time: 10 minutes   •   Cook time: none   •   Serves: 2   •   Serving size 1½ cup

Nutritional Analysis per Serving: Glycemic Index (not significant)   •   Glycemic Load (not significant)   •   Calories 0   •   Protein in grams 0   •   Animal Protein 0   •   Vegetable Protein 0   •   Carbohydrates 0   •   Dietary Fiber 0   •   Net Carbohydrate 0   •   Fat 0 • Saturated Fat 0   •   Cholesterol 0   •   Sodium 0   •   Exchanges free

2 bags decaffeinated green or black tea	¼ tsp. fresh grated orange zest
6 whole cloves	3 cups boiling water
1 cinnamon stick	½ tsp. stevia with FOS or to taste

Place tea bags, cloves, cinnamon stick, and orange zest in a medium saucepan or teapot. Pour boiling water over ingredients and steep for 10 minutes. Remove tea bags, and strain through a fine sieve. Sweeten with stevia to taste.

Palate Preview
Cloves, cinnamon, and orange zest give this tea a sweet taste and restful appeal to enjoy during your quiet moments.

Red Tea with Mint Punch

Prep time: 10 minutes • Cook time: 5 minutes • Serves: 10 • Serving size: 1 cup

Nutritional Analysis per Serving: Glycemic Index 51 • Glycemic Load 2 • Calories 13 • Protein in grams 0 • Animal Protein 0 • Vegetable Protein 0 • Carbohydrates 3 grams • Dietary Fiber 0 • Net Carbohydrate 3 grams • Fat 0 • Saturated Fat 0 • Cholesterol 0 • Sodium 0 • Exchanges free

3 cups boiling water	¼ cup fresh lemon juice
4 Red Zinger tea bags	2 TB. stevia with FOS
12 fresh mint leaves	6 to 7 cups cold water
1 cup orange juice	

Palate Preview _____ A terrific punch to serve to guests and for parties. The punch is tangy and sweet with citrus juices and Red Zinger tea.

Bring 3 cups water to a boil in a large saucepan. Add tea bags and mint leaves. Remove from heat and steep for 5 minutes. Remove tea bags. Add orange juice, lemon juice, stevia, and 6 to 7 cups cold water. Transfer to a pitcher, refrigerate until chilled and serve.

Raspberry Ginger Ale

Prep time: 10 minutes • Cook time: 10 minutes • Serves: 4 • Serving size: 1¼ cup

Nutritional Analysis per Serving: Glycemic Index 39 • Glycemic Load 2 • Calories 16 • Protein in grams <1 • Animal Protein 0 • Vegetable Protein <1 • Carbohydrates 4 grams • Dietary Fiber 2 grams • Net Carbohydrate 4 grams • Fat 0 • Saturated Fat 0 • Cholesterol 0 • Sodium 1 mg • Exchanges free

1 cup fresh or frozen raspberries, thawed	1 tsp. stevia with FOS
2 tsp. minced fresh gingerroot	4 cups unsweetened sparkling water
¼ cup water	

Mash raspberries and set aside. Press raspberries through a fine sieve to remove seeds, if you prefer.

Place minced ginger with ¼ cup water into a small microwavable container, and microwave on high power for 1½ minutes. Steep, stirring, for 5 minutes. Strain through a fine sieve.

Add ginger water, mashed raspberries, and stevia to a pitcher. Add sparkling water.

Palate Preview
Red raspberries give this homemade ginger ale a bright summery taste.

Cranberry-Apple Drink

Prep time: 10 minutes • Cook time: 2 minutes • Serves: 10 • Serving size: 1 cup

Nutritional Analysis per Serving: Glycemic Index 20 • Glycemic Load 1 • Calories 24 • Protein in grams ½ • Animal Protein 0 • Vegetable Protein ½ • Carbohydrates 6 grams • Dietary fiber 1 gram • Net Carbohydrate 5 grams • Fat 0 • Saturated Fat 0 • Cholesterol 0 • Sodium 1 mg • Exchanges ⅓ fruit

7 cups water	2½ teaspoons stevia with FOS
2½ cups whole fresh or frozen cranberries, thawed	1 cup unsweetened apple juice

Palate Preview

The tang of cranberry and the sweetness of apples are exactly what you need for a breakfast wake-up call. And it's a refreshing treat any time of the day.

In a medium saucepan, boil 1 cup water. Add cranberries and simmer for 5 minutes. Cool.

Pour cooked cranberry mixture and stevia in a blender, and blend until smooth. Pour 1 cup apple juice into a 2-quart pitcher. Add cranberry mixture and 6 cups water and stir well. Refrigerate until chilled. Stir before serving.

Glossary

al dente   Italian for "against the teeth." Refers to pasta (or other ingredient such as rice) that is neither soft nor hard, but just slightly firm against the teeth. This, according to many pasta aficionados, is the perfect way to cook pasta.

all-purpose flour   Flour that contains only the inner part of the wheat grain. Usable for all purposes from cakes to gravies.

allspice   Named for its flavor echoes of several spices (cinnamon, cloves, nutmeg), allspice is used in many desserts and in rich marinades and stews.

almonds   Mild, sweet, and crunchy nuts that combine nicely with creamy and sweet food items.

anchovies (also **sardines**)   Tiny, flavorful preserved fish that typically come in cans. The strong flavor from these salted fish is a critical element in many recipes. Anchovies are a traditional garnish for Caesar salad, the dressing of which contains anchovy paste.

andouille sausage   A sausage made with highly seasoned pork chitterlings and tripe, and a standard component of many Cajun dishes. *Andouillette* is a similar sausage, although smaller and usually grilled.

antipasto   A classic Italian-style appetizer plate including an assortment of prepared meats, cheeses, and vegetables such as prosciutto, capicolla, mozzarella, mushrooms, and olives.

artichoke hearts   The center part of the artichoke flower, often found canned in grocery stores and used as a stand-alone vegetable dish or as a flavorful base for appetizers or main courses.

arugula   A spicy-peppery garden plant with leaves that resemble a dandelion and have a distinctive—and very sharp—flavor.

au gratin   The quick broiling of a dish before serving to brown the top ingredients. The term is often used as part of a recipe name and implies cheese and a creamy sauce.

bake   To cook in a dry oven. Baking is one of the most popular methods of cooking and is used for everything from roasts, vegetables, and other main courses to desserts such as cakes and pies. Dry-heat cooking often results in a crisping of the exterior of the food being cooked. Moist-heat cooking, through methods such as steaming, poaching, etc., brings a much different, moist quality to the food.

baking pans   Pans used for baking potatoes to chicken, cookies to croutons.

baking sheet   A large, thin, flat tray used for baking cookies and other foods.

balsamic vinegar   Vinegar produced primarily in Italy from a specific type of grape and aged in wood barrels. It is heavier, darker, and sweeter than most vinegars.

bamboo shoots   Crunchy, tasty white parts of the growing bamboo plant, often purchased canned.

barbecue   This is a loaded word, with different, zealous definitions in different parts of the country. In some cases it is synonymous with grilling (quick-cooking over high heat); in others, to barbecue is to cook something long and slow in a rich liquid (barbecue sauce).

basil   A flavorful, almost sweet, resinous herb delicious with tomatoes and in all kinds of Italian or Mediterranean-style dishes.

baste   To keep foods moist during cooking by spooning, brushing, or drizzling with a liquid.

beat   To quickly mix substances.

Belgian endive   A plant that resembles a small, elongated, tightly packed head of romaine lettuce. The thick, crunchy leaves can be broken off and used with dips and spreads.

blanch   To place a food in boiling water for about 1 minute (or less) to partially cook the exterior and then submerge in or rinse with cool water to halt the cooking. This is a common method for preparing some vegetables such as asparagus for serving and also for preparing foods for freezing.

blend   To completely mix something, usually with a blender or food processor, more slowly than beating.

blue cheese   A blue-veined cheese that crumbles easily and has a somewhat soft texture; usually sold in a block.

boil   To heat a liquid to a point where water is forced to turn into steam, causing the liquid to bubble. To boil something is to insert it into boiling water. A rapid boil is when a lot of bubbles form on the surface of the liquid.

bok choy (also **Chinese cabbage**)   A member of the cabbage family with thick stems, crisp texture, and fresh flavor. It is perfect for stir-frying.

bouillon   Dried essence of stock from chicken, beef, vegetable, or other ingredients. This is a popular starting ingredient for soups as it adds flavor (and often a lot of salt).

bouillabaisse   A seafood soup with a spicy, tomato base, which originated in France.

bouquet garni   A collection of herbs including bay leaf, parsley, thyme, and others. Traditionally, these herbs are tied in a bunch or packaged in cheesecloth for cooking and subsequent removal. Bouquet garni is often found in the spice section of your grocery store and through specialty spice vendors.

braise   To cook with the introduction of some liquid, usually over an extended period of time.

breadcrumbs   Tiny pieces of crumbled dry bread. Breadcrumbs are an important component in many recipes and are also used as a coating, for example with breaded chicken breasts.

brie   A creamy cow's milk cheese from France with a soft, edible rind and a mild flavor.

brine   A highly salted, often seasoned, liquid that is used to flavor and preserve foods. To brine a food is to soak, or preserve, it by submerging it in brine. The salt in the brine penetrates the fibers of the meat and makes it moist and tender.

broil   To cook in a dry oven under the overhead high-heat element.

broth   *See* stock.

brown   To cook in a skillet, turning, until the surface is brown in color, to lock in the juices.

brown rice   Whole-grain rice with a characteristic pale brown or tan color; more nutritious and flavorful than white rice.

Cajun cooking   A style of cooking that combines French and Southern characteristics and includes many highly seasoned stews and meats.

cake flour   A high-starch, soft, and fine flour used primarily for cakes.

canapés   Bite-size hors d'oeuvres made up of any number of ingredients but prepared individually and usually served on a small piece of bread or toast.

capers   Usually sold preserved in jars, capers are the flavorful buds of a Mediterranean plant. The most common size is *nonpareil* (about the size of a small pea); others are larger, including the grape-size caper berries produced in Spain.

caramelize   The term's original meaning is to cook sugar over low heat until it develops a sweet caramel flavor; however, the term is increasingly gaining use to describe cooking vegetables (especially onions) or meat in butter or oil over low heat until they soften, sweeten, and develop a caramel color. Caramelized onions are a popular addition to many recipes, especially as a pizza topping.

caraway   A distinctive spicy seed used for bread, pork, cheese, and cabbage dishes. It is known to reduce stomach upset, which is why it is often paired with, for example, sauerkraut.

carbohydrate   A food component found in starches, sugars, fruits, and vegetables that causes a rise in blood glucose levels. The rise can be high or low based on how quickly the carbohydrate is metabolized in the digestive system. Carbohydrates supply energy and many important nutrients, including vitamins, minerals, and antioxidants.

cardamom   An intense, sweet-smelling spice, common to Indian cooking, used in baking and coffee.

casserole dishes   Primarily used in baking, these covered containers hold liquids and solids together and keep moisture around ingredients that might otherwise dry out.

cayenne   A fiery spice made from (hot) chili peppers, especially the cayenne chili, a slender, red, and very hot pepper.

cheddar   The ubiquitous hard cow's milk cheese with a rich, buttery flavor that ranges from mellow to sharp. Originally produced in England, cheddar is now produced worldwide.

chevre   The French word for goat cheese, is a typically creamy-salty soft cheese delicious by itself or paired with fruits or chutney. Chevres vary in style from mild and creamy to aged, firm, and flavorful. *Artisanal* chevres are usually more expensive and sold in smaller quantities; these are often delicious by themselves. Other chevres produced in quantity are less expensive and often more appropriate for combining with fruit or herbs.

chickpeas (also **garbanzo beans**)   A yellow-gold roundish bean or legume that is the base ingredient in hummus. Chickpeas are high in fiber and low in fat, making this a delicious and healthful component of many appetizers and main dishes.

chili peppers (also **chile peppers**)   Any one of many different "hot" peppers, ranging in intensity from the relatively mild ancho pepper to the blisteringly hot habanero.

chili powder   A seasoning blend that includes chili pepper, cumin, garlic, and oregano. Proportions vary among different versions, but they all offer a warm, rich flavor.

chives   A member of the onion family, chives grow in bunches of long leaves that resemble long grass. Chives provide an light onion flavor to any dish. Chives are very easy to grow, and many people have them in their garden.

chop   To cut into pieces, usually qualified by an adverb such as "*coarsely* chopped," or by a size measurement such as "chopped into ½-inch pieces." "Finely chopped" is much closer to mince.

chorizo   A spiced pork sausage eaten alone and as a component in many recipes. Used widely in Spain and Latin America and known as chourico in Portugal.

cider vinegar   Vinegar produced from apple cider, popular in North America.

cilantro   A member of the parsley family and used in Mexican cooking and some Asian dishes. Cilantro is what gives some salsas their unique flavor. The seeds of the cilantro are the spice, coriander.

cinnamon   A sweet, rich, aromatic spice commonly used in baking or desserts. Cinnamon can also be used for delicious and interesting entrées.

cloves   A sweet, strong, almost wintergreen-flavor spice used in baking and with meats such as ham.

coat   To cover all sides of a food with a liquid, sauce, or solid.

core   To remove the unappetizing middle membranes and seeds of fruits and vegetables.

coriander   A rich, warm, spicy seed used in all types of recipes, from African to South American, from entrées to desserts.

cottage cheese   A mild, creamy-texture cheese made from curds from fresh cow's milk cheese. Curds vary in size; containers will indicate, for example, "small curd" or "large curd." In its low-fat and nonfat forms, cottage cheese is a useful component of low-fat dips, spreads, and other recipes.

count   On packaging of seafood or other foods that come in small sizes, you'll often see a reference to the count, or how many of that item compose 1 pound. For example, 31 to 40 count shrimp are large appetizer shrimp often served with cocktail sauce; 51 to 60 are much smaller.

coulis   A thick paste, often made with vegetables or fruits, used as a sauce for many recipes.

couscous   Granular semolina (durum wheat) that is cooked and used in many Mediterranean and North African dishes.

cream   To blend an ingredient to get a soft, creamy liquid or substance.

croutons   Pieces of bread, usually between ¼ and ½-inch in size, that are sometimes seasoned and baked, broiled, or fried to a crisp texture.

crudités   Fresh vegetables served as an appetizer, often all together on one tray.

cuisine   A style of cooking, typically reflecting a country or region (such as "Spanish cuisine"), a blending of flavors and cuisines (called "fusion"), or an updated style (such as "New Latin"). Cuisine is a French word that means kitchen and has come to mean a style of cooking.

cumin   A fiery, smoky-tasting spice popular in Middle-Eastern and Indian dishes. Cumin is a seed; ground cumin seed is the most common form of the spice used in cooking.

curry   A general term referring to rich, spicy, Indian-style sauces and the dishes prepared with them. Common ingredients include hot pepper, nutmeg, cumin, cinnamon, pepper, and turmeric.

custard   A cooked mixture of eggs and milk. Custards are a popular base for desserts.

dash   A dash refers to a few drops, usually of a liquid, that is released by a quick shake of, for example, a bottle of hot sauce.

deglaze   To scrape up the bits of meat and seasoning left in a pan or skillet after cooking. Usually this is done by adding a liquid such as wine or broth and creating a flavorful stock that can be used to create sauces.

devein   The removal of the dark vein from the back of a large shrimp with a sharp knife.

dice   To cut into small cubes about ¼-inch square.

Dijon mustard   Hearty, spicy mustard made in the style of the Dijon region of France.

dill   A unique herb that is perfect for eggs, salmon, cheese dishes, and of course, vegetables (pickles!).

double boiler   A set of two pots designed to nest together, one inside the other, and provide consistent, moist heat for foods that need delicate treatment. The bottom pot holds water (not quite touching the bottom of the top pot); the top pot holds the ingredient you want to heat.

dough   A soft, pliable mixture of liquid and flour that is the intermediate step, prior to cooking, for many bread or baked-goods recipes such as cookies or bread.

dredge   To cover a piece of food with a dry substance such as flour or corn meal.

dressing   A liquid mixture usually containing oil, vinegar, and herbs used for seasoning salads and other foods. Also the solid dish commonly called "stuffing" used to stuff turkey and other foods.

drizzle   To lightly sprinkle drops of a liquid over food. Drizzling is often the finishing touch to a dish.

dry In the context of wine, a wine that has been vinified to contain little or no sugar, so it's not sweet.

dust To sprinkle a dry substance, often a seasoning, lightly over a food or dish.

entrée The main dish in a meal, but in France, and entrée is considered the first course.

essential amino acids These are comprised of nine amino acids that need to be ingested everyday for optimal health. Other non-essential amino acids can be manufactured in the body, but the body can't manufacture essential amino acids.

etouffee Cajun for "smothered." This savory, rich sauce (often made with crayfish) is served over rice.

extra-virgin olive oil *See* olive oil.

fennel In seed form, a fragrant, licorice-tasting herb. The bulbs have a much milder flavor and a celerylike crunch and are used as a vegetable in salads or cooked recipes.

feta This white, crumbly, salty cheese is popular in Greek cooking, on salads, and on its own. Traditional feta is usually made with sheep's milk, but feta-style cheese can be made from sheep's, cow's, or goat's milk. Its sharp flavor is especially nice with bitter, cured black olives.

fillet A piece of meat or seafood with the bones removed.

fish basket A grill-top metal frame that holds a whole fish intact, making it easier to turn.

fish poacher A long, rectangular pan with a separate metal basket designed to hold a fish either above boiling water for steaming or in simmering liquid for poaching. Fish poachers come in varying sizes up to 24 inches, although an 18-inch version will cover all but the largest meals.

flake To break into thin sections, as with fish.

floret The flower or bud end of broccoli or cauliflower.

flour Grains ground into a meal. Wheat is perhaps the most common flour, an essential component in many breads. Flour is also made from oats, rye, buckwheat, soybeans, etc. Different types of flour serve different purposes. *See also* all-purpose flour; bread flour; cake flour; whole-wheat flour.

FOS (also **fruit ogliosaccharides**) A sugar twice as sweet as table sugar that doesn't raise blood glucose levels or cause an insulin release. Helps the good bacteria grow and flourish in your gut, thus improving your health.

fructose Sugar naturally found in fruit, slightly sweeter than table sugar and now available in bulk. Cooks up just as well as table sugar. Fructose is relatively inexpensive and is available at most grocery stores. If you can't find it locally, order over the Internet.

fry   Pan-cooking over high heat with butter or oil.

garlic   A member of the onion family, a pungent and flavorful element in many savory dishes. A garlic bulb, the form in which garlic is often sold, contains multiple cloves. Each clove, when chopped, provides about 1 teaspoon garlic.

garnish   An embellishment not vital to the dish but added to enhance visual appeal.

ginger   Available in fresh root or powdered form, ginger adds a pungent, sweet, and spicy quality to a dish. It is a very popular element of many Asian and Indian dishes, among others.

glucose   The simplest sugar. All natural sugars are broken down into glucose for use by the body for energy and cellular metabolism. Persons with diabetes have high blood-glucose levels because the insulin-modulating system of the body doesn't function correctly.

glycemic index   The values of carbohydrates are measured using glucose as a standard—assigned a value of 100. All other carbohydrates fall either above or below white bread. They range between 0 to about 165. A Glycemic index of 70 or more is high, 56 to 60 is medium, and below 55 is low.

glycemic load   A numerical value that relates the Glycemic Index of a specific carbohydrate-containing food to the amount eaten. It gives a good representation of how a serving of food will affect your blood glucose levels. Glycemic Load is given for every serving in this book. Plan to eat about 70-100 Glycemic Load points per day, divided among three meals and one to three snacks.

grate   To shave into tiny pieces using a sharp rasp or grater.

grill   To cook over high heat, usually over charcoal or gas.

grind   To reduce a large, hard substance, often a seasoning such as peppercorns, to the consistency of sand.

grits   Coarsely ground grains, usually corn.

Gruyère   A rich, sharp cow's milk cheese with a nutty flavor made in Switzerland.

handful   An unscientific measurement term that refers to the amount of an ingredient you can hold in your hand.

haute cuisine   French for "high cooking." Refers to painstakingly prepared, sometimes exotic, delicious, and complex meals (such as one might find at a high-end traditional French restaurant).

hazelnuts (also **filberts**)   A sweet nut popular in desserts and, to a lesser degree, in savory dishes.

hearts of palm   Firm, elongated, off-white cylinders from the inside of a palm tree stem tip. They are delicious in many recipes.

herbes de Provence A seasoning mix including basil, fennel, marjoram, rosemary, sage, and thyme. Common in the south of France.

herbs The leaves of flavorful plants characterized by fresh, pungent aromas and flavors, such as parsley, sage, rosemary, and thyme.

hors d'oeuvre French for "outside of work" (the "work" being the main meal). An hors d'oeuvre can be any dish served as a starter before the meal.

horseradish A sharp, spicy root that forms the flavor base in many condiments from cocktail sauce to sharp mustards. It is a natural match with roast beef. The form generally found in grocery stores is prepared horseradish, which contains vinegar and oil, among other ingredients. If you come across pure horseradish, use it much more sparingly than the prepared version, or try cutting it with sour cream.

Italian seasoning (also **spaghetti sauce seasoning**) The ubiquitous grocery store blend of dried herbs, which includes basil, oregano, rosemary, and thyme, is a useful seasoning for quick flavor that evokes the "old country" in sauces, meatballs, soups, and vegetable dishes.

jicama A juicy, crunchy, sweet, large, and round Central American vegetable that is eaten both raw and cooked. It is available in many large grocery stores as well as from specialty vendors. If you can't find jicama, try substituting sliced water chestnuts.

julienne A French word meaning to slice into very thin pieces.

liver The nutritious and flavorful organ meat from all types of fowl and animal.

marinate To soak meat, seafood, or other food in a seasoned sauce, called a marinade, which is high in acid content. The acids break down the muscle of the meat, making it tender and adding flavor.

marjoram A sweet herb, a cousin of and similar to oregano, popular in Greek, Spanish, and Italian dishes.

marmalade A fruit-and-sugar preserve that contains whole pieces of fruit peel, to achieve simultaneous sweetness (from the sugar) and tartness (from the fruit's natural acids). The most common marmalades are made with citrus fruits such as orange and lemon.

medallion A small round cut, usually of meat or vegetables such as carrots or cucumbers.

meld A combination of *melt* and *weld,* many cooks use this term to describe how flavors blend and spread over time throughout dips and spreads. Melding is often why recipes call for overnight refrigeration and is also why some dishes taste better as leftovers.

meringue A baked mixture of sugar and beaten egg whites, often used as a dessert topping.

mince To cut into very small pieces smaller than diced pieces, about ⅛-inch or smaller.

monounsaturated Fats that are liquid at room temperature and can help lower high blood cholesterol levels when they are part of a lower-far diet. An unsaturated fat has room in its chemical structure for additional hydrogen atoms, which tends to make it more biologically active and healthy.

mushrooms Any one of a huge variety of *edible* fungi (note emphasis on "edible"; there are also poisonous mushrooms). *See also* crimini mushrooms; porcini mushrooms; portobello mushrooms; shiitake mushrooms; white mushrooms.

nutmeg A sweet, fragrant, musky spice used primarily in baking.

nuts Shell-covered seeds (or fruits) whose meat is rich in flavor and nutrition. A critical component in many dishes, many nuts are tasty on their own as well. *See also* almonds; hazelnuts; pecans; walnuts.

olive oil A fragrant liquid produced by crushing or pressing olives. Extra-virgin olive oil is the oil produced from the first pressing of a batch of olives; oil is also produced from other pressings after the first. Extra-virgin olive oil is generally considered the most flavorful and highest quality and is the type you want to use when your focus is on the oil itself. Be sure the bottle label reads "extra-virgin." An important oil for persons with diabetes. The oil is monounsaturated and always cold-expeller pressed. It's healthy for everyone.

olives The fruit of the olive tree commonly grown on all sides of the Mediter-ranean. There are many varieties of olives but two general types: green and black. Black olives are also called ripe olives. Green olives are immature, though eaten widely.

oregano A fragrant, slightly astringent herb used in Greek, Spanish, and Italian dishes.

oxidation The browning of fruit flesh that happens over time and with exposure to air. Although it's best to prepare fresh fruit dishes just before serving, sometimes that's not possible. If you need to cut apples in advance, minimize oxidation by rubbing the cut surfaces with a lemon half.

paella A grand Spanish dish of rice, shellfish, onion, meats, rich broth, and herbs.

pan-broil Quick-cooking over high heat in a skillet with a minimum of butter or oil. (Frying, on the other hand, uses more butter or oil.)

paprika A rich, red, warm, earthy spice that also lends a rich red color to many dishes.

parboil To partially cook in boiling water or broth. Parboiling is similar to blanching, although blanched foods are quickly cooled with cold water.

pare To scrape away the skin of a food, usually a vegetable, as part of preparation for serving or cooking.

Parmesan   A hard, dry, flavorful cheese primarily used grated or shredded as a seasoning for Italian-style dishes.

parsley   A fresh-tasting green leafy herb used to add color and interest to just about any savory dish. Often used as a garnish just before serving.

pâté   A savory loaf that contains meats, spices, and often a lot of fat, served cold spread or sliced on crusty bread or crackers.

peanuts   The nutritious and high-fat seeds of the peanut plant (a relative of the pea) that are sold shelled or unshelled and in a variety of preparations, including peanut butter and peanut oil. Some people are allergic to peanuts, so care should be taken with their inclusion in recipes.

pecans   Rich, buttery nuts native to North America. Their flavor, a terrific addition to appetizers, is at least partially due to their high unsaturated fat content.

pepper   A biting and pungent seasoning, freshly ground pepper is a must for many dishes and adds an extra level of flavor and taste.

peppercorns   Large, round, dried berries that are ground to produce pepper.

pesto   A thick spread or sauce made with fresh basil leaves, garlic, olive oil, pine nuts, and Parmesan cheese. Other new versions are made with other herbs. Rich and flavorful, pesto can be made at home or purchased in a grocery store and used on anything from appetizers to pasta and other main dishes.

phytonutrients   Found in fruits and vegetables. These molecules play an important role in disease prevention. They neutralize free radicals that can cause diseases such as cancer, diabetes, skin cancer, heart disease, and minor colds and flu.

piccata   A Northern Italian method for preparing light meats, such as chicken or veal. The ingredients often call for lemon juice, white wine, and capers.

pickle   A food, usually a vegetable such as a cucumber, that has been pickled in brine.

pilaf   A rice dish in which the rice is browned in butter or oil, then cooked in a flavorful liquid such as a broth, often with the addition of meats or vegetables. The rice absorbs the broth, resulting in a savory dish.

pinch   An unscientific measurement term that refers to the amount of an ingredient— typically a dry, granular substance such as an herb or seasoning—you can hold between your finger and thumb.

pine nuts (also **pignoli** or **piñon**)   Nuts grown on pine trees, that are rich (read: high fat), flavorful, and, yes, a bit pine-y. Pine nuts are a traditional component of pesto, and they add a wonderful hearty crunch to many other recipes.

pita bread   A flat, hollow wheat bread that can be used for sandwiches or sliced, pizza style, into slices. Pita bread is terrific soft with dips or baked or broiled as a vehicle for other ingredients.

poach   To cook a food in simmering liquid, such as water, wine, or broth.

portobello mushrooms   A mature and larger form of the smaller crimini mushroom, portobellos are brownish, chewy, and flavorful. They are trendy served as whole caps, grilled, and as thin sautéed slices. *See also* crimini mushrooms.

preheat   To turn on an oven, broiler, or other cooking appliance in advance of cooking so the temperature will be at the desired level when the assembled dish is ready for cooking.

presentation   The appealing arrangement of a dish or food on the plate.

prosciutto   Dry, salt-cured ham, that originated in Italy. Prosciutto is popular in many simple dishes in which its unique flavor is allowed to shine.

psyllium   A very low-glycemic grain used for its high fiber content. Used in baked goods to add fiber and lower glycemic load.

purée   To reduce a food to a thick, creamy texture, usually using a blender or food processor.

ragout (pronounced *rag-OO*)   A thick, spicy stew.

red pepper flakes   Hot yet rich, crushed red pepper, used in moderation, brings flavor and interest to many savory dishes.

reduce   To heat a broth or sauce to remove some of the water content, resulting in more concentrated flavor and color.

reserve   To hold a specified ingredient for another use later in the recipe.

rice vinegar   Vinegar produced from fermented rice or rice wine, popular in Asian-style dishes.

roast   To cook something uncovered in an oven, usually without additional liquid.

Roquefort   A world-famous (French) creamy but sharp sheep's milk cheese containing blue lines of mold, making it a "blue cheese."

rosemary   A pungent, sweet herb used with chicken, pork, fish, and especially lamb. A little of it goes a long way.

roux   A mixture of butter or another fat and flour, used to thicken sauces and soups.

saffron   A famous spice made from stamens of crocus flowers. Saffron lends a dramatic yellow color and distinctive flavor to a dish. Only a tiny amount needs to be used, which is good because saffron is very expensive.

sage An herb with a fruity, lemon-rind scent and "sunny" flavor. It is a terrific addition to many dishes.

salsa A style of mixing fresh vegetables and/or fresh fruit in a coarse chop. Salsa can be spicy or not, fruit-based or not, and served as a starter on its own (with chips, for example) or as a companion to a main course.

satay (also **sate**) A popular Southeast Asian dish of broiled skewers of fish or meat, often served with peanut sauce.

sauté Pan-cooking over lower heat than used for frying.

savory A popular herb with a fresh, woody taste.

scant A measurement modification that specifies "include no extra," as in 1 scant teaspoon.

sear To quickly brown the exterior of a food over high heat to preserve interior moisture (that's why many meat recipes involve searing).

search engine An Internet tool that, based on keywords you type, helps find related websites on the topic you searched for. A good search engine such as Google or Yahoo! will suggest sites that are close to what you seek.

shallot A member of the onion family that grows in a bulb somewhat like garlic and has a milder onion flavor. When a recipe calls for shallot, you use the entire bulb. (They might or might not have cloves.)

shellfish A broad range of seafood, including clams, mussels, oysters, crabs, shrimp, and lobster. Some people are allergic to shellfish, so care should be taken with its inclusion in recipes.

shiitake mushrooms Large, dark brown mushrooms originally from the Far East with a hearty, meaty flavor that can be grilled or used as a component in other recipes and as a flavoring source for broth.

shred To cut into many long, thin slices.

short-grain rice A starchy rice popular for Asian-style dishes because it readily clumps for eating with chopsticks.

simmer To boil gently so the liquid barely bubbles.

skewers Thin wooden or metal sticks, usually about eight inches long, that are perfect for assembling kebabs, dipping food pieces into hot sauces, or serving single-bite food items with a bit of panache.

skillet (also **frying pan**) A generally heavy, flat-bottom metal pan with a handle designed to cook food over heat on a stovetop or campfire.

slice   To cut into thin pieces.

slow cooker   An electric countertop device with a lidded container that maintains a low temperature and slowly cooks its contents, often over several hours or a full day.

steam   To suspend a food over boiling water and allow the heat of the steam (water vapor) to cook the food. Steaming is a very quick cooking method that preserves the flavor and texture of a food.

steep   To let sit in hot water. As in steeping tea in hot water for ten minutes.

stevia   Comes from the South American herb, stevia leaf, which is 300 times sweeter than table sugar. Stevia was used as a healing herb by the native peoples. Because it's naturally very sweet, a little goes a long way. Stevia has a slightly odd aftertaste that some people don't like. Manufacturers are now combining it with FOS (fruit ogliosaccharides). This combination doesn't have an aftertaste and is actually good for you.

stevia with FOS   Is about 10 times sweeter than table sugar. Its glycemic index is zero. It holds up fine to both heat and freezing temperatures.

stew   To slowly cook pieces of food submerged in a liquid. Also, a dish that has been prepared by this method.

sticky rice (or **glutinous rice**)   *See* short-grain rice.

Stilton   The famous English blue-veined cheese, delicious with toasted nuts and renowned for its pairing with Port wine.

stir-fry   To cook small bits of food in a wok or skillet over high heat, moving and turning the food quickly to cook all sides.

stock   A flavorful broth made by cooking meats and/or vegetables with seasonings until the liquid absorbs these flavors. This liquid is then strained and the solids discarded. Stock can be eaten by itself or used as a base for soups, stews, sauces, risotto, or many other recipes.

stone ground   Traditionally, grain ground between two stones. Today, roughly ground grain that contains large pieces of grain.

Tabasco sauce   A popular brand of Louisiana hot pepper sauce used in usually small portions to season savory food. The name also refers to a type of hot pepper from Tabasco, a state in Mexico, that is used to make this sauce.

tabouli   A traditional Middle-Eastern dish made with bulghar wheat, mint, garlic, lemon, and parsley.

tahini   A paste made from sesame seeds that is used to flavor many Middle Eastern recipes, especially baba ghanoush and hummus.

tandoori   An Eastern Indian roasted meat dish.

tarragon   A sweet, rich-smelling herb perfect with seafood, vegetables (especially asparagus), chicken, and pork.

teriyaki   A delicious Japanese-style sauce composed of soy sauce, rice wine, ginger, and sugar. It works beautifully with seafood as well as most meats.

thyme   A minty, zesty herb whose leaves are used in a wide range of recipes.

toast   To heat something, usually bread, so it is browned and crisp.

toast points (also **toast triangles**)   Pieces of toast with the crusts removed that are then cut on the diagonal from each corner, resulting in four triangle-shape pieces.

tofu   A cheeselike substance made from soybeans and soy milk. Flavorful and nutritious, tofu is an important component of foods across the globe, especially from East Asia.

tomatillo   A small, round fruit with a distinctive spicy flavor. Tomatillos are a traditional component of many south-of-the-border dishes. To use, remove the papery outer skin, rinse off any sticky residue, and chop like a tomato.

tripe   The stomach of a cow.

turmeric   A spicy, pungent yellow root used in many dishes, especially Indian cuisine, for color and flavor. Turmeric is the source of the brilliant yellow color in many prepared mustards.

twist   A twist (as in lemon or other citrus fruit twist) is simply an attractive way to garnish an appetizer or other dish. Cut a thin, about 1/8-inch-thick cross-section slice of a lemon, for example. Then take that slice and cut from the center out to the edge of the slice on one side. Pick up the piece of lemon and pull apart the two cut ends in opposite directions.

veal   Meat from a calf, generally characterized by mild flavor and tenderness. Certain cuts of veal, such as cutlets and scaloppini, are well suited to quick-cooking.

vegetable steamer   An insert for a large saucepan. Also a special pot with tiny holes in the bottom designed to fit on another pot to hold food to be steamed above boiling water. The insert is generally less expensive and resembles a metal poppy flower that expands to touch the sides of the pot and has small legs. *See also* steam.

venison   Meat from deer.

vinegar   An acidic liquid widely used as dressing and seasoning. Many cuisines use vinegars made from different source materials, such as fermented grapes, apples, and rice. *See also* balsamic vinegar; cider vinegar; rice vinegar; white vinegar; wine vinegar.

walnuts   Grown worldwide, walnuts bring a rich, slightly woody flavor to all types of food. For the quick cook, walnuts are available chopped and ready to go at your grocery store. They are delicious toasted and make fine accompaniments to cheeses.

wasabi   Japanese horseradish, a fiery, pungent condiment used with many Japanese-style dishes, including sushi. Most often sold as a powder; add water to create a paste.

water chestnuts   Actually a tuber, water chestnuts are a popular element in many types of Asian-style cooking. The flesh is white, crunchy, and juicy, and the vegetable holds its texture whether cool or hot.

whisk   To rapidly mix, introducing air to the mixture.

white mushrooms   Ubiquitous button mushrooms. When fresh, they will have an earthy smell and an appealing "soft crunch." White mushrooms are delicious raw in salads, marinated, sautéed, and as component ingredients in many recipes.

white vinegar   The most common type of vinegar found on grocery store shelves. It is produced from grain.

whole-wheat flour   Flour made from the whole grain of wheat. Whole wheat flour is light brown or tan.

wild rice   Actually a grass with a rich, nutty flavor, popular as an unusual and nutritious side dish.

wine vinegar   Vinegar produced from red or white wine.

whipped topping   A nonfat topping used in place of whipped cream. A free food for persons with diabetes.

wok   A wonderful tool for quick-cooking.

Worcestershire sauce   Originally developed in India and containing tamarind, this spicy sauce is used as a seasoning for many meats and other dishes.

yeast   Tiny fungi that, when mixed with water, sugar, flour, and heat, release carbon dioxide bubbles, which, in turn, cause the bread to rise. The yeast also provides that wonderful warm, rich smell and flavor.

zest   Small slivers of peel, usually from a citrus fruit such as lemon, lime, or orange.

zester   A small kitchen tool used to scrape zest off a fruit. A small grater also works fine.

Glycemic Index, Carbohydrate, and Glycemic Load List

The following table lists the Glycemic Index ranking and the carbohydrate content of the ingredients used in the recipes.

Foods	Glycemic Index Value	Amount	Carbs in Grams	Fiber in Grams	Net Carbs in Grams	Glycemic Load
Almond flour	0	1 cup	21	11	10	0
Almonds	0	1 cup	28	15	13	0
Apple juice	40	1 cup	29	0	29	12
Apples	38	1 medium	22	3	19	6
Apples, dried	28	¼ cup	14	2	12	4
Applesauce, unsweetened	40	½ cup	13	3	10	6
Apricots, fresh	57	3 medium	12	1	11	5
Apricots, dried	30	¼ cup	20	2	18	8
Artichokes	0	½ cup	6	4	2	0
Avocado, California	0	1 medium	12	9	3	0
Banana, not over ripe	52	1 medium	27	3	24	12
Barley, pearl, cooked	25	¼ cup	11	2	9	2
Basmati rice, cooked, white	58	¼ cup	12	1	11	6
Basmati rice, cooked, brown	50	¼ cup	12	2	10	5
Baked beans	50	½ cup	27	7	20	11
Beef	0	any amount	0	0	0	0
Black beans, boiled	30	½ cup	20	8	12	4
Black-eyed peas, canned	42	½ cup	16	4	12	5
Bouillon, chicken or beef	0	½ cup	2	0	2	0
Bran, 100%	30	½ cup	23	13	10	3
razil nut	0	6 large	4	2	2	0
Broccoli, raw, chopped	0	½ cup	3	1	2	0
Brown sugar	59	1 oz.	28	0	28	17
Bulgur (course wheat kernels)	52	¼ cup	15	5	10	5
Buttermilk	31	1 cup	12	0	12	4
Butter	0	any	0	0	0	0

Foods	Glycemic Index Value	Amount	Carbs in Grams	Fiber in Grams	Net Carbs in Grams	Glycemic Load
Cabbage, raw, shredded	0	½ cup	2	1	1	0
Cantaloupe, cubed	65	1 cup	13	2	11	6
Capers	0	1 TB.	1	0	1	0
Carrots, raw, shredded	47	½ cup	6	2	4	3
Cashews	22	¼ cup	8	3	5	3
Cauliflower, 1-inch pieces	0	½ cup	3	2	1	0
Celery, diced	0	½ cup	2	1	1	0
Cheese, cheddar and Parmesan	0	1 oz.	0	0	0	0
Cherries, sweet w/pits	22	½ cup	12	2	10	2
Chevre cheese	0	1 oz.	1	0	0	0
Cheese, cottage 2% fat	31	½ cup	4	0	4	1
Cheese, goat	0	1 oz.	1	0	1	0
Chickpeas, canned	42	½ cup	18	7	11	7
Chocolate, unsweeteded	0	1 square	8	5	3	0
Cilantro	0	2 TB.	0	0	0	0
Cocoa powder	55	1 TB.	3	1	2	1
Cornmeal	68	¼ cup	25	3	22	5
Corn, sweet, boiled	60	½ cup	23	5	18	11
Couscous	65	¼ cup	13	2	11	7
Cranberries, dried	48	2 TB.	12	1	11	6
Cranberries, fresh, unsweetened	0	¼ cup	3	1	2	0
Cream Cheese, non-fat	31	2 TB.	2	0	2	1
Cream Cheese, low-fat	31	2 TB.	1	0	1	0

continues

continued

Foods	Glycemic Index Value	Amount	Carbs in Grams	Fiber in Grams	Net Carbs in Grams	Glycemic Load
Cream, light	31	2 TB.	2	0	2	1
Cream, heavy	0	½ cup	3	0	3	0
Cucumber, sliced	0	½ cup	2	1	1	0
Dates	103	3 dates	15	1	14	14
Eggs, large	0	1 large	0.6	0	0	0
Fennel, sliced	0	1 cup	6	2	4	0
Figs, dried	61	3 figs	30	5	25	15
Flour, whole wheat	73	¼ cup	22	4	18	13
Fructose	19	1 TB.	15	0	15	3
Garlic	0	1 clove	1	0.1	1	0
Ginger root	0	1 TB.	0	0	0	0
Grapefruit	25	½ medium	15	2	13	3
Grapefruit juice	48	1 cup	20	0	20	9
Grapes, green	46	¾	19	1	18	8
Green beans, cooked	0	½ cup	5	2	3	0
Green onions	0	¼ cup	2	1	1	0
Green peas, frozen	48	⅔ cup	12	3	9	6
Hazelnuts, diced	0	1 cup	18	7	11	0
Honey	55	1 TB.	18	0	18	10
Ice cream, low fat, vanilla	50	½ cup	9	0	9	5
Jicama	0	½ cup	5	3	2	0
Kidney beans, boiled	46	½ cup	20	7	13	6
Kiwi fruit	58	1 medium	11	3	8	5
Lamb	0	any amount	0	0	0	0
Leafy vegetables, raw	0	1 cup	2	1	1	0
Lemon/lime juice	0	2 TB.	0	0	0	0
Lentils, cooked	29	½ cup	20	8	12	3
Lima beans, frozen	32	½ cup	22	5	17	7

Foods	Glycemic Index Value	Amount	Carbs in Grams	Fiber in Grams	Net Carbs in Grams	Glycemic Load
Macadamia nuts	0	¼ cup	5	3	2	0
Mango, sliced	51	½	18	3	15	8
Milk, 2%	28	1 cup	12	0	12	4
Milk, skim	31	1 cup	12	0	12	4
Oat bran	55	2 TB.	10	5	5	3
Oatmeal, slow cooking, cooked	42	½ cup	13	2	11	5
Oil, olive	0	any amount	0	0	0	0
Oil, spray	0	1 tsp.	0	0	0	0
Onion, chopped	0	½ cup	7	1	6	0
Orange, sections	42	½ cup	13	2	11	3
Orange juice	53	1 cup	28	0	28	15
Papaya, sliced	56	½ cup	11	3	8	5
Parsley	0	2 TB.	0	0	0	0
Peach, sliced	42	1 cup	14	3	11	5
Peanuts, roasted	14	¼ cup	12	2	10	2
Peas, sweet	48	½ cup	13	4	9	5
Peas, black-eyed	42	½ cup	15	4	11	5
Pear	38	1 medium	25	4	21	4
Pecan flour	0	1 cup	15	15	0	0
Pecans, halves	0	¼ cup	5	5	0	0
Pepper, red or green bell, diced	0	¾ cup	4	2	2	0
Pineapple, fresh	59	½ cup	19	2	17	8
Pine nuts or piñon nuts	0	¼ cup	5	2	3	0
Pinto beans, canned	45	½ cup	18	6	12	7
Plums, sliced	39	½ cup	11	1	10	5
Pork	0	any amount	0	0	0	0
Potato, russet, baked in skin	85	½ cup	15	1	14	12
Raisins	64	¼ cup	31	2	29	18

continues

continued

Foods	Glycemic Index Value	Amount	Carbs in Grams	Fiber in Grams	Net Carbs in Grams	Glycemic Load
Raspberries, fresh	40	1 cup	15	8	7	3
Rice, brown, cooked, steamed	50	⅓ cup	15	2	13	7
Rice, wild, boiled 35 minutes	54	⅓ cup	15	2	13	7
Rice, instant, cooked	74	⅓ cup	15	1	14	10
Rice, white, sticky	98	⅓ cup	15	1	14	14
Salami	0	1 oz.	0	0	0	0
Shellfish	0	any amount	0	0	0	0
Sour cream (see cream)						
Split peas, cooked	32	¼ cup	27	11	16	5
Stevia	0	2 TB.	0	0	0	0
Strawberries	40	½ cup	6	1	5	1
Sucrose, granulated table sugar	68	1 TB.	15	0	15	10
Sweet potato, mashed	61	½ cup	15	3	12	7
Tomato, chopped	0	1 cup	8	2	6	0
Tuna and other fish	0	any amount	0	0	0	0
Veal	0	any amount	0	0	0	0
Walnuts, halves	0	¼ cup	3	2	1	0
Yams, cooked, cubed	37	½ cup	15	3	12	4
Yogurt, lite or unsweetened	31	1 cup	16	0	16	5

Index